大学外语教育国际化与当代化国际学术会议论文集

周 爽 崔诗晴 主编

西北工业大学出版社

西 安

【内容简介】 本书从教育国际化背景下的跨文化教育、外语专业人才培养目标与路径、外语教学理念革新与实践、外语教学模式改革与创新、外语语言与教学研究等不同领域,对大学外语教育过程中的问题进行了广泛、深入的思考和探讨,这对于进一步推动大学外语教育教学改革、持续探索大学外语教育教学发展新方向有着积极的意义,对于广大大学外语教育者、研究者的教学与研究有一定的借鉴意义。

图书在版编目(CIP)数据

大学外语教育国际化与当代化国际学术会议论文集 / 周爽,崔诗晴主编. — 西安 : 西北工业大学出版社,2021.6
 ISBN 978-7-5612-7747-8

Ⅰ.①大… Ⅱ.①周… ②崔… Ⅲ.①外语教学-教学研究-高等学校-文集 Ⅳ.①H09-42

中国版本图书馆 CIP 数据核字(2021)第 115294 号

DAXUE WAIYU JIAOYU GUOJIHUA YU DANGDAIHUA GUOJI XUESHU HUIYI LUNWENJI
大 学 外 语 教 育 国 际 化 与 当 代 化 国 际 学 术 会 议 论 文 集

责任编辑:	隋秀娟 李 欣	策划编辑:	梁 卫
责任校对:	曹 江	装帧设计:	李 飞

出版发行:西北工业大学出版社
通信地址:西安市友谊西路 127 号　　　　邮编:710072
电　　话:(029)88491757,88493844
网　　址:www.nwpup.com
印　刷　者:西安日报社印务中心
开　　本:787 mm×1 092 mm　　　1/16
印　　张:16.125
字　　数:434 千字
版　　次:2021 年 6 月第 1 版　　2021 年 6 月第 1 次印刷
定　　价:88.00 元

如有印装问题请与出版社联系调换

序

当今世界复杂多变，我们生活在这危机与机遇并存的时代，正经历着百年未有之大变局。一方面，重重危机威胁着人类的持续健康发展，例如，人与自然之间的生态危机、人与社会之间的人文危机、人与人之间的道德危机、人与自己的心理危机、国家与国家之间的安全危机、文化与文化之间的价值观冲突危机等。另一方面，科学技术的迅猛发展带来了前所未有的机遇。相关报告指出，纳米技术、生物技术、信息技术和认知科学等四个领域是21世纪最前沿的科技领域。可以说，这四个领域都蕴藏着巨大的发展潜力，它们的交叉与融合都必将产生无法想象的效能。抢抓机遇，迎接挑战，教育是关键，是重器。

教育作为一种社会现象，自从人类社会形成以来就出现了。在社会的发展过程中，人类积累了知识和经验，并将之一代一代地传承下去，这种传承活动就是教育的雏形。随着人类知识和经验的更新和不断丰富，教育活动也不断发展和完善，并逐渐成为一种组织严密、培养人的正规的社会活动。教育的重要性不言而喻，我国最早的也是世界上最早的一部教育专著《礼记·学记》中就有这样的论述："建国君民，教学为先。"迪斯累里（Disraeli）在1874年曾指出："一个国家的命运取决于这个国家的人民的教育。"联合国教科文组织认为，人类的可持续发展最终要依靠教育，要教育出新一代的人。2020年刷屏的"后浪"，具有可持续发展的理念和可持续发展的能力。

我国的外语教育已有一百多年的历史，且取得了令人瞩目的辉煌成就，但如何进一步提升外语教育的质量，这是当今我国外语教育的核心问题，也是外语教育改革的永恒主题。为了提升教育的质量，落实立德树人的根本任务，回答和解决"培养什么人、怎样培养人、为谁培养人这个根本问题"，教育部先后颁布了《外国语言文学类教学质量国家标准》（2018）、《普通高等学校本科外国语言文学类专业教学指南》（2020）和《高等学校课程思政建设指导纲要》（2020），对我国外语教育人才培养质量标准、课程思政体系建设等做出了总体要求和明确规定。尤其是课程思政，强调要把价值塑造、知识传授和能力培养融为一体，这是新时代我国教育教学的特色，也是落实立德树人的重要举措。

《大学外语教育国际化与当代化国际学术会议论文集》一书，是我国外语教育教学领域中的一项最新成果，紧跟时代大潮，响应国家新文科号召，服务新时代，体现了新时代我国外语教育教学的鲜明特色，无疑是一股重要的学术有生力量。本书的研究内容涉及教育国际化背景下的跨文化教育、外语专业人才培养目标与路径、外语教学理念革新与实践、外语教学模式改革与创新、外语语言与教学研究等。仔细研读全书,我亦受益匪浅。最大的感受是,本书内容翔实,理论前沿,颇接地气,视野开阔,研究视角新颖,分析问题深入,极具启发性,值得大家研读和学习,故特此推荐。

正值腊月三十除夕之际,我为本书作序,高兴之余,不乏诚惶诚恐之感。由于水平有限,时间仓促,不妥之处,请各位朋友方家不吝赐教。

是为序!

2021 年 2 月 11 日

目 录

一、教育国际化背景下的跨文化教育

高校外语专业学生跨文化能力的培养/王守仁 …………………………………………………… 3

俄罗斯一流大学课程语言特点及启示/高 黎 韩东旭 刘玉姣 ……………………………… 9

英国国家语料库及欧洲语料库教学对中国大学语言教学的启示/罗翔宇
　　董俊虹 ………………………………………………………………………………………… 16

及物性视角下中国国家形象对外构建研究——以2015—2019年"中国新闻奖"
　　国际传播类评论报道为例/解梦周 刘美岩 …………………………………………………… 24

中国大学生跨文化交际能力现状调查研究/李朝翔 …………………………………………… 32

《大都会》的政治无意识解读/陈 璐 ……………………………………………………………… 41

二、外语专业人才培养目标与路径

从复合型人才培养到"全人"教育——对我国外语人才培养的再思考/文 旭
　　司卫国 ………………………………………………………………………………………… 49

综合类高校复语复合型人才培养目标下"英语＋丝路语"外语课程建设的思考/陈 洁
　　张 璐 …………………………………………………………………………………………… 59

大类培养下的外语专业人才培养路径——基于北京三校的考察/车向前 …………………… 66

改革文学选读课程,培养外语专业本科生科研能力/麻 蕾 ……………………………………… 72

从学生视角浅谈法语专业课程的改革与创新/李庆亚 臧小佳 ………………………………… 79

基于心理学视角的高校辅导员谈话技巧刍议——以某高校一名大学生学习倦怠案例
　　为例/高 敏 …………………………………………………………………………………… 82

三、外语教学理念革新与实践

社会主义核心价值观引领的外语课程思政研究/汪桃红 ……………………………………… 89

不忘初心·铸魂育人·中西贯通·文化入髓——论大学外语教育中的价值塑造
　　作用/王 倩 …………………………………………………………………………………… 93

大学外语"课程思政"体系建设实践研究/孙 静 ………………………………………………… 98

积极心理学在大学英语混合式教学中的运用研究/刘 勇 ……………………………………… 102

EMI课程的教学理念及通用教学方法/高 契 …………………………………………………… 106

四、外语教学模式改革与创新

大学英语教学游戏的设计与运用/屈江丽 ………………………………… 117
基于移动互联网环境的英语交互式课堂教学模式研究/杨艳卫 …………… 123
基于产出导向法的 MOOC+SPOC 混合教学模式探索——以非英语专业研究生跨
　　文化交流课程为例/周　兰 ………………………………………………… 127
线上线下混合教学模式中的大学英语学习者跨文化意识培养/王　方 …… 133
利用雨课堂进行研究生公共英语课教学的优势与弊端/张　放 …………… 138
口译教学中专题训练和技能训练对比及融合/王　茜 ……………………… 142
过程教学法在德语写作课堂的运用/陈　婧 ………………………………… 145

五、外语语言与教学研究

基于参数参照模式的口译质量及译员能力测评研究/孙　荧 ……………… 151
德语语音入门阶段的理论基础和错误分析/刘无双 ………………………… 161
英语口语教学与评估中的程式化词串/康　坛 ……………………………… 167
英语反身代词习得研究现状及前景展望/栾钧涵　张　奕 ………………… 172
语速对听力理解的影响/赵翊君　党　弋 …………………………………… 179
基于语料库的"BRING"语义韵比较研究/张晓红　董俊虹 ……………… 187
An Evaluation of Postgraduates' Global Competence and its Influencing Factors/
　　Lei Xiaolan ……………………………………………………………………… 192
Conceptualising Vocabulary Knowledge/Wang Xuan ……………………………… 200
Analysis of Squealer's Discourse Strategies in *Animal Farm*/Chen Yindi ………… 212
An Empirical Analysis of Writing Errors of Non-English Majors Based on Error
　　Analysis Theory/Li Fan　Feng Zongxiang ………………………………… 220
The EMI Sphinx—Transforming the Challenge of English Medium Instruction into an Effective
　　Approach to Learning to Meet the Needs of Our Time/Timothy Kingham …… 234

一、教育国际化背景下的跨文化教育

高校外语专业学生跨文化能力的培养

王守仁*

摘　要：本文对跨文化能力内涵提出新的界定，即认知层面的跨文化知识，功能层面的语言融通，行为层面的创造性与主动性，跨文化交流中的责任感和思辨意识。然后讨论外语专业学生跨文化能力培养"融"的途径：优化课程体系，在外语专业教学内容中有机融入中国元素；从语言技能训练上升到话语方式的掌握，融通中外语言、文化和思想；实现培养方式与手段的跨界融合。

关键词：跨文化能力；课程体系；话语方式；培养方式与手段

习近平总书记指出，"当今世界，人类生活在不同文化、种族、肤色、宗教和不同社会制度所组成的世界里，各国人民形成了你中有我、我中有你的命运共同体。"世界的多样性赋予人类社会生活以丰富性，同时也形成各种有形、无形的壁垒或疆界，而不同文化之间的隔阂是国与国之间以及地区之间发生冲突的最为主要的深层次原因之一。在全球化时代背景下，世界各国文化存在竞争性。法国总统马克龙在2019年外交使节会议的讲话中指出：中国、俄罗斯和印度在拥有强大的经济实力后，开始追寻自己的"国家文化"。"当这些新兴国家找到了自己的国家文化，并且开始坚信它时，他们就会逐渐摆脱西方霸权过去灌输给他们的'哲学文化'，而这正是西方霸权终结的开始。西方霸权的终结，不在于经济衰落，不在于军事衰落，而在于文化衰落。"(马克龙，2019)马克龙呼吁法国及其他欧洲国家做出重大调整，去尝试富有想象力的政治策略，努力维持西方霸权及其哲学文化的吸引力。随着我们国家扩大改革开放，进一步融入世界，中国与外部世界交往日益密切，出现了中外文化交流、交锋、交融日益频繁的态势。搭建不同文化平等对话的平台，有效传播中华文化，消除因文化差异而产生的偏见、误解甚至敌意，是推动人类命运共同体建设的基础性工作，而提升我们的跨文化能力是一个关键环节。

外语人才培养要关注跨文化能力，这涉及教学理念的转变，以及对中国外语人才内涵的认识。在中国语境下办外语专业，最显著的特点、不可替代性在哪里？笔者认为应该是"跨文化"。我们的外语专业不同于欧美国家的母语专业，因为我们是为中国的社会主义建设培养人才。我们的外语专业也不同于国内大学的中文系汉语专业，因为我们是为国家改革开放事业培养国际化人才。外语人才是中外沟通的桥梁，连接中外，双向融通。因此，中国一流外语人才必须具备跨文化能力，这是他们独特的关键能力和必备素养。

2018年，教育部颁布了《普通高等学校本科专业类教学质量国家标准》，针对外国语言文学专业类的学生提出了新的主要能力要求：

---

* 王守仁：南京大学人文社会科学资深教授，博士生导师，南京大学教师教学发展中心主任，中国外国文学学会副会长，主要研究方向为英美文学、英语教育。

外语专业学生应具备外语运用能力、文学赏析能力、跨文化能力、思辨能力,以及一定的研究能力、创新能力、信息技术应用能力、自主学习能力和实践能力(教育部高等学校教学指导委员会,2018)。

这是首次在国家层面制定的本科教学质量标准中对外语专业学生提出跨文化能力的要求,必将对高校外语专业教学产生深远影响。

1 跨文化能力的界定

一说到跨文化能力(intercultural competences),人们通常会想到跨文化交际,即 cross-cultural communication 或 intercultural communication。葛春萍和笔者(2016)曾著文讨论在大学英语教学中培养跨文化交际能力的问题,对跨文化交际能力的含义做了概述。跨文化交际能力涉及知识、态度和技能三个层面。在跨文化交际中首先要掌握相关文化知识,包括对中外文化异同的了解。其次要对异国文化持开放、包容的态度,知识和态度可以形成跨文化的敏感性。再次是技能,指跨文化交际时能采取恰当的方式,调适交际策略。衡量跨文化交际能力有两个标准:有效性(effectiveness)和适宜性(appropriateness)。

跨文化交际能力和跨文化能力经常互换使用。戴晓东的《跨文化能力研究》一书被列入"跨文化研究核心话题丛书",该书"导论"部分就有关于"跨文化能力概念的界定"。跨文化能力可以分为一般跨文化能力和特定跨文化能力:"一般跨文化能力是指那些应用于所有跨文化情境的基本的交际能力。特定跨文化能力是指在特定语境中的抑或与特定技能相联系的交际能力"(戴晓东,2018)。这一界定显然是基于"交际能力",而在实际操作中戴晓东也常常将跨文化交际能力等同于跨文化能力,原本是"跨文化交际能力研究的历史回顾"被置换成"跨文化能力研究的历史回顾",如1998年高一虹在《语言教学与研究》第3期发表了论文《跨文化交际能力的"道"与"器"》,戴晓东在他的书中则改换成了"高一虹的'道'与'器'跨文化能力理论"(戴晓东,2018)。孙有中长期以来一直从事跨文化研究,对跨文化能力培养进行了理论思考和实践探索。他在2016年发表的一篇文章中对跨文化能力的核心内涵做了如下的描述:

尊重世界文化多样性,具有跨文化同理心和批判性文化意识;掌握基本的跨文化研究理论知识和分析方法;熟悉所学语言对象国的历史与现状,理解中外文化的基本特点和异同;能对不同文化现象、文本和制品进行阐释和评价;能得体和有效地进行跨文化沟通;能帮助不同语言文化背景的人士进行有效的跨文化沟通(孙有中,2016)。

孙有中对跨文化能力的描述已超越了交际能力的边界,内容比较丰富。他在文中呼吁"外语界在新一轮教育和教学改革中高度重视跨文化能力培养"(孙有中,2016)。南京大学外国语学院近年来关注外语教育与跨文化能力的关系,结合人才培养实际,探索跨文化能力培养的有效路径,取得了显著成绩,笔者主持的"高素质外语人才跨文化能力培养体系创新与实践"教改项目获得了2018年国家级教学成果一等奖。

早在2009年,联合国教科文组织就发布了《投资于文化多样性与跨文化对话》(*Investing in Cultural Diversity and Intercultural Dialogue*)的报告,提出了"文化扫盲"(cultural literacy)的理念,认为文化扫盲已成为今日世界的生命线,是超越"无知之间的冲突"(clash of ignorances)不可或缺的工具(UNESCO,2009)。

2013年,联合国教科文组织发布了《跨文化能力概念与行动框架》(*Intercultural Competences — Conceptual and Operational Framework*)的报告。报告(UNESCO,2013)中运用了树形模型,将涉及跨文化能力的25个核心概念串联起来,组成一个有机的整体。报告将"文化"(Culture)和"交流"(Communication)视为跨文化能力的树根(Roots),其中,"文化"包括身份、价值、态度和信念,"交流"包括语言、对话、非言语行为;"跨文化对话"(Intercultural Dialogue)是树干(Trunk)的一部分,涉及专业领域的对话和非专业领域的对话。值得注意的是,模型中的"跨文化交际能力"(Intercultural Communicative Competence)只是跨文化能力这棵大树的一片叶子(Leave)。因此,在讨论跨文化能力培养时,应把跨文化交际能力和跨文化能力区分开来。

根据对跨文化内涵的研究和观察以及外语人才培养的实践,我们以跨文化交际能力为基础,进行拓展和创新,提出了具有中国特色的跨文化能力的界定:①认知层面的跨文化知识;②功能层面的语言融通;③行为层面的创造性与主动性;④跨文化交流中的责任感和思辨意识。

对外国文化的理解和认识是跨文化沟通的基础。几年前,国内某高校研究人员的科研论文因为文化的"无知",不恰当地使用了"造物主"(creator)一词,被人诟病。该论文研究了人手的构造,认为人手的构造机理是造物主为使人手得以完成无数灵巧功能而做出的精妙设计。因为"造物主"这个词与"神创论"和"智能设计论"的联系,这篇文章得到了源源不断的负面评论,论文作者后因引发"神创论"的辩论而撤稿并致歉。论文作者表示:"很抱歉引起了关于神创论的辩论。我们的研究与神创论毫无关系。英语并不是我们的母语。我们对于造物主一词的理解与母语是英语的人的理解是两回事。我们现在已经明白了是我们误解了造物主这个词。"(井木犴,2016)

要认识和了解西方,需要在认知层面做很多工作。华为总裁任正非(2018)在一次讲话中说:"当前我们还缺乏对西方世界(权力结构、文化与冲突、价值观、社会心理等)的深刻理解和认识。"我们生活在中国走向世界的时代,我们还有讲好中国故事、传播好中国声音、阐释好中国特色的任务。因此,我们要花大力气掌握认知层面的跨文化知识。

功能层面的语言融通是指话语方式的转变,即换位思考,熟谙西方的思维模式、文化传统、价值取向,以对方认知结构能够理解和接受的语言表达方式分享信息、陈述观点、展开辩论、取得共识。

行为层面的创造性与主动性是指在跨文化沟通中要起到主导地位。在构建人类命运共同体进程中,我们要具备跨文化领导力。中国参与全球治理要成为倡导者而不是"跟随"者,要在国际事务中发挥感召力、塑造力和影响力。

跨文化交流中的责任感和思辨意识主要涉及中外文化的交流、交锋和交融,要求我们具备批判性思维,进行比较与分析,坚持自己的文化立场。

2 跨文化能力的培养途径

文化作为民族精神的底色,是一个国家、一个民族的灵魂。党的十九大提出,要"坚定文化自信","坚守中华文化立场"。在这一思想指导下,我们确定以"坚定文化自信、提升跨文化能力"为核心理念,推进外语人才培养体系的改革与创新。

中国高校外语教育目前存在着"三重三轻"的问题。一是重国外,轻本土,单向教授西方历史社会文化知识,对中国文化缺乏必要关注,课程体系中对中国元素的凸显和阐释较为欠缺。二是重语言,微技能,轻话语方式,过于强调工具性的技能操练,缺乏对中外文化融通与话语方式转换重要性的足够认识。三是重知识积累,轻人文思辨,教学一般以知识讲解与积累为主,对跨文化批判性反思能力培养不够。从跨文化能力这一视角审视这些问题,转变教学理念,重构教学内容,更新教学方法与手段,可望找到解决方案。

孙有中(2016)曾就以跨文化能力培养为导向的外语类课堂教学提出五条基本原则:思辨(critiquing)、反省(reflecting)、探究(exploring)、共情(empathizing)、体验(doing)。这五条原则适用于外语类专业课程的教与学,具有针对性。为使高校外语教学从根本上发生变化,提升教育质量,跨文化能力培养的理念还需渗透和贯穿到课程体系、教学模式、每一个教学环节之中,具体可从三个"融"字上进行思考和探索。

第一,改变传统外语教学观念,在外语专业课程内容中有机融入中华优秀文化。重点建设用外语教授的中国思想文化课程,拓宽并加深外语专业学生对中国文化的认知与理解,尤其注重引导学生深化对中华民族经验智慧的认识,提高文化自觉,将推动中华文化"走出去"作为人才培养的重要着力点,使学生具有弘扬中国传统文化、讲好中国故事的意识和主动性。

第二,从语言技能训练上升到话语方式的转变。以"融通"为核心,形成"跨"文化的特点:既要有对中外文化经典的阅读与研习,也要有对文化经典的换位思考及换位表述,同时把握中外文化的本质与内涵,把"和而不同、交流互鉴"的观念贯穿始终。话语不单纯等同于语言,它具有特定思想指向和价值取向:"话语既是思想的外在表现形式,又是构成思想的重要元素"(谢伏瞻,2019)。在跨文化语境下,话语是一个涉及不同主体的"复杂的认知、交际活动",要"充分考量国际受众不同的文化背景,建立我们的话语与国际受众之间通达的主体间关系,以使我们的话语为不同文化受众所认知、理解和接受"(曲卫国,2015)。融通中外语言、文化和思想,方能有效阐释中国立场和观点。

第三,实现方式与手段的跨界,融合第一课堂和第二课堂、线上和线下、国内学习和国外研修,优化开放互动、国际化程度高的人才培养环境,拓展学生的知识结构,树立世界眼光,增强比较意识,发展批判性思维,有效培养学生在真实情景中进行跨文化沟通的能力。

国务院(2015)下发《统筹推进世界一流大学和一流学科建设总体方案》,确定的第一条"基本原则"为:"坚持以一流为目标。引导和支持具备一定实力的高水平大学和高水平学科瞄准世界一流,汇聚优质资源,培养一流人才,产出一流成果,加快走向世界一流"。建设一流学科,应该符合新时期我国高等教育的要求,即中国特色、世界水平和时代特征。南京大学外国语言文学学科入选一流学科建设名单,学校十分重视一流人才培养。笔者(2018)在一次学科建设专题研讨会上曾提出:"学科建设的中国特色充分体现在一流人才的培养上,即中国高校培养的是具有跨文化能力的人才,他们具有中国情怀和全球竞争力,能够融通中外,在中外交往中能够维护祖国利益,提升中国的国际话语权,这些方面是显著区别于其他高校的。"近年来,南京大学实施外语人才培养新方案,围绕提升学生跨文化能力采取了一些有效举措。

第一,通过优化课程体系,打造"中国思想经典""西方思想经典"等跨文化优质课程,在教学内容中充分融入中国元素,融通中外文化,帮助学生增强文化身份意识,提升对文化多元性的认识。

第二，通过构建跨文化能力培养模式，从叙事（narrate）入手，学会讲述故事。切实改变"重语言，微技能，轻话语表达"的传统外语教学方式，按照跨文化能力在认知、功能、行为等内涵构成上的要求，教学重点从强化语言技能训练转移到掌握话语方式，注重在认知和情感体验层面与对方实现历时和共时的互文对接。

第三，通过倡导研究性教学，开展文化经典研习，利用综合性大学的多学科优质资源与跨学科研究平台，实施文史哲多学科融通的"人文社会科学高级研究院本科生驻院研修项目""悦读经典计划"等，培养学生的高阶思维和批判性思维能力，促使学生增强文化自信与文化自觉。

第四，通过创新培养方式与手段，建设精品在线开放课程，使信息技术与课程内容整合、课堂学习与实践探索互动、国内学习与国外研修对接，依托一流国际化教学团队及国际合作项目，开展本科生交换学习、联合培养、开设国际化课程等，凸显跨文化能力培养的特色与有效性。

综上所述，跨文化能力源自跨文化交际能力，但已超越传统意义上的跨文化交际能力，具有丰富的内涵。高校外语教育重视跨文化能力培养，要求我们从新的角度思考外语专业人才培养目标、培养规格和课程体系，促使教学理念、教学模式、教学内容以及方法手段发生变化，对于外语专业主动适应新时代高等教育新形势、新变化、新挑战，加强内涵建设具有深远意义。中国外语教育应扎根于祖国大地，培养服务于社会主义建设和中华民族伟大复兴的外语人才，在真正意义上实现"中国特色世界一流"的外语教育。跨文化能力有助于学生拓展国际视野，看到一个更加完整的世界，具备应对未来社会挑战的全球胜任力。推进和深化以跨文化能力提升为核心的教学改革，无疑是培养高素质外语人才的有效途径。

参 考 文 献

戴晓东，2018，《跨文化能力研究》，外语教学与研究出版社。
马克龙，2019，法国总统马克龙闭门演讲：西方世界霸权已近终结，译者不详，2019-10-14。据凤凰网：https://ishare.ifeng.com/c/s/v002etIRTwu0O7ZW3mkDev7LiQekV9gbfe9d-_EwuQgQiwNk。
葛春萍、王守仁，2016，《跨文化交际能力培养与大学英语教学》，《外语与外语教学》第 2 期。
国务院，2015，《国务院关于印发统筹推进世界一流大学和一流学科建设总体方案的通知》。据中华人民共和国教育部官网：http://www.moe.gov.cn/jyb_xxgk/moe_1777/moe_1778/201511/t20151105_217823.html。
教育部高等学校教学指导委员会编，2018，《普通高等学校本科专业类教学质量国家标准》（上），高等教育出版社。
井木犴，2016，《"造物主"引发的撤稿：责任在谁？》。据果壳网：http://jingxuan.guokr.com/pick/v2/17696/。
曲卫国，2015，《浅谈跨文化话语的传播效率问题》，2015 年第三届国际语言传播学前沿论坛，江苏师范大学。
任正非，2018，《从人类文明的结晶中，找到解决世界问题的钥匙——任正非在公共关系战略纲要汇报会上的讲话》。据新浪网：https://tech.sina.com.cn/csj/2018-12-13/doc-ihmutuec8725806.shtml。

孙有中，2016，《外语教育与跨文化能力培养》，《中国外语》第3期。
王守仁，2018，《建设具有中国特色的一流外国语言文学学科》，《外国语文研究》第2期。
谢伏瞻，2019，《加快构建中国特色哲学社会科学学科体系、学术体系、话语体系》，《中国社会科学》第5期。
UNESCO. 2009. "Investing in Cultural Diversity and Intercultural Dialogue." Accessed from https：//unesdoc.unesco.org/ark/48223/pf0000185202？posInSet＝1&queryId＝a46d5c85-8697-447d-afd3-94abd1be9c27.
UNESCO. 2013. *Intercultural Competencies—Conceptual and Operational Framework*. Paris：UNESCO.

俄罗斯一流大学课程语言特点及启示

高 黎* 韩东旭** 刘玉姣***

摘 要:"世界一流大学建设"和"高等教育国际化"已经使得留学生成为各国争夺的资源,全英课程不仅是英语国家一流大学的实践,英语为第二语言国家和英语作为外语国家的一流大学也竞相开设相关课程。分析俄罗斯一流大学课程教学语言形态,发现这些大学的课程语言不仅有俄语和英语,而且包括法语、德语、西班牙语、意大利语和汉语,具有多样性。其中,全英课程规模最大,已覆盖从本科到研究生等各个层次的课程,且广泛分布于多个学科领域。俄罗斯一流大学的课程语言不仅顺应时代发展,而且针对学位课程目标人群"量身定制",有助于增加留学生的数量和多样性。我国"双一流"大学的课程语言设置既需要放眼国际,增设全英课程,也要立足地区,考虑"一带一路"沿线国家留学生的需要,适当发展用其他语言讲授的学位课程。

关键词:俄罗斯;一流大学课程语言;全英课程;留学生;"一带一路"

"世界一流大学建设"和"高等教育国际化"已然成为近年各国高等教育发展的重点。无论是发达国家还是发展中国家均高度致力于此。这也就使得留学生日益成为各高校竞相争抢的资源。奖学金、签证和就业等因素固然影响留学目的国的选择,课程教学语言(Medium of Instruction,中文简称课程语言)则始终是影响留学决定的首要因素。究竟是选择英语国家的大学,还是非英语国家的大学,选择 A 大学还是 B 大学,课程语言与留学生已掌握语言的一致性必然占有很大权重。英语已经当之无愧地成为世界通用语,非英语国家一流大学的课程语言是否也应是全英教学(English Medium Instruction)以吸引留学生,是一流大学建设绕不过去的问题。分析俄罗斯一流大学学位课程教学语言的特点,可以起到"他山之石"的作用。

1 一流大学课程语言样态

一流大学课程语言样态指的是一流大学使用母语、英语或其他语言进行学位课程教学所形成的课程语言分布形态。此处无意于深究"一流大学"的定义,而是以三大世界大学排名(THE、QS、ARWU)之一的 THE 世界大学排名为依据,将 2019 年世界排名在前 100 名的大学作为本文一流大学的代表。

一流大学的国别归属很大程度上能够反映其课程语言种类。一般来说,英语国家大学的

---

* 高黎:西北大学外国语学院教授,教育学博士,主要研究方向为外国文学、比较文学。
** 韩东旭:西北大学外国语学院硕士研究生。
*** 刘玉姣:西北大学外国语学院硕士研究生。

课程语言理所当然是英语,非英语国家大学的情况则要区别而论。总体来说,这 100 所大学不均匀地分布在 16 个国家/地区。根据国家/官方语言或主要语言使用情况,这些国家/地区可归为 3 类,即英语国家/地区(英语为国语或主要使用语言)、英语为第二语言(English as a second language,ESL)国家和英语作为外语(English as a foreign language,EFL)国家。

第一类的英语国家/地区包括美国(41 所)、英国(11 所)、澳大利亚(6 所)、加拿大(5 所)、中国香港(3 所)和新加坡(2 所)。可以想见,这 6 个英语国家/地区的 68 所一流大学的学位课程(语言类课程除外)语言自然应是英语,即 2/3 强的世界一流大学实行全英教学。

第二类的 ESL 国家有 7 个,分别为荷兰(7 所)、德国(7 所)、瑞典(3 所)、瑞士(3 所)、法国(2 所)、芬兰(1 所)和比利时(1 所)。值得注意的是,这些国家均位于欧洲,并且都签署了《博洛尼亚宣言》,是欧洲高等教育区成员国(European Higher Education Area,2019)。这些国家在博洛尼亚进程中,已经打破了制度藩篱,建立了学分转换体系和三级学位制度,参加了伊拉斯谟等项目来促进师生流动(徐辉,2010)。大量开设全英课程也已成为促进欧洲高等教育区人员流动的重要手段。荷兰和德国作为该组的"领头羊"更是如此。两国的公立和私立大学均开设了全英学位课程(Dearden,2014)。荷兰皇家艺术与科学院(Royal Netherlands Academy of Arts and Sciences)最新调查显示,荷兰高校 70% 的硕士课程语言为英语,而 2015—2016 学年仅有 18% 的硕士生选择课程语言为荷兰语的学位课程(KNAW,2019)。荷兰排名第一的阿姆斯特丹大学的 94 门硕士学位课程和 62 门本科学位课程中,全英课程分别为 72 门和 14 门(University of Amsterdam,2019)。

德国大学全英课程总量虽逊于荷兰,却也高达 1 884 种(Study.eu,2019)。德国政府早在 1997 年就拨专款资助高校开设全英课程来吸引留学生,2002 年全英课程数量为 62 门(许南,2012)。如今,德国排名第一的慕尼黑大学(University of Munich)的 23 门硕士学位课程为全英课程,全英文授课的博士课程则处于不断增长中(LMU,2019)。全英课程显然是德国吸引留学生的一个有效方式,2014 年留学德国的人数已经达到 35 万人。

第三类的 EFL 国家包括中国内地(3 所)、韩国(2 所)和日本(2 所)。全英学位课程在我国还处于有待大幅度增加的阶段(刘志民、杨洲,2017)。韩国和日本一流大学的全英课程如何?韩国于 1999 年提出"智慧韩国计划"(Brain Korea 21 Project)改革高等教育,包括聘请海外教授开设新专业,使用国际前沿教材等方式提升课程国际化程度等(朱春楠,2016)。2008 年起,韩国每年特别评选 13 所大学划拨专款来支持开设全英课程(张雷生,2015)。首尔大学的全英课程已逾 800 门(Seoul National University,2019);成均馆大学则有 40% 的课程用英语讲授(SKKU,2019)。

日本也在大力发展全英课程。日本全国已在 40 个本科专业、150 个硕士和 122 个博士学位课程中实行全英教学(牟宜武,2017)。东京大学和京都大学这两所世界一流大学的全英课程已蔚然成风。前者有 22 门研究生学位课程(University of Tokyo,2019)和部分本科生课程用英语讲授,后者的土木工程专业本科课程和 25 门研究生学位课程也是如此(Kyoto University,2019)。

2 俄罗斯一流大学课程语言特点

英语已经毫无疑问成为世界通用语,甚至学术通用语。THE 世界排名前 100 名的大学的课程语言样态无疑表明了这一点。俄罗斯一流大学的课程语言特点是本文要重点分析的。搜索俄罗斯官方留学网站留学俄罗斯(Study in Russia)、5-100项目高校协会网站(Association of Global Universities)以及各大学网站信息,可以发现俄罗斯一流大学课程语言呈现如下特征。

2.1 课程语言多样化:多语授课并行

俄罗斯一流大学课程语言呈现的第一个鲜明特征,就是多样性,不仅包括俄罗斯的国语(即俄语)和英语,还有其他课程语言。莫斯科国立大学的课程语言有3种,包括俄语、英语和汉语(Lomonosov Moscow State University, 2019)。圣彼得堡国立大学的课程语言多达6种,有俄语、英语、德语、法语、西班牙语和意大利语(St. Petersburg University, 2019)。跨文化交际中德俄对话、言语交际理论与实践和同声传译三门硕士学位课程使用德语讲授,翻译技术创新这门硕士学位课程语言则可使用法语、西班牙语或意大利语讲授。

俄罗斯其他一流大学的学位课程语言同样也呈现多语化的特征。俄罗斯国立科技大学(National University of Science and Technology)除了开设了俄语和英语授课的硕士和博士学位课程,还开设了法语授课的工商管理硕士学位课程;高等经济学院(Higher School of Economics)和西伯利亚联邦大学(Siberian Federal University)既有俄语和英语授课的学位课程,还分别开设了德语授课的文化思想史和德俄法律这两门硕士学位课程(Study in Russia, 2019)。

值得注意的是,俄罗斯人民友谊大学(People's Friendship University of Russia)不仅开设了俄语、英语、西班牙语(世界政治课)和德语(公共管理课)为课程语言的研究生学位课程,还开设了俄语、英语和法语授课的学士学位课程,并提供了专家层次的全英课程(见表1)(RUDN University, 2019)。塞切诺夫大学(Sechenov University)和新西伯利亚州立大学(Novosibirsk State University)也是如此。

表1 俄罗斯人民友谊大学多种语言课程分布

层次	教学语言	专业
专家	英语	3
本科	法语	1
	英语	6
硕士	英语	20
	法语	4
	西班牙语	1
博士	英语	17

资料来源:根据俄罗斯人民友谊大学网站信息整理而成。

可以看出,这些一流大学的课程语言已涵盖多种语言,不仅有俄语和英语,还有德语、法语、西班牙语、意大利语和汉语。整体而言,这些一流大学的课程语言虽以俄语和英语为主,但针对具体专业则"量身定制"课程语言,形成了一道多语授课"风景"。

2.2 全英课程规模化:多学科多层次

俄罗斯一流大学课程语言显然具有多样性,其中全英课程的规模化尤其让人瞩目。从学科分布来说,莫斯科国立大学在生物学、地质学、政治学、商学、经济学等 7 个学科领域开设了全英学位课程(Lomonosov Moscow State University,2019)。圣彼得堡国立大学的全英课程分布于 9 个学科领域,分别为应用数学和信息学、物理学、生态学与土地利用、社会学、国际关系、政治学、管理学、经济学和文化研究(St. Petersburg University,2019)。远东联邦大学(Far Eastern Federal University)这一在俄率先开设全英硕士课程的大学,已有建筑、国际关系、管理、法律等专业使用英语授课(FEFU,2019)。罗巴切夫斯基大学(Lobachevsky University)全英课程分布于数学与计算机科学、神经科学、超级计算机技术与高性能计算等专业,以及经济学、信息技术和国际关系等专业(UNN,2019)。塞切诺夫大学和喀山国立大学(Kazan Federal University)开设的全英课程包括药学、牙科学和医学 3 个学科领域(Study in Russia,2019)。显见,俄罗斯一流大学全英课程不仅涵盖了自然科学、工程技术、医学,而且广泛分布于人文社会科学领域。

从层次来说,俄罗斯高校的全英课程已涵盖本科到研究生所有层次的学位课程。在本科层次开设较多全英课程的大学有高等经济学院、康德波罗的联邦大学(Immanuel Kant Baltic Federal University)、莫斯科工程物理学院(Moscow Engineering Physics Institutes)、圣彼得堡理工大学(St. Petersburg Polytechnic University)和萨马拉大学(Samara University)等 10 所大学。相比于本科层次,硕士层次的全英课程数量更多。俄罗斯一流大学均开设了数量不等的硕士全英课程,这些课程是全英课程的主体。开设博士层次全英课程的大学较少,主要有乌拉尔联邦大学(Ural Federal University)、高等经济学院、莫斯科工程物理学院、俄罗斯人民友谊大学和新西伯利亚州立大学。除了以上各层次的全英课程,俄罗斯人民友谊大学、塞切诺夫大学和新西伯利亚州立大学在专家层次也开设了全英课程。

从数量来看,俄罗斯一流大学全英课程的规模的确可观。硕士层次的全英课程数量最多,共有 284 门。其中,高等经济学院的这类课程数量最多(55 门),俄罗斯人民友谊大学、圣光机大学和莫斯科工程物理学院的数量分别为 35 门、27 门和 24 门(Study in Russia,2019)。博士层次的以乌拉尔联邦大学的全英课程居首,有 93 门,涵盖了自然科学与数学、工程技术、社会科学、人文以及艺术文化领域(UrFU,2019)。高等经济学院、莫斯科工程物理学院和俄罗斯人民友谊大学在该层次的全英课程数量分别为 55 门、30 门和 20 门。

3　启示

上面的分析显示,俄罗斯一流大学课程语言与 ESL 国家(如荷兰和德国)和 EFL 国家(如日本和韩国)一流大学的课程语言既有共性,又有差异。共性表现在对于全英课程的"青睐",而差异性可从多语授课并行上看出。无论采用何种语言授课,俄罗斯近 6 年的一流大学建设成效还是成绩斐然(The Times Higher Education World University Rankings:Russia's Success Story,2019)。那么,俄罗斯的经验对于我国"双一流"大学建设和高等教育国际化有何启示?

3.1　建设全英课程,吸引优质留学生

全英课程显然成为世界一流大学建设和高等教育国际化的"加速器",是吸引留学生(尤其是学力留学生)的"利器"。荷兰、德国、韩国和日本一流大学的经验和实践如此,俄罗斯亦然。

具体来看,高等经济学院的社会学和数学专业排名不仅在俄罗斯数一数二,在全世界也是排在前 100 名(HSE,2018)。5-100 项目实施时,高等经济学院全英课程不足 5%,留学生比例不到 3%,2013 年这两方面占比分别增至 9.7% 和 3.61%;次年分别达到 10% 和 5.34%(HSE,2018);2018 年则升为 51%(245 门学位课程中本科、硕士和博士的全英课程分别为 15 门、55 门、55 门)和 17.7%(39 500 名学生中 7 000 人为留学生)(HSE,2018)。显然,全英课程与留学生数量、高等教育国际化、世界大学排名之间存在密切联系。非英语国家一流大学使用何种语言教学,定然影响留学生的留学决定。欧洲大学曾经凭借拉丁语实现知识生产传播和人员流动,今天的世界选择了英语作为通用语,开展全英课程已是一流大学建设的必由之路。

相比于俄罗斯,我国一流大学的全英课程有待大力发展。以清华大学和北京大学为例,前者在 THE 2019 年的世界排名为 22 名,但其 2018—2019 年仅有 16 门硕士学位课程和 4 门博士学位课程实行全英授课(清华大学,2018);后者的世界排名为 31 名,仅提供 11 门硕士全英课程,如国际关系、中国法、公共政策、工商管理等专业(北京大学,2018)。我国一流大学全英课程虽有发展,但与其他世界一流大学全英课程的规模相比,仍是任重道远。

全英课程既是如此,我国留学生数量如何?从来华留学生人数来说,我国已是亚洲最大的留学目的国,但具体分析一流大学留学生人数占比,与其他世界一流大学仍存在较大差距。清华大学留学生数量与学生总体数量之比仅为 11%,北京大学的留学生比例略高,为 17%。相对照的是,世界排名第 1 位和第 2 位的牛津大学和剑桥大学的该项比例却分别高达 40% 和 37%(THE,2018)。此外,我国留学生教育质量亟待提高。目前来华留学生以非学力学生为主,多是为了文化交流和语言学习,而不是攻读学位。这些未来的"友好使者",显然难以提供科学技术创新所需的高水平智力支持。大力建设全英课程更加具有必要性和迫切性。

世界已经进入争夺留学生的时代。无论是为补给人力资源、发展教育服务贸易,还是开展教育外交和文化传播,各国均出台了各种优惠政策来吸引留学生。传统的留学市场在一定程度上也随之发生了一些变化。推拉因素中的学费和安全等因素固然重要,不过一流大学的教育质量仍是留学生最为看重的,建设多学科、多层次的全英学位课程是制胜的重要条件。

3.2 创设多语并行课程,增强留学生来源多样化

高等教育的国际化是要实现师生、课程和研究的国际化,而不是"英语化"。奈特(Jane Knight)对于高等教育国际化下的定义表明,课程国际化是将国际的、跨文化的和全球的维度融入课程的全过程,即目标、内容、实施和评价。英国高校课程国际化采取了开设专门国际性主题(如国际文化)和地区研究(如亚太地区),学科内容中融入国际新发展的知识以及课程交换学习等不同方式(沈陆娟、张婷、蔡建平,2012)。美国高校课程国际化则通过强化外语学习与课程的整合等方式,即使用当地语言讲授历史、政治和世界文化等课程(钱小龙、汪霞,2012)。

这些做法显然说明了课程国际化绝不等于课程语言英语化。英语国家大学课程的国际化既有使用特定语言讲授特定课程的,也有使用本族语在课程中融入国际维度的。语言作为"思想的外壳"自然不如思想本身重要。英语成为学术通用语,使得英语国家学生可以不学其他语言,而通过有国际维度的课程内容来获取世界公民所需能力。

不过,对于非英语国家一流大学来说,无论是出于推动课程国际化还是吸引留学生的目的,开设多种语言并行的课程,可以增强本国学生的语言技能,拓展国际视野,并为不同国家的

不同语言使用者提供课程学习的便利。如果说,非洲留学生青睐法国的一个重要原因是共通法语,独联体成员国学生留学俄罗斯也会享有俄语作为族际语的便利,"一带一路"沿线国家主要使用的语言或许也能成为我国一些大学可以建设的学位课程语言,来促进地区人员流动。

实现留学生来源多样化,提高留学生教育质量,加速高等教育国际化,加快建设世界一流大学,是我国"双一流"高校建设工作的历史使命与挑战。俄罗斯一流大学的经验已经揭示,全英课程和多语教学在一流大学建设和高等教育国际化方面具有显著促进作用,我国一流大学亦可有所作为。

参 考 文 献

北京大学,2018,留学申请。据北京大学国际合作部留学生办公室官网:http://www.isd.pku.edu.cn/lxsq.htm。

刘志民、杨洲,2017,《2001—2014 年八大留学目的国位序变化的成因分析与启示》,《黑龙江高教研究》第 8 期。

牟宜武,2017,《全球化时代日本高等教育之国际化战略》,《外语界》第 5 期。

钱小龙、汪霞,2012,《美国大学课程国际化之路》,《高教发展与评估》第 3 期。

清华大学,2018,发展概况。据清华大学官网:http://www.tsinghua.edu.cn/publish/newthu/newthu_cnt/education/edu-3-1.html。

沈陆娟、张婷、蔡建平,2012,《21 世纪以来英国高等教育课程国际化策略和实践》,《内蒙古师范大学学报》第 5 期。

徐辉,2010,《欧洲"博洛尼亚进程"的目标、内容及其影响》,《教育研究》第 4 期。

许南,2012,《高等教育国际化:德国经验及其对中国教育和经济发展的启示》,《教育与经济》第 3 期。

张雷生,2015,《韩国高等教育国际化办学战略政策述评》,《高校教育管理》第 2 期。

朱春楠,2016,《高等教育国际化视阈下的韩国创新型人才培养分析》,《东北师大学报》第 3 期。

European Higher Education Area. 2019. "Full Members." Accessed from http://www.ehea.info/page-full_members.

FEFU. 2019. "Master's Degree Programs in English." Accessed from https://www.dvfu.ru/en/admission/master-studies/master-s-degree-programs-in-english/.

HSE. 2018. "Facts and Figures." Accessed from https://www.hse.ru/en/figures/.

HSE. 2018. "Stage Two of the Roadmap Summary." Accessed from https://strategy.hse.ru/en/documents5-100.

Dearden, Julie. 2014. "English as a medium of instruction—a growing global phenomenon." British Council.

KNAW. 2019. "Nederlands en/of Engels?" Accessed from https://www.knaw.nl/nl/actueel/publicaties/nederlands-en-of-engels.

Kyoto University. 2019. "English-taught Degree Programs." Accessed from http://www.opir.kyoto-u.ac.jp/study/en/curriculum/inenglish/.

LMU. 2019. "Factsheets:LMU at a glance." Accessed from http://www.en.uni-muenchen.de/about_lmu/introducing-lmu/factsheets/index.html.

Lomonosov Moscow State University. 2019. "Prospective Students." Accessed from https://www.msu.ru/en/admissions/.

RUDN University. 2019. "Education." Accessed from http://eng.rudn.ru/education/educational-programs/?level_of_training=489&language=83&mode_of_study%5B%5D=493.

Seoul National University. 2019. "Why NU." Accessed from http://www.useoul.edu/apply/whySNU.

SKKU. 2019. "Why SKKU?" Accessed from https://admission-global.skku.edu/eng/about/why.html.

St. Petersburg University. 2019. "Master Degree Programmes in English/German/French/Spanish/Italian." Accessed from http://english.spbu.ru/education-at-spbu/graduate/master-in-english.

Study.eu. 2019. "Germany again 1st for International Students before UK, France, in Study.EU Country Ranking 2018." Accessed from https://www.study.eu/press/germany-again-1st-for-international-students-before-uk-france-in-study-eu-country-ranking-2018.

Study in Russia. 2019. "Educational Programmes." Accessed from https://studyinrussia.ru/en/study-in-russia/programs/level-is-master%27s%20degree/langs-is-german/type-is-main/duration-from-0-to-100/apply/.

THE. 2018. "Peking University." Accessed from https://www.timeshighereducation.com/world-university-rankings/peking-university.

THE. 2018. "Tsinghua University." Accessed from Accessed from https://www.timeshighereducation.com/world-university-rankings/tsinghua-university.

THE. 2018. "University of Cambridge." Accessed from https://www.timeshighereducation.com/world-university-rankings/university-cambridge.

THE. 2018. "University of Oxford." Accessed from https://www.timeshighereducation.com/world-university-rankings/university-oxford.

"The Times Higher Education World University Rankings:Russia's Success Story, 2019." Accessed from https://5top100.ru/en/news/87872/.

University of Amsterdam. 2019. "Degree Programmes." Accessed from http://www.uva.nl/en/about-the-uva/about-the-university/facts-and-figures/facts-and-figures.html.

University of Tokyo. 2019. "Degree Programs Offered in English for Graduate Students." Accessed from https://www.u-tokyo.ac.jp/en/prospective-students/graduate_course_list.html.

UNN. 2019. "Degree Programmes in English." Accessed from http://eng.unn.ru/academic-programmes/degree-programmes.

UrFU. 2019. "Doctoral Programs in Russian." Accessed from https://urfu.ru/en/international/programs-and-courses/doctoral-programs-in-english/.

英国国家语料库及欧洲语料库教学对中国大学语言教学的启示

罗翔宇*　董俊虹**

摘　要：本文通过介绍和剖析欧洲语料库的发展现状、英国国家语料库以及语料库教学在欧洲大学教学中的应用，提出英国国家语料库及欧洲语料库教学对中国大学语言教学发展具有启示意义。从学生角度来看，需要加强对语料库的了解和具体应用，并且学校应为学生提供一些便利的语料库资源；从教师角度来看，教师应加强语料库和语料库相关计算机技能以及语料库相关教学技能。

关键词：英国国家语料库；欧洲语料库教学；中国大学语言教学

1　引言

计算机技术的发展，存储介质的开发和储存容量的扩大；互联网技术的发展，以电子文本为形式的众多文献在网上传播；共享语料库索引的开发，索引软件能应用于不同类型语料库的开发，这些因素为语料库的发展提供了相应的技术支撑。加上语料库逐渐体现了其极大的应用价值，人们对语料库的需求逐渐增大。1999年，29个欧洲国家于意大利博洛尼亚提出了欧洲高等教育改革计划。这个计划的目标是整合欧盟的高等教育资源，打通固有的教育体制，此计划被称为"博洛尼亚进程"。自从博洛尼亚进程启动，欧洲大学对语料库的建设速度加快，语料库教学在欧洲发展迅速。再看中国，为了更好地发展教育，国家一直在进行教育方式的改革，而欧洲语料库教学对中国外语教学具有较大的借鉴意义。本文从英国国家语料库（British National Corpus，BNC）入手，尝试分析欧洲语料库教师教学培训，并尝试得出欧洲语料库教学对中国大学语言教学的一些借鉴和启示。

2　欧洲语料库发展现状

欧洲议会于2001年通过了《欧洲语言参考框架》（Common European Framework Reference For Language，CEFR），主要作用是为描述个人语言技能提供一个统一的参考标准，其目的是为语言课程纲要和课程指导方针的制定、教学材料的设计和外语水平评估提供透明、一致和全面的基础。它用于欧洲，也用于其他地区，已包括39种语言（刘建达、周艳琼，2017）。《欧洲语言参考框架》在外语水平评估方面有着对交际背景、主题、任务和目的的详细

---

*　罗翔宇：西北工业大学外国语学院硕士研究生。
**　董俊虹：西北工业大学外国语学院教授，主要研究方向为认知语言学、二语习得、高等教育管理等。

分析,以及交流时所要求能力的详细描述。这意味着欧洲语言有了较为统一的评估标准,为语料库建设时的语料搜集整理和划分都提供了一定的便利。与此同时,因为统一评估标准的出现,语料库的使用价值更为凸显,即人们更容易利用语料库的大数据的收集统计来分析语言现状、语言使用的规范以及其他语言研究和教学。可以说,《欧洲语言参考框架》在一定程度上推动了语料库的发展。

目前,欧洲较为成熟的语料库有英国国家语料库(BNC)、兰开斯特-奥斯陆/卑尔根语料库(Lancaster-Oslo/Bergen Corpus,LOB Corpus)、国际英语语料库(International Corpus of English,ICE)、欧洲议会平行语料库(European Parliament Proceeding Parallel Corpus,EPC)等,欧洲语料库的语料内容涉及口语语料以及文本语料,其范围涉及双语、多语、中介语等。语料库在欧洲语言教育教学方面发展十分迅速。语料库教学的应用体现在以下两个方面。一是间接应用,主要基于目标语言的语料库,描述和分析学习者的语言和语言特征语的词典编纂,语法书和教科书的编写;二是直接应用,包括语料库知识的讲授、教授如何利用语料库做相关研究以及基于语料库的教学等(张晓姗,2017)。

3 英国国家语料库

3.1 英国国家语料库简介

英国国家语料库始建于1991年,并于1994年完成。该语料库收集了各种来源的书面和口语样本,词容量约为1亿个,代表了20世纪后期英国英语,包括口头和书面语言。最新版本是2007年发布的BNC XML版本。

英国国家语料库的书面语言部分(90%)收录了包括来自许多地区和国家的报纸、适合各年龄段和不同兴趣人员的专业期刊、学术书籍、流行小说、已发表和未发表的信函和备忘录,以及散文等许多其他类型的文本。口头语言部分(10%)收录了非正式的对话(由志愿者录制,由不同年龄、地区和社会阶层以人口均衡的方式记录)和在不同背景下收集的口语,包括正式商业活动或政府会议以及广播节目。自项目完成以来,2个BNC材料的子语料库已发布:BNC取样器和BNC宝贝。

3.2 英国国家语料库的数据构成

3.2.1 英国国家语料库的实际构成

英国国家语料库的实际构成类型有以下几种:
(1)文本:不超过45 000字的不同样本的数量。
(2)s单位(s-units):由CLAWS系统识别的⟨s⟩元素的数量(约等于句子)。
(3)w单位(w-units):由CLAWS系统标识的⟨w⟩元素的数量(约等于单词)。
BNC的XML版本包含4 049个文本,占5 228 040 KB,或约5.2 GB。它总共包含不到1亿个正字(96 986 707),但w单位(带POS标签的项目)的数量略高于98 363 783。标记区分了另外13 614 425个标点符号字符串,110 691 482个字符串。标记的s单位总数约为600万(6 026 284)。

表1给出了所有计数的绝对计数和百分比。

表 1 文本类型

Category	texts	w-units	percentage/%	s-units	percentage/%
Book	1411	50 293 803	57.18	2 887 523	57.88
Periodical	1208	28 609 494	32.52	1 487 644	29.82
Miscellaneous published	238	4 233 135	4.81	287 700	5.76
Miscellaneous unpublished	249	3 538 882	4.02	220 672	4.42
To-be-spoken	35	1 278 618	1.45	104 665	2.09

3.2.2 文本所涉及的主题

英国国家语料库把所有涉及的主题分配到9个范围中(见表2),其中8个是信息性文本。但根据主题进行分类很难适用于文学或创意类文本,因此,这些文本都被标记为创意文本,并没有被分配到特定的主题范围中。

表 2 文本所涉及主题

Category	texts	w-units	percentage/%	s-units	percentage/%
Imaginative	476	16 496 420	18.75	1 352 150	27.10
Informative: natural & pure science	146	3 821 902	4.34	183 384	3.67
Informative: applied science	370	7 174 152	8.15	356 662	7.15
Informative: social science	526	14 025 537	15.94	698 218	13.99
Informative: world affairs	483	17 244 534	19.60	798 503	16.00
Informative: commerce & finance	295	7 341 163	8.34	382 374	7.66
Informative: arts	261	6 574 857	7.47	321 140	6.43
Informative: belief & thought	146	3 037 533	3.45	151 283	3.03
Informative: leisure	438	12 237 834	13.91	744 490	14.92

3.2.3 文本媒介

文本媒介主要包括图书、期刊、已出版的杂项类、未出版的杂项类和书面口语类(见表3)。其中,已出版的杂项类包括小册子、传单、手册、广告;未出版的杂项类包括信函、备忘录、报告、会议记录、散文;书面口语类包括脚本、电视资料、剧本等。

表 3 文本媒介

Category	texts	w-units	percentage/%	s-units	percentage/%
Book	1411	50 293 803	57.18	2 887 523	57.88
Periodical	1208	28 609 494	32.52	1 487 644	29.82
Miscellaneous published	238	4 233 135	4.81	287 700	5.76
Miscellaneous unpublished	249	3 538 882	4.02	220 672	4.42
To-be-spoken	35	1 278 618	1.45	104 665	2.09

3.3 英国国家语料库的特点

第一,单语。它主要涉及现代英式英语,而不是英国人使用的其他语言。不过,非英国的英语和外语单词确实也存在于语料库中。

第二,共时性。它涵盖了20世纪后期的英国英语,而不是研究语言产生的历史发展时期。

第三,普遍性。它包括许多不同的风格和种类,并不限于任何特定的主题或者流派。特别是它包含口头和书面语言的例子。

第四,样本涵盖范围广。关于书面语言来源,45 000个单词的样本来自单个作者文本的各个部分。最多包含45 000字的较短文本,或杂志和报纸等多作者文本全部包含在内。抽样允许在1亿限制范围内扩大文本的覆盖范围,并避免过度表现特殊文本。

第五,混合性。由口头和书面语言共同组成。

3.4 英国国家语料库的应用

3.4.1 应用领域

在"英国国家语料库 BNCW02 计划使用"的工作文件中,确定了以下可能适用于英国国家语料库的领域,笔者将结合实例进行分析。

(1)参考书的出版。

出版商可以使用语料库进行字典编辑、语法书籍的撰写并出版。绝大多数的参考书都或多或少地借助了语料库。以字典为例,BNC取样器有100万个书面单词的集合,BNC宝贝有400万个单词样本,出版商可以将这些数据作为字典编辑出版的参考数据,如词性搭配、词语例句等。

(2)语言学研究。

人们可以使用语料库研究语言学。语料库会提供如词汇、语法、形态、语义、语篇分析、文体学、社会语言学的原始数据,学者可以通过这些原始数据进行语言学研究,如图1、图2所示。

No	Filename	Hits 1 to 50　Page 1 / 9
1	A0D 1308	She wore peach **satin** camiknickers and no stockings — it was breath-taking.
2	A0L 281	But Woodstock and the sunshine hippies broke through the clouds of small-town standards, and Jay scoured the Oxfam shop for silk and **satin** and velvet.
3	A0X 171	Roncraft are producing a range of clear and coloured versions, but I suspect that the clear gloss and **satin** finishes will be of most interest.
4	A0X 283	The varnishes are available in gloss, **satin** and matt and the floor coating in gloss and satin.
5	A0X 283	The varnishes are available in gloss, satin and matt and the floor coating in gloss and **satin**.
6	A16 124	Which one to use depends, to some extent, upon the appearance which you wish to achieve, which may be an oiled or waxed appearance, a high gloss, **satin** or matt finish, and on what is being finished.
7	A16 161	If the desired shade is obtained with one coat of varnish stain, then further protection should be given with extra coats of clear gloss, **satin** or matt varnish.
8	A16 175	Alternatively, the surface can be rubbed with grade 00 or 000 steel wool and wax polish to produce a smooth **satin** or matt finish.
9	A16 182	**Satin** and matt varnishes and varnish stains must, however, be thoroughly stirred before use until there is no more sediment on the bottom of the container.
10	A16 230	Left: Gloss and **satin** varnishes applied to a panelled hallway (Ronseal).
11	A16 594	Ronseal Pine **Satin** Varnish
12	A16 595	Ronseal Clear **Satin** Varnish
13	A16 601	If you wish to antique new wood, apply one coat of Ronseal pine coloured **Satin** Varnish.
14	A16 911	Available in gloss and **satin** finishes, the new paints result in a lower odour than traditional solvent-based paints, making home decorating a more enjoyable task for both the applier and the occupants.

图1　Satin 的搜索结果

BNC header information for file A0D	
Title:	A classic English crime. Sample containing about 36147 words from a book (domain: imaginative)
Spoken or Written:	Written
Number of Words (tagged items):	37,033
Average sentence length (<w>-tags per <s>-unit):	12.3526
Derived text type:	Fiction and verse
Genre:	W:fict:prose
Text type:	Written books and periodicals
Publication date:	1985-1993
Age of Author:	unknown
Domicile of Author:	unknown
Sex of Author:	unknown
Type of Author:	Multiple
Age of Audience:	Adult
Text Domain:	Imaginative prose
Perceived level of difficulty:	Medium
Medium of Text:	Book
Place of publication:	UK: South (south of Bristol Channel-Wash line)
Text Sample:	End sample

图 2　文件 Satin A0D 文件的具体信息

笔者以单词"Satin"在语料库中进行搜索,便出现了 Satin 相关搭配的语料,学者可以利用其中例句、搭配和这个词所出现的文献的具体出处进行语言现象研究。

(3)人工智能。

英国国家语料库还能运用于人工智能数据测试,主要是基于程序开发的大数据测试平台,通过其庞大的数据总量支持人工智能数据测试平台的开发。

(4)自然语言处理。

英国国家语料库能应用于自然语言处理领域,主要可以应用于标记器、解析器、自然语言理解程序、拼写检查单词等方面。

(5)英语教学。

英语教学过程中也可以借助英国国家语料库。语料库能提供以下语言信息:①词法;②语义/语;③句法;④形态;⑤书写/书面形式/拼写,为课堂教学提供参考,比如要研究定语从句中 which 的用法的话,便可以进行 which 的相关语料搜索,并进行进一步分析,如图 3 所示。同时,还能借助英国国家语料库进行教学大纲和教材设计,可供课堂参考和独立学习者进行研究。

No	Filename	Hits 1 to 50　Page 1 / 7307
1	A00 21	there are nearly 5,000 reported cases of AIDS, of which nearly 3,000 have already died.
2	A00 42	Below I've listed some ideas which many people have already carried out.
3	A00 179	Anthony Kasozi's work as ACET's Director in uganda has recently received financial support form Tear Fund which has enabled him, together with ACET General Manager, Maurice Adams, to identify a number of church-based projects for the coming year.
4	A00 181	Returning from a visit to Uganda, where he met with patients in the villages and with other agencies, Maurice Adams said,　'It is a beautiful country which is being devastated by a disease which can be stopped.'
5	A00 181	Returning from a visit to Uganda, where he met with patients in the villages and with other agencies, Maurice Adams said,　'It is a beautiful country which is being devastated by a disease which can be stopped.'
6	A00 200	I have far fewer friends and I am partially sighted, which makes me a lot more vulnerable; but whatever happens physically, I have always said that it was what happened mentally that mattered.
7	A00 202	I have also campaigned for the Government to give AIDS greater recognition, not as a disease affecting specific sectors of the community, but as a social problem for which there must be adequate welfare provision.
8	A00 251	MAJOR CHANGES in the pattern of HIV disease occurring in the capital which are not obvious from published statistics.
9	A00 295	'I was impressed by the care given to our clients in London and elsewhere,'　explained Peter,　'and the lengths to which ACET staff go to try and meet the needs of clients.
10	A00 305	In the experience of ACET staff and volunteers, practical care in the home not only benefits the HIV infected individual but the whole family, which can often mean three generations.

图 3　which 的查询结果

4　语料库教学在欧洲大学教学中的应用

4.1　语料库教学在欧洲大学的总体情况

在语言教育中人们已经认可了语料库的价值。在某种程度上,语料库逐渐进入现实生活的教学当中。欧洲大学在语言课堂语料库教学中,往往注重真实性和学习者的自主性,将语料库咨询和分析纳入语言学习、教学研究和实践的主流,注重整合学习者语料库与自然语言处理方法,从而通过协调技术复杂性达到教学效果。Chris Greaves 和 Martin Warren 主张一种"计算机驱动的学习英语短语的方法",展示了一种更复杂的协调软件如何能够为学习者提供不同的词典——语法模式的数据而不是搜索词,换句话说,计算机提供的数据如何帮助学习者学习和发展自主性(Alex and Pascual,2014)。Sabine Braun 主张"将语料库工作纳入中等教育:从数据驱动的学习到需求驱动的语料库"。在《用语料库学习英语语法:在大学语法课程中试验协调》一文中,Maria Estling Vannestål 和 Hans Lindquist 阐述了用语料库学习英语语法并强调教师反思在行动研究中的重要性。最后,Katherine Ackerle 和 Francesca Coccetta 在《使用多模协调工具进行材料开发》一文中展示了语料库数据如何在初学者水平上适用于学习者,并且使用多模态语料库将非语言信息包含在语言学习资料中(Anthony,2013)。

除此之外,语料库教学还体现在其他领域中,如平行语料库、文学教学和语言教师教育以及翻译研究等领域的语料库。

4.2　关于语料库的教师培训课程

在杜伊斯堡-埃森大学英语系,Breyer 提供了一个 22 小时的课程,主要是"从两个角度为学生教师创造一种不一样的学习体验,使他们作为学习者和教师"。参与者不仅要对语料库分析有基本的了解,还要对语料库在课堂中的应用有所了解。学生先完成基于语料库的语言任务,然后根据作为学生和教师的双重经验身份进行反思。他们还必须完成一些小型项目,包括撰写反思性文章、审查协调计划,以及完成基于语料库的相关语言练习(Reppen,2013)。

Hüttneret 等人在维也纳大学英语系提出了一个创新型教师教育项目。这种专门用途英语(English for Specific Purpose,ESP)教学模块包括了四个学期的课程,每门课程约 28 节课。基于语料库的体裁分析模型,该模块产生了两个核心课程,其目标是教授学生应用语料库语言学和体裁分析技术,以便探究新的多样化的 ESP 课程设置,并在语言教学中应用这些分析的结果。参与者需要完成项目,依据可能发生的教学情景,剖析自选风格的语料库,并为特定的学习群体准备材料。作者强调,他们的目标不是发展明确预定的能力和技能来应对可预见的教学情况,也没有促进日常教学(如课堂管理、课堂教学规划、给予反馈等)。与之不一样的是,他们是以"让学生培养所需的能力和语言教学专业人员的能力,以熟悉潜在未知的 ESP 类型,与此同时,对教学目的有新的见解"为目标。

华沙大学在应用语言学研究所开设了语料库课程。该研究所的使命是培训语言学家、翻译和外语教师。该课程旨在向学生介绍语料库的概念并对语料库进行分析,概述语料库在语言教学环境中的各种应用,特别强调课程、课堂活动和教材的准备。希望学生熟悉语言教学方法,熟悉各种语言教学技巧。另外,他们并没有预先与语料库有任何联系(Agnieszka,2014)。

因此,课程的重点不在于教学过程本身,例如决定课程目标或者规划课程,而是关于各种语料库,以及以语料库的展示和探索为基础的资源和工具,并展示他们的语言教学潜力。

4.3 关于语料库课程评估

除了制订相应的语料库课程,还要评估它们的有效性。评估手段主要有以下两点。

第一,在课程框架内创建学生项目,检验参与者在课程中获得的能力。

第二,注重学生的直接反应,如检查其中一个课程单元的简短反思文章的数据,以及记录学员对涉及创建语言练习项目的反馈的问卷调查语词等(Angela,2007)。

5 英国国家语料库及欧洲语料库教学对中国大学语言教学的启示

英国国家语料库和欧洲语料库教学的经验对中国大学语言教学有以下几点启示。

5.1 学生方面

第一,很多学生对语料库十分陌生,缺乏对相关知识的了解。教师应该多介绍一些语料库的相关概念,并概述语料库在教学中的各种应用。同时,需有效整合学习者、语料库和与自然语言处理技术之间的关系,充分利用当前计算机技术为语言教学提供有力支持。

第二,学生使用语料库的主动性不强,其重要原因是缺乏易于获得的资源。大多数语料库需要收取费用,而且访问时系统的可靠性和稳定性也差强人意。教师可以尝试与校方协商,获得校方相应的资金支持或者推动校方与相关语料库合作,使学生能较为容易地使用语料库的资源,以此提高学生运用语料库学习的自主性。

5.2 教师方面

第一,很多时候,语料库的使用对硬件和计算技能需求巨大,而对其使用缺乏信心是教师不利用语料库教学的一大原因。因此教师需要加强自身计算机技能的培训,熟练掌握使用语料库教学中所需的相关技能。

第二,为了确保语料库更大规模地进入语言教学,教师需要成为有相当能力的语料库用户,即熟悉不同语料库操作及其相关具体应用,利用好一切可利用的资源和工具。

第三,在中国,教师不在语言教学中利用语料库,很有可能是因为他们对不同的大型语料库在教学中的使用方式的相关知识缺乏了解。语言系教师在语言教学期间可能听说过甚至浏览过语料库,他们甚至可能在课堂中使用过语料库。但是,这并不意味着他们知道如何在教学中应用语料库。因此,认识到学习和教学与应用语料库之间存在显著差异,并帮助学生及教师培养所需的技能非常重要。在教学过程中,教师还需要具备与利用语料库相关的教学技能,创建合适的教学语料库和数据驱动的任务,并将语料库与其他教学技术及其所在教学环境进行良好结合。

6 总结

本文通过介绍和分析欧洲语料库的发展现状,英国国家语料库以及语料库教学在欧洲大学教学中的应用,认为欧洲语料库及其语料库教学对中国大学语言教学具有一定借鉴意义,并对中国大学语言教学带来了一些启示。笔者认为,从学生角度来看,需要加强学生对语料库的理解和具体应用,并为学生提供一些方便使用的语料库资源;从教师角度来看,教师应加强语料库的使用和语料库相关计算机技能以及相关教学技能的培养。

参 考 文 献

刘建达、周艳琼,2017,《〈实践中的欧洲语言共同参考框架〉述评》,《外语教学与研究》。

张晓姗,2017,《〈欧洲语言共同参考框架:学习、教学、评估〉评析》,《学周刊》A 版第 7 期。

Agnieszka, Lenko-Szymanska. 2014. "Is this enough? A Qualitative Evaluation of the Effectiveness of a Teacher–training Course on the Use of Corpora in Language Education." *ReCALL*, Volume 26, Issue 2.

Alex, Boulton, and Pascual, Pérez-Paredes. 2014. "Researching Uses of Corpora for Language Teaching and Learning." *ReCALL*, Volume 26, Issue 2.

Angela, Chambers. 2007. "Integrating Corpora in Language Learning and Teaching." *ReCALL*, Volume 19, Issue 3.

Anthony, L. 2013. "Developing AntConc for a New Generation of Corpus Linguists". Proceedings of the Corpus Linguistics conference (CL 2013). Lancaster University.

Archive. 2018. "What is the BNC?" Accessed from http//www.natcorp.ox.ac.uk/corpus/index.xml.

Reppen, R. 2013. *Using corpora in the language classroom*. Cambridge: Cambridge University Press.

及物性视角下中国国家形象对外构建研究
——以 2015—2019 年"中国新闻奖"国际传播类评论报道为例

解梦周*　刘美岩**

摘　要：随着"讲好中国故事，传播好中国声音"思想的不断传播，中国国家形象对外构建成为符合新时代发展要求的官方命题。本文以 2015—2019 年获得"中国新闻奖"一、二等奖的国际传播类官方评论报道为样本，在及物性理论的框架下，探讨及物性系统各要素在获奖作品中的分布情况和及物性在构建国家形象中发挥的作用。研究发现，物质过程和关系过程是最主要的过程关系，其次是心理过程和言语过程。在这四类过程的共同作用下，获奖作品以客观的叙事，传达了中国立场，塑造了一个有担当、有风范，既强硬又开放包容的大国形象。

关键词：及物性；国家形象；新闻报道

1　引言

国家形象就是外部公众对一国情况的总体认知和总体评价（董青岭，2006）。影响国家形象构建的因素有多种，其中舆论是支撑国家形象的最强大力量，也是反映国家形象的最主要载体（范红、胡钰，2015）。在信息全球化快速发展的今天，一个国家官方新闻媒体的报道形式对于发表本国立场，树立对外国家形象具有巨大的影响力。就国家形象而言，新闻媒体所传达出的国家话语的力度，体现着一个国家在国际上话语权的掌握份额（董青岭，2006）。近年来，随着中国综合国力和国际地位的不断提升，中国在国际事务中获得了更多的话语权，中国新闻媒体的报道也展现出更为积极、有担当的大国风范。与此同时，随着"讲好中国故事，传播好中国声音"思想的不断传播，中国对外国家形象的构建成为符合新时代发展要求的官方命题。因此，对我国新闻媒体国际传播类报道构建国家对外形象这一命题的研究具有实践意义，也符合时代发展趋势。

及物性是系统功能语法中语言的三大元功能之一——概念功能框架下的语义系统。它描述的是小句中各种类型的过程，包括物质过程、心理过程、关系过程、行为过程、言语过程和存在过程。就及物性分析而言，"同一事件可能表达为不同的语言过程，同一语言过程也会有不同的表达方式，过程类型的选择通常取决于说话者的交际意图和他对事件的看法"（柳桂媛，2019）。因此对官方新闻报道进行及物性分析，可以洞悉官方媒体对于新闻事件的态度，这对于国家形象的塑造具有重要的意义。本文将以 2015—2019 年获得中国新闻奖一、二等奖的国

---

*　解梦周：西北工业大学外国语学院硕士研究生。
**　刘美岩：西北工业大学外国语学院教授，主要研究方向为对比语言学及翻译。

际传播类文字评论官方报道为样本,在及物性理论的指导下对其进行文本分析,找出其中各类过程的分布特点,以及这些媒体是如何运用及物性"讲好中国故事,传播好中国声音"从而构建出一个良好的中国形象的。

2 文献综述

系统功能语言学及物性研究最早由语言学家韩礼德开展,他首次将及物性的研究对象从动词扩展到小句,并对小句进行及物性分析(赵苗,2019)。其中,概念功能指语言对人们在现实世界中的各种经验片段及逻辑关系的表达,反映主客观世界中所发生的事、所牵涉的人和物以及与之有关的时间、地点等环境因素(张志彬、张雷,2019)。概念功能中又包含两个子功能:经验功能和逻辑功能。经验功能是关于人们在主客观世界中经历的表达,主要由及物性系统体现。及物性主要包含三个要素:过程(process)、参与者(participants)和与过程相关的环境成分(circumstances)。及物性包括六种过程:物质过程、心理过程、关系过程、行为过程、言语过程和存在过程。换言之,通过对新闻报道进行及物性分析,可以发现新闻语篇小句的构成特点和逻辑关系。

韩礼德在其著作《语言功能与文学问题》中对作品《继承者》进行及物性分析,这是使用及物性分析语篇的开端(赵苗,2019)。此后,及物性理论被应用于新闻、翻译、文艺、学术等多个类型语篇的研究中。针对新闻报道方面的研究,以往人们对新闻语篇的及物性探讨多数存在于新闻标题的研究、西方新闻媒体对中国国家形象的"他塑"、中西方媒体对于中国形象构建的异同研究。如司显柱(2010)对中英两国媒体对于英籍人阿克毛在中国贩毒获死刑一事的报道,进行了及物性对比分析。王宁(2013)从及物性的角度对比分析中西网络媒体有关"利比亚事件"的新闻报道标题,从而揭示了新闻语言的选择体现媒体背后的政治集团的利益诉求和权力斗争。韩艳方(2018)基于及物性系统理论对国内外多家新闻媒体有关"中国梦"的报道进行了分析,探究了中国梦新闻语篇中的中国形象建构。曾艳(2019)和柳桂媛(2019)分别对《纽约时报》对中国经济的报道和对英国《卫报》、美国有线电视新闻网对中国"一带一路"倡议的经济新闻报道进行了及物性研究,探究了英语经济新闻语言使用的特点及其背后的意识形态。另外,关于中国国家形象构建方面的研究还有康俊英(2019)对美国政府文件涉华话语的及物性分析,和张志彬、张雷(2019)对习近平总书记 2018APEC 主旨演讲(英文版)的及物性分析。通过以上分析可以看出,运用及物性分析对中国英文新闻媒体报道在构建国家形象方面的研究还比较有限,对其实践效果的分析也不够深入,因此本文将从及物性入手,对这方面的研究进行补充。

3 评论报道的及物性分析

3.1 研究设计

本研究的语料搜集是通过检索中华新闻传媒网 2015—2019 年近 5 年获得中国新闻奖一、二等奖的目录,找出国际传播类文字报道,分别是 *China Daily* 2019 年二等奖报道"Rest of the world must stand together to prevent trade war"、*China Daily* 2018 年一等奖报道"US

Navy becoming a hazard in Asian waters"、新华社 2018 年二等奖报道"Commentary：Is China's B&R initiative just hegemony in disguise?"和 *China Daily* 2015 年一等奖报道"Silk Road initiatives fit into EU recovery goals",共计 2 612 个单词。以下对此四篇报道依次编号为 R1、R2、R3、R4(R 代表 Report)。R1 和 R2 分别针对美国发起的贸易战和美国所谓的"自由航行"在南海"寻衅滋事"的国际事件进行了分析评论。R3 和 R4 对质疑"一带一路"倡议的报道进行了评论分析,有力地抨击了国际上的质疑之声,达到了进一步宣传"一带一路"倡议的效果。这四篇报道通过主动出击,有效发声,传达了中国立场,引起了海外媒体的广泛关注,大大提高了中国声音在国际舆论场的传播力和影响力。同时,China Daily 和新华网作为两大中国新闻媒体,也在着力打造"讲述中国故事,传播中国声音"的文化品牌,因此其新闻报道具有研究和借鉴意义。

本文将根据韩礼德关于小句的定义,对四篇报道进行小句划分,然后再根据相关理论对各个小句进行过程分类统计,主要解决两个研究问题：①及物性系统的各个过程在获奖的国际传播类文字评论报道中是如何分布的？②这些报道是如何运用及物性构建出一个积极有担当的大国形象的？

3.2 研究过程

通过对这四篇报道进行小句划分,共得到 153 个小句。表 1 是对四篇新闻语篇中各个过程类型出现的频率及百分比的统计。由此表可以看出,物质过程在四篇报道中出现的频次最高,分别是 65%、70.8%、50% 和 48.9%,总计比例 54.9%,超过一半。物质过程表示做某件事的过程,是及物性系统中数量和变化形式最多的过程(聂薇,2018)。评论类新闻中的物质过程大多符合新闻报道客观性的特征,能够体现出官方媒体对于新闻真实性的重视,从而体现出国家关注事实的形象。占比较大的是关系过程,分别是 15%、16.7%、45.2% 和 29.8%,总计比例 32%。关系过程体现了事物与事物之间的关系,包括归属类和识别类。归属类指某个实体具有哪些属性或归于哪种类型；识别类指一个实体与另一个实体是统一的。评论类新闻注重表达对新闻事件的界定与看法,符合关系过程的特点。另外,心理过程占比仅次于关系过程,分别是 10%、8.3%、1.6%、10.6%,总计比例 6.5%。心理过程是表示一种感知的过程,是关于"感觉""思考"和"感知"的心理过程,而评论类新闻中的心理过程则可以反映出官方媒体的立场与态度,能够明确传达一个国家的官方话语。此外,少数的言语过程能够表明报道的来源,从而加强报道的权威性。在这四篇报道中均未出现行为过程。由于行为过程体现生理和心理的行为,如呼吸、做梦、微笑、咳嗽一类的活动过程,不太符合官媒评论类报道严肃的基调,因此在这四篇报道中,并未出现以行为过程类型描述的小句。因此本文将着重分析物质过程、关系过程和心理过程,简要展示言语过程,存在过程和行为过程将不作为重点进行分析。

表 1 四篇新闻中六大及物性过程分布情况

过程类型	R1		R2		R3		R4		总计	
	数量	百分比/%	数量	百分比/%	数量	百分比/%	数量	百分比/%	数量	百分比/%
物质过程	13	65	17	70.8	31	50.0	23	48.9	84	54.9
关系过程	3	15	4	16.7	28	45.2	14	29.8	49	32.0
心理过程	2	10	2	8.3	1	1.6	5	10.6	10	6.5

续表

过程类型	R1		R2		R3		R4		总计	
	数量	百分比/%	数量	百分比/%	数量	百分比/%	数量	百分比/%	数量	百分比/%
言语过程	2	10	0	0	1	1.6	4	8.5	7	4.6
存在过程	0	0	1	4.2	1	1.6	1	2.1	3	1.9
行为过程	0	0	0	0	0	0	0	0	0	0

3.2.1 物质过程与中国国家形象对外构建分析

物质过程是做某件事的过程。这个过程一般由动态动词来表示，此外还包含"动作者"(Actor)和动作的"目标"(Goal)(赵雪爱，1999)。在 R1 和 R2 中，动作的发出者多为与美国相关的群体和事物，这些作为动作者的群体成了话语评价的对象。与之相关的动态动词大多具有消极的语义，更多地向大众传达了美国扰乱世界别国经济和军事发展的实际目的，从而向大众传递出中国勇于承担国际责任、敢于发声的国家形象。

例(1) With **Washington** threatening to take more unilateral actions after imposing restrictive tariffs on imports of steel and aluminum products.

例(2) By avoiding direct wording in opposition to Washington's escalation of disruptive trade measures, **the other G20 members** showed they are yet to reach a consensus on how to tackle the US' beggar-thy-neighbor moves.

例(3) But **it(the U.S.)** needs to adjust to the developments, rather than bring all to ruin through a misguided belief it can hold on to the past.

以上三例来自 R1。例(1)和例(2)分别描述了美国及 G20 其他成员国对贸易战的态度，"threatening""avoiding"等词语，直接展示出美国发动贸易战的居心叵测，以及其他国家还未认识到美国发动的贸易战的目标不只是中国的事实。例(3)中"needs to adjust"和"rather than bring all to ruin"体现了说话人反对贸易战的决心，直接阐述了美国应当如何去做而不应当如何做。这些直接表达态度的话语能够反映出我国官媒反对贸易战的决心，也向世界其他各国传达出强硬的中国态度。

例(4) ... **the guided missile destroyer USS John S. McCain** collided with an oil and chemical tanker in waters east of the Strait of Malacca.

例(5) **The latest incident** occurred just two months after **the USS Fitzgerald and a Philippine container ship** collided in waters off Japan, killing seven US sailors.

例(6) But **investigations** into the cause of the USS Fitzgerald collision shed some light on the way **US warships** tend to sail without observing maritime traffic rules and the sloppiness of their crews.

以上三例来自 R2。在这三例中，美国海军的"destroyer""the USS Fitzgerald""the US warships"成为主要的动作实施者，主要展示了美国近几月在亚洲海域发生的海上事故，并阐释了此类事故责任方主要是美国方面的事实。这样平铺直叙的客观陈述，既能体现出报道的真实性以引起各方的重视,同时也在事实的累加过程中传达出中国对美国海军威胁亚洲航行安全不满的态度。

在 R3 和 R4 中,主要的动作者则是"the Belt and Road initiative""China""Xi"和"Beijing"。这主要是由于发表这两篇报道的目的在于抨击国际上的质疑之声,从而向世界各国更清晰地传达"一带一路"倡议的实际意义,建立一个负责、无霸权主义倾向的大国形象。

例(7) China opposes hegemony … China harbors no intention to control or threaten any other nation. China needs no puppet states. China does not indulge in "regime change" either regionally or globally … Nor will China use the success of the initiative to undermine the influence of others …

例(8) … the B&R initiative prioritizes infrastructure, the number one requirement of so many countries struggling for development.

以上两例来自 R3。例(7)中,动作实施者"China"与"opposes""needs no …""does not indulge in""Nor will … use"这些具有否定意义的动词或动词词组连用,体现出中国政府提出"一带一路"倡议是毫无建立霸权之心的。例(8)用"prioritizes"一词表现出"一带一路"倡议首要的内容特点。

例(9) Xi made public the Silk Road Economic Belt initiative in Astana, Kazakhstan … Since then, China has gone all out to make it a reality.

例(10) The initiatives directly will affect 3 billion people in Asia and Europe and have drawn attention worldwide.

例(11) Beijing and Moscow have been working on plans to link to each other by high-speed rail.

以上三例来自 R4。例(9)中,动作实施者为"Xi"(指代习近平总书记)和"China",更加能够体现中国对"一带一路"倡议的重视。例(10)中"The initiatives"和"will affect"搭配阐释了"一带一路"倡议所带来的积极影响。例(11)中的动作者为"Beijing and Moscow",与"have been working"搭配显示出中国积极寻求与其他各国合作共建"一带一路"的态度。

3.2.2 关系过程与中国国家形象对外构建分析

关系过程指的是反映物质间具有何种关系的过程,可以分为"归属"和"识别"两大类。归属类指某个实体具有哪种属性,或者归于哪种类型。识别过程体现了两个参与者之间通过一个参与者来识别另一个参与者的身份的关系(胡壮麟,2005)。在四篇报道的 153 个小句中,描述关系过程的小句也占据了一定的篇幅,共 49 个,占比 32%。在这之中,具体的分布情况见表 2。

表 2 四篇新闻中关系过程类别分布情况

关系过程	R1		R2		R3		R4		总计	
	数量	百分比/%	数量	百分比/%	数量	百分比/%	数量	百分比/%	数量	百分比/%
归属类	2	66.7	2	50.0	22	78.6	13	92.9	39	79.6
识别类	1	33.3	2	50.0	6	21.4	1	7.1	10	20.4

由表 2 可以看出,在描述关系过程的 49 个小句中,归属类共计 39 个,占比 79.6%,识别类共计 10 个,占比 20.4%。这主要是由于本文选取的四篇报道为评论类文章,注重对事件进行定性,因此更多的是使用关系过程小句来描述事物的特点或者性质,但是识别类过程同样可以显示出媒体对于事件间逻辑关系的判定。

例(1) ... the looming trade war would be a "negative sum game".

例(2) It is a reflexive response by the US to changes in the global trade order that are not to its liking.

以上两例来自 R1,属于归属类过程。例(1)和例(2)主要反映了中国对美国发动的贸易战的定性,这是一场"负和博弈",也是美国不接受贸易秩序改变而产生的本能反应。明确反映出中国对此场贸易战的反对立场。

例(3) ... the collision was the result of "poor seamanship and flaws in keeping watch" on the part of the warship.

例(3)来自 R2,属于识别类过程。它主要回答了美国海军军舰发生撞击事故的原因,是对问题的解释和识别。

此外,在 R3 中还有众多归属类过程的例子,用来描述中国"一带一路"倡议的性质特点,即反对霸权主义、殖民主义,并主张开放、合作务实。如:

例(4) The hegemony concern is groundless and unnecessary.

例(5) The new Silk Road plan is not and will never be neocolonialism by stealth.

例(6) This is an open and inclusive plan rather than a selfish strategy to serve China's own interests at the expense of others.

例(7) A community of shared future is not just an empty idea, it is a fact of nature.

在 R4 中,更多的关系过程用来描述欧盟目前的处境。这种客观的分析实际上更能够传递出中国真实、稳健、有能力与担当的形象。如:

例(8) The EU is on the verge of slipping into its third economic recession in six years ...

例(9) ... Europe now has similar reasons—and opportunities—in dealing with its economic disparities.

例(8)与例(9)实际上阐释了"一带一路"倡议给欧盟带来的重大机遇,即可以缓解经济的衰退和经济差距。

例(10) But the EU ... is still conservative when it comes to expanding its relationship with China.

例(11) ... the EU will have not just one but two great chances to put its cards on the table with China next year.

例(10)和例(11)实际上是在机遇提出之后,对欧盟接受"一带一路"倡议抛出的橄榄枝,反映出中国积极寻求合作的态度,展现出一个开放的大国形象。

3.2.3 心理过程与中国国家形象对外构建分析

心理过程是表示"感觉"(perception)、"反应"(reaction)和"认知"(cognition)等心理的活动。表示感觉的词有 see、look 等;表示反应的词有 like、please 等,表示认知的词有 know、believe、convince 等(胡壮麟,2005)。通过对四篇报道的心理过程分析可以看出,此处的心理过程多是通过借用他人的心理行为来表达自己的态度。如：

例（1）The Trump administration will not be satisfied by what it has done.（R1）

例（2）The US Navy, which likes to claim its presence can help safeguard "freedom of navigation" in the South China Sea …（R2）

例（3）… but only the fearful see a threat where none is intended.（R3）

例（4）If the published reports are to be believed, Juncker, whose main priority should be to drive growth by expanding investment, failed to even mention the Silk Road Economic Belt and the 21st Century Maritime Silk Road when he met Xi.（R4）

可以看出，例（1）和例（2）运用的分别是表示反应的动词"satisfied"和"likes"。例（1）描述了特朗普政府并不满足于当前所设置的贸易保护主义措施，表现出中国对现实情况清晰的认知。例（2）中感觉者为"The US navy"，与"likes"搭配，表述出美国经常扰乱亚洲海上航行安全的事实。这两个心理过程实际上都反映出中国对美国行径的不满。例（3）运用了感觉动词"see"，这实际上是对称"一带一路"倡议是新的霸权主义的反驳，传递出中国对此类说法愤慨的情绪。例（4）运用认知动词"believed"，而后阐释了一个"可以被相信的"事实——欧盟并没有十分积极地参与"一带一路"倡议。这也就顺利地引出后面报道中"说服"欧盟积极参加的其他过程。

3.2.4 言语过程与中国国家形象对外构建分析

在新闻报道中，利用言语过程的目的之一是力证报道的客观性，目的之二则是用他人之口来支持作者的观点（柳桂媛，2019）。在这四篇报道中也存在少数的言语过程。

例（1）the finance ministers and central bankers of the world's 20 biggest economies only said they agreed to the declaration on trade from the 2017 Hamburg Summit …（R1）

例（2）As Bank of Italy Governor Ignazio Visco said during the G20 meeting in Buenos Aires …（R1）

例（3）"They clearly have a strategy," said Coats.（R3）

可以看出，例（1）～（3）主要展示消息的来源，目的是增强报道的客观性和真实性。此外，在R4中也存在言语过程，这不仅增强了报道的权威性，更多的是用他人之口来支撑整个报道的立场，如例（4）所示。

例（4）Xi said last September that the initiatives are aimed at increasing the flow of trade, investment, capital, people and culture while focusing on infrastructure projects.

例（4）借习近平主席对"一带一路"倡议内容的解读，想要表达"一带一路"倡议是一个能够真正给国家带来发展的项目，从而向别国传达出中国开放、合作的形象与态度。

4 结论

本文借助及物性理论，详细分析了2015—2019年获得中国新闻奖一、二等奖的国际传播类文字评论报道。通过分析可知，物质过程和关系过程为最主要的过程关系，接着是心理过程和言语过程。其中物质过程通过大量事实的叠加，客观公正地传达出中国的立场与态度；关系过程大多运用归属类，对事件进行判定和定性，从而反映出中国媒体对事件的评价和倾向；心理过程则是通过借用他人的心理行为来表达自己的态度;言语过程增强了报道的权威性和真实性,同时也存在"用他人之口来支持作者的观点"的情况。China Daily 和新华社两家新闻媒体阐述客观事实,传达中国立场,塑造出了一个有担当、有风范,既强硬又开放包容的大国形象。在外部环境复杂多变的时代背景下,中国的新闻媒体更应坚定立场,扛起"讲好中国故事,传播好中国声音"这面大旗,在国际舆论场上为中国发声,塑造良好的中国形象。

参 考 文 献

董青岭,2006,《国家形象与国际交往刍议》,《国际政治研究》第 3 期。
范红、胡钰,2015,《如何认识国家形象》,《全球传媒学刊》第 4 期。
胡壮麟,2005,《系统功能语言学概论》,北京大学出版社。
韩艳方、陈令君,2018,《及物性系统与中国形象建构——基于语料库的中西方"中国梦"新闻语篇研究》,《当代外语研究》第 1 期。
康俊英,2019,《基于及物系统的中国国家形象"他塑"批评性分析解读——以美国官方文件涉华话语为例》,《山西师大学报(社会科学版)》第 5 期。
柳桂媛,2019,《英语经济新闻中意识形态的及物性分析》,《内蒙古财经大学学报》第 4 期。
聂薇,2018,《从功能语言学看英国主流媒体对"一带一路"倡议的态度变化》,《解放军外国语学院学报》第 6 期。
司显柱、方草,2010,《从及物性视角看英、汉"阿克毛事件"新闻语篇及其背后的意识形态》,《北京交通大学学报(社会科学版)》第 4 期。
王宁,2013,《及物性视角下的中西网络新闻标题批评性分析》,《常州大学学报(社会科学版)》第 6 期。
赵雪爱,1999,《现代英语理论语法》,西安地图出版社。
赵苗,2019,《SFL 视域下探析特雷莎 2018 脱欧谈判演讲的及物性》,《海外英语》第 18 期。
张志彬、张雷,2019,《及物性视角下中国国家形象的构建研究——以习近平主席 2018APEC 主旨演讲(英文版)为例》,《江西电力职业技术学院学报》第 3 期。
曾艳,2019,《从及物性系统看美国媒体对中国经济发展的意识构建——关于〈纽约时报〉的个案研究》,《佳木斯职业学院学报》第 12 期。
Halliday, M. A. K. 1994. *An Introduction to Functional Grammar (2nd ed)*. London: Foreign Language Teaching and Research Press.

中国大学生跨文化交际能力现状调查研究

李朝翔[*]

摘　要：本文基于Byram、文秋芳等学者提出的跨文化交际能力模型，以及钟华等构建的跨文化交际能力自测量表，设计了大学生跨文化交际能力自测量表，包括跨文化能力和交际能力方面的2个一级指标及7个二级指标，对西北工业大学在校生进行线上问卷调查。研究发现，学生的社会语言能力、策略能力、跨文化意识和跨文化态度分值普遍较高，而语言能力和跨文化知识分值较低，虽然大多数学生能够经常使用衔接手段使语篇连贯，但还是缺乏得体、自然地发起话题、维持话题和结束话题的能力。

关键词：跨文化交际能力；中国大学生；现状调查

1　引言

1.1　研究背景

跨文化交际能力在全球化时代成为跨学科研究的主要概念之一，具有不可或缺的重要作用。跨文化交际能力是恰当运用语言文化知识与异文化成员进行有效而得体交际实践的能力，是跨文化交际活动中的决定性因素（张卫东、杨莉，2012）。中国在人才培养方面日趋重视学生跨文化交际能力的培养与提高，《高等学校英语专业英语教学大纲》(2000)和《大学英语课程教学要求(试行)》(2004)都明确提出了培养学生跨文化交际能力的要求。高校响应号召并大力倡导对学生跨文化交际能力的培养，一大批学者以及一线教师为之做出了巨大努力，广大师生意识到跨文化交际能力是外语教育的最终目的（贾玉新，1997）。

为了使跨文化交际能力的培养工作更加高效、井然有序，相关人员就需对学生的跨文化交际能力及时评估，把握进度、发现问题并找出应对之策。只有这样，当代大学生才能更快地提高自身跨文化能力，更好地面对全球化带来的挑战，担负起时代赋予的责任与义务，为国家和社会做出更多的贡献。

1.2　研究问题

近年来，国内大学英语教学尤其重视对学生跨文化交际能力的培养。目前中国大学生的跨文化交际能力如何？还存在着哪些问题？对此，本文以西北工业大学在校生为调查对象，对西北工业大学在校生的跨文化交际能力进行调查研究，在此基础上了解全国高校大学生跨文化交际能力的现状。调查和分析的结论，在一定程度上具有普适性。

---

[*] 李朝翔：西北工业大学外国语学院硕士研究生。

1.3 文献综述

国内外关于跨文化交际能力的文献不在少数,这里主要阐述有代表性的研究成果。

很多学者认为,跨文化交际能力(intercultural communicative competence)是交际能力(communicative competence)的扩展和延伸,如 Lasar(2007)。一般而言,跨文化交际能力指的是成功的跨文化交际所需的能力和素质(陈俊森、樊葳葳、钟华,2006),本文即采用这一较宽泛的定义。

学者们对跨文化交际能力包含的要素众说纷纭。Spitzberg 与 Cupach(1984)提出了跨文化交际能力的三要素,分别指动机、知识和技能。动机指与别人交际的愿望;知识指对交际的意识与理解,包含国家层面的各种文化变量以及个体认同;技能指从事交际行为应具备的一些能力,包括留意能力、模糊容忍能力、自我平静能力、移情能力、自我行为调节能力以及准确预测与解释对方行为能力。陈国明(2006)认为,跨文化交际能力包含 3 个相互依存的层面:①认知层面,指跨文化理解;②情感层面,指文化敏觉力;③行为层面,指跨文化效力。

总之,学者们对跨文化交际能力的讨论从未间断,跨文化交际能力模型层出不穷,但不管学者们如何划分,跨文化交际能力至少应包括 Chomsky 指出的语言能力(linguistic competence)和影响语言使用的社会文化能力(高永晨,2006),本文即按照这一方式进行划分。

国内外学者对跨文化交际能力是可测评的说法已达成共识(Deardorff,2006;钟华、白谦慧、樊葳葳,2013),但目前尚未出现普遍认可的跨文化交际能力测量工具(钟华、白谦慧、樊葳葳,2013)。

在我国跨文化交际研究中,实证性论文只占很小的比例,一般论述和思辨性文章居于多数(胡文仲,2005)。近年来虽然实证性文章有所增加,但系统收集数据做出分析研究的文章仍占少数。本文尝试以西北工业大学在校生为调查对象,利用问卷调查的方法,调查中国大学生跨文化交际能力的现状。

2 理论基础与研究框架

2.1 跨文化交际能力评估理论基础

关于跨文化交际能力包含的要素,国内外学者众说纷纭。英国学者 Byram(1997)构建了一个跨文化交际能力模式,在国外具有很大影响力。Byram 提出跨文化交际能力由知识、技能、态度和性情、行为取向构成,语言能力、社会语言能力及语篇能力与这些构成因素相结合才能形成跨文化交际能力,且它们之间是互动的关系。中国学者文秋芳(1999)认为,跨文化交际能力包括交际能力和跨文化能力两个部分,其中交际能力包括语言能力、语用能力和策略能力 3 个子能力,跨文化能力包括对文化差异的敏感性、对文化差异的宽容性和处理文化差异的灵活性 3 个层次。

2.2 跨文化交际能力自测量表理论框架

跨文化交际能力分为两个部分:①交际能力。美国社会语言学家 Hymes(1972)最早提出交际能力的概念,之后经过多次修改和补充,认为交际能力包括语言能力和语用能力。Chomsky(1965)提出语言能力包括语音、词汇和语法等。语用能力又包括社会语言能力、语篇能力和策略能力。②跨文化能力。跨文化能力包括知识、态度和意识。

基于以上分析,本文构建了大学生跨文化交际能力模型(如图1所示)。

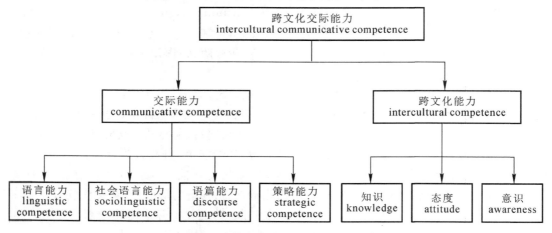

图 1　大学生跨文化交际能力模型

3　研究设计与实施

3.1　跨文化交际能力自测量表

依据大学生跨文化交际能力模型中的 7 个二级指标,并在国内外经典测量量表的基础上,制作此次调查的量表和调查问项。通过问卷预测做信效度检验,对问卷进行修改与调整,增加、删除或修改选项,以期为之后的调查操作和数据分析做好充足的前期工作准备。

问卷内容包括 7 个指标的题项,共有 44 个量表测量型题项。测量题项采用 Likert 5 级量表,范围从 1~5 表示"同意"的程度,即"很不同意"到"很同意"。以下具体阐述问卷中的量表定义及测量题项。

(1)语言能力。

Chomsky(1965)是第一个提出"语言能力"这个概念的,他认为语言能力应包括语音、句法和词汇等。本文主要针对口头跨文化交际,因此题项中只涉及口语和听力两个方面。听力技能部分设置 3 题,口语技能部分设置 4 题,分别包括对自己外语听力、口语的整体评价和所遇困难的原因。

(2)社会语言能力。

社会语言能力指理解语言使用受社会环境因素影响,并根据社会环境调整自己语言行为的能力(Van Ek,1986),共设置 5 个题项,包括对自己外语社会语言能力的整体评价和具体评价。

(3)语篇能力。

语篇能力指"将话语组成衔接、连贯、完整语篇的知识和运用这些知识的能力",包括如何得体地开始、维持及结束交谈的能力(文秋芳,1999),共设置 6 个题项。

(4)策略能力。

策略能力指"交际者运用语言或非语言手段克服由语言能力不足引起的交际困难的能力"(Canale and Swain,1980),共设置6个题项。

(5)跨文化知识。

跨文化知识指"跨文化交际过程中交际者应该具备和运用的知识",包括有关国家、社会和个人层面的知识(Byram,1997),共设置9个题项,包含大众文化和深层文化。

(6)跨文化态度。

跨文化态度指"跨文化交际活动中应具有的积极的态度",包括交际者对于文化差异的敏感,对于不同文化的包容,对自己文化的深刻理解以及对于其他文化的尊重,而不是持厌恶和仇视的态度。本部分共设置5个题项,涉及交往意愿、尊重、宽容文化差异等。

(7)跨文化意识。

跨文化意识包括跨文化敏感度和批判性文化意识两部分。钟华等(2013)构建的初始的量表中,跨文化意识要素仅有3个题项,导致跨文化意识分量表信度很低,因此本文增加了意识要素部分的题项,共设置4个题项,涉及文化敏感度和批判性文化意识。

3.2 量表信度、效度检验

量表编制完成之后,以线上问卷的形式发放,收集小样本数据用于信效度检验。共收集到50份答卷,其中5份为无效问卷(所选选项呈规律性分布),因此最终的有效问卷是45份。

将问卷数据进行数据整理和反向题重新计分,录入SPSS 21.0,进行信度检验、探索性因子分析和效度检验。

(1)信度检验。

总量表和各个分量表的内在一致性检验结果见表1。总量表的信度系数($\alpha=0.890$),交际能力量表的信度系数($\alpha=0.817$)和跨文化能力量表的信度系数($\alpha=0.869$)都在0.8以上,说明量表所测数据的一致性和稳定性较好,问卷本身具有较高的可靠性和可信度。

表1 总量表和分量表的内在一致性检验结果

量表名称	Cronbach's α 系数	题项数
跨文化交际能力总量表	0.890	44
交际能力量表	0.817	26
语言能力分量表	0.894	7
社会语言能力分量表	0.899	5
语篇能力分量表	0.712	6
策略能力分量表	0.417	8
跨文化能力量表	0.869	18
知识分量表	0.951	9
态度分量表	0.801	5
意识分量表	0.717	4

说明:Cronbach's α 系数高于0.8,则问卷信度高;介于0.7~0.8,则问卷信度较高;介于0.6~0.7,则问卷信度可接受;低于0.6,则问卷信度不够,需要对问卷做修改。

在交际能力量表中,语言能力、社会语言能力和语篇能力要素的信度都比较高(分别为 0.894、0.899 和 0.712)。但策略能力的量表信度仅为 0.417,因此删除某项后,Cronbach's α 系数度量结果见表 2。比较删除前后每项的 α 系数得出,若删除 Q19(第 19 题),则策略能力的量表信度大大提高($\alpha=0.610$),因此考虑删除 Q19。

表 2 删除某项后 Cronbach's α 系数度量结果

	项已删除的刻度均值	项已删除的刻度方差	校正的项总计相关性	项已删除的 Cronbach's α 值
Q19	24.60	13.109	−0.357	0.610
Q20	23.89	10.465	0.025	0.451
Q21	23.58	8.477	0.491	0.254
Q22	23.69	7.446	0.540	0.185
Q23	24.82	12.513	−0.285	0.598
Q24	23.69	7.856	0.559	0.203
Q25	23.62	8.286	0.453	0.255
Q26	23.60	8.200	0.500	0.238

在跨文化能力分量表中,知识和态度的量表信度都较高(分别为 0.951 和 0.801,均大于 0.8),意识要素的量表信度($\alpha=0.717$)与原始量表信度($\alpha=0.498$)(钟华等,2013)相比也大大提高。

(2)效度检验。

对量表进行探索性因子分析(Exploratory Factor Analysis,EFA)旨在检验量表测量理论模型的准确程度,即量表的结构效度(钟华等,2013)。

对总量表的 44 个题项进行探索性因子分析。结果显示,量表的 KMO 值大于 0.6(KMO=0.624),且 Bartlett 球形检验显著性水平小于 0.05(sig.=0.000),因此本量表适合做因子分析。根据系数绝对值大于 0.5 的标准,用主成分分析法共析出 10 个因子,累计解释总方差为 80.866%,旋转在 15 次迭代后收敛。

对交际能力分量表的 26 个题项进行探索性因子分析。结果显示,量表的 KMO 值大于 0.6(KMO=0.676),且 Bartlett 球形检验显著性水平小于 0.05(sig.=0.000),因此本量表适合做因子分析。根据系数绝对值大于 0.5 的标准,用主成分分析法共析出 7 个因子,累计解释总方差为 74.588%,旋转在 9 次迭代后收敛。

对跨文化能力分量表的 18 个题项进行探索性因子分析。结果显示,量表的 KMO 值大于 0.6(KMO=0.852),且 Bartlett 球形检验显著性水平小于 0.05(sig.=0.000),因此本量表适合做因子分析。根据系数绝对值大于 0.5 的标准,用主成分分析法共析出 4 个因子,累计解释总方差为 79.404%,旋转在 6 次迭代后收敛。

综上,删除某些测项后,问卷具有很好的内部一致性和内容效度,即具有较好的信度和效度。

4 数据分析与讨论

正式调查共获取 78 份问卷,剔除漏答、没有回答和明显具有 S 型等规律性倾向的无效问卷 8 份,得到有效问卷 70 份,有效样本比例为 89.74%。

将问卷进行数据整理和反向题重新计分,各题项均值、标准差、偏度和峰度等数据见表 3。

表 3 描述统计

	N	均值	标准差	方差	偏度		峰度	
		统计量	统计量	统计量	统计量	标准误	统计量	标准误
Q1	70	2.10	1.079	1.164	0.723	0.287	−0.149	0.566
Q2	70	2.10	1.038	1.077	0.676	0.287	−0.322	0.566
Q3	70	2.47	1.100	1.209	0.310	0.287	−0.496	0.566
Q4	70	2.09	1.032	1.065	0.476	0.287	−0.644	0.566
Q5	70	2.01	1.070	1.145	0.629	0.287	−0.916	0.566
Q6	70	2.23	1.106	1.222	0.655	0.287	−0.393	0.566
Q7	70	2.41	1.245	1.551	0.364	0.287	−1.078	0.566
语言能力	70	2.20	—	—	—	—	—	—
Q8	70	3.34	1.166	1.359	−0.144	0.287	−0.808	0.566
Q9	70	3.36	1.130	1.276	−0.316	0.287	−0.689	0.566
Q10	70	3.43	1.084	1.176	−0.513	0.287	−0.330	0.566
Q11	70	3.47	1.086	1.180	−0.553	0.287	−0.246	0.566
Q12	70	3.54	1.045	1.092	−0.548	0.287	−0.118	0.566
社会语言能力	70	3.43	—	—	—	—	—	—
Q13	70	2.94	1.102	1.214	0.183	0.287	−0.538	0.566
Q14	70	2.64	1.008	1.016	0.339	0.287	−0.230	0.566
Q15	70	2.96	1.042	1.085	0.167	0.287	−0.338	0.566
Q16	70	4.01	1.367	1.869	−0.202	0.287	−1.186	0.566
Q17	70	3.40	0.907	0.823	−0.292	0.287	0.204	0.566
Q18	70	3.01	0.909	0.826	−0.029	0.287	0.412	0.566
语篇能力	70	3.16	—	—	—	—	—	—
Q20	70	3.53	0.959	0.919	−0.033	0.287	−0.904	0.566
Q21	70	3.79	0.849	0.722	−0.592	0.287	0.701	0.566
Q22	70	3.59	1.014	1.029	−0.369	0.287	−0.251	0.566
Q24	70	3.66	0.931	0.866	−0.031	0.287	−0.890	0.566
Q25	70	3.77	0.854	0.730	−0.398	0.287	−0.319	0.566
Q26	70	3.71	0.919	0.845	−0.776	0.287	0.871	0.566
策略能力	70	3.68	—	—	—	—	—	—
Q27	70	3.06	1.115	1.243	−0.051	0.287	−0.665	0.566
Q28	70	2.94	1.075	1.156	−0.028	0.287	−0.510	0.566
Q29	70	3.00	0.978	0.957	−0.096	0.287	−0.128	0.566

续表

	N	均值	标准差	方差	偏度		峰度	
	统计量	统计量	统计量	统计量	统计量	标准误	统计量	标准误
Q30	70	3.07	1.040	1.082	−0.305	0.287	−0.443	0.566
Q31	70	2.83	1.103	1.217	0.150	0.287	−0.610	0.566
Q32	70	2.93	1.054	1.111	0.069	0.287	−0.467	0.566
Q33	70	2.87	1.076	1.157	0.047	0.287	−0.406	0.566
Q34	70	3.00	1.103	1.217	−0.267	0.287	−0.703	0.566
Q35	70	2.93	1.026	1.053	−0.102	0.287	−0.615	0.566
跨文化知识	70	2.96	—	—	—	—	—	—
Q36	70	3.43	0.957	0.915	−0.250	0.287	−0.091	0.566
Q37	70	3.26	1.059	1.121	0.064	0.287	−0.448	0.566
Q38	70	3.49	1.018	1.036	−0.427	0.287	−0.048	0.566
Q39	70	3.30	1.040	1.083	−0.002	0.287	−0.326	0.566
Q40	70	3.91	0.897	0.804	−0.449	0.287	−0.541	0.566
跨文化态度	70	3.48	—	—	—	—	—	—
Q41	70	3.66	1.048	1.098	−0.353	0.287	−0.405	0.566
Q42	70	3.89	0.925	0.856	−0.784	0.287	1.012	0.566
Q43	70	3.39	1.195	1.429	−0.376	0.287	−0.611	0.566
Q44	70	3.43	1.174	1.379	−0.459	0.287	−0.622	0.566
跨文化意识	70	3.59	—	—	—	—	—	—
有效的 N（列表状态）	70	—	—	—	—	—	—	—

4.1 交际能力结果分析

(1)语言能力。

语言能力分值整体较低(均值为2.20)，且听力和口语得分差别不大。可以发现，听力和口语都是阻碍跨文化口语交际活动顺利进行的因素。大多数大学生仅仅具备了"应试"语言能力，与实际从事跨文化交际要求的能力还相距甚远。

(2)社会语言能力。

社会语言能力均值较高(均值为3.43)，且各题项均值都超过3。由此看来，大多数大学生都能够根据社会环境的变化调整自己的交际行为。

(3)语篇能力。

虽然语篇能力总体均值较高(均值为3.16),但各题项均值差别较大。Q13、Q14和Q15的均值都小于3,而Q16的均值大于4,这表明大多数大学生在开始交谈、维持交谈和结束交谈方面的能力比较弱,而更善于使用衔接手段使语篇更连贯。

(4)策略能力。

策略能力总体均值较高(均值为3.68),且各题项均值都较高,表明大学生善于运用语言手段或非语言手段来弥补语言能力不足引起的缺陷。

4.2 跨文化能力结果分析

(1)跨文化知识。

跨文化知识均值较低(均值为2.96),表明大多数大学生缺乏对不同文化知识的了解,从而影响自身的跨文化交际能力。

(2)跨文化态度。

跨文化态度均值较高(均值为3.48),表明大多数学生都能够对跨文化交际活动持有积极的态度,有意愿主动参与跨文化交际活动。

(3)跨文化意识。

跨文化意识均值较高(均值为3.59),表明大多数大学生都有一定的跨文化敏感度和批判性文化意识。

5 结论与展望

5.1 结论与启示

本文基于Byram、文秋芳等学者的研究成果,构建跨文化交际能力模型,通过问卷调查,以西北工业大学在校生为调查对象,进行了大学生跨文化交际能力的现状调查研究。本文得出以下结论:

第一,学生的社会语言能力、策略能力、跨文化意识和跨文化态度普遍较强,愿意主动参与跨文化交际活动,对不同文化持有尊重和宽容的态度,而且会采取一定的策略,使跨文化交际活动顺利进行。

第二,学生的语言能力和跨文化知识不足。这是影响大学生跨文化交际能力的主要因素。这一点启示我们:英语教育不能只培养"应试能力",还要注重学生在跨文化交际活动中的语言及知识的运用能力。

第三,大多数大学生缺乏得体地提起话题、维持话题和结束话题的能力,但善于使用连词等衔接手段使语篇连贯。

5.2 研究不足

本文的不足之处主要有:

第一,调查样本有待扩展,在以后的调研中,应该扩大样本量,使样本更具有代表性;

第二,目前国内外还没有普遍认可的测量工具,本文量表还有许多欠缺之处,有待改进;

第三,自测有一定的主观性,需要补充他测方法进行综合判定。

参 考 文 献

陈国明,2009,《跨文化交际学》,华东师范大学出版社。
陈俊森、樊葳葳、钟华,2006,《跨文化交际与外语教育》,华中科技大学出版社。
高永晨,2006,《大学生跨文化交际能力的现状调查和对策研究》,《外语与外语教学》第11期。
胡文仲,2005,《论跨文化交际的实证研究》,《外语教学与研究》第5期。
贾玉新,1997,《跨文化交际学》,上海外语教育出版社。
文秋芳,1999,《英语口语测试与教学》,上海外语教育出版社。
张卫东、杨莉,2012,《跨文化交际能力体系的构建——基于外语教育视角和实证研究方法》,《外语界》第2期。
钟华、白谦慧、樊葳葳,2013,《中国大学生跨文化交际能力自测量表构建的先导研究》,《外语界》第3期。
Byram, M. 1997. *Teaching and Assessing Intercultural Communicative Competence*. Clevedon: Multilingual Matters.
Canale, M., and Swain M. 1980. "Theoretical bases of communicative approaches to second language teaching and testing". *Applied Linguistics*.
Chomsky, N. 1965. *Aspects of the Theory of Syntax Cambridge*. Cambridge: M. I. T. Press.
Deardorff, D. K. 2006. "Identification and Assessment of Intercultural Competence as a Student Outcome of Internationalization". *Journal of Studies in Intercultural Education*.
Hymes, H. D. 1972. "On Communicative Competence." In J. B. Pride and J. Holmes, (eds.) *Sociolinguistics*. England: Penguin Books.
Lasar, I. 2007. "Developing and Assessing Intercultural Communicative Competence: A Guide for Language Teachers and Teacher Educators." Strasbourg: Council of Europe.
Spitzberg, B., and Cupach, W. 1984. *International Communication Competence*. Beverly Hills: Sage.
Van Ek, J. A. 1986. *Objectives for Foreign Language Learning* (Vol. 1: Scope). Strasbourg: Council of Europe.

《大都会》的政治无意识解读

陈 璐*

摘 要：本文尝试以詹姆逊的政治无意识理论的三层次阐释对德里罗的《大都会》进行解读。从政治历史观来看，主人公埃里克的破产与身亡体现了资本主义社会矛盾以个人命运终结的方式得到一定程度的想象性解决。从社会观来看，社会骚乱与动荡体现的"恐怖"意识形态彰显了阶级对话中的矛盾升级。从历史观来看，跨国资本主义的发展与资本的投机活动最终导致埃里克个人的破产以及美国金融体系的混乱与崩溃，然而与此同时危机的出现也意味着新的变革与发展的机遇。

关键词：《大都会》；政治无意识；三层次；阐释矛盾

唐·德里罗著有小说及剧作十余部，以其后现代主义文学风格逐步成长为当代美国较有影响力的作家，并被哈罗德·布鲁姆称为"当代美国最重要的四大小说家"之一。1985年，其代表作《白噪音》的问世使得德里罗一时名声大噪，并荣获"美国国家图书奖"。此外，他的多部作品还获得了"美国福克纳/笔会奖""以色列耶路撒冷奖"等国际知名的文学奖项。德里罗有着敏锐的意识和社会洞察力，他认为我们现在身处的社会及时代充满危机，恐怖无处不在（陈俊松，2010），也正因如此，他的作品多着眼于当代美国社会形态，描述美国社会及人民的生活，且在一定广度和深度上体现了社会内在的冲突和危机。2003年他发表了小说《大都会》，该作品一方面继承了其对后现代社会各种现象及危机的表现和思考，另一方面也尝试采取了与以往不同的创作风格并借鉴乔伊斯《尤利西斯》的一日典型叙事方式，通过浓缩的叙事时间与空间展现"异化与妄想狂，艺术与商业，现实与想象，性与死亡，全球市场与恐怖主义等主题"（德里罗，2011）。

2012年，大卫·柯南伯格将《大都会》的故事搬上了荧幕，成功地让更多的人了解和关注到这部优秀的作品，与此同时也掀起了人们对《大都会》文学研究的热潮。目前学者们对该小说的研究多集中于叙事、语言、空间视域、物化异化、异托邦和科技等角度。如孙灏楠（2016）以例证法解读了作品中后现代文学叙事技巧的运用；郭四春（2014）分析了小说写作语言呈现出的"陌生化"特征及其审美效果与价值。从空间理论上看，张琦（2017）着重分析了作品中"车"这一典型空间的三大隐喻，探讨其在人物塑造和体现社会生活等方面的文本寓意；王雪梅（2014）分别从虚拟空间、精神空间及空间寓意的这三个"第三空间"角度探讨了《大都会》中与资本主义危机相关联的隐喻使用及其含义；桂娴（2018）则是从物理空间、心理空间及第三空间三方面探讨了城市空间对人类主体意识的影响，以至于产生主体的压抑、异化和妄想。此外，赵丽（2017）从宗教、科技、心理等方面探究了作品呈现出的异化问题及其现实意义。从科技的角度，李楠（2014）探讨了科技进步带来的大量机器与信息产生的"物化"现象及其对都市人生

---

* 陈璐：西北工业大学外国语学院硕士研究生。

活的影响；彭阳辉（2015）从技术哲学的角度指出了作品中体现的技术泛化导致的物化和异化的新态，引人深思；左银（2019）则以福柯的异托邦理论为切入点，通过探究作品中具有异托邦特征的空间来解读其背后的隐喻意义，发现《大都会》实质上是后现代社会中的一个巨大的异托邦，展现出都市人的生活和精神面貌，从而进一步揭示出这所异托邦中存在的内在冲突和精神危机。黄向辉（2012）从时间—空间切入展现了纽约大都市中的城市社会生活景象，并进一步从城市与性别的关系出发，探究了全球化发展浪潮中的美国城市危机及科技导致的人的异化问题和精神危机。陈思宇（2019）则另辟蹊径，从存在主义的视角出发，探讨了《大都会》中体现的存在状态，包括社会的、个人的以及人际间的存在状态，由此指出这其中存在状态的不正常形态及由此引发的扭曲、异化乃至痛苦。不同于以上的研究视角，本文欲从西方马克思主义知名学者弗德里克·詹姆逊（Fredric Jameson）的政治无意识理论的三层次阐释框架切入，尝试解读《大都会》文本中的政治无意识体现。

1 政治无意识阐释的三层次

弗德里克·詹姆逊的著作《政治无意识——作为社会象征的叙事》综合了卢卡奇、阿尔都塞、德里达、拉康等一大批西方学者的观点，还有形式主义、精神分析、结构主义及后结构主义等文化批评流派的思想，总体性地构建起其马克思主义阐释学的新模式。他的叙事政治阐释将政治视角看作一切阅读和阐释的绝对视域，将文学文本当作对历史的重写，旨在把被压制和埋没的这种基本历史现实复归到文本的表面当中（詹姆逊，1999），历史的文本化以及政治无意识的叙事化，使得文学作品的阐释成为可能（詹姆逊，1999）。

为达成文本叙事政治的阐释目的，詹姆逊构建了三个同心圆组成的阐释框架，即"首先是政治历史观，即狭义的定期发生的事件和颇似年代顺序的系列事件；然后是社会观，在现在已经不太具有历史性和时间限制的意义上指的是社会阶级之间的构成性张力和斗争；最后是历史观，即现在确认为是最宽泛意义上的一系列生产方式以及各种不同的人类社会构造的接续和命运。"（詹姆逊，1999）

根据詹姆逊的解读，第一个视域指的是将文本看作社会象征行为并被理解为对真实矛盾的想象性解决；第二个视域则从个别来自集体或阶级话语中的"言论"，在社会阶级的范畴强调阶级对话，而由于这种较大的阶级话语从来不是完全呈现的，詹姆逊认为其可以说是围绕意识形态，这一社会阶级在本质上不相容的集体话语的最小可读单位来组织的（詹姆逊，1999）；第三个视域构成了"形式的意识形态"角度的解读，包括对一切社会现象、一切社会结构层面都有与之相关的具有总体统摄地位的"生产方式"以及文化客体与生产方式的关系等的理解。由此可以看出，这整个阐释框架是一个以文本为圆心逐层扩大及拓展的同心圆构架，以此来构成詹姆逊对文本进行由小及大的逐渐总体化的阐释。

2 一日之间的生死变换

小说《大都会》在叙事空间上可以说是流动的，故事讲述的进展随着主人公埃里克的行程而徐徐展开，不论是在行驶的车上，下车去到餐馆、影院，还是遇到反全球化的示威游行等，德里罗顺着行程的动态变换来描述埃里克在相应情景下的一天中的所看所做所想，进而由此视角切入反映都市生活中的人物与场景。作为交通工具且配备有多种设备仪器的豪华轿车及作为终点的目的地理发店则是串联埃里克在市区穿行行踪的两条叙事空间线索。在叙事时间方面,德里罗尝试借鉴乔伊斯的写作方式对小说的叙事时间进行了压缩,描述了28岁的主人公——亿万富翁、外汇交易与基金管理商埃里克,在大都市纽约市区中穿梭一天的历程。在这不长不短的一天中,他执着要去往目的地,即去熟悉的理发店理发,尽管这必须要穿过当日由于总统行程导致交通堵塞严重的纽约市区。埃里克乘坐豪华的白色加长轿车,在行驶的一路不断地在车上会见各部门主管,查看研究报告并探讨日币的涨跌情况及货币行情等。途中他设法发生了三次性行为,经历了由反全球化的示威游行演变而来的一场骚乱,目睹了一男子自焚,听闻两位商业巨头遇刺而亡,穿过了一支送葬的队伍。此外,他还遭遇了两次袭击,而后一次显然是致命的。而他最终的死亡一半是由于前雇员精心谋划的刺杀,一半却也因为其在货币投机中失利导致破产后逐步走向自我放弃和自毁,最终倒下,走向生命的终结。

压缩在这一天的叙事时间里,围绕着埃里克的行程出现了众多的人物和事件,要想更深刻地考虑这些,尤其是主人公生死变换及集体事件爆发的意义,必须结合作品中所表现的这一天的时间及背景来更进一步地探讨。在小说的开始,作者给出了故事发生的时间设定,2000年4月的一天,这一天好像没有什么特别的,这时读者需要把时间放到更大的时间及时代背景里去考察其特征。德里罗在一段采访中说,"这部小说被阈限于冷战时代结束与恐怖时代开始之间"(德里罗,2011)。这里所说的"恐怖时代"开始的标志即是震惊世界的发生于2001年的"9·11事件"。小说的故事发生时间的设定恰在这之前的不久,正是在这样的背景下,主人公埃里克,一位超级资本家,在繁华的纽约都市,一天之内便经历由高峰到谷底的巨大变化,而最终导致由生至死的命运转变。

尽管这个故事经过作者叙事压缩的处理,把现实中或许数年才可能发生的一位资本家经历的挑战或者命运反转压缩在一天之中,形成了一种较为强烈的反差对比。因而引发了这样的一个思考,即在故事设定的时间及时代背景下,埃里克的最终命运意味着什么?书中的主人公埃里克是德里罗笔下一个网络资本巨头的代表,他的跨国资本遍布全球,然而这种资本的投机并未产生实际的生产效益,其中潜藏着资本泡沫的巨大危机。一旦资本市场失衡,出现短时间的大幅度波动,很容易造成资本的极度缩水从而爆发危机。主人公埃里克过度的自信,在日元暴跌的情况下疯狂买入巨额日元,不听从旁人的建议,认为到头来日元不会继续下跌而是出现涨幅,以期在这场投机中赚得盆满钵满。不料资本市场变化无常,日元的持续走低使得他在一日之内走向破产,且在前雇员的刺杀和自我放弃中走向生命的终点。然而这样一场生死变换,却也不得不说和埃里克的性格息息相关。身为一个大资本家,坐拥高耸豪华的住宅大楼,豪华轿车内数据可视设备、微波炉、心脏检测仪等各式设备应有尽有。然而他冷酷地将所有厉害人物视为自己的威胁,内心对其他企业巨头惨遭刺杀的消息暗自欣喜,且以不明所以的自尊威胁为缘由枪杀了自己的安保主管托沃尔。他视婚姻为富豪间的联姻,为了自己的贪欲最终也赌上了对方的财产,尽管他的货币分析师认为他现在在"正在进行盲目的投机",是"在下一个大赌注"(德里罗,2011),还有财务主管对他说"我们怀里揣着的日元可以在数小时内把我们压垮(德里罗,2011)",他藏不住的贪婪之心使得他为日元的预期下跌而窃喜,丝毫未察觉危机的来临。他的情人之一将他的金钱观解读为金钱的意义,是"提醒你,你还活在这个世界上","内心有感受种种奥秘的欲望","感到自己容光焕发"(德里罗,2011)。即使如此,埃里克对金钱和财富的追逐又怎能停得下脚步。在前雇员的眼中,埃里克是高傲自大的,有"巨大的野心,对别人不屑一顾","践踏别人,无视别人,迫害别人,唯我独尊,缺乏悔恨之心"(德里罗,2011)。他的这些行为最终为他自己埋下了恶果。由此可以看出,有着如此秉性的资本投机者的失败及生命终结或成必然。

根据詹姆逊政治无意识中的第一层政治历史观的阐释,文本被看作是社会象征行为。纽约大都会的一日故事是实际社会和繁华都市生活的缩影和象征,主人公大资本家埃里克在资本市场中一日的起伏及命运变换象征着资本市场的变幻无常和潜藏的泡沫危机,而最终埃里克的生命终结也是德里罗对资本主义发展中残酷无情而又贪婪无度的资本家命运的预测,彰显着其对跨国资本主义发展过程中危机与矛盾在埃里克这样一个资本家身上的结果预测和想象性解决方式。正如杰里格斯认为的那样,在这一天里,帕克从一个经济人变成一具尸体,一副空空的骨架,这象征着资本主义体制具有死亡驱动力。(Cristina,2015)

3　一日之中的动荡与骚乱

一日的叙事时间是对纽约这一大都会的社会生活的缩影。然而在这一日的故事中,城市中的一切并不太平。在埃里克出行之前,托沃尔便报告了由于总统出行而造成的市区严重的**交通堵塞**问题,因此读者更能感受在市区内埃里克出行的速度之缓慢,并将注意力更加集中于当日随之发生的各种事件,而交通堵塞好似只是艰难一日的开端。国际货币基金总裁被刺杀身亡,说唱歌手被枪杀以及俄罗斯最大的传媒企业巨头在他的别墅前遭枪杀,这一则则事件的发生为故事笼罩了一层恐怖氛围。俄罗斯最大的传媒企业巨头的死亡更是被解说隐晦地将他的死与他名声不太好的生意伙伴、反全球化分子,以及地区战争联系起来(德里罗,2011)。此外,由一场骚乱发展而来的抗议活动更是祸及埃里克和他的豪华轿车,车外发生了打砸商店及车辆、放老鼠进商店、向警察投掷烟幕弹等恐吓及暴力行为,而身处骚乱中的埃里克目睹了这混乱的场景以及一男子的自焚,自己的轿车外部也被泼漆,被搞得五颜六色,且遭打砸现出几处凹陷。由此,刺杀的频繁出现及社会暴乱的混乱场面,凸现出资本主义发展至当下的不稳定因子及恐怖因素及其对社会生活的不利影响。大资本家在这般的社会背景中,也因其自身秉性等缘由并未能逃出恐怖的阴影。埃里克先是受到了馅饼刺客——安德烈·彼得雷斯库的非致命馅饼攻击,在一番搏斗中他的头顶受伤了,再者便是前雇员化名本诺·莱文的计划性刺杀,最终以埃里克的死亡拉下故事的帷幕。由此可见,这一日之间发生了众多事件,充斥着社会不安定的因素,也蒙上了恐怖的面纱。根据德里罗政治无意识理论的第二层社会观,在这个一日故事之中,"恐怖"便构成了这个故事的意识形态,呈现出整个文本所示的社会不同阶级间的矛盾和碰撞。

4　夜幕降临,期待白昼

德里罗认为,社会生产方式的变革不是一朝一夕的事,在同一共时阶段实际上同时共存着多种不同生产方式。只有当落后的生产方式和先进的生产方式之间的矛盾不可调和之时,所谓的文化革命才会随之发生。崩溃、变革与发展,其实就在事物发展的过程之中。所谓物极必反,危机出现的同时也意味着变革与发展的机遇。

如前所述,纽约大都会的一日故事呈现了恐怖的意识形态,在这样一日缩影的氛围中,或因贫富的两极分化严重,或因大资本家的过度垄断与剥削,阶级矛盾越加凸现,由此可以看到,一日之内爆发了五桩刺杀事件,还有游行和骚乱的发生,都说明社会的不稳定现状以及恐怖因子的不断加剧。其中值得注意的一点是,在游行示威之中,一幢大楼的电子屏幕显示了一条信息,"一个幽灵在全世界游荡——资本主义的幽灵"(詹姆逊,2011)。这是化用了马克思恩格斯的《共产党宣言》开篇中的经典,表明了他们为揭示资本主义的今日弊端而奔走呐喊的行为及目的,而此次或许是一次先声,反映了在恐怖日甚的资本主义下求变革的要求与愿望。故事的最后以资本市场的无常变化,及从事资本市场投机活动的主人公、跨国资本家埃里克的破产及死亡为结局,表现了在阶级矛盾凸出的背景之下跨国资本主义发展的严峻局势和艰难困境,或许其正处在一个崩溃的边缘。

就这一结局及其寓意而言,Erich(2013)认为,德里罗描绘了一个美国超级大反派的死亡。Alessandra(2015)更是认为小说主人公埃里克是投机资本的化身,通过其自我走向毁灭的结局,体现了德里罗对金融体制的结构和秩序的质疑,并进一步预言了2008年首先由美国金融体制崩溃而引发的随后波及各个领域以及影响全球的金融危机。这一观点也正印证了小说故事中资本主义发展中的困境与瓶颈,是黑暗来临的前夕,期待冲出黑暗的破局重生。

5 结语

瓦伦提诺评价"《大都会》是一部路上小说"(Kuaaell,2007)。德里罗将故事的叙事压缩在一天之内,从主人公埃里克的行踪出发,讲述了其一天的境遇及所看所想,鲜明地表现出其自私贪婪、冷酷无情的性格特征,以及其所主导经营的跨国资本市场货币投机活动因变化无常而潜藏的泡沫危机。两相结合,埃里克的命运似乎已经注定,最终他在一日之内走向破产和崩溃,视为作者对跨国资本主义发展背景中颇具代表性的个人命运预测及对矛盾的想象性解决。然而埃里克作为跨国大资本家同样逃脱不了社会矛盾中的"恐怖"因子。一日之内纽约大都市爆出包括对埃里克在内人物的五次刺杀行径,严重的骚乱引起暴力反抗行为和示威游行活动,由此显出由阶级矛盾的激化带来的社会不安定,并为大都市的人物命运及社会生活蒙上了"恐怖"的面纱。因此,"恐怖"是该故事中体现的意识形态。身处恐怖之中的埃里克最终也难逃一死的结局,他的破产与遭刺杀而亡进一步体现了资本主义发展中的危机与困境,使之已处于崩溃的边缘,因而可将其视为"9.11"恐怖事件发生后社会恐怖氛围的延续体现,以及对2008年金融风暴来临及其带来的严重危机与后果的预言。《大都会》中一日的都市生活是城市和时代的缩影,其中隐藏着人物命运的变化,冥冥之中人物自身的性格及时代的发展背景、趋势和危机已经为一切奠定了结局。

本文从德里罗政治无意识理论的三个层面对《大都会》进行了解读。主人公埃里克的破产与身亡体现了资本主义社会矛盾以个人命运终结的方式得到一定程度的想象性解决。社会中骚乱与动荡体现的"恐怖"意识形态进一步彰显出阶级对话中的矛盾升级。最终,跨国资本主义市场投机发展表现为埃里克个人及金融体系逐步走向崩溃与黑暗,只有一场变革才能迎来新的光明。

参 考 文 献

陈俊松,2010,《让小说永葆生命力:唐·德里罗访谈录(英文)》,《外国文学研究》第 1 期。
陈思宇,2019,《现代主义困境——〈大都会〉的存在主义解读》,学位论文,东北师范大学。
弗雷德里克·詹姆逊,1999,《政治无意识——作为社会象征的叙事》,王逢振、陈永国译,中国社会科学版社。
桂娴,2018,《压抑·妄想·异化——唐·德里罗〈大都会〉中主体意识的空间隐喻》,硕士学位论文,河北农业大学。
郭四春,2014,《论〈大都会〉中语言的"陌生化"》,《当代教育理论与实践》第 6 期。
黄向辉,2012,《穿越都市的迷宫——解读唐·德里罗的〈大都会〉》,《英美文学研究论丛》第 2 期。
李楠,2014,《〈大都会〉:机器与死亡》,《外国文学》第 2 期。
彭阳辉,2015,《技术哲学主要思想在唐·德里罗〈大都会〉中的回响》,《当代外语研究》第 6 期。
孙灏楠,2016,《唐·德里罗〈大都会〉后现代叙事技巧分析》,硕士学位论文,长春理工大学。
唐·德里罗,2011,《大都会》,韩忠华译,人民出版社。
王雪梅,2014,《空间视域下的〈大都会〉研究》,硕士学位论文,天津师范大学。张琦,2017,《德里罗〈大都会〉车的空间意象》,《当代外国文学》第 3 期。
赵丽,2017,《论唐·德里罗小说〈大都会〉中的异化问题》,硕士学位论文,深圳大学。
左银,2019,《唐·德里罗〈大都会〉中的城市异托邦研究》,硕士学位论文,四川外国语大学。
Alessandra, D. M. 2013. "Morbid Tiers of Immortality: Don DeLillo's Players and the Financialisation of the USA." *Textual Practice*. Vol. 27: 875 – 898.
Cristina, G. 2015. "Death Drive and Desire in Cronenberg's Adaptation of DeLillo's Cosmopolis." *Critique: Studies in Contemporary Fiction*. Vol. 56: 519 – 530.
Erich, H. 2013. "A Bruised Cartoonish Quality: The Death of an American Supervillain in Don DeLillo's Cosmopolis." *Critique: Studies in Contemporary Fiction*. Vol. 55: 438 – 451.
Kuaaell, S. 2007. "Valentino From Virtue to Virtual: De Lillo's Cosmopolis and the Corruption of the Absent Body." *Modern Fiction Studies*. Vol. 53: 140 – 162.

二、外语专业人才培养目标与路径

从复合型人才培养到"全人"教育
——对我国外语人才培养的再思考

文 旭* 司卫国**

摘 要：我国复合型外语人才培养的改革与实践历史悠久，成绩显著，但同时也存在一些问题。本文在回顾复合型外语人才培养发展历程的基础上，详细阐述了现阶段复合型外语人才培养面临的问题与挑战，并提出了一些思考和建议。围绕解决"外语专业为谁培养人才""培养什么样的外语专业人才""怎样培养外语专业人才"这三个根本问题，本文主张在外语专业人才培养中实施"全人"教育，提出培育创新型外语专业"全人"的目标，尝试构建"通德通识、博雅精专"的外语专业"全人"培养模式。为此，需要从教育理念、课程体系、教学资源、实践平台和评价体系等维度进行外语专业人才培养模式改革，建立健全人才质量监控长效机制。

关键词：复合型外语人才；外语专业；全人；全人教育

1 引言

复合型外语人才主要是指掌握了两种专业实用技能的人才（戴炜栋，1999）。培养复合型外语人才的试验是我国外语教育中影响最大、涉及范围最广的一次改革（胡文仲，2008）。复合型外语人才培养的改革与实践在我国已有近80年的历史，取得了令人瞩目的成就，不仅满足了我国经济社会发展的需要，而且还带动了外语学科的发展，提高了我国外语教育事业的整体水平。

外语学科是讲好中国故事、传播好中国声音、构建中国对外话语体系的重要学科。全球化时代、互联网时代、大数据时代，国家和社会对外语人才的需求发生了新的变化，呈现出"多元化"趋势（张绍杰，2015；胡文仲，2014；文秋芳，2014；仲伟合，2014）。尽管复合型外语人才培养的改革与实践成效显著，但仍然面临一些问题和挑战。因此，有必要重新审视外语专业人才培养的目标和培养模式。

2 复合型外语人才培养的发展历程

我国复合型外语人才培养的改革与实践大致经历了四个阶段：第一阶段从20世纪40年代到改革开放，属于萌芽阶段；第二阶段从改革开放初期到1999年，是复合型外语人才培养的

---

* 文旭：西南大学外国语学院党委书记，二级教授，博士生导师，主要研究方向为认知语言学、认知语用学、认知翻译学、外语教育学等。
** 司卫国：西南大学外国语学院硕士研究生。

试验与形成阶段;第三阶段从 2000 年到 2010 年,属于确立与成熟阶段;第四阶段从 2010 年到今后若干年,是批评与反思阶段。

2.1 萌芽阶段

我国复合型外语人才培养萌芽于 20 世纪 40 年代(汪家树,2002)。早在国立东方语文专科学校,学生除了学习外语之外,还要必修经济学、社会学、民族学和法学等人文社会科学基础课程。中华人民共和国成立后,为了满足外交、外贸对外语人才的需求,北京对外贸易专科学校开设了外贸翻译专业,北京广播学院开设了外语播音专业,逐渐探索出了"外语+外贸""外语+外交"等复合型外语人才培养模式(胡文仲,2014)。但是,从全国范围来看,这一时期的复合型外语人才培养模式非常单一,绝大多数高等院校外语专业走的仍是单一的外国语言文学道路,沿用传统的教育方式和苏联外语教学模式,仍然采用以培养学生语言技能为主的外语教学模式。虽然复合型人才培养模式的探索才刚刚起步,但这一时期培养出来的复合型外语人才在我国特殊时期的政治、经济和外交等领域做出了不可磨灭的贡献。

2.2 试验与形成阶段

党的十一届三中全会后,我国开始实行改革开放政策。为了适应经济社会发展对外语人才的需求,1983 年,上海外国语学院率先开始了复合型外语人才培养的试验,开始招收新闻学等非语言类专业的本科生,并革新教学思路和办学模式,从单科型外语专业院校转变为多科型应用学科类外国语大学(胡文仲,2014)。之后,北京外国语学院在英语系开设经贸、新闻等方向的专业课程,进行复合型外语人才培养模式的教育教学改革。20 世纪 90 年代,随着改革开放的深入和社会主义市场经济的发展,外语界、教育界及其他社会各界人士逐渐意识到单一外语培养模式已难以适应时代和社会发展的要求。越来越多的外语院校、综合性大学和理工科大学也陆续加入复合型外语人才的试验(汪家树,2002),开始探索"外语+专业"或"专业+外语"等复合型人才培养模式,强调外语语言技能与相关专业知识的复合培养,许多院校除开设外语基础课程外,还增加了经贸、商务、新闻、法律和旅游等专业课程。

这一阶段,复合型外语人才培养基本已经形成相对固定的培养模式:外语+专业倾向课程、外语+专业、专业+外语等(胡文仲,2014)。经过十几年的试验和探索,多所高校在培养复合型外语人才方面积累了一些经验,逐渐形成一定的格局。北京外国语大学、上海外国语大学和广州外国语大学等都已经发展成为具有多种学科门类的外语综合型大学。复合型模式培养出来的外语专业毕业生与其他学院同等专业的毕业生相比有着明显的外语优势,也深受用人单位欢迎。此外,师范类高校、综合性大学和理工科大学等也都摸索出了一套适合自身类型和特色的复合型外语人才办学模式(胡文仲、孙有中,2006),复合型外语人才培养模式的改革与实践方兴未艾。

2.3 确立与成熟阶段

到 20 世纪末,复合型外语人才培养经过几十年探索与实践已初具规模,也取得了阶段性成果。《高等学校英语专业英语教学大纲》(2000)(以下简称《大纲》)明确指出,21 世纪是一个国际化的知识经济时代。我们所面临的挑战决定了 21 世纪我国高等学校英语专业人才的培养目标和规格:"高等学校英语专业培养具有扎实的英语语言基础和广博的文化知识并能熟练地运用英语在外事、教育、经贸、文化、科技、军事等部门从事翻译、教学、管理、研究等工作的复合型英语人才"。这是首次以正式文件的形式确定高校英语专业的任务是培养"复合型英语人才"。其他语种也按照教育部文件的精神对复合型外语人才的培养做了进一步探索。至此，培养复合型外语人才成为国家意志，有了纲领性文件和行动指南。各高校开始依据《大纲》，注重差异，因地、因校制宜，制订外语专业人才培养计划和实施方案。

2001年，我国加入世界贸易组织，对外贸易和交流进一步频繁。国家急需一批具有国际视野、通晓国际规则、能够参与国际事务和国际竞争的国际化人才。复合型外语人才培养又迎来了新的发展契机，逐渐走向成熟，出现了新的特点。人才复合的形式趋于多样化，出现了新的培养模式，如辅修专业、双学位、双专业、双语教育及"多语＋"模式等。此外，国内很多高校还与国外相关专业高校开展合作与交流，实施本科生、研究生联合培养等。英语专业也由原来单一的英语语言文学专业拓展为包括英语、翻译、商务英语等在内的英语类专业（文秋芳，2014；仲伟合，2014）。外语专业在培养层次上也逐步发展成集本、硕、博于一体，兼具全方位、多层次、立体化特色的人才培养体系。

2.4 批评与反思阶段

经过数十年的努力，我国外语专业发展迅速，招生规模不断扩大。单就英语类专业而言，到2012年底，我国1 448所本科院校（1 145所普通本科、303所独立学院）中设有994个英语语言文学点、146个商务英语点、106个翻译点（文秋芳，2014）。随着规模不断扩大，外语专业发展过程中也暴露出诸如外语专业学科属性趋于模糊、人才培养质量下降等问题。外语界和教育界人士纷纷开始重新审视复合型外语人才培养模式（戴炜栋，1999；汪家树，2002；胡文仲，2014；文秋芳，2014；仲伟合，2014；孙有中，2017；束定芳，2017；王文斌、李民，2018）。2010年，国家出台了《国家中长期教育改革和发展规划纲要（2010—2020年）》（以下简称《规划纲要》）。《规划纲要》明确指出，要狠抓本科教育人才培养存在的主要问题，切实提高人才培养质量。2012年教育部颁布的《普通高等学校本科专业目录和专业介绍》把英语专业的培养目标重新定位为培养"英语专业人才"。新颁布的《外语类专业本科教学质量国家标准》（以下简称《国标》）对外语专业的培养目标做了修改，将其定位为"具有良好的综合素质、扎实的外语语言基本功、厚实的外国语言文学知识和必要的相关专业知识，适应国家经济建设和社会发展需要的外语专业人才"（王巍巍、仲伟合，2017）。对比2000年《大纲》可以发现，国家层面已经不再使用"复合型外语人才"这一说法。由"复合型外语人才"到"外语专业人才"的转变不仅是学界对"复合型外语人才"所带来问题的反思，也反映了外语专业需要强化外语专业教育的思想（胡文仲、孙有中，2006；胡文仲，2008；孙有中，2017）。

纵观我国复合型外语人才培养改革与实践近80年的发展历程，可以发现复合型外语人才由萌芽到正式确立是一个渐进的、发展的过程。每一阶段都是社会发展的产物，都带有时代的烙印，外语系都充当了复合型人才培养的"孵化器"（戴炜栋、张雪梅，2007）。然而，虽然复合型外语人才培养的改革与实践成绩显著，但仍面临一些问题和挑战，需要进一步反思和探索。

3 复合型外语人才培养面临的问题与挑战

复合型外语人才培养面临的问题和挑战集中表现在以下五个方面。

3.1 外语专业性质弱化,学科属性趋于模糊

复合型外语人才的基本培养模式是"外语+X",即是说,复合型外语人才除了需要精通外语之外,至少还需要掌握一门其他专业知识。从理论上讲,"外语+X"应该突出外语的基础地位。但是,由于复合型人才培养加重了高等教育的职业化倾向和功利主义倾向,在实际操作中,高校为了追求培养复合型外语人才的效率,不惜压缩外语专业的课时量,而用更多的课时开设诸如经济、金融、外贸、法律、新闻、旅游等其他专业课程。有些高校虽然开设了一定数量的外语专业课程,但更多的也只是语言技能课,用于培养学生听、说、读、写、译等技能,忽视了其他人文课程设置。此外,外语教师在教育教学过程中缺少对学生进行人文精神和人文素养的渗透,导致外语学科人文属性降低,学科意识逐渐淡化。加之学生需要花费更多的时间学习其他专业知识,对外语专业的基本知识、基本技能掌握不足,学生外语实践能力较弱,远远达不到"精通"外语的要求,直接导致外语专业流于为其他专业服务的"工具"。1998年,教育部批准下发的《关于外语专业面向21世纪本科教育改革的若干意见》指出,"从根本上来讲,外语是一种技能,一种载体;只有当外语与某一被载体相结合时,才能形成专业。"这种把外语看作是一种技能和载体的看法带有很明显的时代印记,在一定程度上符合当时国家、社会对外语人才的要求。但是这种"外语专业不是专业,而是一种工具"的论断直接导致外国语言文学的学科内涵受到其他学科的冲击,外语专业性质弱化,学科属性趋于模糊(冯光武,2017)。

3.2 教育理念和教学方式相对落后

2017年,习近平总书记在庆祝中国人民大学建校80周年的贺信中指出,高校应该围绕解决"为谁培养人、培养什么样的人、怎样培养人这个根本问题"办学。"为谁培养人"是中外教育史上长期争论的话题,主要形成两种论断:"社会本位论"和"个体本位论"。纵观我国复合型外语人才培养的发展历程,不难看出在很大程度上培养复合型外语人才是教育目的观中"社会本位论"的体现。也就是说,培养复合型外语人才是国家和社会发展的需要。这一主张无可厚非,但不可否认的是,它在一定程度磨灭了学生的个性需求,阻碍了个体的全面发展。习近平总书记在党的十九大报告中多次提出,要不断促进人的全面发展。显然复合型人才在协调国家需求、社会需求和个人需求方面还有进一步探索的空间。此外,在现有复合型外语人才培养模式下,很多高校外语教师依然采用"一言堂""满堂灌""填鸭式"等教学方式,不能因材施教,仅仅扮演着知识传授者的角色,导致学生的外语实践能力训练被忽视,学生的语言基本功下降。对于其他专业知识,学生也只能被动接受,造成似懂非懂的局面。另外,部分外语教师授课形式也比较单一,缺乏互动式、启发式、探究式教学,不能很好地发挥学生的主观能动性和激发学生的创造性。这些都不利于学生创新意识,逻辑思辨能力和分析、解决问题能力的提高。

3.3 课程设置不合理,与培养目标不匹配

课程设置直接影响人才培养质量。目前我国各高校外语专业课程设置与复合型外语人才的培养目标不是很匹配。具体表现为以下几点:①外语专业课程内容形式单一,以语言技能训练课程为主,缺少有利于拓展学生知识面和学科视野的课程;教学内容和教材知识结构单一,内容陈旧老化,导致培养出来的学生普遍存在视野狭窄,只对自己的学习领域略知一二的思维局限,远远达不到"通德通识、博雅精专"的要求。②缺乏通识教育,人文教育的传统被弱化,致

使外语专业教学沦落为追随市场风向、过于职业化和着眼于短期办学效益的培训机构。③复合的专业课程难度较大,由于课时有限,学生很难掌握其精髓。很可能会导致学生外语专业知识没有学好,其他复合的专业课程知识也没有掌握好,导致培养出来的学生达不到预期效果。④大部分高校缺乏有利于提高学生创新能力的跨学科、跨方向的方法论课程,也少有高校开设有利于拓展学生知识面和学科视野的跨学科课程,不利于外语专业学生创新思维的形成和创新能力的培养(张绍杰、杨忠,2009)。

3.4　教学质量和人才培养质量下滑,学生的思辨能力和创新能力不足

《规划纲要》指出,提高质量是高等教育发展的核心任务,是建设高等教育强国的基本要求。当前我国的外语专业教育已由原先的精英教育演变为大众教育,外语专业招生规模扩大,学生数量增加。我国已有994所普通本科高校设有英语专业(文秋芳,2014),英语专业体量之大可见一斑。但据统计,我国英语专业四、八级考试只有50%~60%与40%~50%的合格率(邹申、方秀才、陈炜,2012),这在一定程度上反映了外语教学质量和人才培养质量的退步。近年来外语专业的毕业生就业也比较困难,优质就业率低,英语专业连续3年高居"最难就业"榜的前三名(束定芳,2015)。但是,目前国家和社会对外语人才的需求还远远没有达到饱和的地步,高端外语人才仍然稀缺。高校培养出来的外语专业学生难以满足市场对人才综合素质的要求。此外,注重语言技能训练的课程体系导致学生在思想深度、知识结构及分析问题能力等方面的严重不足,学生的思辨能力一直被诟病。外语专业学生还普遍存在"思辨缺席症"(文旭,2013)。"思辨缺席症"根源于直觉性思维和顺从性思维的藩篱。教学双方习惯于固守教学套路形式,教学内容缺乏层次和特色,只注重形式的传授,忽视对现有问题的批评与反思以及对学生个性化的培养。

3.5　师资队伍建设有待加强

培养复合型外语人才对外语教师的综合素质有了更高的要求。一方面,任课教师必须精通外语,具备扎实的外语基本功、厚实的外国语言文学知识和必要的相关专业知识;另一方面,还要有其他专业特长。但是在实际教学过程中,外语专业的师资队伍基本上都是由有外国语言文学专业教育背景的教师构成,他们大多都缺乏诸如经济、外贸、法律、新闻等专业知识,有的教师虽然有相关专业的学习或培训,但依然很难达到复合型外语人才培养对师资的要求。高校外语专业在师资力量不足、教学硬件和环境所限的条件下,忽视外语专业基础教育,一味追求多学科的复合,很可能导致最后的复合流于形式。此外,部分高校外语教师没有协调好教书和育人的关系及教学、科研与社会服务的关系。教育教学水平和人才培养质量得不到保证。在新的形势下,信息技术的新发展、信息技术对教育的影响等,也对外语教师提出了更高的要求(叶兴国,2017)。

综上所述,复合型外语人才培养面临着一些问题和挑战,一定程度上已经不能适应新形势下国家、社会和个人发展的需求。新《国标》已经将外语专业的培养目标修改为培养"外语专业人才"。围绕解决"外语专业为谁培养人才""培养什么样的外语专业人才""怎样培养外语专业人才"这三个根本问题,笔者认为,外语专业人才培养应该以国家、社会和个人需求为导向,以培育创新型外语专业"全人"为目标,以"立德树人"为根本,以人才质量为核心,以"协同育人"为保障,构建"通德通识、博雅精专"的外语专业"全人"培养模式。

4 "全人"教育思想

"全人"教育(holistic education),顾名思义,是关于"人"的教育,兴起于20世纪六七十年代,是一种带有强烈批判主义色彩的教育思想流派(文旭、夏云,2014)。"全人"教育理念最早可追溯到我国古代儒学大师孔子的教育思想。孔子认为,教育应该以培养德才兼备的"君子"为目标,而培养"君子"的途径是倡导德育和智育并重,但要以德育为根本。此外,孔子还倡导"君子不器"这一主张,意思就是君子要全面发展,具有广博的学识和才能,不能受限于一技。孔子的教育思想是"全人"教育的发端,近代著名教育家蔡元培则继承了这一思想。蔡元培在《对于新教育之意见》一文中提出了"五育并举"的教育思想,主张要培育全面发展的优秀人才。西方教育界也有类似的主张,如亚里士多德在自由教育论中倡导自由人的教育,以促进人的全面发展。然而,第一个现代意义上提出"全人教育"的则是美国教育思想家米勒(Ron Miller)。"全人"是指全面发展的人,具有主体性且能够把握自己命运的人。因此,"全人"教育强调人的整体发展,尊重个体的多样性,其目的就是培养有道德、有知识、有纪律、有能力,和谐发展的"完人"(Forbes,2003;文旭,2013;文旭、夏云,2014;文旭,2014,2016;蒋洪新、简功友,2017;文旭、滕超,2018)。

党的十九大报告指出,我国正处于决胜全面建成小康社会的时代。在新时代,"全人"教育被赋予了新的内涵。习近平总书记在党的十九大报告中明确指出,"要全面贯彻党的教育方针,落实立德树人根本任务,发展素质教育,推进教育公平,培养德智体美全面发展的社会主义建设者和接班人"。我们认为,新时代的"全人"教育可以包含以下几个方面的内容。①以"立德树人"为根本任务,落实以"学生为本"的教育理念。"立德树人"就是要重点培养矢志不渝、严于律己、责任心强、德才兼备的优秀人才。②注重全员、全过程、全方位育人。"全人"教育重视育人过程,育人要始终贯穿教育教学全过程,需要整合培养单位、家庭、企业及社会各方面的力量,形成协同育人和协同评价机制(靳诺,2017),以增强"全人"教育的持续性、有效性和整体性。③侧重人文精神和人文素养的培养和融合。"全人"教育既强调科学知识的重要作用,又主张在教育教学过程中加强人文精神和人文素养的渗透。人文性主要体现在:一方面,既关注个人的物质世界,又重视其精神世界,倡导物质世界与精神世界的平衡;另一方面,既关注跨学科的人文性,又强调跨文化的人文性,倡导人文教育(孙有中,2017)。④重视个体"双能"的全面挖掘。培养"完人"需要重视个体才能和潜能的充分挖掘,激发个体成为"全人"的潜质,侧重自我实现,关注个体人生体验,重视体验学习,强调体验认知在"立德树人"过程中的重要作用。⑤强调跨学科、跨领域和跨方向的知识整合与互动。"全人"教育倡导不同学科间的整合学习,整合不同学科之间的教学资源,打破学科壁垒,侧重以跨学科的整合学习促进人的跨学科思维能力、批判性思维能力和创新思维能力的提高。

总之,新时代的"全人"教育理念整合了"以人为本"和"以社会为本"的两种教育观点,既重视个人自身发展的需求,又兼顾社会和国家对人才的需求,力求人才培养服务于国家发展战略;既重视培养专业能力,达到"博雅精专",又倡导"立德树人",以求"通识通德"。"全人"教育为我们全面审视和深入反思当前我国外语专业人才培养现状提供了新的视角。

5 "全人"教育在外语人才培养中的现实化

《规划纲要》明确指出,要"培养具有国际视野、通晓国际规则、能够参与国际事务和国际竞争的国际化人才"。很多外语界学者提出,外语专业人才培养应该适应国家、社会及个体发展的需要(胡文仲,2014;文秋芳,2014;束定芳,2017;王文斌、李民,2018)。这一主张与"全人"教育的理念不谋而合。为此具体可从教育理念、课程体系、教学资源、实践平台、评价体系等维度进行外语专业人才培养模式改革,建立健全人才质量监控长效机制和人才评价体系。

5.1 创新教育理念,构建"全人"教育模式

教育理念,是在高校办学的过程中逐渐形成的对教育发展和教育目标的理性认识,是高校教育教学的行动指南。我国外语专业要实现提高教育质量和人才培养质量的目标,需要树立"全人"教育的外语教育理念。作为外语教师,在教书育人的过程中,不仅要注重学生知识结构、能力结构的建构,更应该尊重学生的个性发展,重视个人"双能"的全面挖掘,全面提高学生的实践能力、批判性思维能力、创新能力以及社会责任感。践行"全人"教育理念,还要倡导不同学科间的整合学习。整合不同学科之间的教学资源,打破学科界限,促进学生的跨学科思维能力、批判性思辨能力和创新思维能力的提高。因此,针对复合型外语人才培养中存在的问题,我们把"全人"教育理念与外语专业教育教学的实际结合起来,确定培育创新型外语专业"全人"的教育目标。主张以"立德树人"为根本,以"通德""通识"为基础,提出"教外语、育全人""教单科、育全人"的教育理念,明确外语专业教育教学的内容与方法,构建"通德通识、博雅精专"的外语专业"全人"培养模式。

5.2 重构课程体系,推行"全人"教学方式

很多外语界学者呼吁外语专业人才培养应该回归"学科本位",强化人文教育,在人文教育和技能培养中寻找平衡点(胡文仲、孙有中,2006;金利民,2010;胡文仲,2014)。围绕"全人"教育的核心思想,我们需要改革外语专业培养方案,重新构建符合"全人"培养模式的外语专业课程体系。外语专业的课程设置应体现人文性与科学性、基础性与综合性、前沿性与交叉性,既重视语言基本技能的训练,又重视人文外语教育,倡导跨学科课程学习。具体而言,外语专业课程设置可分为外语专业基础课程、发展课程和支撑课程(见图1),有针对性地开设通识课程、学科交叉课程和其他跨学科课程,增加批判性思维训练课程、实践教学课程和个性发展课程等。依托课程体系,重视跨学科培养,让学生在多学科的交叉中博采众长,注重培养学生的创新能力、思辨能力和教学能力(Gambril and Gibbs,2017)。此外,在变革现有课程体系的同时,教师还应该践行"科教结合"的育人理念,"以研促教"(teaching by researching),推行"全人"教学方式,重新理解专业导师的角色。在"全人"培养模式下,"教师不再是知识的唯一占有者和提供者,而变为课堂的组织者和学习的引导者"(刘润清,2014)。外语专业教师应重视"讨论式""探究式""合作式""批判式""体验式"等教育教学方法,发挥引路人和启发者的作用,在各专业课程中加强人文渗透,确保"全人"培养模式的有效实施。

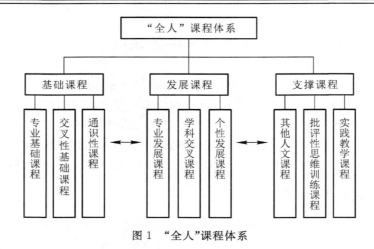

图1 "全人"课程体系

5.3 丰富教学资源,注重通识教育和跨学科知识的学习

目前我们培养出来的外语专业学生存在视野有限、知识狭窄的问题,远远达不到"通德通识、博雅精专"的要求。外语专业"全人"的培养更要注重通识教育,倡导跨学科、多学科知识的学习。通识教育也称博雅教育,是相对于专业教育而言的非专业教育(文旭,2016)。我们认为,通识教育应与专业教育均衡发展,最终实现"全人"教育。外语专业"全人"培养模式还要求重视跨学科培养。跨学科培养有利于学生在多学科的交叉中博采众长,有利于改善学生的知识结构、能力结构和思维方式,有利于学生创新能力的提高。

5.4 搭建实践平台,拓展"全人"培养路径

外语专业"全人"培养模式要求外语人才培养坚持"一个中心"和"三个结合"。"一个中心"是指坚持以人才培养质量为中心,"三个结合"是指课内与课外相结合、教学与实践相结合、学校办学与社会需求相结合。要想实现"一个中心"和"三个结合",就必须搭建实践平台,让学生"动手做"(hands on)并在"做中整体学"(holistic-learning by doing),拓展"全人"培养路径。对于外语专业本科生,一方面高校可利用自身优势资源,如附属中学或实习基地,安排外语专业学生进行实践教学;另一方面,学校可为学生与实习单位牵线搭桥,安排学生到有外语专业人才需求的单位实习,近距离了解社会对外语人才综合素质的要求。对研究生而言,每几名研究生可配一名实习导师,实习导师和科研导师共同指导研究生完成实践教学任务,以达到理论联系实践、实践反馈理论的目的。实践环节已经不能局限于实践教学,而应该包括参加学术活动、做学术报告等环节,突出创新能力、科研能力和实践能力的培养(杜占元,2014)。

5.5 优化师资,建设"全人"师资队伍

百年大计,教育为本;教育大计,教师为本。教师质量在很大程度上决定了人才培养质量。"全人"培养模式需要"全人"师资队伍,为此需要强化师资队伍建设。一方面,外语教师要树立终生学习理念,不断提高自身的专业素养和业务水平,以满足新形势下培育创新型外语专业"全人"对教师综合素质的要求。另一方面,强化师德建设,加强对外语专业教师的监督与评价,建立健全教师质量监督机制。在教师评价层面,采用全方位评价模式和科学的层次分析

法,对教师的教学实践能力、研究创新能力、服务奉献意识、品德修养等方面进行评价,从根本上解决"导师不导,指导不力"等问题。

5.6 完善人才质量监控和评价体系,确保"全人"培养质量

质量是高等教育的生命线,追求质量、内涵发展是高等教育最核心、最本质的要求(刘延东 2012)。2017年12月28日,教育部学位中心正式对外发布了全国高校第四轮学科评估结果。在本次学科评估中,人才培养质量成为衡量和评价一个学科整体发展水平的重要指标。确保"全人"培养质量,需加快人才质量保障体系建设,建立健全外语专业人才质量监控机制和评价体系。

首先,建立健全内部质量监控和保障体系。培养单位是教育质量保障的第一责任主体。培养单位需完善外语专业学生质量监管制度,构建外语专业教育自我评估体系,切实将质量监控贯穿于外语专业人才培养的各个环节。加强对学生的过程性考核和全程性评价,注重考核形式的多元化、有效性和可操作性,加强对学生专业素养、思辨能力、综合素质的考查。其次,切实强化外部质量评价与监督,发挥社会监督、政府监督和第三方监督的作用,形成全员协同监督和协同评价机制。在学生评价层面,结合传统评价方式,将职前和职后评价、个体与社会评价、阶段性与全程性评价相结合。根据学生个体、家庭、社会反馈,及时调整教育教学方式。构建外语专业已毕业学生质量追踪机制,加强与已毕业学生的互动与交流,不断提高"全人"培养质量。总之,质量是外语专业人才培养的生命线,贯穿于"全人"培养模式的全过程,需要全员、全过程、全方位的参与和监督。

6 结语

外语专业"全人"培养模式以国家、社会和个人需求为导向,以"立德树人"为根本,以人才质量为核心,以"协同育人"为保障,围绕解决"外语专业为谁培养人才""培养什么样的外语专业人才""怎样培养外语专业人才"这三个根本问题,致力于培养创新型外语专业"全人",从根本上解决复合型外语人才面临的问题。培养"全人"需要全员参与,贯穿于外语专业教育的各个环节,需要从教育理念、课程体系、教学资源、实践平台和评价体系等维度进行外语专业人才培养模式改革。唯有如此,才有利于育"完人"、育"全人"培养目标的实现,外语专业才能在"双一流"建设中占有一席之地,从而为新时代中国特色社会主义事业培养更多德才兼备、全面发展的创新型外语专业"全人"。

参 考 文 献

杜占元,2014,《深化高校科技体制改革——促进质量提升和创新驱动发展》,《中国高等教育》第11期。
戴炜栋,1999,《关于面向21世纪培养复合型高级外语人才发展战略的几个问题》,《外语界》第4期。
戴炜栋、张雪梅,2007,《对我国英语专业本科教学的反思》,《外语界》第4期。
冯光武,2017,《把握国标精神、找准学校定位、突出专业特色——〈高等学校英语专业本科教

学质量国家标准〉的实施建议》,《外语界》第 1 期。
胡文仲,2008,《英语专业"专"在哪里?》,《外语界》第 6 期。
胡文仲,2014,《试论我国英语专业人才的培养——回顾与展望》,《外语教学与研究》第 1 期。
胡文仲、孙有中,2006,《突出学科特点,加强人文教育:试论当前英语专业教学改革》,《外语教学与研究》第 5 期。
蒋洪新、简功友,2017,《全人教育与个性学习——英语专业〈国标〉课程体系的研制与思考》,《外语教学与研究》第 6 期。
金利民,2010,《注重人文内涵的英语专业课程体系改革》,《外语教学与研究》第 3 期。
靳诺,2017,《坚持立德树人 培养优秀人才》,《光明日报》4 月 10 日。
刘润清,2014,《大数据时代的外语教育科研》,《当代外语研究》第 7 期。
刘延东,2012,《深化高等教育改革——走以提高质量为核心的内涵式发展道路》,《求是》第 10 期。
束定芳,2015,《高校英语专业"复兴"之三大路径》,《中国外语》第 5 期。
束定芳,2017,《社会需求与外语学科建设》,《中国外语》第 1 期。
孙有中,2017,《人文英语教育论》,《外语教学与研究》第 6 期。
王文斌、李民,2018,《外语教育属于什么学科?——外语教育学构建的必要性及相关问题探析》,《外语教学》第 1 期。
王巍巍、仲伟合,2017,《"国标"指导下的英语类专业课程改革与建设》,《外语界》第 3 期。
汪家树,2002,《21 世纪复合型外语人才培养的思考》,《同济大学学报(社会科学版)》第 2 期。
文秋芳,2014,《英语类专业实践多元人才观面临的挑战与对策》,《外语教学与研究》第 1 期。
文旭,2013,《以"思"为基础的外语教育思想》,《当代外语研究》第 1 期。
文旭,2016,《全人教育与外语专业人才培养》,《东北师范大学学报(社会科学版)》第 3 期。
文旭、滕超,2018,《英语专业"全人"培养模式探索与实践》,《中国高等教育》第 6 期。
文旭、夏云,2014,《全人教育在外语教育中的现实化》,《外语界》第 5 期。
谢安邦、张东海,2011,《全人教育理论与实践》,华东师范大学出版社。
叶兴国,2017,《外语教师面临的新形势新问题》,《外语教学与研究》第 2 期。
张绍杰、杨忠,2009,《外语学科博士研究生教育——问题与对策》,《中国外语》第 1 期。
张绍杰,2015,《践行开放性、融合型、多元观的外语人才培养理念》,《现代外语》第 1 期。
仲伟合,2014,《英语类专业创新发展探索》,《外语教学与研究》第 1 期。
邹申、方秀才、陈炜,2012,《2011 年英语专业四、八级考试分析报告》,《外语测试与教学》第 1 期。
Forbes, S. H. 2003. *Holistic Education: Its Nature and Intellectual Preceden*. Brandon: The Foundations for Education Renewal.
Gambrill, E., and Gibbs, L. 2017. *Critical Thinking for Helping Professionals: A Skills-based Workbook*. Oxford: Oxford University Press.

综合类高校复语复合型人才培养目标下"英语+丝路语"外语课程建设的思考

陈 洁* 张 璐**

摘 要：在"一带一路"倡议背景下，综合类高校应结合自身专业优势，重视"英语+丝路语"的复语人才培养，以应对该类人才紧缺的局面。本文借鉴国外复语人才培养的经验及重点关注的问题，探讨新复合型人才培养目标下综合类高校复语人才外语课程建设需要重点考虑的多元弹性课程体系、学生学习心理动机干预及互联网辅助丝路语教学。

关键词："一带一路"；综合类高校；复语人才；人才培养；课程建设

1 背景

在"一带一路"倡议和"双一流"高校建设背景下，我国高等教育国际化发展的方向和复合型人才的培养方案再次成为关注的焦点。在此背景下，人才的定义也具有较强的特殊性，指"可以很好地服务'一带一路'倡议的需要、具有良好的国际视野和多元文化背景，同时接受过某一领域较高的专业知识和技能方面教育的人。应是知己知彼的政策沟通人才；精通多国家和民族语言的翻译人才；熟稔'一带一路'沿线国家国情的复合型人才；深谙宗教社会的跨文化人才；实践操作层面的技术型人才"（穆正礼等，2017）。现阶段的"走出去"战略与我国对高校学生外语能力的需求从"内需型"向"外向型"转变相契合。但是我们过去在外语人才培养过程中主要关注西方发达国家语言的弊端已经显现，对丝路沿线国家的文化和历史情况知之甚少，语言沟通只依靠英语间接交流所造成的沟通不便与误解会造成巨大的能量与资源损耗。沿线国家语言及文化、制度的不同所带来的种种问题都需要在增进了解的基础上通过磋商交流解决，而语言的沟通则成为一切问题解决的起点和基础。随着与丝路沿线国家贸易、金融及基础设施建设方面的合作需求的进一步加强，掌握多门外语（主要为"英语+丝路语"）以适应工作交际应用的需要也成为越来越多高校学生的迫切需求，这对提升学生竞争力、提高工作效率、减少工作摩擦，从而创造良好的工作环境、创造更大的价值等方面都具有深远的影响。

面对此培养目标及丝路语人才紧缺的局面，外语课程建设所面对的机遇与挑战巨大。许多学者就此展开了研究和讨论，但依据的理论多是基于新形势下高等教育策略和思路的探讨，鲜有对具体制度的可行性和具体实践策略实施及路径的研究。通过查阅近期国家核心期刊（CSSCI）发现，对于如何在非语言类高校开展丝路语教学的研究论文很少，多数有关开展复语教学的论文都是讨论如何在外语类高校中开展教学的，内容偏重第二外语课堂建设。专业外

---
* 陈洁：西北工业大学外国语学院副教授，主讲大学英语读写、口语、英汉翻译等课程。
** 张璐：西安外国语大学出国留学人员培训部教师。

国语大学主要培养精通和熟练的语言人才,主要的复合人才培养方案几乎都是外语专业与经济管理专业的结合,专业虽有复合却很单一,学生毕业后主要从事语言专业能力要求较高的翻译等相关工作。近期一些外语类院校的复合型人才培养已加入了新的内容,即"复语型"外语人才,教育部对其的定义为"所培养的人才除母语之外,能够比较熟练地掌握两种以上的外语,具有跨文化多外语交流能力"。"我国开展'复语型'外语人才培养的学校已有不少,如大连外国语大学、天津外国语大学、上海外国语大学等,也取得了较好的效果,尤其是在'一带一路'倡议过程中,这类复语型外语人才已经变得更加炙手可热。"(蒋洪新,2019)但是,单凭各外语院校的单一语言类课程显然无法在短期内及更长远的未来解决跨文化人才存量不足的问题。因此,当务之急应积极利用各综合类院校的专业人才培养优势,设置大语言类课程模块,扩充学生选择学习一至两门非通用语(主要为丝路语)的条件,因为丝路语人才培养和教学发展创新直接关系到我国未来长期对外交往、国家经济建设和综合实力。综合类高校虽有专业选择方面的优势,但在与语言专业结合这方面稍滞后,对社会需求和按需培养的方案还未进行调研,目前适用于综合型高校的研究普遍集中在政策与规划研究上。

因此,本研究将结合国外复语人才培养路径,探讨新复合型人才培养目标下综合类高校复语人才外语课程建设需要重点考虑的几个方面。

2 国外复语人才培养现状及我国"英语+丝路语"人才培养路径

全球的语言研究视角已从双语转向多语种教育。很多地区抓住语言学习的黄金时期,从孩子低龄时期就开始推广除英语以外的民族语言和地区性语言。维护语言的多样性,促进语言学习和多语种沟通被视为改善沟通和减少文化间误解的基本要素。国外双外语教学开展得较早,有一些成功的经验可供我们参考,同时也有一些出现的问题值得我们在人才培养规划时予以规避。联合国教科文组织公布的《世界文化多样性宣言》(2001年)和教育立场文件《多语种世界中的教育》(2003年)特别呼吁鼓励语言多样性,在尊重各级母语教育的基础上,鼓励人们从小学习一门以上外语。

2.1 国外复语人才培养现状

澳大利亚在多语种教育方面贡献突出,规定所有儿童都需要接受外语教育(2007年开始有40多种语言选择),政府有多种文化相关政策予以支持(Yağmur and Extra,2011)。印度的外语政策为:学校教授至少三种语言,这被称为三种语言公式。这三种语言包括印地语、英语及特定州的官方语言。在完成十年中学教育后学生将至少学习了三种语言。欧盟致力于从国家层面建立语言决策机构,推动外语教育的长远发展。欧盟会议的翻译或口译员要求至少同时精通两门外语。在过去的几十年中(自1995年),欧盟委员会就在白皮书中设定了多语种教育目标,从而促进欧盟公民的语言知识的积累,旨在教育欧洲公民,使他们除了掌握母语之外,每个欧盟成员国应提高学生至少对两种外国语言的熟练应用程度。英语可被用作教学语言,既强化了英语的学习,又便利了第二门外语的学习(Wu,2017)。这个思路为我国丝路语教学师资提供了一个思路,即教授丝路语的教师不一定是国内相关外语专业毕业的中国教师,也可以通过引进国外教师,将英语作为授课语言,缓解近期师资不足的问题。1994年,美国政府颁布的《2000年目标:美国教育法案》明确将"外国语"定为核心课程之一。同年,《改进美国学校法案》又将"外国语"推至"对国家经济竞争和国家安全至关重要"的地位。2006年1月,美国时任总统布什宣布启动"国家安全语言"计划(National Security Language Initiative,NSLI),加紧培养美国的外语人才,其中汉语与阿拉伯语、俄语、印地语、波斯语一起,被列为美国最急需相关人才的"关键"(critical)外语(王慧,2008)。美国的复合专业的设置已成为美国高校的专业结构体系的一部分,也是高校教育教学运行中的常态。在美国排名前50位的大学中,都有复合专业培养人才的体制(Thormann and Zimmerman,2012)。语言专业也是和众多专业结合最多的专业,并且给予语言专业的学分一般也是最高的,各大学所提供的语言种类也较多,一般的社区大学也有十门左右的语言课程可供选择,可满足不同学生的多样化学习需求,从中可以看出各个大学对语言学习的重视,体现出对学生学习语言所付出的努力和时间的肯定与扶持。

2.2 我国"英语+丝路语"人才培养路径

2.2.1 复语人才培养背景

参考国外复语人才培养的经验与做法,我国丝路关键语人才培养路径要充分结合我国发展现状,和"一带一路"倡议目前及未来的经济增长与文化交流的迫切需求,以及"一带一路"倡议基础设施建设互联互通的优先领域。目前,以新亚欧大陆桥经济走廊为引领,以陆、海、空立体通道和信息高速路为骨架,以铁路、港口、公路、通信等重大工程为依托,中国与中东欧国家间日趋成熟的基础设施网络正在形成,双边投资的领域也不断拓宽,由较为单一的领域扩展至机械、化工、信息技术、电信、新能源、物流商贸、研发、金融、农业、旅游等多个行业,特别是中国的优势产能和技术装备输出的比例越来越大(穆正礼等,2017)。近期,合作沟通的领域已从基础设施建设开始扩展至金融、教育、医疗健康等"民心相通"领域,所涉及的专业数量大大增多,人才需求持续旺盛,也体现出"走出去"战略的深入发展。中国教育部于2016年7月发布了《推进共建"一带一路"教育行动》,进一步明确了教育互联互通合作、开展人才培养培训、共建丝路机制等三方面重点合作,对接"一带一路"沿线各国意愿,互鉴先进教育经验,共享优质教育资源,全面推动各国教育提速发展。比如,协力推进教育共同体建设,实现学分互认、学位互授联授;鼓励"一带一路"沿线国家学者开展或合作开展中国课题研究;鼓励"一带一路"沿线各国高等学校在语言、交通运输、建筑、医学、能源、水利、生态保护、文化遗产保护等沿线国家发展急需的专业领域联合培养学生等(穆正礼等,2017)。

2.2.2 课程模式及配套条件

各综合院校要抓住契机引领教育发展改革方向,并结合自身优势专业特长,分析学生就业走向及用人单位长期需求,建设多元化、弹性化的课程体系,开展相关丝路语课程的建设并引导学生在四年大学学习过程中加入语言学习的重要内容,为毕业后的就业积极准备、拓宽其就业面并增加竞争力和适应能力。高校应从人才培养和教育规划两个方面着手,在充分了解学生的认知能力接受度的基础上,利用互联网辅助非通用语教学,推动多样化的语言教育政策的制定,更多考虑到双语双言或多语多言社会的现实和未来,促进多元外语教学发展并改进外语教学模式。

积极创造优质配套教学条件和语言环境。可利用高校的少数民族学生和留学生资源让同学们结成学习小组,进行互帮互助学习,进一步了解当地文化和社会生活知识;定期聘请专家教授对学生进行语言指导并举办讲座,增加学生学习的兴趣和动力;等等。考核标准中的考试内容要以实用性为主,综合考虑听说读写几个应用方向,而不能过分偏重学术性。为开发更多更好的国际化课程,我们可以参考国外已有的经验,同时也可以结合国内大学的情况开设适合学生和社会需求的课程。在校内教师比较匮乏的情况下,可以利用其他高校、社会和国际资源,如进行国内大学校际合作,从经验和师资较丰富的外语专业院校聘请几位或多位专家教授组成教学团队进行授课,还可以聘请国际专家学者,单独授课或与国内同行进行合作,采用线上、线下相结合的形式引进丝路语国家已使用的较成熟的语言学习软件进行网络学习,以作为我国高校语言课程的重要补充。

在学生中开展调研,采取分层式教学。教师可从学生在大学一年级时就在部分相关专业中授课,学习时间为两年。因其难度较大,需要投入的时间较多,在学分方面可有所倾斜或奖励;在学生三、四年级时可为学习成绩优异的学生开设语言提高班,并与相关国家高校进行联系,开展短期交流项目,进一步提高学生的学习积极性并帮助学生实地了解当地文化,增强学习的目标感和方向感。在课程内容方面也可加入英语的内容,如教师用英语介绍和讲解语言课程,学生将英语作为和教师沟通的媒介,此方法尤其适用于外籍教师授课内容的开展,既兼顾了学生的英语学习,同时也为师生的交流创造了便利。

3 以合理先进的外语课程及学分设置增加学生学习多门外语的自信心及学习动力,减少其焦虑情绪

3.1 学生心理建设

众所周知,中国学生学习第一门外语即英语的学习周期漫长,但到大学阶段仍有很多学生对英语学习缺乏自信心,焦虑情绪颇重。如果这时再让其学习第二门外语,学生的畏难情绪会加重,同时也担心外语学习耗时耗力,影响专业课程的学习。学生的心理准备、态度和动力是决定学习成功的关键。动力、自尊和焦虑相互作用并共同影响学习过程和效率,因此教师应着重关注如何降低学生外语学习的焦虑情绪。减少焦虑的方法有二:其一是学生的积极正面评价及正确的学习动机;其二是提供更好的学习环境,如合作学习法以及计算机网络辅助学习(He,2018)。教师应采取积极措施缓和课堂气氛,利用幽默与友好的评价与学生互动交流,注重形成性评价,减少较严厉的评价性词汇在课堂的使用频率;增加学生准备课堂活动的时间,使学生准备充分从而对参与课堂活动更有信心,输出效果更好;注重学生互动与小组讨论的质量提升,为学生更好地使用语言,设计有针对性、有建设性的课堂活动。利用互联网在外语教学中强调多模式、多维和互动式体验。

如学生明白所学语言在社会生活或职业生涯中有用,他们将会充分认识到外语的交流价值,从而更有学习动力。同时,这种积极的态度也会促使学生更积极主动地使用这门外语,从而形成一种良性循环。这些因素都是保证外语学习成功的关键。相应地,如果学生学习外语只是因为外在压力,那么学习的动力将会很小,同时学习的态度也常常是负面的(Lightbown and Spada,2000)。基于此,学校需要加大宣传力度并及时跟进,进行学业指导,帮助学生掌握社会需求信息,并且设置有别于英语学习学制的第二外语学习鼓励性政策,将已经通过大学英语四、六级考试,学有余力并且对外语学习较有兴趣、有信心的学生作为重点培养对象。但是

需要注意的是,外语教师对学生学习的动力的影响是比较小的,尤其是成年学生,教师对学生学习动力的影响主要是尽力创造支持鼓励的学习环境,让学生感到被鼓励并经常体验到成功的喜悦,从而形成语言学习的良性循环(Lightbown and Spada,2000)。

3.2　学习动机培养

根据二语习得理论,语言学习动力直接影响学习者的努力程度、学习态度及情感。语言学习动力分为四种类型:工具型动机(instrumental motivation),即学习语言的目的是通过考试或找到更好的工作等;融合型动机(integrative motivation),即学习语言是因为对目标语国家的人民或文化感兴趣;结果型动机(resultative motivation),即学习的动机来源于之前成功的学习经验;内在动力(intrinsic motivation),即学习者保有对外语的好奇心与兴趣并自觉参与到各种学习活动中去(Ellis,1997)。所有这些动因并不是孤立甚至对立的,而是互为补充并且不断变化的,可见,外在环境对语言学习过程的影响是巨大的,为学习者创造产生积极动因的学习条件和环境对外语学习的成败至关重要。在就业竞争压力的驱动下,学校应对人才市场中对专业与语言要求较高的就业方向做好深入调研,增强学生学习第二外语的信心和动力,争取与企业定向培养,在提升人才利用率的目标下提前进行实践能力培养,提升学生适应能力。

4　互联网辅助丝路语教学

4.1　互联网辅助教学的最新发展

国际上,国际教育技术协会(International Society for Technology in Education,ISTE)已对从学前到高等教育的技术使用标准进行了界定;TESOL(Teaching of English to Speakers of Other Languages)组织也发布了针对教师和学生的相关技术标准,并对技术与语言教学的相互贯通做了专门的说明。众所周知,大学阶段的语言学习是针对有成熟思想的成人的,但是学习一门新语言意味着要经历初期的反复而单调的基础语言知识练习,这个过程很容易使学生觉得枯燥无趣,而且这个过程往往持续数月甚至一个学期,学习者通常需要有相当的毅力和决心才会有所收获。因此,将互联网融入学生的学习过程为教学提供了一个有效途径。浸入式外语教学已应用几十年,但新的浸入式教学利用3D技术创造新的语言环境体验,提供新的可能性,例如帮助提高绩效评估,与智能影像进行虚拟互动,以及将应试者浸入3D虚拟环境中以执行语言任务(Kessler and Ware,2013)。互联网辅助语言学习(Computer Assisted Language Learning,CALL)在一定程度上可以克服面对面的语言学习的局限,但是需注意将语言学习在国际信息资源与社交媒体的背景下与科技、理论与教学法的有机结合。

4.2　互联网辅助教学应关注的内容建设

科技不仅仅是工具和设备,更是体验,我们更应该关注使用科技的过程。它能够以其设计与所创造的场景吸引学习者,包含认知学习策略以及批判性思维能力的培养等,其过程应当包含叙事(narrative)、互动(interactive)、适应(adaptive)、交际(communicative)和生产(productive)这五个要素(Hinkelman,2018)。研究表明,用图像帮助记忆单词比用单纯的翻译效果要好。同样的方法也适用于阅读与写作教学,图像使学习者更直接地与目标语交流。图像和同源词使得语言初学者也能在更高的水平上利用互联网信息,并且浸入式的网上学习对语言技能的提升大有裨益。总结起来共有5点好处:①成年语言学习者对有一定深度的内容更感兴趣;②学生对自己的学习过程负责,学习者不仅仅是被动的接受者,而变为积极主动的指导参与者;③原汁原味的课文可在互联网的辅助下使学习者尽早接触学习;④文本、文化和语言可以互为补充;⑤更有意义的内容可以提升语言的习得(Hennessee,1999)。语言学习需要创造更多的与该语言接触的机会并且频繁地使用该语言进行对话,所以作为当面授课的有益补充,互联网辅助教学具有相当有利的条件。我们可以利用网络进行师生和学生之间的课前对话交流、小组活动、课后练习互动,也可将个人作业提交到网上,进行一系列小组活动、朗读模仿与纠错、学术论坛等,都可以增加学生使用语言的机会和乐趣,同时也体现了使用语言的最终目的——沟通与交流。只有在交流中才能认识到学习中的不足,并能提升相当的语言学习动力(Cenoz and Genesee,1998)。同时,网上讨论可以弥补在课堂上小组讨论时学生总是习惯用母语交流的不足。

  网上内容选择的原则方面,第二外语教学的互联网资源应注意使用社会文化评估(social-cultural assessment)以适应学生不同文化背景的客观情况。在帮助学生学习外语的同时强调社会与个人知识共建过程中的相互依存关系。要依据学生的文化背景来考查学生的学习情况,如利用学生的母语知识经验来反思外语学习过程中的一些话题。授课教师不能无视学生母语及本国文化在其外语学习中的影响,而是应该结合这个背景来教课和考查学生(白丽新、张乐,2015)。很重要的一点是,使学生能够认知并能够结合自己熟悉的母语知识去理解新的外语内容,评价的内容应与核心内容及认知技能相关。考查的顺序依据的原则是从简单到复杂,从具体到抽象,从熟悉到不熟悉,从特殊到一般。教师在评价时应尤其关注学生将语言与文化和内容相结合的能力,不应只过分关注内容,例如应注意收集学生在处理熟悉与不熟悉的语言背景下独立作业和指导后的作业,个人与小组作业的不同表现,以此发现学生在哪种语言背景下的表现更好,哪些情况下需要更多的练习和帮助。教师安排的各种互联网活动基本可以归纳为三类:信息交换(information exchange)、比较/分析(comparison/analysis)以及协作/产品创建(collaboration/product creation)(Kessler and Ware,2013)。教师应当了解学生的需要,给予学生积极的鼓励和具体的反馈。在利用互联网资源的同时,教师一定要做好安排与规划,及时关注每个学生的个性化问题,并实时反馈和沟通(Thormann and Zimmerman,2012)。毕竟,所有语言教师的目标应该是帮助学生进行现实生活中的沟通,包括使用检索到的信息以及分析和综合技能。老师可以通过监控过程来观察学生的参与程度,并公开或私下地向学生提出建议,也可以在定期的视频会议上选择典型案例组织集体讨论,从而使有共性或需要特别注意的问题引起全班同学的注意。教师的安排和想法是起决定性作用的一个因素,教师通过组织的活动和提供的材料使学生使用语言资源并利用目标语言进行互动交流。日益完善和丰富的互联网为我们的改革提供了便利条件,尝试利用互联网学习丝路语,这对已经具备自学能力的大学生来说是非常便利的。我们应持续关注计算机辅助外语学习的最新进展和技术的应用及效果分析,发现并利用合适的教学平台和服务平台。

参 考 文 献

白丽新、张乐，2015，《美国大学中的复合专业设置体系研究》，《国家教育行政学院学报》第10期。

蒋洪新，2019，《新时代外语专业复合型人才培养的思考》，《中国外语》第1期。

穆正礼、罗红玲、蓝玉茜、魏珮玲，2017，《"一带一路"背景下的人才需求及人才培养模式》，《海外华文教育》第7期。

王慧，2008，《美国外语教育研究之管见》，《理论视野》第9期。

Cenoz, J, and Genesee, F. 1998. *Beyond bilingualism: Multilingualism and multilingual education*. Clevedon: Multilingual Matters.

Ellis, Rod. 1997. *Second Language Acquisition*. New York: Oxford University Press.

He, Deyuan. 2018. *Foreign Language Learning Anxiety in China: Theories and Applications in English Language Teaching*. Singapore: Springer.

Hennessee, Hella. 1999. "Forging the Link Between Idea and Language: Teaching German with Web-based Materials". *South Central Review*.

Hinkelman, Don. 2018. *Blending Technologies in Second Language Classrooms*. UK: Palgrave Macmillan.

Kessler, G, and Ware, P. D. 2013. "Addressing the Language Classroom Competencies of the European Higher Education Area Through the Use of Technology". *Competency-based Language Teaching in Higher Education*. Netherlands: Springer. pp 93–105.

Lightbown, P. M, and Spada, N. 2000. *How Languages Are Learned*. NewYork: Oxford University Press.

Thormann, J, and Zimmerman, I. K. 2012. *The Complete Step-by-Step Guide to Designing and Teaching Online Courses*. New York: Teachers College Press.

Wu, Ruilin. 2017. "Trilingual Education for Ethnic Minority Groups in China with Special Reference to Trilingual CLIL Education in Europe: an Exploratory Study". *European Journal of Language Policy*. Vol. 9:203–226.

Yağmur, Kutlay, and Extra, Guus. 2011. "Urban multilingualism in Europe: Educational responses to increasing diversity". *Journal of Pragmatics*. Vol. 43: 1185–1195.

大类培养下的外语专业人才培养路径
——基于北京三校的考察

车向前*

摘　要：大类招生、培养是当前高等教育改革的热点。通过对北京三所高校的培养改革进行调研、反思后发现，外语专业大类培养改革应处理好大类课程群与专业课程群的关系、外语专业的一般性和特殊性关系、学生自主选择与专业需求及学科发展的关系，以及外语专业工具性和人文性特征的关系。基于此，外语类专业大类培养在路径上应注意挖掘语言类学生资源、把握语言类学生志趣、建立健全模块化课程体系、突出课程博雅人文特质等。

关键词：大类培养；外语专业；通识教育

1　引言

《周易》云："引而伸之，触类而长之，天下之能事毕矣"。当前，大类招生、培养已然是我国高等教育改革的一个重要趋势和热点。大类培养旨在建设通识、大类、专业三位一体的课程体系，具有基础知识宽厚、交叉，专业知识精深的特点。通过人文科学、社会科学、自然科学等多学科知识学习，强化人才培养的通识性和社会性。作为通识教育和专业教育融通的重要环节，大类培养为学生提供了更广阔的选择空间。就外语大类专业而言，其在实践过程中也面临着一定程度的改革阵痛，如大类培养下的外语专业学生的通识课程与专业课程的平衡关系、大类培养对专业人才培养带来的冲击等。本文通过对国内较早实施大类招生、培养的三所北京高校——北京理工大学、中国人民大学、北京航空航天大学外语专业改革状况的详细考察，反思其改革模式与经验，以期为当下外语专业大类招生改革提供一些借鉴。

2　北京三校外语专业大类培养改革概况

2.1　北京理工大学外语专业大类培养改革概况与特色

北京理工大学外语类专业包括英语、日语、德语与西班牙语。该校推行大类招生，同时实行书院制管理。外国语学院、人文与社会科学学院、法学院所有专业学生划归"社会科学"大类，组成"社会科学实验班"，所有学生均纳入明德书院进行管理。语言（外语）类专业的改革措施有以下特色。

第一，入学后即选定专业意向。为使学生在大学期间能够达到本科专业类教学国家标准，

---

*　车向前：西北工业大学外国语学院教师，主讲欧美文化等课程。

社会科学实验班新生在入学时进行语言类专业意向确定,由学生自愿报名,接受外国语学院语言类特色课程培养,同时与明德书院学生一起修读大类公共课程。此部分学生一年后进行专业确认时,可以根据学习兴趣选择语言专业或选择书院内非语言类专业(外语类保送生除外)。社会科学实验班未进行语言专业意向确认的学生,如对语言学习有浓厚的兴趣,可在一年后书院整体确认专业时选择语言类专业,外国语学院根据各专业可接收人数进行接收。

第二,英语专业基础阶段教学计划完备。英语专业在前两个学年(四学期)形成了"公共基础课+素质(大类)通识课+专业必修课+专业选修课"的基本框架,最大限度地平衡了大类培养与语言专业特殊性之间的关系。其中,专业必修课模块"综合英语+英语阅读+英语听力+英语口语+英语写作"持续贯穿前四学期教学;必修大类通识课分为"人文素质通识(哲学与历史、文学与艺术、健康与社会、经济与管理、科学与技术、创新与创业类中,任意4类,每类2个学分)、实践通识(艺术实践、科技实践、文化实践类,任意2类,每类1个学分)",前两年共计8个学分,从第二学期开始修习。

第三,小语种专业基础阶段教学计划凸显特色。日语、德语与西班牙语等小语种因其学习的特殊性,在基础阶段特别强调基本能力的训练。以德语为例,德语专业在大一两学期除安排必修课之外,其专业必修课为基础德语Ⅰ/Ⅱ(各20学时/周,总计640学时),最大限度地为学生打好基础提供保障。

2.2 中国人民大学外语专业大类培养改革概况与特色

中国人民大学语言类专业包括英语、日语、俄语、德语、法语、西班牙语等专业。该校外国语学院有着完善的本、硕、博培养体系。外国语学院所有专业单列为"外国语言文学大类"进行培养。该校语言(外语)类专业培养改革措施有以下特色。

第一,设置独立的"外国语言文学大类"。中国人民大学主要有6个学院,按学院大类招生,针对人文学科设置了"人文科学实验班",依托该校文学院、历史学院、哲学院、国学院、马克思主义学院等学院进行招生和培养,但外国语学院并未参与,而是单列出"外国语言文学大类"。根据语言教育特点,学院在新生入校后2周内完成专业分流,分流专业包括日语、俄语、德语、法语、西班牙语、英语,充分考虑到外语教育教学的特殊性和独立性,保障了专业培养质量。外国语学院同时要求各语言类专业修读11个学分的通识核心课[①]。

第二,英语专业培养计划的人文性特色突出。该校大力提倡英语专业的"人文性",坚守人文教育。入学后前两年均设置"人文经典阅读(Ⅰ—Ⅳ)"课程,贯穿前两学年,学习内容包括文学、哲学、社会学等经典文献;大二学年开设英国文学史及选读、美国文学史等课程,增强学生的文学文化修养;大三后的高年级阶段开设莎士比亚戏剧、英国维多利亚时期文学选读、十九世纪美国文学选读、现代主义与后现代主义文学导读等课程,更为专业、难度更大,人文性的特点更突出(中国人民大学外国语学院,2019)。

第三,英语作为第二专业/学位建设完善。从2013年起,该校每年从非英语专业本科新生中挑选英语口语及写作能力突出的学生组成实验班。实验班学生除了学习各自的专业课程

---

① 通识核心课包括哲学与伦理、历史与文化、思辨与表达、审美与诠释、世界与中国、科学与技术、实证与推理以及生命与环境八大类。

外,还要完成实验班的学习任务。为期3个学期的学习结束后,成绩合格者可获得实验班结业证书,成绩优异者则可继续进入以英语作为第二专业的学习阶段。这种培养模式旨在为优秀学生提供英语学习的全新平台,使其将来不但能够娴熟地运用英语进行业务活动,而且具有国际化视野。

2.3 北京航空航天大学外语专业大类培养改革概况与特色

北京航空航天大学现有的文科学院包括人文与社会科学高等研究院(下辖知行文科实验班)、法学院(法学专业)、人文社会科学学院(经济学和行政管理专业)和外国语学院(英语、德语和翻译专业)。为了提升文科的整体能力,北京航空航天大学文科专业采用"社会科学实验班"大类招生模式。实验班隶属于人文与社会科学高等研究院。大类学生实行一年的通识教育和交叉学科基础教育。该校语言(外语)类专业培养改革措施有以下特色。

第一,英语与翻译专业大类培养第一学年的"通识+交叉学科基础+专业基础"课程设置完善。该校已经实行了较为长期的大类培养,形成了比较完善的培养模式。学生入校后学习一年的通识课程(如中国文明文化史、西方文明文化史、艺术史)和交叉学科基础课程(如经济学、法学、行政管理),该两类课程为全汉语讲授。对于选择英语专业的学生,开设核心专业类必修课程,第1~2学期课程为英美经典要义(1-2)、中西交流概要(1-2)、国际时事(1-2),该类课程为全英文讲授。

第二,德语专业不参与大类培养。小语种专业学生的德语基础几乎为零,在大一入学确定德语专业意向后,进行专门培养,不再参与社会科学实验班课程。

第三,协议保障外语类专业学习。在专业决定方面,实行各学院与学生的双向选择机制。"既充分尊重学生对专业的自主选择,又恰当考虑学院的专业要求"。外国语学院在学生自主选择的基础上,考虑到外语类专业的实际情况和对学生素质的特殊要求,与初步选定英语、翻译、德语专业的学生签订协议,进行有针对性的培养。第一学年结束后根据前期课程选择、学习成绩和综合表现进行二次选择。

第四,确定"人文与社会科学高等研究院"精英文科人才培养创新模式。"北航高研院"是北京航空航天大学特设的融教学与科研为一体的高等学术机构,定位于精英文科人才培养、文科的通识教育、大文科的博雅教育、高水平学术研究。培养面向未来、汇通古今中西的高层次领导型、领军型精英人才,并在此过程中探索该校精英文科人才培养的创新模式。每年从社会科学试验班中择优录取30人,在进行专业教育的同时,强化通识教育和交叉学科教育。

3 北京三校经验对外语类本科专业培养的借鉴

基于对以上三校的调研,对于大类培养下专业改革的思路,笔者对如下四对关系有了基本认识。其一,应处理好大类培养与专业培养的关系。人才大类培养更加符合素质教育要求,有助于"厚基础""宽口径"培养模式的实行,大类培养与学科/专业的特殊性密切相关,二者皆不可偏废,特别是在培养方案上,不能借大类通识课之名行专业课教学之实,更不能用大类通识课替代专业/学科基础课。其二,应处理好外语类专业的一般性和特殊性关系。大类培养语境下,外语专业培养目标与其他专业都有跨学科、创新型、国际化、高辨识度、应用复合型等普遍特点。但同时,语言教育有其特殊性,要遵循外语专业人才培养规律,将专业教育与素质培养融为一体。遵循外语类本科专业教学国家标准,在低年级阶段,要特别注重夯实学生外语语言基础;在扎实的语言能力的基础上,再在学生高年级阶段,培养其中西跨文化能力与国际视野、学术视野。前者是后者的根本奠基,后者是前者的纵深发展。在三校调研中,各校负责人均表示,英语专业学生若在低年级阶段无专业技能类基础课训练,不利于高年级分方向后的深入专业学习,不利于专四、专八等专业证书的考取;离开扎实的语言基本功,外语学生的全面发展、学科的人文特质便无从谈起。其三,基于第二点认识,应处理好学生自主选择与专业需求及学科发展的关系。如学者郭英剑(2019)所言,"'专业'是学科人才培养的基地,'学科'是专业持续发展的基础"。语言类专业需要保障一定数量的有兴趣、有意向的新生在低年级完成基础语言学习,因此应该在学生入校后,在大类专业内进行摸底,基本明确大部分学生的语言学习意向,既充分尊重学生对专业的自主选择,又恰当考虑学院的专业要求,既有利于学生发展,又有助于学科建设。其四,应处理好外语专业工具性和人文性的关系。在大类培养思路下,掌握外语不仅是国际竞争的需要,也是受教育者全面发展的需要。在新形势下应该全面理解外语教育的价值,既看到其工具性,又认识其人文性。

基于上述认识,本文提出如下六点对策。

第一,充分挖掘语言类学生资源,把握语言类学生志趣与专业发展、学科建设的平衡。首先应加大宣传,提高外语类保送生比例。进一步提高招收符合教育部规定的具有推荐保送生资格的外国语中学的优秀应届高中毕业生的比例。通过加强在全国各知名外语类高中的走访与宣传力度、积极召开外语类保送生家长见面会等方式,向有兴趣的学生、教师及家长们介绍学校和学院详细信息,吸引学生报考外国语学院外语类专业,该批学生进入学校后必须选择英语、德语专业。其次是入校后确定学生语言专业意向。入学第一个月内通过宣传、走访、互动、交流,展示外语类专业优势,在此基础上通过志愿填报、面试等手段确立学生外语类专业意向,签订第一学年专业培养协议,最大限度地照顾学生兴趣与发展,保障专业发展与学科建设需要。具体操作上,学生入学初,外国语学院首先在专业意向上确认各专业拟接收人数,学生可选择填报一个或多个语言类专业志愿,根据测评结果依次进行专业意向确认。各专业根据学生意向填报情况,结合高考英语成绩,进行综合语言学习能力测评。测评方式为学院组织专家组进行面试(专家提问,考生回答)。所有被确认为语言类专业意向的学生,将按照含有相关语言类特色的教学计划学习一年。一年后依然有权在社会科学实验班各专业内进行专业确认。而在一年后申请进入小语种专业学习的学生,如无语言基础,则与下一届新生一起进行语言学习。申请进入英语专业的学生,要对其英语能力进行测试,按其能力情况安排进入同级班级进行语言专业学习,或与下一届新生一起进行语言学习。

第二,英语专业课程设置方面,大类培养第一学年应形成"公共必修课程(思政、军理、体育)+大类核心通识课(博雅、人文)+学科专业核心基础课(语言基本能力)"的完备的核心课程群。在北京三校的第一年大类培养中,均有2~4门相应的专业基础技能必修课。因此,在大类培养的第一学年,应在保持现有课程的基础上,适当减少核心通识课的比例,转换或设立3门(每门2~3学时/周)左右的学科专业基础技能必修课,以夯实学生基本功,为后期的学习打下良好基础。具体课程安排见(不包含选修课)表1。

表 1 课程安排

学 期	公共必修课程 （汉语讲授）	大类核心通识课 （汉语或双语讲授）	学科专业核心基础课 （英语讲授）
1	思政、军理、体育等课程	博雅类通识课3门，含欧美文化或西方文明史1门	综合英语1 人文经典阅读1 英语听说1（外教） 英语写作1
2	思政、军理、体育等课程	博雅类通识课3门，含跨文化交际1门	综合英语2 人文经典阅读2 英语听说2（外教） 英语写作2

德语专业课程设置方面，学生入校以后，专业基础知识几乎为零，需要大量的基础训练保障其基本语言能力的培养，因此应最大限度地降低大类通识课的比例，保证听说读写等基础课的开设。应以语言基础能力培养为主，而大量修习大类培养课程占用了学生基本功训练的时间与精力，因此第一学年应安排每周20个学时左右的专业基础课，不参与大类培养课程，或者每学期大类培养课程学分应减小到2个学分，或者在中高年级以选修形式组织。

第三，大类核心通识课应突出博雅、人文特质。大类培养的目的，在于培养学生的人文情怀与科学素养、历史眼光与国际视野、道德底蕴与法治理念、审辩思维与创新精神。因此，大类核心通识课程应该特别重视其博雅性、人文性。目前，很多学校的大类招生存在哲学社会科学大类平台课程整体专业性过强、人文性较弱的问题，应结合专业方向的特色，设置能够兼具人文情怀普遍性与专业科学性的课程。英语专业可开设西方文明史、跨文化交际、中西交流概要等课程，夯实核心通识和宽厚学科基础。博雅、人文特质同样应体现在专业基础课的设置上。应为外语专业大一、大二学生开设人文经典阅读或英美经典要义课程，替代传统的泛读课，内容可包含难度一般的文学、社会学、哲学等英文原典，以开阔学生视野，突出学科的人文性特征，为高年级学生的培养打下基础。

第四，高年级培养特色应兼具人文性与工具性，可设置"翻译"和"文学文化"等方向。在专业特色方面，课程体系和结构设计应强调专业教育与个性化发展并重，本科到硕士、博士上升发展路径通畅，同时为学生提供多种学业成长路径，使其拥有良好的发展空间。考虑到不同学校英语专业学生人数及师资总量，建议设置"翻译"和"文学文化"等方向。如翻译方向可在开设翻译理论、科技英语等基础课程的同时，通过与理工科专业教师合上等方式开设专业实践实训课，使学生具有较强的用外语进行科技信息交流与传播的能力。文学文化方向先修课程应为英美文学、西方文化等课程；对高年级学生应提供更为专业、详细的课程，结合专业教师研究方向，开设如西方批评理论、圣经文学、二十世纪英国/美国小说、中西语言对比、中西文化对比等课程，进一步突出人文特质，加强思辨能力培养。在两个核心方向之外，同时可为学生开设语言学概论/西方语言学流派、英语教学法、商务英语等选修课程，满足其未来专业/职业发展的需要。

第五，加强第二学位建设。具体而言，一是继续鼓励外语专业学生进行第二学位修读。拓展外语专业学生的复合特征，继续突破传统单一的语言培养模式，可借鉴北京理工大学的培养经验,充分鼓励学生参加管理学、经济学、法学等双学士学位专业学习,并支持学生们修读其他专业的数学、统计等课程。提高本科生攻读双学位的比例,培养其扎实的英语语言基础和广泛的科学文化知识能力。二是加强英语作为第二专业/学位的作用。可借鉴中国人民大学培养经验,每年可从非英语专业本科新生中挑选50名左右的英语口语及写作能力突出的学生,组成英语实验班。实验班学生在学习各自的专业课程的同时,还要完成一年左右的实验班的学习任务,学习结束后,成绩合格者可获得实验班结业证书,鼓励其进入以英语作为第二专业的学习阶段,部分学分可进行替换。

第六,打造精英人文社科人才培养创新模式。可考虑对人文社科类优秀本科生实施"拔尖创新人才培养"计划,单独设立学院管理,建设人文社科专业本科教学最高平台,培育具有深厚人文底蕴、扎实专业知识、强烈创新意识、宽广国际视野的精英人才。模式上可借鉴北京航空航天大学高等研究院,一、二年级实行大类通识教育,学生主要修读校级模块课程、依托所在学院的院级大类通识教育模块课程和学科基础模块课程,学生从大一第二学期开始进行研究能力培养,参与导师的研究课题。三、四年级实行宽口径的专业教育。每位学生配备一名高水平教师担任导师。在导师指导下,学生可根据自己的兴趣特长和意愿自主确认人文社科类主修专业,制订个人修读计划,修读专业模块课程、专业拓展模块课程和实践教育模块课程。学习期间,学生将获得更多的机会参与导师的科研课题,在研究实践中进一步夯实专业知识。

4 结语

"强化通识教育,推进大类培养,已经成为创建高水平研究型大学的当务之急"(谢桂红、颜洽茂、金娟琴,2008)。总体来看,外语类专业大类培养要不断创新人才培养模式,建立适应学生自由选择专业和个性化发展的机制,要紧紧围绕"厚语言基础、宽发展口径"的中心,结合学校办学特色,强化学生自主学习的意识和能力,不断培养学生的语言能力、专业拓展能力和跨文化交际能力,确保专业人才的培养规格和质量。唯有如此,才能真正实现学生成长路径多样化,才能培养出兼具国际视野和人文情怀的高素质复合型人才。

参 考 文 献

郭英剑,2019,《新中国英语专业教育70年——历史考察与反思》,《语言教育》第4期。
谢桂红、颜洽茂、金娟琴,2008,《强化通识教育 推进大类培养》,《中国大学教学》第3期。
中国人民大学教务处,2019,本科生培养方案(2019级):外国语学院。据中国人民大学外国语学院官网:http://fl.ruc.edu.cn/docs/2019-09/c58bd110e34a44b0a034841da717c189.pdf。

改革文学选读课程,培养外语专业本科生科研能力

麻 蕾*

摘 要:近年来,随着我国高等教育与国际接轨以及国家"双一流"建设的持续推进,各高校对本科生科研能力培养提出了更高要求。而外语专业本科生科研能力培养尚未形成有效培养机制。本文依托文学选读课程实践,建议整合跨媒介教学资料、改革课程教学模式、构建课程评价体系,将本科生科研能力培养嵌入单门课程,以实现外语专业本科生科研能力培养目标。

关键词:外语专业本科生;科研能力培养;嵌入单门课程;文学选读课程

1 本科生科研能力培养综述

科研能力是指一个人在其所从事的专业中,以科学的思维和适当的方法,对未知领域进行科学探索的能力。科研能力主要包括发现并提出问题的能力,获取及搜集资料的能力,对研究对象及其相关资料进行分析的能力,运用创造性思维提出新思想、新方法和新结果的能力,以及对科研活动的过程与结果进行表达的能力。它是一个人专业知识深度和广度的综合体现。

21世纪是知识经济时代,世界各国的研究型大学都在本科教育阶段致力于培养具有创新意识和创新能力的高级人才。我国教育部在高等教育"质量工程"中明确指出,要推动学生自主学习、研究性学习和改革实践教学,提高学生的学习和研究兴趣,培养学生的动手能力和创新精神。2008年发布的《国家中长期教育改革和发展规划纲要》在"高等教育"部分明确提出:"提高人才培养质量,支持学生参与科学研究,强化实践教学环节"。2015年党中央、国务院做出了"双一流"建设的重大战略决策,提出培养拔尖创新人才的具体任务,要求全面提升学生的综合素质、国际视野、科学精神和创业意识、创造能力。

在实践层面,清华大学实施"学生研究训练"计划、上海交通大学推出"本科生研究计划"、浙江大学推出"大学生科研训练计划"、"文科/理科基地"项目、"君政基金",还有各研究型大学联合共建实习平台,都为本科生提供了科研训练的机会,使本科生接触学科前沿,了解学科发展动态。但是,由于各专业有不同的发展状况和培养模式,本科生科研能力培养在不同专业之间存在不均衡发展的状况。

2 外语专业本科生科研能力培养的问题

仇云龙(2018)通过对国内英语专业本科生学术研究能力培养的回顾与展望,发现国内英语专业本科生学术研究能力培养的先行研究存在局限,在未来研究中,应加强培养内涵研究,

---

* 麻蕾:西北工业大学外国语学院副教授,主要研究方向为德语文学。

深化培养要素研究。关秀娟(2013)指出,外语专业本科生的科研意识落后于其他学科的学生,科研训练起点低,外语专业本科生科研能力培养仍未形成有效举措。目前的外语教学应以构建外语学科意识为主导,在培养学生专业综合能力的基础上,进一步优化培养方案和课程模式,着力培养外语专业本科生的科研能力,促进外语专业内涵式发展。但是我国外语专业本科生科研能力培养尚存在一些问题。

第一,理论层面。与我国外语专业本科生的科研能力相关的理论研究不足。我国学界有关本科生科研能力培养的研究尚处于起步阶段,且当前研究多从本科生科研的制度、管理、体制等宏观方面进行理论探讨(邬家瑛、钱辉,2009),而外语专业本科生科研能力培养的相关研究不足,且理论认识不够深入。

第二,实践层面。我国多数高校在外语专业本科生科研能力培养方面尚未形成切实有效的培养机制。我国很多大学都设置了相应的本科生科研管理机构,拥有专项经费及展示平台,且有些高校已将本科生科研训练纳入正规的课程体系,但实施效果欠佳。例如,近年来国内研究型大学通过实行本科生导师制,在教师和学生之间建立"导学"关系。但是,我国本科生导师制度由于起步较晚,在实施过程中仍存在师生之间沟通不畅及导师职责不清等问题(石荣传,2016),这些问题在外语专业本科生培养中尤其突出。此外,因其专业的特殊性,外语专业本科生特别是小语种专业本科生在低年级阶段的学习,目前仍以提升外语语言能力为重点,学生参加课外科研训练和申请校内科研课题的参与度普遍不高。我国外语专业本科生目前仍主要通过参与实习及社会实践、参加学术报告会议、完成毕业论文等方式获得科研训练。

第三,教学层面。本科生科研应以培养学生创新能力为目的,从本质上讲是教学的一种形式。应把现有的本科生科研管理模式由课余化、研究化和结果导向逐渐转向教学化、必修化和过程导向(邬家瑛、钱辉,2009)。我国外语专业本科生科研能力培养目前仍存在将科研能力培养和本科教学割裂开来的问题。

3 依托文学选读课程进行教学模式改革,培养外语专业本科生的科研能力

刘皓(2018)指出,本科生科研的本质属性是学习而不是研究,尤其需要加强的是嵌入单门课程的研究与探索。外语专业本科教学应该充分发挥外语专业课程类型多样、教学方法灵活的先天优势,深化以本科生科研能力培养为导向的课程改革,将科研能力培养嵌入外国文学、语言学导论、相关国家国情历史概论、跨文化交际等外语学科专业课程。将学生科研能力培养嵌入单门课程,能够有效解决外语专业本科生科研能力培养过程中遇到的现实问题。笔者以文学选读课程的教学模式改革实践为基础,探讨外语专业本科生科研能力培养的可行性方案。

文学选读课程是高校外语专业各语种在本科高年级开设的学科专业课,一般开设在第五或第六学期,高校按照自身的专业设置特色将其分为专业必修课或专业选修课。文学选读课程涵盖外国文学史、文学类型学、文学理论、文学批评理论等多方面的外国文学学科知识。文学选读课程有助于提升学生的语言运用能力、开阔其文学视野、丰富其文化知识、增强其多元文化意识;有助于培养学生的文学鉴赏力和文学批评能力;有助于培养学生的思辨能力、自主学习能力和创新能力。以英语专业为例,根据《高等学校英语专业英语教学大纲》可知,英美文学选读课程的教学目标在于:培养学生阅读、欣赏、理解英语文学原著的能力,帮助学生掌握文

学批评的基本知识和方法。通过阅读和分析英美文学作品,增强学生对西方文学及文化的了解,促进学生语言基本功和人文素质的提高。

笔者认为,依托文学选读课程的教学改革,通过整合跨媒介教学资料、优化课程教学模式、构建过程性评价体系,将本科生科研能力培养嵌入单门课程,外语专业本科生的科研能力培养目标就能实现。

3.1 贴近科学研究,整合跨媒介教学资料

传统文学课堂以提高学生的语言能力和培养学生的文学鉴赏力为目标,较少兼顾学生科研意识和科研能力的培养。改革后的文学选读课程在提高学生综合语言能力基础上,抛弃"知识传授型"课程的固有思维,将培养学生的科研能力设定为课程培养目标。

信息技术背景下,教学内容不再是封闭、一成不变的知识点,而是开放、灵活的知识网,学生可以随时通过网络快速获取外国文学知识的相关信息。新时代的文学阅读可采用文本与图片、音频、视频相结合的"文本+"方式。教师在准备教学资料的过程中,首先应该继续发挥纸质文本作为文学研究第一手资料所具备的准确、科学、权威等优势。在此基础上充分利用多媒体技术的跨媒介手段,挖掘更丰富的图片、音频、视频等多媒体化教学材料,保障文学资料的多样性,为"文本+"的跨媒介阅读方式构建文献基础。在对教学内容合理取舍与跨媒介整合过程中,教学材料要突出问题意识且要贴近科学研究。

在传统的文学选读课堂上,教师大多会在分析作品之前将作家及作品相关信息讲述给学生,但学生很难真正掌握,更谈不上融会贯通。究其原因,主要是学生在此过程中仍是被动地获取知识。信息技术背景下,教师完全可以将搜集文学资料的任务交给学生。若要围绕一个作家或一部作品进行相关研究,学生可利用互联网、数据库等资源搜集相关文学史、文学流派、作家生平、作品风格、作品批评等各类资料,并对所搜集到的资料进行分类整理,从而获得翔实且全面的文学文献。在文献搜集过程中,学生成为学习的主体,既获取了相关知识,又提高了基本的文献搜集能力。

3.2 参考科研工作步骤,优化文学选读课程教学模式

3.2.1 传统文学选读课程模式

如前文所述,传统的文学选读课主要侧重于学生语言能力和文学鉴赏力的提升,文学文本仅作为提升学生两个能力的阅读材料,文本所蕴含的文学学科相关知识没有被充分挖掘。传统文学选读课或按时间,或按流派,或按体裁将课堂划分为若干个教学单元。每一个教学单元又被划分为课前、课中、课后三个环节。课前,教师将文学作品节选以及提前设计好的问题发给学生,引导学生带着问题提前阅读作品节选,并针对问题进行思考。课中,教师简要介绍作品所涉及的文学史、文学理论、作家背景等相关知识;教师就所提出的问题与学生交流想法,通过课堂讨论,帮助学生掌握文学鉴赏的相关方法,这一环节同时也起到了帮助学生提炼观点、提高语言表达水平的作用。课后,教师就具体文学问题,布置相关书面或口头作业,例如朗诵、角色扮演、续写故事、撰写作品批评等。一方面帮助学生提高口语及书面语表达能力,另一方面增强学生对文学的兴趣。

传统模式在提高学生语言综合能力和文学鉴赏力方面的成效是值得肯定的,但是传统教学模式也存在一定弊端。其一,教师在三个环节中均处于课堂中心地位,学生要完全按照教师

的安排和思路进行文学阅读和思考,学生的主动性和积极性没有被完全调动起来。其二,课堂教学侧重语言技能提升,在文学理论、文本分析、文学批评等文学研究方面较少涉及,很难将课程教学与外语专业本科生科研能力培养有效结合。

3.2.2 改革后的文学选读课程模式

(1)文学选读课程的课程目标

本课程的教学模式改革以形成开放的、研究性的文学课堂为基础,提高学生的综合语言能力,培养学生的文学鉴赏力和文学研究能力,帮助学生形成文学学科意识、掌握文学研究基本方法,以培养学生的科研能力为目标。改革后的文学选读课程将课堂教学环节重新调整,采取小组活动、专题研讨、文学讲座、论文写作、专题汇报、文学沙龙等多种方法,让学生在主动参与的过程中获取文学知识,初步具备科研能力。

(2)课程设计的基本原则

教师在设计课程方案时确定了小组工作原则、"X+1+1"原则和实时反馈原则。

小组工作原则是指将全体学生按照总人数划分为若干文学小组,每组由3~4名学生组成,学生以小组成员的身份参与本学期全部课堂活动。

"X+1+1"原则是指课程文本阅读量,即各小组本学期需要完成X篇作品节选+1篇作品节选+1部完整作品的阅读与研究任务。其中X一般为6~9篇作品节选,教师根据课程人数变化和教学内容调整节选作品的总量。学生按照"X+1+1"原则,选择相关作品作为自己本学期的研讨和研究对象,通过小组合作方式,完成X项课堂研讨任务、1项口头汇报任务和1项论文设计任务。教师全程参与三项任务,进行点评和补充,布置各项后续工作及任务。

实时反馈原则是师生之间的联系与沟通。教师通过线上交流群实时关注各小组工作进度,并进行有效监督,确保各小组准时、高效地完成学习及科研任务。此外,各文学小组组内利用线上、线下多种方式协同工作,及时解决组员在文本阅读、组内研讨、口头汇报、论文准备等若干环节中遇到的各种问题。

(3)课程模式的具体实施阶段

参考科研工作的四个基本步骤:科研选题、资料收集、研究试验、论文撰写,按照每学期16个教学周,将教学过程细化为学期初(科研选题阶段)、学期中(科学研究阶段)、学期末(成果呈现阶段)、结课后(反思反馈阶段)四个阶段。四个阶段给学生安排不同的学习及科研任务,突出学生自主性。

第一阶段:学期初,即第1教学周,为科研选题阶段。

教师根据学生总人数及学生各自的文学兴趣,确定文学小组总数和各小组具体人数。各文学小组通过集体商议,最终确定X篇作品节选,各小组选择1篇作品节选、选定1部完整作品。教师在前期文学作品选择过程中采取兼顾文学时期、文学流派、作品体裁及学生兴趣的原则,有侧重地提供多部完整作品和若干作品节选。笔者在前期调查时注意到,多数作品选读课程主要选取不同时期外国文学作品节选为阅读材料。诚然,作品节选能够让学生在一个学期内阅读到不同体裁、不同作家的各类作品,保证了学生阅读的广度,也有助于学生搭建初步的外国文学体系。对于整部作品的选取,特别是长篇经典作品,限于学时和难度,教师和学生大多都会望而却步。事实上,整部作品的完整阅读,既能保证学生阅读的深度,又有助于学生对文学作品的整体理解和阐释。本着"回到文学作品本身"的原则,阅读材料的选择必须重视作品的完整性。基于以上原因,本课程最终确定了"X+1+1"原则,一方面保障学生阅读的广度与深度,另一方面兼顾文本的多样性和完整性。

第二阶段:学期中,即第 2～15 教学周,为科学研究阶段。

在这一阶段,要求每小组制订并填写严格的科研工作进度表,并通过选定小组长进行有效的组内监督,确保科研工作有序进行。同时,要求学生和教师双方严格依照实时反馈原则,确保每个环节中的问题能够及时得到解决。

基于"X+1+1"原则,课程将每个小组此研究阶段的工作划分为三项任务。

任务一:各小组针对 X 篇节选作品,依照"阅读—提问—全员讨论"的进程完成前期准备,参与其他小组的口头报告和之后的全员讨论(每两周完成 1 篇节选)。这一阶段主要训练学生的团队协作能力,文学鉴赏、发现问题、凝练观点等综合语言能力。

任务二:各小组从 X 篇作品节选中选出 1 篇,依照"确定选题—搜集资料—研究讨论—口头汇报—全员讨论"的进程,利用 2 周时间依照两个环节完成 1 篇节选的口头汇报工作。第一个环节,小组基于前期文本阅读和文献搜集工作,针对与作品相关的文学史、文学流派、文学理论、作品分析进行口头汇报,主持并参与全员讨论。第二个环节是口头汇报的延伸环节,针对全员讨论中的焦点问题继续研究讨论,教师基于相关文学理论、文学批评方法对作品进行再阐释,同时设计相关后续课堂活动对课堂口头汇报进行有效补充。例如,通过广播剧欣赏或电影改编、作品朗诵或角色扮演、故事续写或创意写作、文学辩论等多种跨媒介手段,充分调动学生的主观能动性,提升学生的综合语言能力和文学思辨能力。

任务三:各小组另选 1 部完整作品作为研究对象,依照"确定选题(第 1 周)—查找资料(第 2～5 周)—课题研究(第 6～10 周)—撰写论文(第 10～15 周)"的工作进度,完成课程论文撰写工作。

三项任务平行并存且依次递进,各项任务内部又自成体系。前两项任务是第三项任务的基础,第三项任务则是前两个任务链的深化和升华。目的是使学生在提升语言综合能力、文学鉴赏力、思辨能力等各项综合能力的基础上,养成文学学科意识,提升科学研究能力。

第三阶段:学期末,即第 16 教学周,为成果呈现阶段。

各文学小组呈现研究成果——课程论文,并就课程论文完成答辩。论文答辩是本学期学生科研工作和科研成果的集中展现,充分体现学生的综合素养和文学研究能力。

在第 17～18 周,组内学生根据论文答辩过程中的各类问题,进行深入思考并对论文进行调整和修改,修改之后每位学生独立提交课程论文终稿。修改后的课程论文既能充分体现小组的集体智慧,又具有鲜明的个人特色。

第四阶段:结课后,即第 19～20 周,为反思反馈阶段。

一方面,教师在结课后安排 1～2 次工作坊或文学沙龙,就收集到的论文进行评述,指出其中有关文学理论、作品分析、资料搜集、科研方法、论文撰写等各方面存在的各类问题,帮助学生掌握基本的文学批评方法和文学研究方法。另一方面,学生对本学期课堂活动、文本阅读、口头汇报和论文成果等方面的收获和疑问进行总结,同教师深入交流,提出自己对各环节的思考、对课程模式的建议以及对本科生科研训练的认识。

四个阶段围绕外语专业本科生科研能力培养的课程总目标,使学生经过"入手"(即入手做汇报、写论文)、"入脑"(研究及讨论)、"入心"(掌握科研工作方法)的循序渐进过程,养成初步的文学学科意识和科学研究能力。

3.3 革新评价方式,构建过程性评价体系

文学选读课程通常以闭卷考试的方式对学生进行考核,传统的闭卷考试以考查具体知识点为主,问题设置主要围绕具体的文学问题,考核学生对文学知识的掌握程度和对文学问题的评价能力,是一种结果性评价。但因闭卷考试本身的局限性,很难做到对学生文学鉴赏能力、科学研究能力以及学习全过程的投入情况进行全面且客观的评判。针对以上问题,改革后的文学选读课程对评价体系进行革新,不再以考查具体知识点为目的,而是突出对学生综合能力的评价。课程构建过程性评价体系,将学生的文学鉴赏能力、文本分析能力、文学批评能力、科学论文撰写能力纳入考查范围,重点考查学生在课程全过程中各个阶段的素质发展和能力水平。

3.3.1 三种评价方式相结合

本课程学生均以小组成员身份参与全部课程活动,根据过程性评价主体的不同划分,笔者将小组自评、小组互评、教师评价等三种方式相结合,对全体学生在课程全过程中的学习及科研工作的表现、投入及效果进行综合评价。

小组自评和小组互评是指各小组在口头汇报、论文答辩之后对本小组或其他小组在此项工作中的投入及表现进行评价。小组自评和互评是以学生为主体,对自身学习及科研工作的个体反思与互相借鉴的有效方式。

教师评价包括教师点评及教师量化评价两部分。教师点评是指教师就学期中小组口头汇报、学期末小组论文答辩的投入与表现,分别在课后和结课后(即反思反馈阶段)进行点评,帮助学生在语言能力、学科知识、科研方法、研究动态、工作态度等各方面拓展思路、加深认识。教师量化评价是指教师就每项科研任务各环节的完成情况,对各文学小组及小组成员进行量化评分,保证学生最终成绩评定的客观性。教师点评和教师量化评价是将过程性评价与结果性评价完美结合的创新型评价体系,既能保障教师对学生学习研究、课堂组织、教学效果的有效监控和调节,又能保障课程评价体系的客观性及整体性。

3.3.2 运用量化评价工具

制订小组汇报评价量表、小组论文答辩评价量表、学生论文评价量表,其中的评价要素各有侧重。小组汇报评价量表的主要评价要素为作品内容、作品制作、语言及表现、汇报效果;小组论文答辩评价量表的主要评价要素为文献与综述、内容与逻辑、回答问题、语言及表现;学生论文评价量表的主要评价要素为论文选题及意义、查阅文献能力、综合运用知识能力、研究方案与方法、写作与表达能力、写作的规范性等。

三个评价量表相结合,根据20%、35%、45%的权重比例,综合评价学生整个学期中学习及科研的投入和表现。

4 结语

随着高等教育的跨越式发展和高等教育改革的持续推进,提升外语专业本科生的培养质量始终是各高校外语专业本科教学的根本任务,外语专业本科生科研能力培养则是各高校培养高素质创新人才的有效举措。但是,鉴于外语专业的特殊性和外语专业本科生科研能力培

养的具体问题,课外科研训练等相关实践举措很难有效实施。因此,将学生科研能力培养嵌入单门课程是目前外语专业本科生科研能力培养的可行性方案。笔者认为,高校应依据本科外语教学的自身特点,发挥外语课堂的先天优势,通过跨媒介整合教学资料、优化教学模式、重构课程评价体系,将本科生科研能力培养嵌入外国文学作品选读课程,强化外语专业本科生的科研意识,以实现外语专业本科生科研能力培养目标。

参 考 文 献

关秀娟,2013,《外语专业研究生科研能力"三位一体"培养模式探索》,《学位与研究生教育》第9期。

刘皓,2018,《强化嵌入单门课的探究式学习——兼论本科生科研分类》,《高等工程教育研究》第4期。

仇云龙、林正军,2018,《国内英语专业本科生学术研究能力培养研究:回顾与展望》,《外语教学理论与实践》第2期。

石荣传,2016,《本科生导师制:类型、实施现状及完善对策》,《大学教育科学》第3期。

邬家瑛、钱辉,2009,《论本科生科研训练存在的问题及解决思路》,《中国高教研究》第1期。

从学生视角浅谈法语专业课程的改革与创新

李庆亚[*] 臧小佳[**]

摘 要:2018年法语被教育部正式列入高中课程。另据统计,截至2018年底,内地共有144所大学开设了法语专业。法语越来越深入到我们的学习和工作中,但法语人才不定期流失、法语专业毕业生技能单一、高校法语学习平台小等问题给建设特色法语专业带来了很大的阻力。如何解决上述问题,让法语专业走出自己的特色路线?本文拟采用调查法、访谈法等研究方法,以理论为基础,以现实为依据,从学生视角分析大学法语课程的改革与创新,进而推动法语专业走出自己的特色路线。

关键词:学生视角;大学法语课程;改革与创新

教育部在《国家中长期教育改革和发展规划纲要(2010—2020年)》(以下简称《纲要》)中指出要"加强实验室、校内外实习基地、课程教材等基本建设"。深化教学改革,推进和完善学分制,实行弹性学制,促进文理交融。支持学生参与科学研究,强化实践教学环节。加强就业创业教育和就业指导服务。创立高校与科研院所、行业、企业联合培养人才的新机制。全面实施"高等学校本科教学质量与教学改革工程"。大学法语课程应如何改革与创新,进而实现《纲要》目标?本文将从目前高校法语毕业生的发展方向、专业素质以及高校法语课程软件、硬件建设进行探讨,分析大学法语课程的改革与创新,并在此基础上,为让法语专业走出自己的特色路线提出些许建议。

1 目前高校法语毕业生的发展方向问题

根据教育部统计,法语专业是最容易就业的专业之一,也是应届本科毕业生平均收入最高的专业之一。在目前法语专业学生就业的主战场——非洲,据笔者调查,仅中国铁建驻阿尔及利亚项目部基层翻译的底薪不会低于一万元人民币。除此之外,还有就职于中建、中水、中土、中石油等企业的应届毕业生,也有通过公务员考试成为外交部、商务部外派人员,到驻非洲各国的中国大使馆工作的毕业生。这部分学生的收入水平极大地拉高了法语专业应届本科毕业生的平均收入水平。但是,我们要看到高收入之外,这部分学生不得不面临的发展方向的问题。

常驻国外,为祖国的外交事业默默贡献,或者为中国企业"走出去"战略添砖加瓦固然是一种选择,然而,大多数法语专业学生在前期的资金积累完成后会选择回国发展。这时,由于自

---

[*] 李庆亚:西北工业大学外国语学院硕士研究生。
[**] 臧小佳:西北工业大学外国语学院副院长,副教授,主要研究方向为法国现当代文学、文学理论与文学批评、普鲁斯特研究、绘画及美学、法语文学翻译等。

已常驻国外而可能导致的人脉断档、错过发展时机等问题就会显现出来。更有甚者,选择放弃自己所学专业,彻底转行,这样国外的从业经历很难为自己带来优势。除此之外,在个人感情问题上,作为法语专业学生,毕业后只要从事法语相关工作,就无法避免或长或短的出差,甚至是常驻国外,这直接导致了异地恋的产生。据网络调查报告显示,虽然调查方法或样本大小各有异同,但异地恋的成功率基本不高于三成,这对法语专业学生的发展方向必然产生巨大影响。

笔者对周围法语专业毕业生的调查显示,八成以上的毕业生在面临就业时并未对自己的未来发展方向有明确的规划,以毕业后三年为界,他们中的大多数人会做出辞职、考研、转行等选择。法语专业人才流失的问题如何缓解,这就需要我们的专业老师在日常生活中,多关注时事,多关注法语就业前景,通过进修、海外学习以及到相关企事业单位挂职锻炼等方式,提升自己的综合素质,及时向学生解释毕业时的选择在未来的人生中可能会带来的影响,让学生清楚毕业时选择的意义和自己的发展方向,帮助学生在人生的道路上少走弯路。同时,高校在设置课程时,要结合学生理想和就业市场的需求,培养复合型人才,将语言能力培养与专业能力培养紧密结合起来,提升学生的就业能力,拓展学生的就业范围。

2 目前高校法语毕业生的综合素质问题

在"一带一路"倡议的大背景下,我国与亚洲、非洲、欧洲等国的交流合作日益加深,经济合作不断加强,高校的小语种专业越来越受青睐,其中法语尤甚。由于历史原因,57个非洲国家中有26个国家的官方语言或通用语言为法语,这使得相关就业市场对法语专业人才的需求量是巨大的。然而,目前高校普遍只重视对学生的专业语言能力的培养,片面强调语言的工具性,却忽视了对学生思维能力和人文素养的培养。

目前社会亟须的是复合型人才,仅通晓法语一项技能可以满足一时之需,却不利于未来长远的发展。1998年,哈佛大学时任校长陆登庭博士访问北大时指出,大学要重视对"人文"学问的传授。高等教育作为人才培养的更高层次,应该提供无法用金钱衡量的最佳的教育。这种教育不仅赋予我们较强的专业技能,而且还使我们善于观察、勤于思考、勇于探索,塑造健全完善的人格,特别是通过不同学科知识的渗透,使从事科学研究的人开始懂得鉴赏艺术,从事艺术创造的人逐渐了解科学,使我们每个人的生活更加丰富多彩(程建峰、施翔、钟蕾,2000)。陆登庭校长的观点其实可以引申为更加广义的教学方式。所幸,目前被中国高校推崇的"通识教育"与陆登庭校长的观点一脉相承,注重培养学生的综合素质。但是,我们也应看到,目前高校的教育教学方式仍需提高。

在课程设置方面,为了提高学生的人文素质,可以多开设人文课程和人文讲座,作为学生的选修课或者必修课,丰富学生的人文视野,并把这一思想贯彻到任课教师的教学思想中,鼓励教师在授课时,多注重人文精神的熏陶,引导学生树立正确的人生观和价值观。另外,如有条件,高校任课教师在教授法语语言知识的同时,可以适当穿插其他领域的内容,如金融学、建筑学等。甚至可进一步根据学生的兴趣,开设专业的法语相应课程,以培养"一专多能"的复合型人才。

综上所述,高校在课程设置上不仅要有优秀的教师团队作为支撑,还要结合法语的学科特点,在充分尊重学生的差异性的基础上,进行多学科融合,加强配套设施建设。

3　加强实施法语课程的软件、硬件条件建设

　　法语课程的软件建设主要是指师资建设。在传统的法语教学中，往往以教师为本位，这就使得教师自身的素质在很大程度上决定了课堂教学效果。从学生的视角来看，教师的个人魅力是维系课堂效果的关键。如果教师在具备强大法语实力的同时通晓其他专业知识，并能将二者有机结合起来，在法语教学过程中适当穿插，那么这样的法语课将取得一加一远远大于二的效果。这也符合前文提到的陆登庭校长的理念。而从目前的调查来看，高校法语教师这种"兼儒墨，合名法"的杂家素质有待提升。对教师的培养，同样适用"通识教育"的理念。如果"复合型"学生遇到"复合型"教师，根据数学中排列组合的理论，创造出的结果的数量是非常可观的。因此，"于百家之道无不贯通"的教师队伍，是特色法语教学的关键。

　　法语课程的硬件建设主要是指高校积极开展有效的校校合作、校企合作，加强教材建设，整合计算机技术与课程，为学生提供丰富的学习和实践机会。法语学习需要真实的语言环境，只有在这种语言环境下，学生的语言能力才能突飞猛进。校校合作是指有条件的高校可以为学生提供国内外高校联合培养的模式，比如说四川大学法语系设置的"3+2"的模式，即学生先在国内读3年，再到国外读2年，最后可拿到四川大学的本科毕业证书和国外合作院校的硕士毕业证书。校企合作是指高校或学院积极谋求与不同企业的合作，让学生在掌握语言能力之余，获得处理日常事务的能力，让语言成为工作时的工具。加强教材建设是指学生使用的法语教材应该紧跟当今社会的形势发展变化，贴合学生生活，从而激发学生的学习兴趣。整合计算机技术与课程是指将计算机技术看作课程系统的一个有机组成部分，将教师、学生、计算机以及教学内容变成相互联系的整体，让学生成为课堂的中心、学习的主体。

4　小结

　　当前法语课程的制订，片面强调语言的工具性，既不利于学生对未来发展方向的明确，也不利于学生在未来的工作中尽早掌握法语语言能力之外的其他技能。笔者通过与同学、友人交流，查阅文献资料，并结合自身经历，提出以上几点法语课程的改革与创新建议，希望能为解决法语专业学生存在的对未来发展方向不明确、自身综合素养不足以及法语课程的软件、硬件条件建设不完善等问题提供一定的参考，并为让法语专业走出自己的特色路线贡献自己的思路。

参 考 文 献

程建峰、施翔、钟蕾，2000，《知识经济与高等教育的创新》，《江西农业大学学报》第6期。
教育部教材局，2019，普通高中课程方案、课程标准及教材的修订情况。据中华人民共和国教育部官网：http://www.moe.gov.cn/fbh/live/2019/50754/sfcl/201906/t20190620_386630.html。
国家中长期教育改革和发展规划纲要工作小组办公室，2010，国家中长期教育改革和发展规划纲要（2010—2020年）。据中华人民共和国教育部官网：http://www.moe.gov.cn/srcsite/A01/s7048/201007/t20100729_171904.html。

基于心理学视角的高校辅导员谈话技巧刍议
——以某高校一名大学生学习倦怠案例为例

高 敏[*]

摘 要：为了探讨高校辅导员与学生进行谈心谈话的工作方法，笔者结合工作中的实际案例进行分析，对案例谈话中涉及的心理学知识和咨询技能进行了分析和总结，结果表明知心理学知识和心理咨询技术的应用对提升谈话工作的实效性具有积极的作用。

关键词：心理学视角；高校辅导员；谈话技巧

1 引言

谈话是高校辅导员日常工作中最常用的工作方式之一，是与学生沟通、交流和开展工作的必要途径，在思想政治教育、心理危机干预及各类专项指导中具有重要作用和积极意义。相关资料统计，高校辅导员每周与学生面对面的谈话达十余次之多，谈话记录字数有1~2万字。因此，辅导员与学生谈心、谈话的技巧和成效，是反映其工作能力和职业技能水准的重要参考指标。

根据《高等学校辅导员职业能力标准（暂行）》的相关规定，辅导员应具备宽广的知识储备，了解心理学等学科的基本原理和基础知识。该标准还针对初、中、高级辅导员，在心理健康教育与咨询方面分别提出了具体的知识和能力要求。

尽管高校辅导员的年龄、学历、专业均呈现出多样化的特点，但合理运用心理学相关的知识和技巧，能使辅导员的多项工作事半功倍，这在谈心谈话工作中体现得尤为突出。

2 对象、方法、结果

陈某，女，某重点高校大三学生。自幼学习努力，成绩优良；家庭经济宽裕，氛围和睦。该生以优异的高考成绩考入理想的学校，大一结束后，有少数科目不及格，大二结束后出现多门科目不及格的情况，大三第一学期结束时，累计不及格学分已达到学校规定的退学标准。

从2019年10月起，辅导员开始与陈某进行一对一的谈话。经过四次谈话，双方逐步建立起联系和信任，辅导员也开展了心理疏导和自信心重建等工作，帮助学生正视自我，并改善学生的学业倦怠、与父母沟通不畅等问题。该生从被动参与、阻抗，到主动配合、积极应对，最终与辅导员共同探索、寻找并勇敢面对长期困扰其心理的问题。目前该生已经进入新的年级继续学业，与父母的关系和沟通方式有了较为明显的改观，精神面貌逐渐恢复，变得较为开朗和活泼。

---

[*] 高敏：西北工业大学外国语学院党委副书记。

3 讨论

3.1 辅导员要掌握必要的心理学知识和技能

在心理咨询过程中,面对来访者,咨询师可以根据自己擅长的方向、对来访者的判断来选择接诊或是转介。而作为高校辅导员,面对工作要求或是学生求助,一般来说是不能做选择的。但是,这并不意味着,辅导员与学生的谈话工作与心理咨询完全没有相通之处。辅导员在与学生的谈话过程中,可以广泛运用心理学知识和心理咨询方法,达到事半功倍的效果。同时,相关知识可以帮助辅导员对学生的问题进行心理学甄别,如果发现学生有严重心理问题,则需要及时转到专业机构治疗,以免贻误最佳治疗时机,甚至造成不可挽回的后果。

3.2 建立良好的谈话关系

良好的咨询关系是心理咨询工作顺利进行的必要前提。辅导员工作中,常常面临学生意愿和工作要求发生冲突的情况,这就要求辅导员与学生建立良好的谈话关系,对学生不厌倦、不讨好,相互理解,平等对话,真诚沟通。如本案例中,学校要求及时将与学生有关的违纪处分(处理)或者重大学籍变动等信息告知家长,而学生往往对此抵触并且不理解。作为辅导员,首先,不要急于否定和批评学生,而应真诚地表示理解;其次,在肯定学生报喜不报忧的情理后,要注重从事理上引导学生与父母建立良好沟通关系,主动定期联系;最后,要摆明立场和原则,在符合学校规定和遵守职业要求的前提下尽最大努力帮助学生,赢得学生信任。

3.3 遵循"以学生为中心"的谈话原则

根据人本主义疗法主要代表人罗杰斯的"来访者中心疗法"的观点,在谈话过程中,辅导员应该营造良好的谈话环境和氛围,把谈话中可能出现的其他事情提前安排好,对于临时被打断的情况要迅速做出反应,以免干扰谈话过程,错过时机。另外,从神情、动作和语言等各个方面表达对学生无条件的关注,设身处地地理解学生,让学生感受到被关注、被重视、被看到。最后,无论学生是遇到困难或是犯了错误,辅导员都要将其作为一个值得坦诚面对和对待的人,并保持一种不评价的态度,理解学生的困境和难处,从而发掘学生的潜力,激发其自我导向的行为,实现自我价值。

3.4 综合分析,巧妙应对阻抗

辅导员在谈话过程中,时常会遇到谈话进展不顺畅、难以进行的情况,主要表现为有问无答、回答简短、敷衍等。在心理咨询中这是阻抗的一种表现形式。当察觉阻抗时,应尽量做到以诚恳的态度解除对方的戒备心理,使其能开诚布公地谈论问题。甚至可以把这种"阻力"信息反馈给求助者,从帮助对方的角度出发,以诚恳的探讨问题的态度提出。如本案例中,前几次的谈话围绕着学生学业、人际关系等信息展开,辅导员明显感觉到讲话程度和内容中的阻抗,谈话一度陷入僵局。然而阻抗也往往指示着问题的症结所在,这时要抓住契机,把阻力"传递"给学生,巧妙地激发学生先解决辅导员"信息不足"这一问题的动力,最终形成鼓励其正视自己内心的合力,突破问题的关键。另外,遇到阻抗时还可以采用自我暴露技术、具体化提问等多种方法,以触碰到学生的"心弦",切准"心病"的脉。

3.5 坚持"助人自助"的原则

心理咨询通过来访者主动求助以增强其独立自主性、改变看待问题的方式、建立合理情绪从而完善自我,实现自我。辅导员对学生的心理疏导其实也是这样。每个遇到困难的学生,首先都是独自与问题做斗争的,对自己的问题最有发言权和决定权,任何其他人都只能是摇旗呐喊。更多时候,其实学生心里是有答案或者解决办法的,只是一时看不清或者不愿面对,卡在了解决问题的路上,无形中增加了问题的复杂程度和难度。学生本人能够坚持并且想到求助,这本身就是勇敢和值得尊重的。因此,谈话过程中,辅导员要始终坚持以鼓励和引导为主,不要代替学生做决定,当好倾听者和陪伴者而不是决策者,让谈话成为学生认识自我、悦纳自我、完善自我的过程,引导学生依靠自身的知识和力量解决问题。

3.6 保持长期关注,巩固谈话效果

心理学家罗森塔尔通过实验得出:赞美、信任和期待具有一种能量,能改变人的行为。本案例中,当学生失约并拒绝进行直接沟通时,辅导员通过短信的形式进行持续关注,向学生传递了"我一直在关注你""感谢你的信任""相信你是优秀的"等表达关注和期待的信号,有助于唤起学生的信心和力量来面对并解决问题,维持支持的连续性。因此,辅导员在一次或一个阶段的谈话结束后,还应通过多种方式向学生传递"持续关注"的信号,促使学生不断将外界的期待内化为自身的行动,以巩固谈话效果。

参 考 文 献

中国就业培训技术指导中心、中国心理卫生协会,2012,《心理咨询师(基础知识)》,第二版,民族出版社。
朱秀薇、徐芳丽,2008,《高校辅导员谈话工作的洗礼咨询技巧运用》,《文教资料》第4期。

附录

案例材料

陈某,女,大三学生。自幼学习努力,成绩优良。家庭经济宽裕,氛围和睦。该生以优异的高考成绩考入大学,被父母寄予厚望。大一结束后,有少数科目不及格;大二结束后出现多门科目不及格的情况;从大三第一学期起基本不上课,学期结束时,累计不及格学分已达到学校规定的退学标准。

第一印象:衣着、打扮得体适宜;行为举止合乎正常,有礼貌;话语少,回答问题略有闪烁其词;谈到学习成绩问题时近乎沉默。

该生同学介绍情况:大一、大二时活泼开朗,与同学关系融洽。到大三后,与其他同学交往变少,仅与宿舍舍友关系比较亲近。但由于宿舍成员对未来的规划不同,时常只有她一人在宿舍。除了上课,其他时间很少见到她,而且上课也时常不见人。

本案例研究共分为四个阶段。

1. 第一阶段

谈话两次,每次四十分钟,由学习、退学等问题切入话题,进展并不顺利,基本上是辅导员在主导谈话、寻找话题,学生被动应付,或者沉默。

初始阶段的重点应放在增加熟悉程度、寻找共同话题、建立信任等方面。如问一问"能说一说在大学以前你是怎样的吗?""在家里你和谁沟通得相对多一些?""遇到问题或者困难你会想到告诉谁?"等等。对于不善于或者不愿意交流的学生,多一些等待的时间,或者采用封闭式提问:"是和爸爸交流多一些还是和妈妈交流多一些?"。对于学生总是通过简短的语言回答问题的情况,要及时改变提问方式:"当时你是怎么想的?""你觉得都产生了怎样的影响?"。对于学生回答的只言片语,可通过重复的方式共情,拉近情感距离,也给自己和对方留下更多的思考时间。

结束时的约定、作业:请学生认真思考关于退学的问题,自己的打算及如何面对,并约定好下次见面的时间。

获得的信息及分析:陈某表现出一定程度的社交退缩,不愿意对话和沟通,缺乏对话题的探索兴趣。在谈到退学这样重大的问题时,也只是简单地说一句"我不想退学",没有更多的语言表达,情绪上相对平静,仿佛在说他人的事情。在谈到自己打算如何面对这一问题时,她说不知道,表达时感觉她的心情并不沉重。另一个重要信息是,她中学前一直没有跟父母生活在一起,可推测她在十几岁以前与父母是疏远的,情感上存在疏离。

2. 第二阶段

谈话一次,大约持续四十分钟,与上次谈话间隔一周,学生按照约定主动前往。相对于第一阶段,其表现显得放松了一些。在谈话和回答问题时,不那么拘谨和艰难,逐渐流露出同龄女大学生共有的灵巧和朝气。

这个阶段的谈话需要触及问题的实质。她认为自己想好了,愿意退学,甚至还想到了一些退学后的打算。当询问这件事家人是否知情以及他们怎么看待这件事时,学生的回答是:"没有。我觉得这是我的事,不需要跟他们说。"经过进一步的探讨后,该生稍微思考了一下,仍然表示不想让父母知道。此后,便又回到第一阶段谈话时不积极的沉默状态。

结束时的约定、作业:要求学生思考,如果把情况告知父母,他们会有怎样的反应。

获得的信息及分析:该生与父母沟通不畅是长期以来固化的一种状态,她习惯了独自面对困难和问题,认为父母给不了自己任何帮助。与父母沟通不畅、压力无法得到释放,虽然不是其学习成绩不佳的直接原因,但却是长期以来对其造成困扰、导致心理压力成倍增加的一个隐藏问题,在对其帮助的过程中是一个无法回避的问题。这需要建立更进一步的信任,在以后的谈话中逐渐了解。

3. 第三阶段

谈话一次,持续约五十分钟,与上次谈话间隔一周。根据约定,本次谈话的重点是对于父母的态度。但是,在谈及父母时,她显得不情愿,一开始,谈话进行得并不顺利。

"平时和父母交流自己的事情吗?"

她摇头。

"为什么不和父母交流呢?"

"不想。"

"父母是关心你的,怎么不想交流呢?"

她没有说话。

可以考虑转换对话的模式和内容,让学生换位思考:辅导员是想帮助她的,但辅导员首先需要她的帮助。

"陈某,是不想谈到父母吗?还是和父母沟通时有什么不好面对的问题?或者是有什么不方便说的地方?如果有,你可以告诉老师,没有关系的,我们再一起想想办法。"

说到这里,学生的嘴角动了两下,有了一些表情上的回应。

"是他们不和你交流,还是说交流过但让你失望了?"

"失望。"她基本上没有犹豫就说出了失望。

提问的人在给出选项时其实是有风险的,需要谨慎,更需要对谈话对象的特点有所了解并做出判断。敏锐地抓住这个转折以后,小心地切入话题,谈话开始变得顺利。

结束时的约定、作业:这次只约定了下一次谈话的时间,但没有布置作业,因为已经打开心门的她会主动思考。

获得的信息及分析:这次谈话找到了她与父母沟通不畅的症结所在。虽然在谈话结束前,并没有解决"要不要告知父母"的问题,但至少找到了一条可行的路,而且是学生自己的选择。

4. 第四阶段

学生没有如约前来。辅导员主动联系了三次,从接听电话到无人接听,再到关机,学生似乎选择了退缩。于是,辅导员采取了发短信的方式交流,感谢学生对自己的信任,坦诚地讲出了自己的苦恼和困惑,但目前这件事尚未完成,不知是什么原因失去了联系。对于学生提出的请求(不希望辅导员告知家长),辅导员愿意继续与其沟通,但如果就此失去联系,则无法继续提供帮助。真心期待一起把这件事情解决好。

大约三四天后,学生回复了信息,说之前不联系是因为她想一个人好好思考,现在她下定决心,由自己来与父母坦诚沟通退学这件事。目前父母已经知晓,第二天会来学校。另外,还提出希望辅导员帮她对一些与退学事件关系不大的其他信息保密,暂时先不要告知父母。

获得的信息及分析:学生的反馈是令人欣喜的,在退学这件事上,她从一开始的逃避、犹豫,到最终勇敢地做出了选择,而且是自己主动与父母沟通,并请父母到学校来一起面对。可以看到,一个二十岁的女生,在一步步学会坚强面对自己人生中的重大问题,并动用自己全部的智慧和能力去解答。

在这个过程中,辅导员发的信息发挥了重要作用,首先传递了"我在继续关注你"的信息,而且并没有因为学生爽约而生气,或者放弃对学生的帮助;其次给学生留出了一定的空间和时间,没有提出"你看到信息后立即来见我"等刚性的要求,传递了"我仍然信任你"的信号;最后又强调愿意与学生一起解决问题,再次表明了自己作为一个帮助者、合作者的身份,始终传递的是积极友好的信息。

三、外语教学理念革新与实践

社会主义核心价值观引领的外语课程思政研究

汪桃红[*]

摘　要：2016年习近平总书记在全国思政工作会议上的讲话中提出将传统的思政课程向课程思政转变的思路。2018年在全国教育大会上指出，要把立德树人融入思想道德教育、文化知识教育、社会实践教育各环节。时代召唤高等教育人才培养的价值回归，实现人才培养和国家发展的有机协调。"课程思政"成为当前一个热门的教学改革方向。课程思政不是简单的课程加思政的模式，而是一个以教师为主导，教材为依托，课堂教学为载体，课后实践为拓展，制度为保障的系统工程。这也是思政课堂从显性逐步走向隐性，多管齐下的协同育人模式。外语课程思政要实现语言知识技能的学习和价值追求的统一，语言形式与思想的同步，教书与育人目标的和谐统一。

关键词：大学外语教学；课程思政

1　课程思政回归育人本质

教育是人类发展史中永恒的历史范畴，是人类传播和传承生产经验和生活经验的主要方式，其无论是对个人还是国家的重要性都不言而喻。在中国古代，"教育"一词首次出现在《孟子·尽心上》——"得天下英才而教育之"。《说文解字》中阐释"教，上所施下所效也，育，养子使作善也。"在古人的观念中，教导孩子从善是教育的根本目标之一。从善即儒家思想所推崇的"仁爱"观念，注重人的德行修养。正所谓"修身齐家治国平天下"，个人修养高、品行优秀是经营家庭，治理国家，平定天下的基础和前提。中国具有几千多年历史的私塾教育一直实施的是以诵读儒家经典为文化特色的教育模式，科举考试成为选拔从地方到中央各级各类人才的重要方式。古代的教育重视管理者对中国儒家思想的传承，"仁爱"是核心思想。随着近代以来"西学东渐"的盛行，中国的有志之士探索救亡图存的道路，开始向西方学习，废除私塾，创办现代大学，引进西方大学体制，注重科学精神和实用主义。随着中华人民共和国的成立，根据中国社会主义初级阶段的国情，指导思想上重视思想政治教育，思政课成为中国大学课程的重要组成部分，与专业课相互独立。专业课传授与专业相关的知识和技能，思政课集中传授马列主义、毛泽东思想和邓小平理论等传统的意识形态理论。这种教学体制实际上遵循的是工具和技术理性与价值和思想教育两张皮的逻辑结构。不管是专业知识和技能，还是政治思想导向，都集中于育人的根本目标。两者应该是和谐统一，高度一致的。

习近平总书记在全国高校思想政治工作会议上强调，"思想政治理论课要在坚持改进中加强，提升思想政治教育的亲和力和针对性，其他各门课都要守好一段渠，种好责任田"。教育要为经济发展和政治服务，但是教育也是人的权利。教育的本质是培养人，提高人的生命质量和

---

[*] 汪桃红：江苏科技大学外国语学院英语系教师，主要研究方向为英美文学、叙事学等。

生命价值,包括强健的体魄、较高的科学文化素养、崇高的思想品德。课程思政打破了思政课单打独斗的格局,破除了思政课和专业课之间的壁垒,将思政渗透于专业课堂,有助于实现教育育人的本质要求,实现从大学教育的工具理性、技术理性向价值理性、审美理性的根本转变。

2 坚持以社会主义核心价值观为导向,反对文化相对主义

社会主义核心价值观的"富强、民主、文明、和谐,自由、平等、公正、法治,爱国、敬业、诚信、友善",简短的十二个词分别从国家、社会和个人三个层面浓缩了社会主义所倡导的价值导向。它是马克思主义唯物辩证法在当代中国的运用,体现了物质基础与上层建筑、国家和个人、物质文明与精神文明之间的辩证关系。当它被提出来之后,从中央到地方掀起了全民传诵核心价值观和将其制作为标语的热潮,很多人都能够倒背如流,但是有的人在深入理解核心价值观的深刻内涵,以及指导实践并在实践中自觉运用方面比较欠缺。理论的根本力量在于能够为实践提供指导,社会主义核心价值观是"仁、义、礼、智、信"的当代发展,源于有中国特色社会主义改革开放鲜活而生动的社会实践,具有深厚的社会实践基础,在实践中能为社会主义建设者提供理论武器和道义的力量。当代大学生是将来社会主义建设的生力军,他们的价值标准、道德取向直接关系到中华民族伟大复兴的中国梦的实现。对于外语学习者来说,熟练掌握一门外语是题中应有之义,从根本上来看外语学习要着眼于当下全方位的对外开放的国家发展战略。"以专业技能知识为载体加强大学生思想政治教育,具有强大的说服力和感染力,有助于将课堂主渠道功能发挥最大化,扭转专业课程教学重智轻德现象,具有其他教育方式不可替代的优势"(高德毅、宗爱东,2017)。反观当前高校外语学科的教学现状不难发现以下几个问题。

第一,长期以来,中国高校外语教材和学习内容过于强调语言的原汁原味,注重语言的措辞和结构,而思想价值内涵并未得到同等重视。由于外语是以西方语言和文化为载体的实践性很强的学科,语言是思维和思想的载体,学习的材料大多体现了西方国家的文化特征,如地理、社会、历史、人文风情等,传达了西方国家的价值追求、宗教信仰和意识形态。在这样的环境下,在外语教学过程中,更要加强对社会主义核心价值观的讨论与践行。

第二,外语学习者对外界新鲜事物的接受程度高,在多元文化的浸润中容易被文化相对主义所左右。"文化相对主义"由美国人类学之父弗朗兹·博厄斯[①]所推崇,他指出衡量文化没有普遍绝对的评判标准。文化相对主义对于打破种族主义、民族中心主义痼疾,尊重多元文化共存来说有一定的先进性,然而,它也一并否定了科学价值观标准的客观性和独立性。而这样囊括一切的价值观念实际上也否定了一切价值标准,并不利于处在形成期的青年价值观的建立。这就对高校外语教师提出了更高的要求,他们需要有坚定的社会主义价值观立场,并且能够对教学材料的价值内涵进行深入挖掘,能联系实际,结合实践,引导青年学生树立正确的价值观和人生观。

第三,有的外语学习者缺乏思辨力和质疑精神。由于数字时代和信息时代纷繁复杂的多维信息来源以及移动学习和碎片化学习的普及,外语学习者获取学习资源的途径空前丰富,现代人通过网络几乎可以获取任何学习资源。改革开放以来,中国的外语教育获得了长足发展,国人的外语水平也大大提高了。但同时也要清醒地看到当前的外语教育在面向现代化和国际

[①] 弗朗兹·博厄斯(Franz Boas,1858—1942),德裔美国人类学家,现代人类学的先驱之一,享有"美国人类学之父"的称号,提出了文化相对主义的观点。

化过程中的诸多不足。有的外语学习者缺乏对信息来源的求证和质疑精神。黄源深教授[①]曾多次撰文批评英语专业学生思辨力缺乏的顽疾,时至今日,这一问题仍然未得到根本解决。

3 将批判性思考和创新思维融入外语课堂

综观改革开放以来中国的外语教育,"引进来"是主旋律,外语学习的很多教材内容多由国内专家从国外主流书刊中选取。其中不乏通识性的知识和文化,具有普适性的价值,比如科学精神、诚信、道德、环保意识等。这和我们所提倡的社会主义核心价值观的理念相一致,符合社会发展进步的大趋势,也反映了普通大众对幸福生活的向往和追求。但是也有许多与中国主流价值观念迥异的观点,这就需要甄别并进行批判性的思考,绝不能全盘接受。国外主流媒体上的原版文章往往是非常好的外语学习素材,然而需要警惕的是,这些文章的观点、立场以及价值导向往往是跟特定的政治、经济、历史和文化背景相关。课堂上,外语教师要引导学生对这些学习素材进行深入讨论和探究。

我国很多外语学习者缺少反映中国特色和文化精神的教材和学习资料。我国相关专家学者完全有能力编撰承载中国文化和价值追求的教材。用熟练的他国语言,讲述我们自己的故事,这也应该是展示中国文化自信的题中应有之义。

4 用外语讲好中国故事

如今中国经济总量稳居世界第二,综合经济实力令世界瞩目。然而与经济实力的强势相比,文化事业发展相对滞后,中国文化的国际影响力非常有限。由于意识形态、文化背景、价值观念的不同,中国文化在英语国家的传播和接受度非常有限。近年来,随着"讲好中国故事,传播好中国声音"的深入发展,文艺界、传媒界都在积极探索讲好中国故事的方法和策略。从客观条件看外语界,高校外语课堂对于讲好中国故事有得天独厚的优势。形式多样的语言实践是语言知识能力和个人素质、职业素养的融合,能为学生将来的职业发展打下坚实的基础。

英语语言文化知识承载的西方人文思想、文化传统和社会现状等广博的知识,为了解目的语国家文化、公众的认知模式和欣赏品味提供了良好的条件。高校是国家机体中一个重要的机构,也是实现文化交流和合作的重要场所。随着近年来外国留学生来华人数大量增加,以高校为阵地,讲好中国故事,传播中国文化大有可为。外语人在以下三个方面是可以有所作为的。

第一,规范并提升公众场所等地公示语的翻译质量,展现良好的亲近目的语文化的氛围。公共场所的公示语是对外交流的窗口,是展示国家形象的外衣,其重要作用不言而喻。然而长期以来,有的公共场所的外语翻译让目的语国家读者读不懂、读不通,翻译质量不尽如人意。高校外语人应该走出书斋,将书本的理论知识和社会实践相结合,学以致用,用目的语国家的人民能接纳的方式进行翻译。中文公示语多是口号和道德劝诫,其中有关于社会主义核心价值观的表述以及传统道德观念的宣传,如果按照字面意思翻译成目的语很有可能难以引起目的语读者的共鸣和认同,其传播的效果也大打折扣。因此要从普世的价值观和道德观出发,以

---

① 黄源深,上海对外经贸大学教授。1998年首次发表《思辨缺席》一文,2010年发表《英语专业课程必须彻底改革——再谈"思辨缺席"》一文,聚焦英语专业学生缺乏批判性思考的痼疾。

全人类的基本价值取向为尺度,有选择性地对原文进行翻译、改编和再创作。

第二,在第二课堂语言实践中,教师要引导学生充分发挥创造力,将社会主义核心价值观的内容融入生活和学习实际,鼓励学生结合核心价值观的思想,主动地、创造性地丰富核心价值观的内涵,让优良的道德和社会主义价值观贴近学生的生活实际,成为身边具体可感知的文化活动。让课程思政从课内延伸到课外,将知识和技能的训练与文化素养和价值观的提升相结合。开展形式多样的校园文娱活动,以生动形象和观众喜闻乐见的艺术形式再现社会主义建设中涌现出来的先进典型。与千人一面、扁平化的人物形象宣传不同,各种舞台剧、情景剧及以社会主义核心价值观为主题的动漫设计和文化产品,可以对相关人物、事件和思想理念进行多方面、立体化和形象化的呈现。艺术超越语言,超越国界,易于为全世界人民所接受。当然这样的艺术呈现要与目的语国家的文化传统相契合,通过多种方式将典型的人文故事、经典剧目等植入多种多样的艺术表现形式中去。

第三,以中外合作办学为契机,促进民间交流。随着中国对外开放步伐的加快,中外合作办学的规模越来越大。一方面,大量外国留学生来华学习和工作;另一方面,中国高校和外国高校开展联合培养学生的计划,将国内在校生一定时段的学习和生活安排在外国高校。赴外留学的中国学生本身就是中国形象的代表,扮演着讲述中国故事的代言人的角色。因此,加强对"准留学生"的社会主义核心价值观的教育的意义非同寻常。除了合作办学的对外交流渠道,教师和科研机构也应加强对外交流与合作。

5 结论

课程思政教育顺应了教育培养人才的根本目标和要求,是大学科学教育,是工具理性与思想道德和价值理性的融合。社会主义核心价值观成为课程思政的价值坐标导向,课程思政在社会主义核心价值的引领下得以顺利开展。大学外语课堂开展课程思政教育绝非课程与思政的简单叠加,或在语言课堂上对思政内容的生搬硬套。课程思政应该遵循高等教育的规律,通过全程育人、全方位育人,培养具有优良的社会主义道德风尚,能为社会主义建设建功立业的人才。另外,外语课程思政课堂又有其不同于思政课堂的独特性。主要表现在对教学材料的挖掘和更新,这对教材的编写和人员素质提出了较高要求;另外,在具体实施过程中,应避免文化相对主义的误导,以批判性思考的态度理性对待当今世界纷繁复杂的文化现象。最后,语言类专业作为一种实践型学科,大量的课程思政语言实践是外语课程思政的一大特色。高校要将学生的思想道德提升与语言运用能力相结合,开展丰富多彩的具有创新思维的社会主义核心价值观的多样化的表述活动,实现用外语对外讲好社会主义核心价值观和中国故事。

参 考 文 献

高德毅、宗爱东,2017,《从思政课程到课程思政:从战略高度构建高校思想政治教育课程体系》,《中国高等教育》第 1 期。
习近平,2017,《习近平谈治国理政》,第二卷,外文出版社。

不忘初心·铸魂育人·中西贯通·文化入髓
——论大学外语教育中的价值塑造作用

王 倩*

摘 要:博雅教育背景下,"大学之道"的最高境界应该是哺育人类精神情怀,是对人的一种社会改造。大学外语教育的功能除教授外国语言和文化知识外,更重要的是通过语言引领文化传播和影响,促进大学生世界观的形成。本文从"三位一体"(价值塑造、知识传授、能力培养)人才培养理念的核心即"价值塑造"的背景和内涵入手,探讨高校外语教育如何实现对大学生的价值塑造。本文提出外语教育要突出课程教学的育人导向,帮助学生融通中外文化、增强母语文化自信与文化自觉、培养用外语讲好中国故事和阐释好中国特色的能力。这一目标可以通过科学设置课程、深挖教材内涵、革新教学内容,借力于第二课堂育人机制,并通过繁荣校园文化得以实现。

关键词:外语教育价值塑造;文化自觉;人文情怀

1 引言

2016年12月,习近平总书记在全国高校思想政治工作会议上强调,"高校思想政治工作关系高校培养什么样的人、如何培养人以及为谁培养人这个根本问题……要用好课堂教学这个主渠道……使各类课程都要与思想政治理论课同向同行,形成协同效应。"2018年全国教育大会上,习近平总书记又指出,立德树人是教育工作的根本任务和教育现代化的方向目标。以人为本,培养具有健全人格、创新思维、宽厚基础、全球视野和社会责任感的高素质、高层次、多样化、创造性人才是高等教育的根本任务(陈海瑾,2014)。随着"一带一路"倡议的实施,语言在互连互通、经济文化合作中的需求及作用日益增强,这对我国的外语教学提出了更高的要求。践行外语教学活动的主体是外语教师,这无疑对外语教师专业素养的核心,即教学实践能力,带来了更大的挑战。语言是文化的载体,通过外语教育进行人文教育,对学生的价值观塑造有其独特的作用,特别是在当今国际形势错综复杂、不同意识形态碰撞及真伪信息并存的环境下,外语教育如何承担塑造灵魂、培育人才的历史使命,实现英语教学与价值引导的有机统一,达到"以文化人、以文育人"显得尤为重要。

---

* 王倩:西北工业大学外国语学院副教授,主要研究方向为外国语言学及应用语言学。主讲大学英语读写、高级视听说、英语演讲与辩论、留学英语、国际公文写作等课程。

2 以第一课堂为主阵地,用思想聚人力,以文化养人心

随着国内高校逐步进入大类培养模式,通识/博雅教育成为核心议题(吕敏宏、刘世生,2011)。博雅教育强调人文精神,包括责任意识、沟通能力、领导能力,还有德行和品格。"不做一个没有灵魂的专门家,而成为一个有文化的人",应是博雅教育下形成的价值塑造。在高校,特别是理工类院校的文化氛围中,外语作为人文学科,具有其独特的优势,成为博雅教育的学科载体。在这场大类培养模式的改革中,教师也需重塑教育理念,积极思索"培养什么样的人"的问题。外语教育是全球胜任力培养的着力点。全球胜任力包括跨文化交际能力、广博知识、人文素养、家国情怀、民族精神与文化自信。着力于学生全球胜任力的培养,将价值塑造贯穿于教育的全过程,正是外语教育最大的价值所在。

2.1 优化课程体系,使外语教育成为博雅教育的核心

语言是表达思想观念及相互沟通的工具或载体,其内容实质是文化。语言教学与学习过程,也就是文化传播与吸收的过程,同时还伴随着一定的价值取向并构成了文化的精神内核。从一定意义上来讲,语言、文化与价值观三者之间具有不可分割性和相互渗透性。语言教育兼有工具性和人文性双重性质,教学目标中的知识目标(获取语言文化知识)是基础目标,技能目标(获取语言应用技能)是重要目标,而人文素养目标(开阔视野、健全人格,引导学生的价值观、世界观及审美意识)则是终极目标。"教育活动不可能避免价值问题"(叶澜,2002),因为语言教育的主旨在于实现知识功能、交际功能和价值观功能的相互融合。这就不难理解为什么大学阶段的外语教育同样承担着提高大学生思想政治素质的重任。如何将外语教育与思政育人紧密结合,增强学生的价值认同与道路自信,坚定中国立场,面向世界传播"中国声音",是当前高校大学英语教学改革面临的重要课题。

全人教育要求把学生培养成为情智双修、中西兼顾、博古通今的"全人",而全人教育理念的要素之一便是全球胜任力、国际视野,是"三位一体"能力培养的重要组成部分。要具备全球素养,跨文化沟通能力是基础,而熟知中国的国情政情和他国文化是跨文化沟通能力的前提。在通识教育体系中,一方面,通过在技能课程中依托教学材料进行跨文化能力和思辨能力的培养,另一方面,通过开设以语言为媒介的多学科课程,特别是文史哲学科,拓展学生多元知识层次。与此同时,可以通过开设跨文化交际、英语畅谈中国文化、经典文化阅读与赏析、国际交流语篇分析等课程,帮助学生形成自己的文化身份意识,树立文化自信。如中国文化相关课程可以让学生意识到中华优秀传统文化是中华民族的文化根源,可为全球治理提供中国智慧。传统文化教育使大学生能深刻理解中国优秀传统文化的当代价值和世界意义,树立起其对中国传统文化的深刻认同感和自豪感,并能带着中国智慧参与全球治理。如在国际交流语篇分析课程上,教师可以利用国际交往中最新鲜的语料,引导学生通过口语、书面语语篇对比,分析不同文化人群在交流和碰撞思想时的不同表达方式及背后隐藏的不同文化、价值观,自觉引导学生对东西方差异进行批判性阅读、思考、讨论,使学生能够较好地把握交际技巧,在国际交流中适度得体、不卑不亢、从容自若。

大类招生背景下,大类内的通识教育强调培养学生的人文情怀与科学素养、历史眼光与国际视野、道德底蕴与法治理念、审辩思维与创新精神。因此,开设的课程应该特别重视其博雅

性、人文性。应建立良好的大类平台课程体系，将外语、法律、经贸等学科进行有机融合，以价值塑造为引领，共建课程，为培养新型、复合型人才提供保障，在促进哲学社会科学类内部优质教育资源生态流动和优化配置的同时，推动学校人文素养教育，增强学校人文氛围，构建繁荣高校文化的重要渠道。

2.2 深挖教材，重构并革新教学内容，渗透思政教育

随着"全员育人、全程育人、全方位育人"的大思政格局构建在全国高校陆续展开，外语教学与思政教育可以同向同行，形成合力效应。

首先，教师可以将"以人为本""平等参与""互动互补""灵活开放"的课程教学观和"自主、合作、探究、对话"等教学形式融入教学实践过程中，建构知识、品德和情感相融的教学氛围。资源挖掘是课程思政的重要方面，需基于教材，但又不能拘泥于教材（高德毅、宗爱东，2017）。课程思政应与大学英语课程教学目标、学校定位和学生个体需求相结合，与语言教学无缝对接，达到"润物无声"的教学效果。在语言教学的同时，提升大学生的政治认同、价值认同和文化自信。为达到上述目标，外语教师应明确教学目标，研究教材，革新课堂教学内容，挖掘教材中蕴藏的德育元素，结合时事动态、形势和政策，捕捉相关的德育事例，渗透思想教育，使英语学习与思政教育共频共振（康莉、徐锦芳，2018）。如可以利用课文中的主人公在困难逆境中磨炼意志的典型事例对学生进行意志品质教育，引导学生形成战胜挫折、坚持理想信念的勇气和毅力。如在进行东西方文化对比的教学中，一方面，让学生感知西方优秀文化中的道德元素和精髓，丰富和建构自我文化底蕴和道德素质；另一方面，可以培养学生的民族意识，激发他们的爱国主义情愫，培养其文化自省意识、合作意识、集体观念和探究精神等能力，使其养成正确的价值观、遵守道德规范，从而树立用外语向世界传播中国文化思想的意识，讲好中国故事，传播中国声音。教师也可以把外语教育过程与审美教育过程相统一，如利用英语文学作品中丰富的情感来激发学生的情感和思维，提高学生的外语素质和"情商"，培养学生的审美意识和能力。

3 以第二课堂为支撑，用实践磨技能，以活动铸心魂

除在第一课堂主阵地对学生进行价值引领外，还可以充分利用第二课堂的育人功能，将价值塑造融入课堂内外和培养全过程。新形势下，社会思潮涌动、多元文化冲击，这对大学生理想信念教育提出了更高的要求，也为第二课堂思政育人的建设和创新提供了新的发展契机。第二课堂所塑造的实践育人氛围是综合素质形成和发展的重要环境，具有第一课堂不可替代的作用。目前诸多高校都设有外语相关的创新实践基地，是提升学生实践沟通能力、协调能力、语言应用能力及培养思辨能力的主要渠道。在第二课堂中开展的丰富活动，如演讲及辩论比赛、青年领导力论坛等都可以在第二课堂实践教育中实现对学生的价值引领。如有关中国智造、国庆主题演讲或以深挖中国传统文化节日内涵的专题论坛等都可以将理想信念教育和爱国主义教育融入学生的内心信仰和实际行动，引导学生树立正确的世界观、人生观、价值观。同时，这种大范围的和系统的涉及文化类型的教育内容，是多方面促进校园文化建设的重要切入点。这归因于外语教育的功能除了教授外国语言和文化知识外，还具有丰富的文化内涵，更多的是通过语言引领文化传播和影响，促进青年世界观的形成。深化和拓展基于第二课堂的

思政育人体系建设,既符合高校教育的客观需求,也为实践育人制度化、科学化、常态化机制建设奠定了坚实基础。第二课堂是高校思政实践教育的重要平台,只有与传统的思政课堂教学互补互融,才能不断强化教书育人的重要价值,对大学生理想信念的形成和爱国情怀的培养有着极其重要的意义。

4 以文化洗礼为支撑,借助校园文化提升学生人文素养

习近平总书记在 2018 年 9 月 10 日召开的全国教育大会上强调,要"培养德智体美劳全面发展的社会主义建设者和接班人"。教育是国之大计,培养什么的人是教育的首要问题。要增强学生的综合素质,培养其创新思维,就需要提高学生的审美和人文素养。外语学习作为培养人文素质的重要载体,在培养学生优秀文化移情能力、启迪学生心智及拓展学生国际视野方面有着不可替代的作用。目前大学生普遍缺乏思辨能力,欠缺人文素养,这与一流人才培养要求背道而驰。营造校园人文环境,建设校园文化氛围,不仅能够对学生个性培养起到启迪作用,更能从多角度、多层次、多方面提升学生的人文素养。浓厚的人文环境在育人的过程中可以潜移默化地熏陶和感染学生,帮助学生发现真善美。高校可以通过举办人文知识竞赛、外语节、经典阅读读书会、名人(师)讲座等活动活跃校园文化氛围,促进校园文化建设,提升大学生的人文素养,引导大学生发挥特长、主动参与,在活动中相互交流,不断培养大学生良好的集体荣誉感和道德素质。另外,高校可以结合学科特色,举办科技文化节、社团文化节和体育竞赛活动等,帮助大学生在策划活动、管理组织和人际交往过程中提升个人能力,满足学生的精神文化需求。亦可依托学校的外语学科,举办传统文化进校园活动,建设跨文化研究基地、非物质文化传承基地等,重视本民族传统文化氛围的营造。这既为学生创造了传承民族文化的机会,增强了学生的美感体验,又提升了学生的民族文化精神。人文素养与科学素养的深度融合,是培养创新型人才的必由之路。

5 结语

在全球化、后现代主义和国际化等思潮日趋升温并深刻影响社会发展走向的背景下,外语教育俨然成为一个国家最重要的社会资源和文化软实力的隐形标尺。外语教育在理所当然地成为国家与国家、民族与民族、文化与文化沟通和交流的桥头堡的同时,也承载着促进中华民族传统文化价值观传播的重要使命,而且,在维护国家意识形态、民族身份认同、协调社会和谐发展以及达成国际理解中都发挥着重要的作用。外语教育立足于知识的传递、情操的陶冶和精神的培育,而价值塑造应该是贯穿其中的主线。在培养学生的民族情感与民族精神的同时,还需要培养学生成为具有全球意识、宽广胸怀和包容精神的人,培养学生成为"世界公民"。大学外语教育是学生学习英语的高级阶段,学习者已具备感悟语言、欣赏语言、创造性组织语言活动的素质。外语教育应该充分发挥其文化教育功能,引导学生养成良好的道德、充盈的精神和正确的思想观念。毫无疑问,外语课程要突出课程教学的育人导向,促使专业学习与价值观教育同频共振,让课堂成为学生价值塑造的有效载体,显性教育与隐性教育融会贯通;创新教学方法和教学手段,更新教学内容,找出英语教学与思政教育语言素材之间的互补点,同时借力于第二课堂实践体系,全方位帮助大学生养成正确的价值观。除此之外,我们还需要在外语

教材编写、教学模式改革、教师培训、资金扶持、项目研究、机构协作等方面进行进一步思考,因为这些不仅是外语教育提升自身话语权的重要途径,而且有助于提升高校外语教学中师生的价值观的敏锐性和辨别力,实现对大学生社会主义核心价值观的培育。综上所述,高等外语教育只有注重学生的"世界公民"内涵教育,才能充分发挥外语教育的导向作用,把握育人的根基,促进人的全面发展,培养出国家需要的具有全球素养、通晓国际规则的创新型外语人才。

参 考 文 献

陈海瑾,2014,《"卓越工程师"培养背景下理工科高校人文教育路径探究》,《思想教育研究》第 4 期。
高德毅、宗爱东,2017,《从思政课程到课程思政:从战略高度构建高效思想政治教育课程体系》,《中国高等教育》第 1 期。
康莉、徐锦芬,2018,《大学英语教材中的文化自觉及其实现》,《外语学刊》第 4 期。
吕敏宏、刘世生,2011,《会通中西之学,培育博雅之士》,《外语教学与研究》第 2 期。
叶澜,2002,《重建课堂教学价值观》,《教育研究》第 5 期。

大学外语"课程思政"体系建设实践研究*

孙 静**

摘 要:"课程思政"的建设工作是当前高等教育改革工作的重点。把思想政治工作贯穿教育教学全过程是大学外语课程的重要任务。本研究以跨文化理论中的价值取向理论为基础,对大学外语课程"课程思政"体系的搭建进行探讨,以期实现课程的育人功能,挖掘课程的思政元素和德育功能,将价值引领、知识传授、能力培养相统一。

关键词:课程思政;跨文化交际;大学外语

2016年12月,习近平总书记在全国高校思想政治工作会议上强调"把思想政治工作贯穿教育教学全过程",提出了关于"课程思政"的指导意见。2017年12月,教育部印发《高校思想政治工作质量提升工程实施纲要》,明确提出"充分挖掘和运用各门课程蕴含的思想政治教育元素"(教育部,2017)。2018年10月,国务院在《有关进一步强化与完善大学生思政教育的建议》中再次指出,"加强和改进大学生思想政治教育是一项重大而紧迫的战略任务"。"课程思政"的理念倍受关注,是由于思政教育对于大学生的健康成长、价值观取向乃至社会的发展有着至关重要的作用,而"课程思政"可以充分利用"各门课程的育人功能"和"所有教师的育人职责",将核心价值观真正落实到每一堂课的教学工作中。

目前,关于在大学外语课程中开展"思政教育"的相关研究文献主要集中于阐述宏观理论政策、论述在外语课程中进行"思政教育"的可行性和必要性、笼统提出外语"课程思政"教学模式框架、对外语教师"课程思政"教育过程中的角色分析等方面(陈顺利,2018),这些观点对外语课程嵌入"思政教育"有重要的指导作用。但在外语课程中如何具体搭建"课程思政"体系、建立有可操作性的"课程思政"教学模式、设计合理的"课程思政"教学内容等实践操作层面的研究还远远不够。

本研究将以跨文化交际中的价值取向理论作为外语课程"课程思政"体系搭建的理论框架,使用对比分析的教学方法,筛选提炼与外语课程结合度高且普适性强的教学内容,建设适用于各类外语课程的"课程思政"体系,并将该体系应用于各类大学外语课程中,实现在大学外语课程进行"思政教育"的目的。

---

* 本文得到了西北工业大学基础研究与创新发展创新团队类"大学生英语语用能力差异性研究"(G2019KY05402)项目与陕西省社科界2020重大理论与现实研究项目"大学外语'课程思政'教育体系建设的实践研究"(20WY-44)的支持与资助。

** 孙静:西北工业大学外国语学院大学英语教学部系主任,副教授,主讲大学英语读写课程、大学英语听力课程、口语课程。

1 大学外语课程实施"课程思政"的必要性

大学外语课程是开展"课程思政"教育的重要阵地,主要体现在以下3个方面。

(1)大学外语课程是人文课程。

学生在大学外语课程中接触大量的英文原版资料,可以了解到西方国家的政治、文化、历史和风俗等丰富内容,这些素材覆盖了思想道德教育的多个方面,可以利用中西方价值观的共性开展"课程思政"的教育工作,在潜移默化中引导青年学生树立社会主义核心价值观,将语言和思想紧密结合。因此,大学外语教学对于塑造大学生正确的人生观和价值观能发挥重要作用。

(2)大学外语课程是基础课程。

大学外语课程持续时间长、受众广,而且教学形式、教学方法和课堂模式多样。可通过教学设计和全过程的引导将"思政教育"融入教学工作,以课程为载体,将学科资源转化为育人资源,对思政课程的内容进行拓展深化,将传授知识和思政教育相结合,发掘课程思政元素,从而达到"课程思政"的教育目的。

(3)大学外语课程能让学生充分感受东西方价值观的碰撞。

学生在大学外语课程中了解异域文化的同时,也能感受到强烈的东西方价值观差异。当学生对某些观点产生困惑时,外语教师应当担任起"价值引领"的角色,帮助学生树立和培养"文化自信"和"文化自觉",引导学生客观、科学地思考问题,进而深刻认识社会主义核心价值观。

2 大学外语"课程思政"体系建设的理论基础

作为跨文化理论的四大重要理论之一,价值取向理论由美国人类学家克拉克洪提出,主要包括对人性的看法、人类对自身和外部环境的看法、人对自身和他人关系的看法、人的活动导向、人的空间观念和人的时间观念六个方面。东西方文化在这六个方面表现出很大的差异性,这是由地域、文化、价值观等多种因素决定的。通过对价值理论的介绍,可以更好地解释外语课程中所接触到的西方文化中的种种观点和现象,进而水到渠成地引入思政教育的相关内容。跨文化交际理论中的价值取向理论与思政教育的需求不谋而合,适用于外语课堂中辅助"课程思政"的教学工作。在了解六个价值取向差异的基础上,还需要对学生进行思辨能力的塑造,使他们能够运用马列主义批判与思辨观,辨识西方文化中的糟粕,以避免崇洋媚外的现象的出现,汲取不同文化中共性的价值观,理解德育的重要性,进而树立正确的价值观。因此,马克思主义哲学的批判与思辨理论能够有效地帮助学生正确地思考问题。

3 研究价值

(1)本研究可以为外语教师实现语言知识教学与学生思政教育教学相结合提供理论指导。

(2)本研究可以为各类外语课程提供实操性强的思政学习材料。

(3)本研究可以帮助外语教师提高其自身的思想政治素养及思政教育敏感性。

4 大学外语"课程思政"体系建设内容

(1)大学外语"课程思政"体系框架。

本研究以"跨文化交际"为理论基础,依托该理论中的价值取向理论,精选国外原版资料中的思政元素资料、国内思政学习材料以及中国传统文化知识的英文版资料作为教学内容,采取对比分析的教学方法,指导和引导学生对东西方价值观进行辩证理解和认识,培养学生的民族自信和家国情怀。最后,在课程评价体系中将思想政治教育成效纳入考核标准,加快思政教育进外语课堂的步伐。本研究将外语课程思政教育体系构建和课堂实践活动相结合,研究方法主要为观察法和文献研究法,具体研究框架如图1所示。

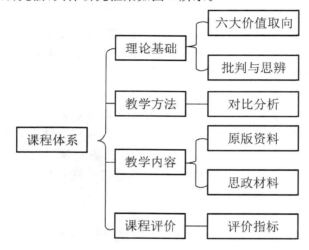

图 1 课程体系研究框架

(2)大学外语"课程思政"体系内容。

1)教学内容建设

在教学内容建设方面,首先要对目前大学外语教学中所使用的教材进行系统分析,并结合六大价值取向,确定六个学习的主题。这主要包括人际关系(人对自身和他人关系的看法)、环境保护(人对自身和外部环境的看法)、自我认知(人的活动导向)、道德伦理(对人性的看法)、关于未来(人的时间观念)和文化文明(人的空间观念)六个方面。

上述六个主题基本涵盖了价值观构建的各个方面,在筛选学习内容时,需要围绕这些主题进行,以便于在开展"课程思政"时找到教学主题和思政教育的结合点,可以实现在课堂教学中对各类话题的切换和延伸,导入包含中国文化和价值观塑造的教学内容,使两者有机融合。党的十九大报告、习近平总书记关于价值观的论述、习近平总书记对青年学生的讲话等内容都是非常好的思政学习内容。

2)主要教学方法

在教学中主要采取对比分析法,这是由外语课程自身的特点决定的。虽然学生能够在外语课堂接触到大量的外文原版材料,但是,在传统的外语教学中,外语教师主要以讲解语言知识、介绍背景文化、培养交际能力等为教学目标,而常常忽略对学生进行思想方面的启发和引导。增加"课程思政"学习内容以后,教师可以将原本学习的语言材料与思政材料进行对比教学,充分、生动、准确地提炼并挖掘学习材料中的思政元素,引导学生树立并践行社会主义核心价值观,坚定社会主义信念。另外,还可以通过开展具体的教学活动,如做报告、仿写、分组讨论等充分培养学生的思辨能力。

3)课程评价体系建设

在课程评价体系建设方面,要对原有的外语课堂的评价体系进行优化,设定合理可行的考核方式,将思政学习方面的评价融入其中。坚持形成性评估和终结性评估并重的原则,设计出与外语课程知识相结合的思政学习考核指标。在学习过程中,要关注学生的学习态度、学习方法及学习效果,教师在评价结果的帮助下,可以及时调整自己的教学方法。另外,应当建立双向评价体系,对教师"课程思政"的教学效果进行评测,以反映出教师在教学中的问题,并利于其及时改进。合理科学的课程评价能真正反映出"课程思政"的教学效果,并有力地促进和保障"课程思政"在外语课程中顺利进行,加快思政教育进外语课堂的步伐。大学外语"课程思政"评价应坚持主观和客观相结合原则、导向性原则、科学性原则、可比性原则和公开性原则等,也可以借助心理学、数学、行为科学等学科的测评量表来设计评价问卷,将自评、互评和师评综合考虑,以得到客观、科学和准确的评价结果。

5 结论

通过发掘外语课程与"课程思政"的结合点,将跨文化交际理论中的价值取向理论作为理论基础,设计"课程思政"的教学体系,可以使"课程思政"教学工作的开展更能有的放矢、事半功倍,让思政教育更具备说服力。在教学方法上,针对外语课程的特点,提出对比分析的有效办法,能够充分地将思政内容融入专业的外语教学中,让思想政治教育无缝嵌入外语课堂。在教学内容设计上,充分考虑到各类外语课程教育主题的共性和价值取向理论指导的六个方面,提供适用于使用不同外语教材的外语课堂的学习内容。这样可以大大节约外语教师搜集思政教育材料的时间,同时也具有很强的实操性。研究成果可以直接应用于大学外语课堂中,作为进行"课程思政"学习的补充材料,在指导外语教师"课程思政"教学工作的同时,提升专业外语教师自身的思政素养和思政理论水平,提高外语教师"课程思政"的教学能力,使外语课堂成为传播马列主义的阵地,让大学生通过思想政治教育,能用正确的价值观指导自己的生活和学习。

参 考 文 献

陈顺利,2018,《大学英语课程思政教育教学的探索与实践探究》,《课程教育研究》第 9 期。
教育部,2017,中共教育部党组关于印发《高校思想政治工作质量提升工程实施纲要》的通知。据中华人民共和国教育部官网:http://www.moe.gov.cn/srcsite/A12/S7060/201712/t20171206_320698.html.

积极心理学在大学英语混合式教学中的运用研究

刘 勇[*]

摘 要：当前的大学英语混合式教学中，学生英语基础参差不齐，明德学院实行分类教学，力求满足学生对外语的需求。受自2019年底爆发的新冠肺炎疫情影响，各大学均采取了线上教学的方式。面对双重挑战，针对学生的积极性和主动性不强的问题，明德学院英语教师认为，将积极心理学运用到大学英语混合式教学中，实行针对性教育就是解决相关问题的一种有效途径。

关键词：分类教学；大学英语混合式教学；积极心理学

外语学习是一个复杂的过程，需要学习者了解并掌握语言知识，使语言知识技能内化，最终达到自动输出语言的效果。西安明德理工学院（原西北工业大学明德学院）英语教师基于克拉申的语言输入假说理论、乔姆斯基语言学的层次性和布鲁姆教育目标分类理论，于2019年打通大学英语教学通道，采取分类教学，针对学生不同的弱项进行强化训练：A类学生专攻四级考试，B类学生进行有方向的专题训练，C类学生夯实语言基础。分类教学的实施是一项系统的工程，涉及教学理念、教学内容、教学方法、教学教材和教学管理等方面的改革，真正做到了把提高学生的语言交际能力作为教学的重要目标，以学生为学习的主体。在教学中，了解学生的需求，科学地组织教学，充分发挥学生的积极性和主动性，培养具有市场竞争力的各行各业的应用型人才。

新冠肺炎疫情对我国大学生的学习和生活都造成了巨大影响。面对重大疫情，全国各大学均采取线上教学模式继续学期教学。在线上学习过程中，大学生经历了由新奇到反感、抵触、忍受再到接受的心理过程。未来的大学英语教学中，线上线下混合式教学将会是必然的发展趋势。混合式教学将传统的课堂教学和互联网自主学习相结合，二者的优势同时得以发挥。这种教学模式深化了"学生为本"的教学观，重视学生的自主学习，学生得以掌握学习的主动权。

在整个教学改革过程中，教育者们既要关注学生的学习效果，也要重视其心理健康。将积极心理学应用到大学英语混合式教学中，也是教育者们关注的重点之一。

积极心理学是美国心理学界于20世纪末兴起的一个新的心理学研究领域，以Seligman（塞利格曼）与Csikzentmihalyi（契克森米哈伊）共同发表的《积极心理学导论》一文为标志，致力于研究人的发展潜力和美德等积极品质。

积极心理学作为一门明确的学科出现于1998年，"是一门有关生命从开始到结束各个阶段的学科，是心理学崭新的一个领域。这门学科着重研究那些使生命更有价值和更有意义的

---

[*] 刘勇：西安明德理工学院语言文化传播学院副院长，教授，主讲英语专业精读、泛读、听力、口语、口译、教育心理学、英语修辞学、雅思阅读等课程。

东西。""人类生命中的优点跟缺点一样,都是真实存在的","生活不只是要避免或解决问题与困扰","积极心理学最基本的假设就是人们的美好和卓越与疾病、混乱和悲痛同样都是真实存在的。""积极心理学的特征可以大致归纳为三个:一是主观层面上的对于积极情绪的体验;二是个人层面上关于积极人格特质研究;三是群体层面上关于积极组织系统研究。以上三个特征是相互关联,密不可分的。"

笔者在教学和科研及与兄弟院校同行的交流中发现,大学英语分类线上教学中确实还存在一定问题。而在众多问题中,其根源都基本指向这几点,即学生英语基础水平参差不齐、两极分化严重,学习的积极性和主动性不强,填鸭式教学现象严重。因此,结合招生情况、课程教学现状及前期理论和实践,笔者发现将积极心理学运用到大学英语分类线上课程,实行针对性教育就是解决相关问题的一种有效途径。

作为线上教学的主导者,英语教师必须意识到线上教学不仅仅应涉及英语语言和文学文化,还应涉及教育学、管理学、心理学等多门学科知识,特别是心理学,在以学生为教学中心的外语课教学中有重要的作用。

积极心理学的研究表明:人的学习和活动的本质与自我的思维和选择密不可分,并且在很大程度上由自我选择所决定;教育教学只有从个体本身出发,充分地凝聚个体的思维,才能在课堂上形成合力,产生有价值的思想,达到良好的教育教学目标。

积极心理学在教育理念上强调个体的主动性,教育者的使命不仅是教授知识,更为重要的是关注学生的闪光点,激发他们身上的潜能。真正有效的大学英语教学,不是简单地让学生"占有"知识(如单词、句子、语法),而是引导学生利用其拥有的知识,使用思维导图,把英语作为工具载体去思考、表达,进而用英语分析问题、研究问题和解决问题。教师作为教学的设计者,必须积极创设教学情境,提高学生主动参与的意识,学生则应该重视自己应有的话语权,积极参与到教学中,使英语教学真正变成师生之间、生生之间的合作教学过程,从而激发学生的潜能,增加其积极的学习体验,培养其主动、合作等积极心理品质。

传统教学中典型的"非人性化特征"造成学生有厌学情绪和教师有职业倦怠感,而将积极心理学的理念广泛融入课堂教学赋予了教学新的意义。培养学生的积极心理品质,包括注意力、思维力、自信心、自制力、心理承受能力、环境适应能力、情绪调控能力、自我管理能力、人际交往能力、同情心、积极乐观、责任感等。它能有效打破传统教学"独白式"的思维方式,将教学归于教师与学生的合作关系中,使得双方都作为参与者进行积极的互动。同时,它也能打破传统的由社会预设的"教师主导"的师生关系,强调了师生之间的平等。在这样的大学英语课堂中,教师的角色发生了根本性的转变,教师从一个传导知识的"绝对权威"变成了学生的"潜能激发者"和"学习辅助者"。另外,英语课堂上积极情感的渗透不同于传统意义上的说服、劝导,而是一种彼此互动的商谈,是对话的各方从各自的角度出发而达成的一种视域融合,是从复制到创造的积极拓展。

教师应通过多样的教学方式关注学生的积极体验。积极心理学认为,积极人格特质主要是通过激发和强化个体的各种已有与潜在的能力,使其变成一种习惯性的行为方式而形成的。教师可以利用多样的教学内容的积极意义影响学生,使他们获得多样的积极体验。英语教学不应拘泥于传统的教材,针对 A、B、C 类学生,教师应努力创造与学生的生活实际紧密联系的教学情景,体现出英语教学的实用性与时代感,引发学生的共鸣并引导他们参与到教学活动中去。如充分利用朋辈学习理论,把学生分组,围绕教学内容布置学习任务。为了完成任务,同组的学生共同参与、分工合作,利用网络或其他渠道搜集教学内容相关知识,制作课件,在教学平台上进行展示与介绍。这样既可以让学生了解到所学知识的背景,也可以让学生表达自己的思想,让他们利用现代化教学平台锻炼各方面的能力,培养学生有重点、有计划地安排学习时间的能力,做到主次分明,减少学习焦虑,提高自信心和自控力,使他们在学习过程中展现个性,并得到积极愉悦的体验。在良好的师生关系中,学生更能体会到教师的关爱与鼓励,形成有信心、有勇气、有毅力等积极人格特质。教师也可以在学生中建立英语课外兴趣合作小组,通过即时交流工具如微信群、QQ 群等,以提问的方式给学生布置课外兴趣作业,并在学生完成作业的过程中引导、启发学生学习。这样就可以解决英语线上教学人数多、时间紧、学生与教师交流不畅等问题。学生可以在课外英语学习过程中形成自我管理、自我导向、同伴监督、教师网络指导的良性学习模式,从而成为具有适应性的学习个体。这样也可以帮助学生养成自主、智慧、创新等积极人格特质,提升其在大学英语学习中的成就感和幸福感。

应用形成性评价可以促进学生学习自主性的形成。教师不仅要关注学生的考试成绩,还要关注学生在大学英语学习过程中的努力和付出,并以平时成绩的形式计入学生的期末总成绩,不能仅根据考试成绩一刀切。只要学生付出了努力,只要比过去有进步,而且有不断进步的愿望,教师都应该给予肯定和激励性的评价,让每位学生在努力后都能获得成功的体验,激发他们进一步进取的愿望和信心。在目前英语教学的课堂组织模式下,为了让学生能更多地参与讨论并被关注,教师可以采取合作学习的方式,在学生中先分组,再通过合作小组具体明确每个组员的学习任务,不能让组员存有偷懒的幻想,督促人人动脑,积极思考。这种小组合作学习带来的不仅是学生个人的成功,而且是团体的胜利,学生所获得的自我价值感更强;同时,也能让学生在小组交流、沟通、分享中学会合作、竞争,提高其社会适应能力。

积极心理学不仅仅是关于疾病或健康的科学,也是关于教育、爱与成长的科学。从积极心理学的理论视角出发,转变大学英语教学理念,优化课堂教学模式,能促进学生心理健康发展,有效消解学生英语学习的"无力感",并能帮助教师构建良好的课堂教学氛围,消除教师教学的"倦怠感",形成教学相长的良性循环。积极心理学的理念对改善大学英语课堂教学效果,提高大学英语教学质量以及对学生的个人成长的重大作用既是对传统教育的一种超越,同时也是实现教育自身价值的一种再平衡。

参 考 文 献

郭鹏飞,2015,《积极心理学在大学英语英语教学中的应用》,《洛阳师范学院学报》第 3 期。
教育部高教司,2004,《大学英语课程教学要求(试行)》。
庞维国,2003,《自主学习——学与教的原理和策略》,华东师范大学出版社。
浦一婷,2017,《教育心理学理论视阈下本科生英语阅读策略的调查研究》,硕士学位论文,南京邮电大学。
尚丽莉,2016,《积极心理学在大学英语教学中的应用》,《山东农业工程学院学报》第 12 期。
束定芳,2004,《外语教学改革问题与对策》,上海外语教育出版社。
杨稣、武成莉,2011,《基于积极心理学的青年学生心理健康教育路径探析》,《理论导刊》第 3 期。
曾纳,2016,《运用积极心理学优化大学英语课堂教学》,《大学英语教学与研究》第 3 期。

张蕴,2010,《混合式学习法在大学英语教学中的实施》,博士学位论文,上海外国语大学。

朱瑞佳、马永辉、刘杰秀,2012,《积极心理学在大学外语教学中的应用研究》,《绥化学院学报》第4期。

Bolte, A., Goschke, T., and Kuhl, J. 2003. "Emotion and Intuition: Effects of Positive and Negative Mood on Implicit Judgments of Semantic Coherence." *Psychological Science*. Vol. 14: 416–421.

Christopher, Peterson. 2010. *A Priner in Positive Psychology*. Qunyan Press.

Krashen, S. D. 1985. *The Input Hypothesis: Issues and Implications*. London: Longman.

EMI 课程的教学理念及通用教学方法

高 挈*

摘 要:EMI(English Medium Instruction)课程近年来在世界范围内受到普遍的关注和推广,成为应对国际化、提升高校国际竞争力的重要途径之一。EMI 课程在我国高校的广泛开设给 EMI 课程的相关教师带来了新的挑战。本文结合作者在牛津 EMI 中心参与教学培训的体验和收获,试图在理清 EMI 课程基本特点的基础上,结合相关教育理论,梳理 EMI 课程教师应当建立的教学理念,提出在相关教学理念指导下不同 EMI 课程可以采用的通用教学方法,以期为 EMI 课程教师的教学提供参考。

关键词:EMI 课程;国际化;语言;教学理念;教学方法

1 引言

EMI(English Medium Instruction)课程是一种用英语向母语非英语的学习者讲授(除英语以外的)专业课程的授课模式(Dearden,2018)。近一二十年来,EMI 课程在母语非英语的国家受到广泛的重视。德国、荷兰、丹麦、西班牙等欧洲国家,在各阶段教育中均开展了 EMI 课程教学,尤其是在高等院校中,EMI 课程呈现出明显的增长趋势(Dearden,2015;Wächter and Maiworm,2014)。在亚洲地区的新加坡、韩国、马来西亚、日本等国,EMI 课程也得到了较广泛的关注和推广。在非洲,一些经济相对发达的国家(如南非等)也十分重视 EMI 课程的建设(Dearden,2015;Kirkpatrick,2014)。

EMI 课程在世界范围内受到普遍的重视和推广与当今日益加深的经济全球化和教育国际化密切相关(谈多娇,2012)。为了应对全球化带来的挑战,教育部于 2010 年颁布了《国家中长期教育改革和发展纲要(2010—2020 年)》,明确提出需要"培养大批具有国际视野,通晓国际规则,能够参与国际事务和国际竞争的国际化人才"(新华社,2015)。高等教育本身的全球化趋势也客观上要求高校通过国际化来提升教育研究水平,吸引国际学生,谋求发展。因此,开设 EMI 课程成为应对国际化、提升高校全球竞争力的重要途径之一(李颖,2012)。

EMI 课程作为推动国际化的重要组成部分,成为高校办学能力的重要指标和参与国际竞争的重要基础(Hu and Mckay,2012)。教育部(2001)印发了《关于加强高等学校本科教学工作提高教学质量的若干意见》,提出要在三年内使重点高校本科教学课程中 EMI 课程所占比提升到 5%~10%。一项针对我国 130 多所高等院校的调查表明,到 2006 年,平均每所高校开设的 EMI 课程已达 44 门(吴平、王根树等,2010)。以西北工业大学为例,截至 2017 年底,全校已开设本科全英文授课专业 11 个,硕士全英文授课专业 32 个,博士全英文授课专业 24 个。课程覆盖全校 16 个学院,其中本科生全英文课程 200 余门,吸收了来自全球 80 余个国家

---

* 高挈:西北工业大学外国语学院副教授,主讲学术英语口语等课程。

的近 2 000 名留学生(西北工业大学国际教育学院,2018)。

　　EMI 课程的快速发展已成全球趋势。快速发展的 EMI 课程一方面有力地推动了高校的国际化进程,顺应了时代的要求,另一方面也给高校和 EMI 课程的相关教师带来了新的挑战。EMI 课程具有哪些特点？EMI 教师需要具备哪些基本素质,树立何种教学理念？EMI 课程需要采用何种教学方法？这些都是摆在 EMI 课程教师面前迫切需要解决的问题。

　　本文结合笔者在参与西北工业大学联合牛津 EMI 中心组织的 EMI 教师培训后的心得体会,主要从教师的角度出发,分析上述问题,着重探讨 EMI 课程教师应当树立何种教学理念,以及在此种理念指导下适用于不同 EMI 课程的通用教学方法。

2　EMI 课程的特点

　　EMI 课程对授课教师的专业知识、英语语言能力以及教学能力都提出了新的要求。一方面,EMI 课程教师必须对课程内容了如指掌；另一方面,还必须精通英语,能够用英语准确表述并清晰阐述学科内容。而如何将内容与语言有效结合,则需要 EMI 教师掌握教学规律,合理应用教学方法。显然 EMI 教师的能力提升不是一蹴而就的,需要经过不断的实践、探索和练习。建立起对 EMI 课程的总体认识,把握 EMI 课程的特点是 EMI 教师走入 EMI 课程教学的第一步。

2.1　内容为本

　　EMI 课程直译过来是"英文媒介课程",也就是说课程内容用英语讲授,课程的中介语言从母语变为了英语。依据讲授课程过程中使用英语的比例,国内一般称之为全英文课程或双语课程。尽管 EMI 课程所采用的知识传输媒介变成了英语,其讲授的知识内容并没有发生根本变化,要求 EMI 教师使用英语作为媒介语言完成传统母语作为媒介语言讲授一门课程时完成所有的教学内容和目标,不能因为使用了非母语语言而改变或者减少教学内容。

2.2　重视语言

　　EMI 课程的语言媒介是英语。对于母语非英语国家的教师和学生而言,他们必须能用英语进行有效沟通,用英语来教授和学习课程内容。课程能否顺利推进,学生能否正确、充分地理解课程内容,都取决于媒介语言(英语)能否准确表达和合理使用,因此英语对 EMI 课程十分重要。EMI 教师不仅要精通自身教学领域,对课程内容了如指掌,还要有语言意识,既能自己清晰、准确地表达课程内容,还要擅于与学生沟通,掌握语言教学的相关技巧。

2.3　跨文化性

　　EMI 课程使用英语作为教学媒介,不管是中国教师还是中国学生,他们对英语授课方式和交流过程、英语教材和参考资料等都需要一个适应的过程,这一过程既是语言的适应过程,也是文化的适应过程。从教师的角度来说,需要斟酌英语授课过程中选择何种语言风格、哪些具体词汇以及何种具体教学方式。对学生来说,需要适应英语的表述逻辑、文化内涵和国际化的课堂互动方式。

　　此外,EMI 课堂还往往面向国际学生,学生文化背景多样复杂,跨文化性是 EMI 课程的重要特点。EMI课程教师必须了解学生的基本文化背景,熟悉多国文化,有较强的文化敏感性。课程必须适应多文化环境,避免文化冲突,消解可能由文化差异导致的课程理解障碍,实现教学过程中的师生、生生跨文化交际。

3 EMI课程的教学理念

上述EMI课程的特点决定了EMI课程的教学理念必然有别于用汉语讲授的课程。笔者认为EMI课程教师可以从以下几方面建立EMI课程的教学理念。

3.1 兼顾内容和语言

EMI课程既要传授专业知识,又要使用英语作为媒介,教学中究竟是内容重要还是语言重要,这是EMI课程教师必须首先厘清的问题。

EMI课程的授课内容是除英语以外的专业课程知识,目的是让学生掌握特定的专业知识,因此EMI课程在课程内容设置、课程进度推进、课程教学目的等方面应当与传统非EMI专业课程基本一致。学生能通过对课程的学习掌握好某项专业知识仍然是检验EMI课程教学效果的最基本标准。

与此同时,EMI课程又是使用英语作为媒介的,是否能够准确有效地使用英语讲授和交流直接决定了EMI课程内容是否能够被有效讲解,教学目标是否能够实现。EMI课程教师的英语水平的高低在很大程度上决定了课程的成败。因此作为讲授媒介的英语必须受到EMI教师的足够重视。与非EMI课程相比,语言的重要性在EMI课程中大大提升。EMI课程教师必须有语言意识,在教学过程中时刻考虑到非母语带来的课程教学障碍(包括教师自身语言水平引发的授课障碍和学生语言水平引发的听课障碍)并采取相应的对策。这也可能是EMI课程教师面临的最大挑战。

EMI课程教师对课程语言的具体规划和选择可以借鉴Coyle et al.(2010)为Content and Language Integrated Learning(CLIL)课程提供的"语言三拼图"(Language Triptych)。Coyle et al. (2010)将CLIL课程所使用的工具语言分为以下三种:①"学习使用的语言(language of learning)",即学习者要学习某种课程内容必须掌握的语言,包括课程内容的关键术语,用于描述、定义、解释、分析和预测相关课程内容或主题的语言;②"辅助学习的语言(language for learning)",即学习者在非母语学习环境中为了进行学习、达成学习目的而使用的语言,包括提问、回答、争论、用于完成小组作业和撰写研究报告所使用的语言;③"通过学习获得的语言(language through learning)",即学习者在学习过程中获得的新语言,包括进行演讲报告、评价、反馈、讨论、查询资料时所获得的语言。在进行课程设计和准备阶段,EMI课程教师可以从这三类语言出发,结合课程内容,梳理学生已经掌握的语言、需要重点讲解的语言、课程进行过程中学生可能自发掌握的语言,对相关语言进行列举、分类和预测,辅助学生在英语环境下更好地学习专业内容。

值得注意的是,EMI课程不是语言课程,英语在EMI课程授课过程中主要是作为一种沟通的媒介。教师在授课过程中较少纠正学生的纯语言问题,如发音、拼写、语法、句法等。对学生语言的关注较多集中在其是否能进行有效的课堂交流、能否有效掌握课程内容等语言应用和理解等层面。EMI课程教师在提升自身语言意识的同时,要避免在纯语言内容上过多浪费时间,避免偏离课程内容中心。

3.2 尊重教学规律

EMI课程教学既要考虑到学科知识自身的特点,也要考虑到学生自身的学习认知规律,要充分尊重认知规律和学科知识发展规律,科学设计,循序渐进。

在设置专业知识领域的课程教学目标时,教师需要依据课程自身的特点、要求和学科知识体系的相关情况,具体课程具体分析。在认知领域的课程教学目标方面,可以参考Bloom认知领域教学目标分类理论。该理论将教育目标分为知识、理解、应用、分析、综合和评价,主张循序渐进、逐层深入地开展教学。2001年,Anderson等人对该理论进行了修订,提出"认知过程"从低级到高级的6个层级,分别为识记(remembering)、理解(understanding)、运用(applying)、分析(analyzing)、评价(evaluating)和创新(creating)(祝珣、马文静,2014),如图1所示。

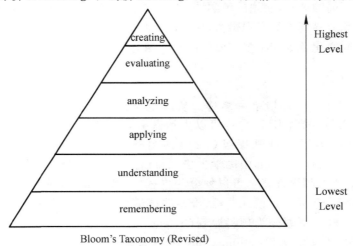

图1 Anderson等人修订的Bloom认知领域教学目标分类

在进行教学设计时可以结合EMI课程内容和定位,明确要达到哪个层级的教学目标,设计相应的教学方案。一方面,EMI教学应当按照认知规律,循序渐进地引导学生从图1中底部的认知层级逐渐过渡到顶部高层级的认知领域。在教学内容的安排上,应当由易到难,讲解由浅入深。另一方面,高校EMI课程教学的最终目标应当是使学生能够综合应用所学知识,激发学生的创造力。因此,教学不应停留在识记、理解的基础层次,而应当增加课程的应用实践和分析评价环节。

3.3 学生需求导向

EMI课程天然具有"内容+语言"的双重难度,还可能面临文化差异带来的第三重难度。无论是教师还是学生都面临着多重挑战,因而EMI课程授课更需要以学生需求为中心,在课程设计、内容设置、教学方法、教学活动等环节充分考虑学生困难和学生需求,降低学生因语言障碍而导致的内容理解偏差,还要注意文化差异造成的理解偏差。

在EMI课程的准备阶段,需要对学生的语言水平和文化背景进行摸底。针对中国学生一般可以采用普及率高的大学英语四六级(CET 4/6)考试成绩作为语言水平评价依据。针对国际学生,在语言水平方面,可以参考雅思(IELTS)考试成绩或托福(TOFEL)考试成绩,也可对照欧洲语言参考标准(Common European Framework of Reference for Languages,CEFR)自测表组织学生自测语言水平或利用英孚标准英语测试(Education First Standard English Test,EFSET)组织学生进行在线测试,从而获得统一标准下班级学生的语言水平参考。针对其文化背景,可以采取问卷的形式进行摸底。针对不同文化背景的学生,教师应当在课前做好"文化备课",合理安排教学内容。EMI 课程的教学安排和语言策略也应当根据学生的英语水平和文化背景的差异有所区别。

在具体的教学过程中,EMI 课程教师要做到以下几点。①关注学生是否能在英语指导下顺利理解课程内容,是否能借助英语有效沟通并顺利完成学习任务,根据学生的反应灵活调整教学策略。②注意语言技巧,如对语言的简化处理,专业术语的重复强调,对重音、断句、语音、语调的运用等。③避免因文化差异引起的理解偏差,例如要考虑选取的教学材料是否在不同的环境中会产生不同的理解,使用的教学词汇是否会产生歧义等。④更具耐心,充分考虑语言障碍带来的思考和应答延长等客观事实,在提问或任务设置过程中给予学生充分的思考和准备时间。理解不同文化背景的学生在面对同一问题时思考角度的差异等。

3.4 因课制宜

EMI 课程的具体教学环境多种多样。从学生(S)、教师(T)、课程领域(F)和班级规模(CS)四个维度来考量,我国 EMI 课程可以大致做出以下划分。按学生构成可以分为多文化背景(Multi-culture)英语非母语班级(L2)(如中外学生混合班)、单一文化背景(Single-culture)英语非母语班级(L2)(如中国学生班)、母语为英语与母语非英语的国际性学生的混合班(Mixed)等。按教师语言背景可以划分为中教(L2 Chinese teacher)授课课程、母语为英语的外教(L1 Foreign teacher)授课课程、母语非英语的外教(L2 Foreign teacher)授课课程。按课程学科方向可以基本划分为理科课程(Science)、工科课程(Technology)、社会科学类课程(Social science)、人文类课程(Humanities)和体育类课程(Physical science)。按班级规模可分为小班(Small)教学(35 人以下班级)和大班(Large)教学(35 人以上班级)。如图 2 所示,我国 EMI 课程的基本教学环境可以是在四个维度 S、T、F 和 CS 上进行的任意组合,如[M-C L2]+[L2 C-T]+[Science]+[Small]型教学环境,由此可以得到 90 种不同的 EMI 教学环境。此外,在具体的授课班级里,学生的英语水平还可能参差不齐,进一步使得教学环境有差异。

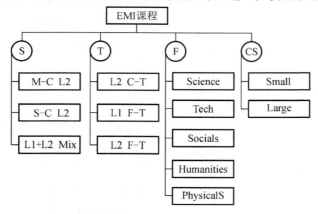

图 2 我国 EMI 课程基本教学环境分类

千差万别的具体授课环境要求 EMI 课程教师必须学会对自身的教学环境综合研判,因课制宜。例如,面对多种文化背景的学生,必须考虑到文化差异和各国学生教育背景。根据学科领域的不同,教师应当注意到课程的教学和认知逻辑,进行课程模块的筛选。如果发现学生存在一定的语言障碍,教师则必须在教学过程中调整教学时间分配并简化讲解的表述。对大班授课时,小班授课的教学方法和课堂设计必然就不再适用。只有进行仔细的课前分析,EMI 课程教师才能制订出有针对性的教学计划和教学方案。

4 EMI 课程教学理念指导下的教学方法

EMI 课程教学需要依具体情况具体设计,但依据上述相关教学理念,也可以找到一些共通的教学方法。

4.1 引入语言课程的交互模式

EMI 课程以英语为主要授课媒介语言,整个教学过程必须时刻考虑语言因素的影响,教学过程也可以借鉴语言课程的交互方式,引入 IRF 话语结构。

IRF 三话步回合交互模式是最具代表性的课堂话语结构,由教师引发(Initiation)—学生应答(Response)—教师反馈(Feedback)三个话步构成。这一话语结构是以 Sinclair 和 Coulthard 为代表的"伯明翰学派"提出的课堂话语分析理论中的重要环节,一直为语言教师和话语分析研究者所重视(范文芳、马靖香,2011)。

教师就某一解题方法发问,学生回答,教师反馈的三话步回合交互模式:

T:Can we use ***1 to solve this problem? (I)
S:No. (R)
T:Good. We can't use it. (F)
(***1 代表某解题方法 1)

此话语结构还可以进行循环和变化。如:

T:Can we use ***1 to solve this problem? (I)
S1:No. (R)
T:No. Then what can we use? (RI)
S1:Maybe we can use ***2 to solve it. (R1)
S2:But I think ***3 is better. (R2)
T:Can you explain why ***3 is better? (RI)
S2:Maybe because … (R)
T:Do you agree with him? (I)
S1:Yes. I agree. (R)
T:Good. Both of them can solve the problem. But obviously ***3 is much better.

                                                                                 （F）

（＊＊＊1、＊＊＊2、＊＊＊3代表某三种解题方法）

上述例子表现了IRF大于三话步回合的会话结构。教师引发话语后未得到满意答复，进一步追问(RI)，直到获取满意的答案，给出反馈(F)。此过程中还出现了一个引发(I)的多个应答(R1,R2)。这种IRF的话语结构模式可以帮助EMI教师启发学生，检验学生对课程知识的理解，同时给予学生明确评价，从而帮助学生确定其理解是否正确，同时对学生进行积极评价和鼓励，增强其学习动力。

4.2　重视互助式学习

由于EMI课程较传统母语讲解课程有内容和语言的双重难度，课堂推进上可能面临更大的困难。部分学生可能存在英语带来的理解障碍，使用英语回答教师问题和进行课堂交流也会加重一部分学生的紧张感，互助式学习可以在很大程度上解决这些问题。

互助式学习在课堂上可以通过小组活动实现。采用分组的方式，可以使学生经常处于共同学习的状态，增加学生间的讨论机会。学生可以通过讨论澄清疑问，锻炼语言交流能力，同时用集体的智慧更有效地解决课程问题。学生在全班同学面前发言之前先在小组中进行讨论，既可以增加学生交流的机会和思考时间，也可以帮助学生克服公开发言的紧张情绪，增强自信，营造一个更加轻松的课堂氛围。

分组的方式多种多样，如抽签分组、根据学生的语言水平分组、根据学生的性格分组、让学生自由组合等。小组活动一般可有双人小组和多人小组的形式，为保证每名小组成员都能充分参与讨论，小组人员不宜过多，可控制在6人以内。在整个教学过程中，教师应当注意经常调整分组，使学生产生新的互动。在进行小组任务设计时，还应当合理分工，注意观察学生的表现，避免小组中出现过度积极分子和过度消极分子，依据实际情况，及时做出调整。

课下的互助式学习更加灵活。教师可以通过布置小组任务的方式促使学生进行课下交流和合作。还可以通过软件建立班级群，合理利用不受时间和空间限制的网络交流平台，如微信群、QQ群、在线课程平台等。学生在这样的网络群组中可以互相交流学习，常常会自发地寻求帮助或者给予帮助，形成互帮互促的学习氛围。

4.3　结合现代教学技术

现代技术已经越来越广泛地与教育结合，应用于课堂教学。EMI课程可以充分利用现代技术手段，辅助课程教学，增加学生对课程的兴趣，提升课程效率。

现代技术与EMI课程的结合可以渗透到包括课前准备、课堂教学、课后练习、教学测验和课程评价的各个环节。例如，在课前准备和课后评价环节，教师可以借助问卷星、KwikSurveys等在线平台就学生基本情况、意愿等进行调查，可以借助EFSET在线测试工具对学生的语言水平进行科学评估。教学过程中可以使用"雨课堂""微助教""Kahoot"等教学系统或在线答题系统进行电子签到，组织课堂游戏，进行随堂测试，布置作业、推送学习资料并记录学生学习的相关数据。教师还可以借助MOOC或SPOC资源开展"翻转课堂"教学，或者要求学生利用现代技术手段自制学习小作品进行课堂展示。

在互联网和手机普及的当今时代，EMI教师只有学会有效利用现代技术，创造出自己的

"智慧课堂",才能把现代科技带来的干扰因素转换成对课程有利的因素,把学生的电脑和手机由娱乐工具变成学习工具。EMI 教师还要注意把现代技术的应用与 EMI 课程的实际需要相结合,在现代技术和传统方法间找到平衡。既要增加课程的互动性和趣味性,也要避免弱化主题或者由于技术问题而出现课程时间和内容控制上的问题。

5 结论

EMI 课程的推广已成趋势,这是各国高校寻求国际化和发展的重要手段,也是各国在全球化趋势中谋求竞争优势的需求。EMI 课程近些年在我国高校渐受重视,渐成气候,EMI 课程教师也逐渐增多。EMI 课程教师在自身能力培养、课程教学理念的建立和课程教学方法的选择上都和传统课程有所区别。本文初步探讨了 EMI 课程的特点,重点分析了 EMI 课程的教学理念和通用的教学方法,具体结论如下:

第一,EMI 课程和传统专业课程的根本区别在于语言媒介的不同。内容是 EMI 课程的根本,语言则是有效呈现内容的途径。合格的 EMI 教师必须做到内容与语言并重,不仅要有扎实的专门学科知识,还要有语言能力和跨文化能力,将内容与其语言载体完美融合,在授课过程中充分认识到学生面临的非母语环境和学生的文化背景差异,不断磨炼自己的讲授技巧,提升课程的教学效果。

第二,EMI 课程的教学过程需要将科学性与艺术性相结合。一方面,EMI 课程教学需要遵循认知规律和课程规律,制订合理的教学目标,循序渐进地引导学生完成学习内容。另一方面,EMI 课程教师也应当不断探索,在课程设计上下功夫,积极采用新技术手段,增加课程的互动性,让课程既有挑战性又有趣味性,以提升学生的学习兴趣和动力,增强学生克服内容与语言双重困难的信心。

EMI 课程是否能够取得良好效果,EMI 课程教师起着决定性的因素。EMI 教师必须不断提升自身能力,才能适应 EMI 课程的教学需求。EMI 教师不仅要精通专业知识,还必须有良好的语言功底,具备跨文化能力,同时也要熟悉教学法。这就对 EMI 教师提出了专业、语言、文化和教学上的四重要求。开设 EMI 课程的高校应当为 EMI 课程教师提供多种学习机会,帮助 EMI 教师提高语言水平,学习先进教学法。西北工业大学教师教学发展中心常年开展的各种教师发展项目,有效地推动了该校 EMI 教师全方位素质的提高,树立了一个很好的范本。广大 EMI 课程教师也应当勇于面对新的挑战,主动提升自我综合能力,积极适应 EMI 课程的需求。

参 考 文 献

范文芳、马靖香,2011,《中国英语课堂上的 IRF 会话结构与交际性课堂教学模式研究》,《中国外语》第 1 期。
教育部,2001,《关于加强高等学校本科教学工作提高教学质量的若干意见》。据中华人民共和国教育部官网:http://old.moe.gov.cn//publicfiles/business/htmlfiles/moe/moe_1623/201006/88633.html。
李颖,2012,《高校双语/EMI 课堂调查与分析》,《外语界》第 2 期。

谈多娇,2012,《双语教学:中国高等教育国际化的战略选择》,《教育研究》第 11 期。
吴平、王根树等,2010,《高等学校双语教学的现状研究和实践探索》,高等教育出版社。
西北工业大学国际教育学院,2018,《学院介绍》。据西北工业大学国际教育学院官网:http://gjjyxy.nwpu.edu.cn/xin/gywm/jshao.htm。
新华社,2015,《国家中长期教育改革和发展规划纲要》,据新华社官网:http://www.gov.cn/jrzg/2010-07/29/content_1667143.htm。
祝珣、马文静,2014,《鲁姆教育目标分类理论对大学英语阅读教学的启示》,《中国大学教学》第 9 期。
"CEFR 及 EF SET." Accessed from http://www.efset.cn/english-score/cefr/#nav-2.
Coyle, D., Hood, P., and Marsh, D. 2010. *CLIL: Content and Language Integrated Learning*. Cambridge: Cambridge University Press.
Dearden, J. 2018. "A systematic review of English medium instruction in higher education". *Language Teaching*.
Dearden, J. 2015. "English as a medium of instruction—a growing global phenomenon. British Council." Accessed from https://www.britishcouncil.org/sites/default/files/e484_emi_cover_option_3_final_web.pdf.
Hu, G., and McKay, S. L. 2012. "English language education in East Asia: Some recent developments". *Journal of Multilingual and Multicultural Development*.
Kirkpatrick, A. 2014. "The Language(s) of HE: EMI and/or ELF and/or Multilingualism?" *The Asian Journal of Applied Linguistics*. Vol. 1: 4-15
Wächter, B, and Maiworm, F. 2014. *English-Taught Programmes in European Higher Education: The State of Play in 2014*. Bonn: Lemmens.

四、外语教学模式改革与创新

大学英语教学游戏的设计与运用

屈江丽[*]

摘　要：大学英语教学游戏具有较强的趣味性和互动性，能够有效激发学生的学习动机、兴趣和内驱力，消解学生的心理压力和焦虑感，从而增强学生的自信心，提高其学习效率。针对大学英语教学游戏的设计与运用，归纳出理应遵循的基本原则，给出了具体方式及注意事项，并列举出若干实例，诸如词语接龙、句子传递、名篇背诵、课堂讨论、演讲辩论、角色扮演、故事续接、戏剧表演、影视剧配音比赛等，都可供英语教师们参考借鉴。实践证明，将英语技能训练和英语国家文化融入教学游戏，在培养学生跨文化交际能力的同时，还能寓教于乐，潜移默化地影响学生的学习和生活。

关键词：大学英语；教学游戏；设计；运用

1　引言

我国的英语教师们多年来积累了丰富的教学经验，不断发展和完善着英语课堂教学的方式方法，并取得了一定的教学成效。但是以往所有的教学方法，大多是建立在传统的英语课堂教学模式之上的。如何在英语课堂教学中兼顾全体学习者，集中全体学生的注意力，因材施教，寓教于乐，始终是英语教学设计中的重点和难点问题（刘爽，2013）。为适应新时期英语课堂教学改革的需要，不少英语教师采取了多种多样的教学方式以增加课堂教学的趣味性，而游戏教学法便是其中行之有效的一种。实践证明，课堂教学会因为游戏活动而变得更加丰富多彩，相对于枯燥、机械的传统学习过程而言，更能体现出语言学习的趣味性和互动性。

近几年来，游戏教学法在中小学教育中得到了广泛应用。然而据笔者了解，大学英语教师普遍还不够重视教学游戏的设计与运用，这实际上是忽视了当今大学生的实际状况和心理需求。调查发现，不少大学生很希望在轻松愉快的游戏氛围中习得英语读写及口语交际能力。笔者认为，教师如能将富于文化特征的英语知识蕴含在教学游戏之中，会给大学英语课堂增添诸多趣味性，使学生因为兴趣大增而克服畏难情绪，从而提高英语学习的质量和效率。

---

[*] 屈江丽：西北工业大学外国语学院教师，主讲大学英语Ⅱ/Ⅲ、大学英语（文化与思辨）、演讲与辩论等课程。

2 大学英语教学游戏的设计和运用细则

2.1 大学英语教学游戏设计与运用的基本原则

2.1.1 趣味性

趣味性原则是英语课堂教学游戏设计与运用中最为重要的原则之一(范文芳,2010)。毋庸赘述,中国自古以来就有寓教于乐的教学思想。对于中国学生而言,英语作为第二语言,难学难练,如果课堂教学缺乏趣味性,教学效果会大打折扣。因此,教师在教学过程中以恰到好处的游戏设计引入或辅助教学,可以为英语课堂增添很多乐趣,从而激发学生的学习内驱力,使其积极主动地学习英语。

2.1.2 目的性

游戏设计与运用终究只是大学英语教学的辅助手段,每一个环节都要与大学英语教学的重点和难点相对应,游戏的内容和形式要针对相应的语言技能操练而编排,游戏的难易程度也要与学习者的英语语言能力、学习水平相契合(白琳,2009)。

2.1.3 多样性

同样的游戏形式,在不同的课堂教学中反复出现,即"换汤不换药",会使学生感到乏味,也就在很大程度上丧失了趣味性。因此,大学英语教师要不断积累新的经验,不断创新游戏内容和形式,使课堂游戏朝着多元化、多样性的方向发展。

2.1.4 竞争性

大学英语课堂教学游戏设计与运用要想足够吸引学生,就需要设计一些竞争性、激励性游戏,以便充分调动学生参与游戏活动的积极性,使其在游戏中渴望取得胜利,始终以饱满的激情和昂扬的斗志投入其中。

2.1.5 公平性

英语课堂教学游戏设计与运用要面向全体学生,在兼顾所有学生现有水平的同时,还要给英语水平偏低或者性格较为内向的学生提供更多的参与机会,尤其要注意循序渐进,难易相间,以避免学生因学习水平不足而逐渐丧失参与的热情和信心。

2.2 大学英语教学游戏设计与运用的一般方式

2.2.1 卡片类游戏的设计与运用

英语课堂上较为常用的游戏方式是传统的卡片类游戏,比较适合于语音、词汇、句型、语法等教学板块。实际应用时可以和竞赛式游戏配合使用,让学生快速认读、记忆,然后抢答,这样运用的效果往往是很好的。例如,可以将卡片类游戏和猜词游戏配合起来运用,具体做法是:由学生们自由分成若干小组,每组选出一位同学到讲台前,面对大家;这时老师只向他展示卡片内容,由他向小组的其他同学做出提示,可以用动作、声音或用英语来解释,但是不能直接说出卡片上的词汇,而是要由组内其他同学根据接收到的信息猜测出来。教师可以给每个小组均分5张卡片即5个词,猜出全部词汇同时费时最少的小组获胜。

四、外语教学模式改革与创新

2.2.2 写作类游戏的设计与运用

写作类游戏一般需要学生拥有一定量的词汇和句型知识积累,运用起来才能达到预期效果(温西梅,2010)。因此,写作类游戏是英语教学游戏设计与运用中的难点之一,但是学生一旦体会到游戏的乐趣,参与英语写作的热情就会在游戏中得到充分显现。比如,对于教师给出的同一段开头语,学生们可以写出很多内容不同的主体和结尾。也可以让学生相互修改作品,在规定的时间内找出错误或给出评价,还可以在已经成形的段落基础上进行改写。学生在游戏中,通过对文本的理解和再创造,更为深刻地理解了作品所蕴含的意义,同时提高了英语表达能力。

2.2.3 益智类游戏的设计与运用

益智类游戏有益于训练词汇、句型的识别、认读和记忆能力等,设计运用这类游戏时,常与图表、拼图、综合能力训练类游戏结合起来,进行单词记忆、遣词造句、句型转换、读写和口语交际能力的训练。例如,让学生依次复述他看到的视频或文字材料内容,类似于看图说话,以此加深对句型、段落或语篇的理解。

2.2.4 情景式游戏的设计与运用

英语教师们在教学中常常使用情景教学法,我们不妨将情景教学法变通拓展,使课堂教学成为游戏活动。比如预先设定言语交际的背景,让学生通过表演、模仿等方式表达相关的知识点。在情景游戏中,学生能够快速提高其听力、口语乃至综合能力。例如戏剧表演、诗歌朗诵、辩论、演说、书面报告等,都可以用于语言练习。也可以通过模拟拍电影,在游戏过程中学习拍摄短片。这类游戏需要教师给定任务,让学生根据要求设计剧本并进行演绎(朱文,2006)。特别是对于听力训练,情景游戏是再合适不过的,在情景中训练听力,能够使学生感受到真实的语言环境,对于英语语言能够应用自如。

2.2.5 表演类游戏的设计与运用

表演类游戏的设计与运用,可以和歌舞、小品、短剧、演讲、辩论结合起来,有助于理解英语句型、句段、语篇等,或进行口语交际能力训练。例如,在大学英语教学中,可以尝试举行英语歌曲演唱比赛,以富有浪漫色彩的内容和形式进行语音和口语表达能力训练。参与者通过学唱英语歌曲来达到学习英语和运用英语的目的,这不失为一种生动活泼的学习方式。

2.3 大学英语教学游戏设计与运用的注意事项

2.3.1 游戏设计要运用在课堂教学过程中的适当时间(周艳芳,2010)

大学英语课程特定的教学任务,要求教师在运用课堂游戏辅助教学时把握适时的原则,确保其有益于提高课堂教学质量。因此,在教学中要针对具体的学习任务和不同时段,将游戏分为课前导入游戏、课程穿插游戏、巩固教学内容游戏、课后练习游戏设计等。换言之,选择进行游戏的时间要恰到好处,一般应选在刚开始上课的时候运用,以便激发学生学习英语的欲望,使其集中注意力,这就是所谓的 warm-up。也可以选在学生注意力不集中、产生疲倦感之前开始游戏,这样既能活跃课堂气氛,又能提高学习效率,这在英语教学中叫作 wake-up。

2.3.2 游戏设计与运用要与学生的英语水平相匹配

一方面,设计和运用教学游戏时要以学生为中心。另一方面,大学英语课堂上进行的游戏活动必须以语言的演练为主,要能够使学生不断突破自己的语言水平,自我更新语言知识,通过自我实现来体验运用英语语言的乐趣,保持积极向上的学习动机和态度。因此,游戏的内容和形式都要符合大学生的年龄特点、心理特征和学习进度,要尽量多做一些探索性、对抗性强的游戏。

2.3.3 游戏设计与运用要营造出英语学习的语言环境

游戏教学法被认为是情景教学的分支,其主要目的之一便是营造一种模拟的语言环境,减少学生的畏难情绪,使学生在游戏中充分感受语言情境以及英语所承载的文化内涵。大学英语教学游戏的场景和道具应该是千变万化的,以此营造英语学习的语言环境,可增进学生对英语国家文化的直观了解和感性认识。

2.3.4 游戏设计与运用要与大学英语教学目的相契合

大学英语教学游戏的设计与运用应针对具体的学习任务而进行,并且要与语言技能训练相对应。游戏的情节与任务,要能够帮助大学生利用课堂上学到的英语语言知识完成游戏过程中的各项任务,灵活地巩固学到的语言技能并用目的语解决游戏中的问题,进而更好地理解英语知识和抽象的英语国家文化,全面提高英语素养。

2.3.5 游戏设计与运用要体现循序渐进的教学原则

只有学生能够主动接受教育,才能取得最好的效果。大学英语教师要一步步引导全体学生,使他们都能充分参与到教学游戏中去,就必须坚持循序渐进的原则。在设计和运用游戏教学法时,应根据教学内容,在不同的游戏点设置相关的提示,使游戏和学习能够顺利进行,从而达到英语教学的目的。

2.3.6 游戏设计与运用要注意融入文化元素

中国学生对英语国家的名胜古迹、自然风光非常感兴趣,外国很多的节日、饮食和民俗文化等都深深吸引着他们。教师要注意把各种文化元素融入英语教学游戏,让学生在课堂上完成相应的学习任务、掌握相应的语言技能,同时潜移默化地感受到英语语言所承载的文化内涵。

2.4 大学英语教学游戏设计与运用的若干实例

大学英语教师可以借鉴图书、杂志以及网络上现有的游戏资源,尤其是网络上的教学游戏资源,目前已是极为丰富的,比如用一些搜索引擎输入"Games for English Teaching",只需敲一下回车键,就会发现有大量网页推介英语教学游戏,可以有所选择地使用。但是为了更好地贴近学生实际情况,教师自行设计教学游戏也是非常必要的,下面提供若干实例,以供教师们参考和借鉴。

2.4.1 词语接龙

用英语进行词语接龙,就是把前一单词的最后一个字母作为下一个单词的首字母,一个单词紧接着一个单词说下去,每个参与者都要力求做到发音准确、口齿清楚。这种游戏的参与人数可多可少,时间安排也比较灵活,可根据教学过程中的实际情况,或要求全体同学一起参与,或选择部分同学参与。需要注意的是,游戏的时间不宜太长,以免影响教学进度。

2.4.2 句子传递

游戏步骤:教师将全班同学均分成若干小组,然后让每组选出一位代表到讲台上,由教师把英语句子小声说给各组代表,各组代表回到所在小组,小声将句子依次告知下一位组员,每组的最后一位组员到讲台上大声说出原定的句子,其中语音语调最准确的学生所在的小组获胜。随后,教师可以让全班同学大声朗读所有的句子。值得注意的是,教师告知各组代表的句子应该是不一样的,这样既可避免学生之间互相询问而影响实际效果,又能使全班同学在游戏结束后学会说更多的英语句子。

2.4.3 演讲和辩论

游戏步骤:教师给定一个演讲题目,并且将全班同学分成正方和反方两个大组,然后由每组成员推选一个口语水平较高的学生作为主辩手,代表所有组员陈述观点,其余同学随之展开自由辩论,最后由教师就双方表现做出评价和总结。值得注意的是,演讲和辩论在英语口语训练中属于难度较大的项目,要求学生具有相当娴熟的口语表达能力。因此,教师给定的题目必须贴近学生的学习和生活实际,同时要给学生提供一些可能会用到的词汇或句子,以降低游戏难度。

2.4.4 角色扮演

游戏步骤:教师指定口语课上学过的对话材料,或是精读课上学过的课文,按照角色扮演的要求将全班同学分为若干小组,给他们一定的时间做准备,然后让各组学生根据所扮演的角色进行表演,教师在游戏结束后做出评价和总结。值得注意的是,课堂时间是有限的,教师应安排学生在课后做好准备工作,使课堂上的表演活动有声有色。教师在评价学生表现时,不仅要纠正学生在英语语音语调方面的错误,更要认真观察学生的表演是否符合角色特点,从整体上给出恰如其分的激励性评价。

2.4.5 故事续接

故事续接游戏能用来培养学生的观察、分析能力,既可用于口语练习,还可用于写作训练,相应的游戏形式也是多种多样的。例如,教师给学生提供一个开头,然后要求学生通过思考和想象续接故事。这种游戏形式自由但难度较大,学生只有充分运用其理解力、判断力和想象力,续接的故事情节才会有逻辑性。只要有部分学生才思敏捷、反应灵活,同时又能发挥丰富的想象力,就会给大家带来意外的惊喜。

2.4.6 戏剧表演

学生可自由分组,每组选出一个导演,在教师指导下选择学生自己比较感兴趣的戏剧剧本,并由导演负责安排全组同学表演。演出结束后可由全班同学投票选出最佳导演、最佳表演小组和最佳男女主角等。教师要特别关注那些性格内向、容易紧张的学生,鼓励他们积极参与到集体活动中去。

2.4.7 影视剧配音比赛

大学里有条件的班级,可以在教师指导下举行影视剧配音比赛。由学生自由组合成若干小组,选择全体组员共同喜爱的影视剧片段,对其进行消音处理后分角色进行配音,时间上以10分钟左右为宜,游戏结束后由教师或全班同学评选出优胜的小组。一般来说,影视剧配音比赛越是紧张,课堂气氛就越是热烈,这样的大学英语教学游戏会使所有参与者由衷期待并经久难忘。

3 结语

大学生在进行跨文化交际时,往往会不自觉地产生一种心理压力和焦虑感,而在轻松、有趣的游戏环境中,心理上的压力和焦虑感会慢慢减轻,随之而来的是对英语国家文化的欣赏和体验。实践证明,运用游戏教学法能够有效增强大学英语教学的趣味性和互动性,有助于培养学生对英语知识的探索、体验和应用能力,以及解决实际问题的能力。但是需要特别注意的是,教学游戏的设计与运用终究是辅助手段,在具体实施过程中要避免过犹不及的现象发生。大学英语教师要根据具体的教学目的和任务,将那些渗透着文化因素的英语语言知识转化为教学游戏的内容,使所有学生都能积极参与互动,从而全面提升英语学习的质量和效率。

参 考 文 献

白琳,2009,《游戏在大学英语口语课堂上的设计与应用》,《华章》第 19 期。
范方芳,2010,《课堂游戏与大学英语教学》,《和田师范专科学校学报(汉文综合版)》第 4 期。
刘爽,2013,《拯救独立学院英语课堂的神器——游戏教学法》,《课程教育研究》第 1 期。
温西梅,2010,《基于情感角度的游戏教学法在高职英语教学中的应用分析》,《海外英语》第 10 期。
周艳芳,2010,《游戏在大学英语教学中的应用》,《科技信息》第 13 期。
朱文,2006,《英语课堂游戏教学法的实践探索》,《新课程(下)》第 6 期。

基于移动互联网环境的英语交互式课堂教学模式研究

杨艳卫[*]

摘　要：基于移动互联网环境的交互式课堂教学模式，将网络资源、移动技术、课堂教学、课堂互动等融为一体，为英语教学的发展提供了新的平台和媒介，可以提升学生的英语交际能力、课堂的参与度、英语学习的主动性等，助力学生英语语言能力的提升。

关键词：移动互联网；交互式课堂；课堂参与度

1　引言

在传统英语课堂模式中，教师是课堂的中心，学生课堂参与度较低、学习积极性不高，很难有效实现课程教学目标和语言的交际目的。另外，统一的教材、统一的练习，不利于不同层次学生的语言能力的快速提升。课程评价体系也很难做到多次客观评价学生的语言能力发展。移动互联网时代，网络媒体技术的发展速度惊人，每天都有海量的文件、视频材料上传到网站，学习资源的获取方式产生了质的变化，兼具时代感和历史性，适合不同层次、不同需求的学习者。在有移动互联网的情况下，学生可以随时随地阅读材料，观看视频，进行讨论、分析、测试等，结合应用程序、网站等可以记录学生的语言能力发展过程，实现有效的交互式学习。

2　移动互联网环境下的英语交互式课堂教学模式

2.1　交互式课堂教学模式

Rivers（2000）认为语言学习与教学是交互的过程。语言教学中，教师要为学生创造机会和情景来活用语言规则，实现语言应用能力的提升。教学中教师应以学生为中心，为学生提供具有现实有意义的材料，模拟真实语言环境，提高学生语言交际能力（姜冬艳，2018）。

交互式教学模式是以学生为中心的课堂教学模式。交互式课堂教学模式存在三种交互形式：学生与移动互联网之间的交互、学生与学生之间的交互、教师与学生之间的交互。教师和学生、学生与学生之间是平等关系（雷琼华，2017）。教师应根据学生的个体差异，规划教学内容，组织教学活动，实现多种形式的交互，如学生与教学内容、学生与学生、老师与学生之间的交互，促进学生语言能力的发展。

2.2　移动互联网环境下的英语交互式课堂模式

随着移动互联网的发展，网络覆盖面更加广泛，网络知识材料的获取手段、工具等更加丰

---

[*] 杨艳卫：西安明德理工学院语言文化传播学院副教授，主讲高级英语、英语语法、英语精读等课程。

富。人们可以借助智能手机、电脑等设备,随时随地通过互联网获取各种信息。移动互联网同时也为学习者提供了虚拟的语言学习环境,使语言教学突破时空限制,学生可以在教室内外实时地进行人机互动、师生互动、生生互动,进行各种语言能力的训练。移动互联网环境将移动互联网技术和英语教学融入英语课堂,符合现代教育发展的趋势。在交互式课堂教学模式下,教师引导学生参与交互式教学活动,充分调动学生的语言学习兴趣,最大程度发挥学生的主观能动性,使学生成为学习的主角。基于移动互联网,学生学习的内容更具多样性、时代性、实用性,文本更具真实性和可操作性,学生参与的积极性、兴趣以及学习效果都会得到大幅度提高(雷琼华,2011)。

3 基于移动互联网环境的英语交互式课堂教学模式研究

3.1 实验对象

本研究以西北工业大学明德学院语言文化传播学院 17 级英语专业 1 班和翻译专业 1 班的学生为实验对象,两个班学生的高考成绩、人数、性别比例基本相同。使用《现代大学英语教材》学生用书 1、2 为实验教材。翻译专业 1 班为实验班,使用交互式课堂教学模式;英语专业 1 班为对照班,使用传统课堂教学模式,以教师讲解为主。通过为期一年的教学实验,对学生的语言交际能力、课堂参与度、交互式练习参与度、练习完成质量、学习态度、学习积极性和自主性等方面进行对比研究。

3.2 实验方法

基于移动网络环境,使用钉钉、微信、QQ、云课堂、Kahoot 平台等实现交互式课堂的构建,设计课程讨论互动话题,组织多样的生生互动、师生互动课堂活动,提升学生课程参与度,利用合理的资源,提升学生参与的热情,使他们成为学习的主体,提升他们的思辨能力和沟通能力。利用网络,查找视频、音频、图文等各类资源,使用问卷星、iTest、云课堂等,设计新颖的、具有时代特色的分层课程练习、课堂或课后小测试,更好地服务于不同层次的学生。对网络数据进行统计对比,发现学生在语言交际能力、参与度等方面的差异。

3.3 拟解决问题

打破纸质学习资源的限制,利用网络资源提高教学内容的时效性和英语教学效果;弥补纸质课堂练习、测试的不足,实现学生测试结果的快速统计。在移动互联网环境下,使用现代技术,进行多样化的交互活动,实现教学目标。移动互动讨论方式使所有学生都能参与讨论、互评、辩论等,提升学生课堂参与度、思辨能力、语言交际能力等;利用 iTest、问卷星、Hot Potatoes、Kahoot 平台等制作课堂、课后测试,快速、准确统计学生测试结果,发现学生学习中存在的问题,对语言错误及时进行纠正和指导。转变以教师为中心的课堂模式,提高学生的参与度,改变学生被动学习的模式,激发学生学习动机,调动学生学习的积极性,构建以学生为主体的课堂,培养学生的语言交际能力。

3.4 交互课堂教学模式

3.4.1 课前交互

教师根据课堂教学内容设计课前预习材料、形式，如背景知识分享、视频观看及问答、课文相关话题讨论、词汇查阅、语法点的解读、文章的赏析等。学生通过网络查找资料，在钉钉、微信、QQ 等平台进行小组讨论，完成生生互动，为课堂的分享做好准备。在课前讨论过程中，教师可以随时参与，进行有效的辅导，为高质量的课堂分享打下基础。

3.4.2 课堂交互

课堂的交互形式多样，其中包括课前预习内容分享、小测试、问答、讨论、演讲、表演等。学生通过教师的引导完成各种形式的课堂活动。在课堂活动开展过程中，所有学生可以借助云课堂、QQ 等平台进行课堂交互，通过大屏幕将所有的学生分享的内容展示出来，实现全班全员参与。教师可以对互联网中学生分享的内容进行点评，或邀请学生点评，实现高质量的交互和学生语言能力的整体提升。

3.4.3 课后交互

课后交互的主要目的是巩固所学内容，在交际中学会使用新知识。教师使用 iTest、问卷星、Hot Potatoes 等，对学生对知识的掌握程度进行测试，对出现的高频问题进行强化练习。测试结果体现学生的部分语言能力。要求学生完成写作、戏剧表演、演讲、互评等不同形式的活动，在真实的环境下使用语言，提升沟通能力、交际能力、思辨能力等。

3.5 实验的结果

3.5.1 提升教学资源的时代感

与对照班相比，实验班所分享的内容、话题讨论中的论据往往更具时代性，学生更擅长在移动互联网上查找最新的资源，从新闻时事中查找有效的信息，丰富讨论的话题，论证自己的观点，语言更具时代特色。

3.5.2 提高学生教学活动参与度

实验班学生教学活动参与度高。交互式课堂教学模式在语言教学中能有效地提升学生教学活动的参与度，能提高生生互动、师生互动的质量，进而提升教学效果；交互式课堂教学模式能提升学生的学习热情，使学生成为学习的主体，提高学生的语言能力、沟通能力、协作能力等；交互式课堂教学模式能拓展学生探索知识的能力和途径，能帮助学生形成长期学习、随时随地学习的理念。

3.5.3 丰富英语教学的形式

基于移动互联网环境下的英语交互式课堂教学模式中使用的教学形式包括测试、总结、分析、自评、小组互评、生生互评、讨论、辩论等，形式灵活多样，学生发言机会均等，不会受人数、时间、空间的限制，能最大限度地满足学生参与的热情，实现交互式学习。

4 结论

互联网时代背景下，英语课堂教学的模式需要与时俱进，社会对学生英语语言能力的要求也逐渐提高,学生不仅仅要具有传统意义上英语口语和写作能力,还要有一定的交际能力、沟通能力、思辨能力、探索能力等。如何在英语交际中更好地传递思想,更好地形成有效的交际？移动互联网络为我们提供了媒介,有效地解决了教学资源滞后、课堂参与度低等问题,能有效促进学生语言能力、沟通能力等的提升,有利于促进英语教学的全面发展。基于移动网络的英语交互式课堂教学模式,对课堂硬件设施、网络环境、智能手机等的配置要求相对较高,对教师教学组织能力、知识储备、现代技术掌握能力、学习能力等都有更高的要求。如何使移动互联网更好地服务于英语交互式教学,从而提升英语教学质量,仍需相关人员做进一步的研究。

参 考 文 献

姜冬艳,2018,《基于移动互联网络环境下的〈综合英语〉交互式教学模式研究》,《吉林工程技术师范学院学报》第 8 期。

姜冬艳,2018,《基于移动互联网络环境下的大学英语交互式教学模式研究》,《科技资讯》第 15 期。

雷琼华,2017,《基于移动互联网络环境下的大学英语交互式教学模式浅析》,《黑河学院学报》第 2 期。

Wilga, M. Rivers,2000,《交互性语言教学》,吴本虎导读,人民教育出版社。

基于产出导向法的 MOOC＋SPOC 混合教学模式探索
——以非英语专业研究生跨文化交流课程为例

周 兰*

摘 要：本文采用"产出导向法"指导 MOOC＋SPOC 混合式线上教学，探讨疫情期间线上外语教学新模式。研究发现，产出导向法以教师为中介的三段式教学流程，即驱动、促成和评价，在社交软件、直播、录播、网络云平台等信息技术的辅助下，能有效确保学生线上线下的学习需求得以满足。

关键词：POA；SPOC；MOOC；外语教学

1 引言

受到新冠肺炎疫情影响，教育部发文要求全国高校"停课不停教、停课不停学"，鼓励教师充分利用慕课和优质在线课程资源，积极开展在线教学活动。由此，2020年春季学期，国内高校全面铺开线上教学活动。据CNNIC(China Internet Network Information Center，中国互联网络信息中心)第45次报告显示，截至2020年3月，中国在线教育用户规模达4.23亿，较2018年底，增长了110.2%。信息技术在教育领域迅速发展，无论是辅助教学的相关硬件设备，还是5G技术驱动下的直播教学，以及在线教育依托的云平台建设，都在疫情的推动下日趋完善。诚然，我国在线教育呈爆发式增长，但面对突发疫情如何制订适合的在线教学实施方案，有效利用线上资源、提高教学效率、确保学习效果，仍值得进一步探讨。本研究以"产出导向法"(Production-Oriented Approach，POA)为理论指导，利用 MOOC＋SPOC 开展混合式线上教学，探索适合研究生公共英语教学的新模式，旨在培养学生的跨文化交流意识和提升学生的口头表达能力。

2 理论依据

POA 是以"输出驱动假设"(Output-driven Hypothesis)为原型(文秋芳，2008，2013)，充分汲取了中国传统教育理论与西方教学理论精华(文秋芳，2015，2016)。作为中国本土理论，POA 在以分析中国特色外语教学为主的同时还加强与国际的交流合作，经过十余年的发展与完善，为解决我国高校外语教学存在的问题提供了重要理论依据，并涌现了一批教学科研成果(张文娟，2015，2016；曹巧珍，2017；常小玲，2017；邱琳，2017；孙曙光，2017；张伶俐，2017；张艳，2019；唐美华，2020)。

---

* 周兰：暨南大学外国语学院教师，主要研究方向为外语教学、教学理论与实践研究等。

POA 教学理念提倡以学习为中心、学用一体和全人教育。"以学习为中心"（learning-centered）即课堂教学应以实现教学目标为导向并促成有效教学的发生，而非"教师中心说"和"学生中心说"（learner-centered）。POA 还倡导"学"与"用"结合，即学用一体，用英语做事，培养学生运用英语的综合能力，拒绝哑巴式英语。POA 的"全人教育说"则是通过教师对任务话题、输入材料和教学活动的巧妙设计来实现的（文秋芳，2015）。

POA 教学流程以教师为中介分为：驱动（motivating）、促成（enabling）和评价（assessing）三个阶段。在驱动阶段，由教师激发学生学习输入动力，明确教学目标和产出任务；在促成阶段，教师发挥脚手架作用，引导学生完成产出任务；在评价阶段，采用合作评价，由师生共同完成。

MOOC（Massive Open Online Course，大规模在线开放课程）是信息化技术应用于高等教育的突出成果之一，也是近期在线教育的主要形式之一。但随着 MOOC 的广泛应用，其潜在问题也逐渐显露。课堂内容过于简单，教学模式单一，缺乏挑战性、趣味性和互动性，学生辍学率高；此外，MOOC 线上评估体系不够完善，学生问题也得不到及时反馈等，极大地影响了线上教学的成效。在此背景下，加州大学伯克利分校的阿曼多·福克教授提出了 SPOC（Small Private Online Course）的概念，即小规模限制性在线课程，对学生范畴、课堂准入条件加以限制，便于教师更精确地掌握学生学习情况（康叶钦，2014）。通过线上教育、线下课堂相结合的混合式教学模式来弥补单一 MOOC 线上学习的不足，实现线下课堂和在线学习的优势互补。面对疫情，线下面授课程难以开展，为满足学生线下学习的要求，本研究利用直播、录播和网络云分享等手段远程协助构建线上模拟课堂，增加与学生的多维度对话和互动。

当前，POA 研究主要集中于设计驱动—促成—评价各教学环节，或是某个单元教学任务产出，又或是任务型教材编写，研究范畴也仅限于大学英语教学。疫情时期，面向研究生的将产出导向法应用于 MOOC+SPOC 的线上教学，还是一次较为全新的尝试。本文基于产出导向法，通过视频直播和网络教学双系统模式，重构线上虚拟课堂，初步总结教师在教学过程中的发现，在教学实践基础上进行教学反思并提出优化课程设计的建议。

3 研究设计

3.1 研究对象

本研究对象为全校（暨南大学）2019 级非英语专业的研究生，共 100 位，年龄范围在 21～25 岁，其中 80% 已通过全国大学英语六级考试。

3.2 研究问题

疫情期间如何在 MOOC+SPOC 线上课程中有效地、分阶段开展 POA 教学流程（驱动、促成和评价）？如何设计课前任务以有效刺激驱动？线上学习时，如何在学生产出任务时予以及时指导？如何激励学生课后进行师生互评？

3.3 POA 教学程序

研究生公共英语课程为期 16 周，2 个班，每班每周 2 课时，共计 48 课时。第 1、2 周为导学课程,主要向学生介绍疫情期间的课程设计调整、本学期的学习目标与计划、POA 教学模式、MOOC 和 SPOC 线上课程注册、相关线上平台操作流程介绍、直播软件的选用、填写问卷、分组及 QQ 群组建等。第 15、16 周为口语测试。POA 教学法从第 3 周开始至第 14 周结束,共持续 12 周。

3.3.1 学情分析

(1)学习条件分析。

线上教学对于网络环境和硬件设备有一定要求,因此,在课程开始前对学习对象及其所处的环境是否适合进行网络教学展开了问卷调查。

问题一:学生是否具备网络学习的硬件条件?

从问卷调查得知,学生基本都具备开展网络学习的条件,但也存在部分学生上网设备性能不佳、网络流量有限等问题,具体情况见图 1。

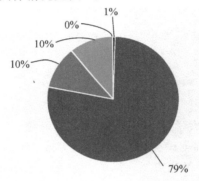

■ 有网络,有电脑且有智能手机,完全能正常开展　　■ 有网络,无电脑但有智能手机,能正常开展　　■ 其他
■ 无网络,但有智能手机且有流量,基本能正常开展　　□ 无网络,且智能手机无流量,不能保证能正常开展

图 1　学生开展远程网络学习条件

问题二:学生所处环境对网络学习的影响?

问卷显示,24%的学生认为学习条件较好,67%的学生认为学习条件一般,9%的学生认为学习条件简陋。由此可见,疫情期临时构建的线上学习可能会存在小部分学生无法保证学习进度的问题。

问题三:学生进行网络学习可能遇到的困难有哪些?

根据问卷可知,仅有 4%的学生认为远程网络学习不存在问题,51%的学生认为外界环境对网络学习干扰较大,40%的学生担心网络不稳,自己跟不上教师节奏,具体问题见图 2。

根据以上学情调查分析可知,大部分学生能进行网络学习,但还存在着一定问题,其中硬件设备不足、网络环境和学习环境不佳为主要问题,因此在课程设计上需要根据学生反馈的困难做出适当调整。

(2)学生特点分析。

1)本校研究生语言学习的特点为听说能力较弱,他们将大部分的时间集中于词汇和语法知识的学习,忽略了语言产出的重要性。

2)有的研究生更专注于专业领域内的知识,对英语学习要求不高,导致有的研究生的英语学习态度模棱两可,学习动力不足甚至缺失。

3)研究生具备一定的自学、检索能力,知识构成相对成熟,且富有一定的深度和广度。

综合上述学情分析,在教学的具体实施过程中,教师需要考虑网络环境的干扰、充分调动学生自觉参与产出任务的积极性,确保线上课程能够顺利、高效进行。

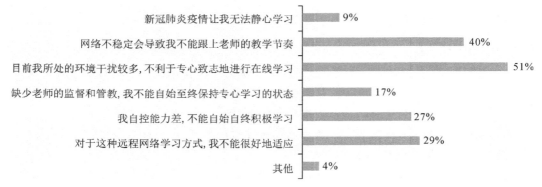

图 2 学生进行网络学习所遇到的困难

3.3.2 教学过程

(1)驱动。

学生在课前自行登录中国大学 MOOC 观看慕课学习视频,教师通过中国大学 MOOC 创建的 SPOC 平台,上传文本案例创设交际情境,学生完成 MOOC 学习后,分组讨论 SPOC 文本案例中的文化冲突,尝试提出解决方案。以第一单元"Comparing Cultures"为例,该章节内容主要涉及中西文化对比,通过分析中西思维的差异引出跨文化交流中可能遇到的障碍。MOOC 视频讲解关键知识点,其中涵盖了一定量的文化理论和专业词汇,给学生的学习带来困难与挑战,教师通过文本案例创设跨文化交际中的冲突,使学生明确需要完成的交际目标和要学习的重点词汇。本门课程需要学生在具体的跨文化交流情境中尝试用相关的文化理论进行分析,理解文化现象背后的深义,激发学生进行深度思考,培养学生的辩证思维能力。

(2)促成。

在前期学情调查中发现,部分学生的网络环境不佳、硬件设备性能不佳,很可能会直接影响直播效果。因此,每周 2 学时的直播课主要以录播＋QQ 互动的形式进行。第 1 周至第 4 周,教师提前录制视频,以第一单元"Comparing Cultures"为例,SPOC 文本案例来自中美贸易往来中发生的真实事件,美方坚持采用美国计量单位而不愿使用国际标准计量单位所引发的冲突,案例中已经利用 MOOC 中介绍的跨文化交流障碍民族中心主义(ethnocentrism)对美方行为进行了简要分析,教师的录播视频会重点强调民族中心主义的来龙去脉,帮助学生理解运用,进一步思考如何克服障碍的策略,最后达到产出任务的目的。学生在观看视频中遇到问题可以在 QQ 上与教师实时互动,研究生所具备的自学和检索能力,使得在线答疑较以往面授课堂更加深入、全面,且更具批判性。通过观看录播视频和 QQ 实时互动的形式,学生清楚了解完成产出任务的步骤和每一步的具体要求,开始分组产出任务,并将小组讨论录音并上传到云分享平台,为下一步的师生互评做准备。教师整个过程都利用网络,根据学生反馈的问题及时提供帮助。从第 5 周开始,学生已逐渐适应教学节奏,教师开始减少一些资料的推送,有意识地逐步降低自己的"脚手架"作用,提升学生学习的主动性和责任感。

(3)评价。

课后产出"评价"。教师在课前将本学期任务评价标准以录播视频的方式发布到慕课网,供学生参考。线上学习时,教师无法像面授课堂一样实时检查、及时反馈,因此,本次课程的所有评价均为延时"检查"。课程结束后,教师会在云分享平台听学生录音并撰写评语,每周每班挑选两组进行详细点评,剩余组进行评分。研究生为大班制,每班人数约53人,分9组,每组5～6人,两班共计18组。学生互评按照对应组号在两班之间相互评分,即一班一组与二班一组互评。网课阶段学生学习任务重,学生的课后评价部分应尽量缩减,只需了解标准进行评分即可。通过互评,学生能够掌握学习流程和评分标准,学生评分的过程不仅加深了知识的巩固与内化,通过对比还能及时发现自身的问题并及时调整学习策略,达到以评促学的效果(见图3)。

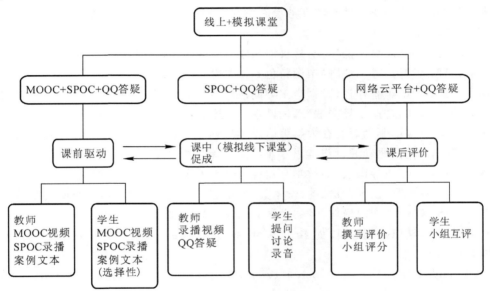

图3 产出导向法与MOOC+SPOC相结合的教学设计

4 结论

基于产出导向法的MOOC+SPOC混合式教学模式能够处理疫情期间的教学困境,指导教师组织学生进行线上混合式学习。学生在线上发生的学习行为,平台以数据报告的形式发送给教师,量化的学习进度和学习成效更能直接地反馈学生对知识点的掌握程度,方便教师及时调整教学进度。此外,疫情期间,教师在实战训练中积累了相当丰富的线上教学经验,对进一步推进信息化教学在国内的发展意义深远。尽管产出导向法中教师作为协调者和主导者,对于疫情期间缺乏引导的线上教学和学习动力不足的学生具有现实指导意义,但在具体的教学实施中仍存在几个问题:①疫情阻断了师生、生生之间的人际交互,公共课学生间不熟悉,教与学呈孤立状,因此课程开始前需多方位了解学生及其所处环境,构建师生、生生间多工具交互平台;②线上学习任务易超载,需简化任务设计,指导学生提高实施效率。由此可见,基于

POA 线上教学的新模式仍需进一步探索与实践。

参 考 文 献

曹巧珍，2017，《"产出导向法"之教师中介作用探析——以〈新一代大学英语〉第二册第四单元为例》，《中国外语教育》第 1 期。
常小玲，2017，《"产出导向法"的教材编写研究》，《现代外语》第 3 期。
康叶钦，2014，《在线教育的"后 MOOC 时代——SPOC 解析"》，《清华大学教育研究》第 1 期。
邱琳，2017，《"产出导向法"语言促成环节过程化设计研究》，《现代外语》第 3 期。
孙曙光，2017，《"师生合作评价"课堂反思性实践研究》，《现代外语》第 3 期。
唐美华，2020，《"产出导向法"与"任务型教学法"比较：英语专业精读课单元教学设计案例》，《外语教学与研究》第 1 期。
文秋芳，2018，《"产出导向法"与对外汉语教学》，《世界汉语教学》，第 3 期。
文秋芳，2017，《"产出导向法"的中国特色》，《现代外语》第 3 期。
文秋芳，2016，《"师生合作评价"："产出导向法"创设的新评价形式》，《外语界》第 5 期。
文秋芳，2015，《构建"产出导向法"理论体系》，《外语教学与研究》第 4 期。
文秋芳，2013，《输出驱动假设在大学英语教学中的应用：思考与建议》，《外语界》第 6 期。
文秋芳，2008，《输出驱动假设与英语专业技能课程改革》，《外语界》第 2 期。
张伶俐，2017，《"产出导向法"的教学有效性研究》，《现代外语》第 3 期。
张艳，2019，《基于"产出导向法"的〈学术英语〉泛在学习模式研究》，《外语电化教学》第 3 期。
张文娟，2016，《基于"产出导向法"的大学英语课堂教学实践》，《外语与外语教学》第 2 期。
张文娟，2015，《学以致用、用以促学——产出导向法"促成"环节的课堂教学尝试》，《中国外语教育》第 4 期。
Wen, Qiufang. 2016. "The production-oriented approach to teaching university students in China". *Language Teaching*. Vol. 1:1—15.
Wen, Qiufang. 2017. "The production-oriented approach: A pedagogical innovation in university English teaching in China". In *Faces of English Education: Students, Teachers, and Pedagogy*, edited by Lillian, Wong and Ken, Hyland, London & New York: Routledge.

线上线下混合教学模式中的大学英语学习者跨文化意识培养

王 方*

摘 要：本文从论述跨文化意识的定义入手，在比较分析了两种跨文化沟通模式后，提出跨文化沟通技能的培训必须是文化知识结合情景下的课堂活动来完成的，因此线上线下混合式教学模式是比较理想的跨文化类课程模式。其后，文章以暨南大学的西方礼仪课程为例，对线上线下混合式课程的规划提出了基本设计思路。

关键词：跨文化意识；线上教学；混合模式；大学英语

1 引言

"跨文化交际"（亦称"跨文化沟通"）这一概念自20世纪70年代美国学者爱德华·霍尔等人提出至今，五十多年间，国内英语教育界关于这一领域的研究蓬勃发展。胡文仲、孙有中等人早在2006年就提出要将跨文化研究融入英语教学，由此产生了一系列高质量的英语教材和理论著作。2017年教育部发布的《大学英语教学指南》分别从外语教育人文性和外语学科核心素养出发，将跨文化能力培养列为外语教育的重要目标之一。基于这一思想，国内公共英语纷纷引入跨文化类课程，以应对越来越广泛的国际交流和避免文化差异带来的各种沟通问题。然而，文化类课程依靠讲座形式的知识输入显然是不够的，教育者们提出应结合实操性练习，让学生在清晰的社会场景中感受文化的意义，更好地解读文字符号，从情感和经历中去操控和使用语言（刘丹，2015；秦丽莉、戴炜栋，2013；许国彬，2009）。自2012年开始的慕课建设为跨文化教学带来新的思路，从翻转课堂到慕课，教师们尝试将知识输入网站，实操性的练习提前布置成课堂任务让学生完成，从而开始了新的教学尝试。这种教学方法在2020年春季疫情期间显示了线上教学的优越性和未来教育发展的前瞻性。线上教育不再是可有可无的选择，而是必不可少的重要组成部分。本文旨在讨论如何将线上和面授两种方式相结合，构建混合式的教育模式，以培养学习者的跨文化意识。

2 对跨文化意识的定义和阐释

目前，为了提高学习者的跨文化沟通能力，国内外许多传播学和语言学学者提出众多跨文化沟通能力理论模型，这些模型形式不一，但各有千秋，总结起来，其目标与我国《大学英语教学指南》目标相一致，均为了提高学习者认知，加深对其他文化的理解，并将其升华为对他国价

---

* 王方：暨南大学外国语学院教师，研究生公共英语教研室主任，主要从事大学英语教学、翻译和跨文化研究。

值观的概念性认识。目前,国内外以实证做基础最新最完整的跨文化沟通模式有两种,一种是美籍传播学者陈国华等人提出的跨文化沟通三层面模式,另一种是国内学者张卫东等人提出的适应中国国情的跨文化交际能力体系。陈国华(2009)的三个层面是指认知层面(跨文化理解力)、情感层面(跨文化敏觉力)和行为层面(跨文化效力)。而张卫东和杨莉(2012)所提出的三个跨文化体系同样包括三个部分,文化意识、文化知识和交际实践。将这两种模式对比就会发现两种模式有不少共同之处,比如它们都涉及学习者的认知、情感和行为层面,具体见表1。

表1 跨文化沟通能力模式对比

跨文化模式名称	认知层面	情感层面	行为层面	训练方法
跨文化沟通能力模式（陈国华）	跨文化理解力（第一层表层文化知识,第二层对立性文化特征,第三层移情特征）	跨文化敏觉力（沟通时个人情绪或情感变化）	跨文化效力（跨文化沟通技巧）	文化通则法、文化特殊法
跨文化交际能力体系（张卫东、杨莉）	文化知识（中国与异国文化知识）	文化意识（心理和情感的综合体,跨文化交流的思想准备）	交际实践（交际的实际工具和手段）	语言交流、非语言交流、交际策略和技能

从上表可以看出,这两种模式在三个层面上有许多相似之处,都强调了文化知识、心理变化和培训方法。所不同的是对于文化理解力(cultural awareness)的定义,陈国华的模式认为,跨文化理解力涵盖的内容广泛,除了掌握本国和他国文化知识外,还需学习者有一定的移情能力,也就是能设身处地为对方考虑;张卫东的模式则将文化知识和文化意识(cultural awareness)分开单独描述,强调学习者主观的学习态度,即在沟通中是否有意识地理解对方的思维方式。虽然分类稍有不同,但很明显两位学者都认为跨文化所需理解的知识和学习者的主观动力都是跨文化沟通的重要组成部分,两个模型只是描述不同而非内容不同。笔者认为,对于在校生来说,他们中大多数人仍处于提高语言能力的阶段,无法将知识从理解力中完全分隔开,所以陈国华的跨文化理解力和张卫东的文化意识以及文化知识都是本文中教学法所要培训的目标,即跨文化意识。概括起来,就是在掌握本国和他国文化知识的前提下培养学生有意识地预防或解决沟通危机,避免文化休克(cultural shock)。文化休克表现为对于他国文化现象的理解存在误区,头脑里的刻板印象,更严重的还有民族中心主义(胡文仲,1997);即使这种问题没有出现,有些教师通过教学也发现某些学生跨文化能力的偏差,即态度走极端的现象,不是顽固不化,就是完全沉迷,盲目崇拜(王松,2016)。这种现象在本质上和文化休克一样都是跨文化理解力不足。因此,对学生进行跨文化意识的培养是十分有必要的,拥有跨文化意识可以使学生更深层次地理解他国文化知识,顺利完成跨文化沟通。

3 线上线下混合式教学模式的必要性

微课、慕课和SPOC作为线上教育的主要代表,相对于传统的知识输入型课堂而言,具有以下优点。

首先,线上教学有立体化可反复查阅的完整记录。这些教学记录保存在网站上,学生可以无限次回放,通过其中的微课理解每单元重点难点。这种做法的优点是,学习者能够按照自己的学习节奏有侧重点地复习理解,这能帮助他们形成独立的学习风格,培养其独立思考的能力,由被动学转为主动学。其次,线上资源的累积性建设。慕课一经建好,教学内容、形式、辅助练习、题库等被数字固定化,常年会以规范有体系的课堂形式呈现。教师不用再像以往一样不断重复地搭建教学框架,可以在这一基础上定期进行资源补充、技术优化,以及学习效果数据累计,节省了人力物力,是教育方法的重大进步。再次,这也是线上教学最具特色的一点:学生的学习轨迹可以量化为数据进行统计和保存。这将结束期末"一考定终身"的总结性评估方式,而是以形成性评估来判定学生的成绩,结果更客观公平,令人信服。最后,线上教育的发展也更加符合未来社会的工作和生活方式。在大数据的时代,知识更新空前加速,联合国教科文组织曾经做过调查,宣布人类的知识更新速度已经由18世纪的80~90年更新一次到如今2~3年就更新一次,学习将不再局限于在校的几年,而是随时随地终身制的。因此,这种以技术为依托的自主学习意识的培养可以满足学生今后终身学习的愿望,这也是大学教育的长期目标(黄琳琳,2016)。

线上教育有以上优势,也能弥补因大班教学与学生交流造成的种种不便(孙有中、唐锦兰、蔡静,2017),2020年春季的疫情使它瞬间成为唯一的教学形式,但这又让大多数老师措手不及。虽然网上已有大量的慕课资源可以借鉴,但单纯依靠网络进行教学暴露出许多问题,例如,网络信号不佳、连线太慢甚至掉线,还有不少教师反映互动不及时。如果学生自己不提问,教师很难发现学生的困难并及时予以帮助,而且学生之间也难以沟通互动。这些情况都说明,线上线下混合式课程模式互为补充才能为学习者提供良好的学习保障。

纵观混合式慕课的发展,其总趋势也是由单纯的线上微课转为线上和面授相配合的课程。目前最新的线上线下混合式慕课(Hybrid MOOCs)起源于2012年,是在关联主义学习理论的慕课(Connectivist MOOCs)和行为主义理论的慕课(XMOOCs)的基础上发展起来的,但较之前两种,混合式慕课将两种学习理念联合使用,既重视知识的复制,又重视知识体系的建立,同时更兼顾师生互动。在这种学习模式中,重点知识以翻转课堂呈现,课堂成为答疑、讨论并发现问题的场所,课外学生根据自身特点培养自主学习习惯。教师负责提供资料,观察学习进度,答疑并组织在线练习(黄琳琳,2016)。概括来说,混合式慕课在允许每人采取不同学习策略的前提下,更高效且有针对性地帮助个人完成学习任务,培养其自主学习能力,并使这种学习意识和习惯始终保持下去。

4 线上线下混合课程模式设计与跨文化意识的培养

跨文化意识是建立在对本国文化知识理解的基础上对他国文化价值观的客观分析,也是学习者从主观角度上对他国文化的主动思考并尝试跨越文化障碍的思想动力。跨文化意识既包含本国和他国的文化知识,同时也包含一种思维方式,一个学习过程。陈国华(2009)提出文化通则法和文化特殊法的教育方式,例如文化同化案件,角色扮演、区域研究和经验学习法等。这类课堂活动具有一个共性,都是采取任务型教学,创造一种环境或描绘一种场景,让学生在非常具体的社会生活里通过亲身实践来培养自身的思维,提高跨文化沟通的意识。在接下来的内容中,笔者将以自己任教的暨南大学跨文化类课程为具体案例引入课程设计。

暨南大学是中国最大的华侨大学,每年招收来自一百多个国家、地区的华侨和海外学生。作为国内最著名的"侨校",暨南大学站在培养海外学生的第一线,跨文化沟通策略和技能培训是其大学外语教育不可或缺的重要组成部分。

西方礼仪课是我校自2012年开始设立的跨文化类课程的代表,由于该课程兼具向学生介绍国际礼仪知识和提高学生文化理解力的特点,所以它深受本科各年级学生的喜爱。课程内容涵盖了现代西方社会各方面的礼仪原则,内容大致有见面礼仪、着装礼仪、电子通信礼仪、餐饮礼仪、面试礼仪、会议礼仪、国际礼仪和特殊场景礼仪等,配套还有原版西方生活案例。

西方礼仪课程内容有如下特点。①中西文化对比。在长期的授课过程中,教师们发现,由于我国幅员辽阔,地区差异明显,学生对国内通用的传统礼仪知识概念尚且比较模糊,一味学习西方知识会使知识的理解显得苍白、空洞,使用起来也无法做到灵活机动,随机应变。因此,课程内融入了部分中华传统礼仪,比如《论语》和《仪礼》的翻译片段,使课程同时具有向海外传播中华文化和显示民族凝聚力的社会意义。②学习任务类型多样。学习任务主要以任务型项目为导向,同时兼具探究式的学习方式。以下有具体方法的详细介绍,这里不再赘述。

依托以上的教学经验,混合式教学模式(见图1)的具体规划应涵盖以下几点。

第一,线上教学内容(占总课程的2/3):SPOC+教师个性化资源导入。教师可依托中国大学慕课的精品课程开设校内SPOC,可选课程有哈尔滨工业大学的国际交流英语课或厦门大学的《论语》英译鉴赏课,在线上每章节中教师根据学生学习情况再加入课堂习题或讨论。通过对传统文化经典《论语》《仪礼》中相关篇章或名句的欣赏和翻译,学生获得了跨文化意识中的文化知识,体会西方文化差异,从而加深对他国文化的理解,提高跨文化沟通的意识。除了SPOC,教师也可利用超星学习通或Blackboard平台,它们同样可以分章节发布学习内容。教师还可通过录屏的方式自制微课,进行重点问题讲解。另外平台

图1 混合式教学模式

还可安排全班或小组内进行论坛讨论。以上的平台都有记录学生学习情况和测验成绩的功能,以便期末形成性评估使用。

第二,线下教学内容(占总课程的1/3):身临其境的体验方式。面授课程可在开始前两周布置教学任务,比如翻译对比、情景再现、角色扮演、案例分析、交换身份、报告展示、校内调研、与知名企业家座谈等,利用交际法教学和任务驱动型教学,使学生形象地理解文化差异之所在,保持学习过程从线下到线上的动态延续,使学生将实际场景融会贯通,形成固定的跨文化意识(许国彬,2009)。由于暨南大学本科学生背景多元化,其中有国内的应届毕业生,有海外的应届华侨毕业生,更有工作数年"回炉教育"的港澳台往届毕业生,还有众多母语非中文的海外学生等,师生和生生之间的合作交流都会因成长和文化背景擦出不同的火花,单是对学习活动的反思与讨论就是很好的跨文化意识培训了。

第三,教师反馈需及时,同学之间的交流更频繁。教师每次看过作业或测试后可根据学生的掌握情况在线进行反馈,对个别学习有困难的学生还要给予额外关注。这样做,一来可以督

促学生完成学习任务,二来也可及时处理学习中的问题。同学之间的相互沟通由于有了软件也变得快捷、容易和丰富许多,学习小组的团队协作更体现了集思广益的作用(孙有中、唐锦兰、蔡静,2017)。

第四,确定形成性的评估方式。教师通过各类软件的统计结果整合学期成绩,而不是考勤加卷面考试的结果式评估。这种方式是对学习过程的记录,更准确快捷,结果更客观。

5 结语

跨文化沟通和线上线下混合式教育模式相对于外语教学来说都是比较新颖的,但一出现就生机勃勃,这与当前国际交流增多、电子技术飞速发展是分不开的。二十一世纪以来,无论是人的观念还是技术革新都以前所未有的崭新面貌登上舞台,社会生活的方方面面也随之发生着极大变化。相对而言,不变的是源远流长的各国传统文化和基本语言知识,然而如何以更包容的心态和更广阔的心胸来分析和理解他国文化是英语教育者的工作目标之一。在这样一个离开了智能手机和电脑几乎寸步难行的时代,教学生利用这些科技优势为学习服务,而非沉溺于科技本身带来的短期愉悦感也是教育者需要反复思考并实践的。在全球英语水平逐年提高的时代,当字词句的教学不再成为大学英语最核心的教学内容之时,线上教育将承担基础知识输入的任务,而在混合式教学中,线上与线下的比例如何分配,怎样更好地分配学习任务、检查学生的完成情况,以及如何培养更适合个体的自主学习风格应是未来英语教育工作者继续关注的一系列问题。

参 考 文 献

陈国华,2009,《跨文化交际学》,华东师范大学出版社。
黄林林,2017,《MOOCs 资源与大学英语课程教学:理论·技术·实践》,外语教学与研究出版社。
胡文仲,1999,《跨文化交际学概论》,外语教学与研究出版社。
刘丹,2015,《跨文化交际能力构念与培养研究——跨文化、跨文本、跨主体视角》,《外语学刊》第 6 期。
秦丽莉、戴炜栋,2013,《以培养"多元文化"意识为导向的跨文化交际学课程研究》,《外语电化教学》总第 154 期。
孙有中、唐锦兰、蔡静,2017,《英语专业人文通识教育混合教学模式研究》,《外语电化教学》总第 173 期。
许国彬,2009,《大学生跨文化学习能力与文化忧患意识的培养》,《外语与外语教学》第 12 期。
王松、刘长远,2016,《外语学习者的跨文化意识培养》,《外语学刊》第 5 期。
张卫东、杨莉,2012,《跨文化交际能力体系的构建——基于外语教育视角和实证研究方法》,《外语界》第 2 期。

利用雨课堂进行研究生公共英语课教学的优势与弊端

张 放[*]

摘 要:近几年来,各种借助网络开展的课堂教学新模式在高校中开始被广泛应用,其中雨课堂因其设计灵活、便于操作的特点受到了很多教师的欢迎。雨课堂教学模式的优势在于其将微信和幻灯片相结合,教师和学生双方只需要携带有微信的手机和一个安装雨课堂插件的电脑,便可开展教与学的活动。通过雨课堂模式,教师可以将课前—课上—课后的每一个环节相串合,学生通过课前预习和课后作业练习,可以巩固和强化课上的学习效果。然而,在研究生公共英语课的实际教学中,雨课堂模式的弊端也得以暴露,其根本问题在于:学生年龄群和英语课上课形式的特点,学生在课堂上使用手机存在较大的不可控性;雨课堂有灵活多样的授课方式,学生的注意力反而会被雨课堂的有些功能所干扰;与面对面的口头交流方式相比,雨课堂的模式在一定程度上剥夺了教师与学生的直接互动,从而减少了语言学习的乐趣和效率。

关键词:雨课堂;优势灵活;弊端不可控性;干扰性

1 引言

近些年,由于网络和智能手机的高速发展与应用,大学课堂已经不再拘泥于传统课堂模式,各类基于新媒介的翻转课堂、慕课、微课等模式席卷而来(胡杰辉,2014),并被越来越多的大学教师接受和喜爱。其中,由清华大学与学堂在线共同开发的"雨课堂"智慧教学工具因其明显的优势受到了广泛的推崇。

2 雨课堂的优势

雨课堂是一种利用网络、幻灯片课件和微信平台进行教学的智慧课堂工具。其特点和优势在于:利用微信推送教学幻灯片,因此雨课堂对课堂的硬件设施要求非常简单——只需要一台连接互联网的电脑,学生们和老师每人一部智能手机;课堂互动随时随地。开启雨课堂后,教师可以建立网上班级,学生们除了可以在线上和老师进行课堂的教与学互动,学生们也可以在课前完成老师在网上推送的预习题,在课后完成老师布置的课后作业与练习,参与网上的交流讨论。使用雨课堂,教师也可以将带有视频、习题、语音的课件推送到学生手机,课堂上学生可以实时答题,弹幕互动,这在一定程度上解决了师生之间缺乏交流这一传统课堂存在的问题(多依丽,2017)。这就意味着,雨课堂可以使课堂从教室里延展到教室外,上课时间得到弹性延长,教师与学生可以一直保持联系,教师可以随时检查学生的作业完成情况。总之,这种课

---

[*] 张放:西北工业大学外国语学院教师,主讲研究生公共英语读写和听说等课程。

前预习—课堂教学—课后复习相串合的形式可以使得教与学的活动永不下线(李鹏,2018)。

得益于这一优势,雨课堂解决了一些大学传统的教学模式历年来积攒的弊病。这些大学教学模式一直无法规避的问题主要集中在:学科课时少,但课程任务重,教学内容多;教师少,学生多,教师与学生配比严重不协调,因此师生双方课堂无互动,缺乏交流(姚洁,2017);由于教学内容繁杂,师生人数配比失衡,教师难以操作量化与考核。而雨课堂的使用使教学时间从课堂里延续到课堂外,教师可以成为教学的组织者与参与者,他们不仅可以在课上讲授内容,还可以在课下与学生广泛互动,同时可以利用灵活的网上教学模式对学生进行考核与测评,使学习时间得以科学化利用,学习效率得以提升。

3 雨课堂的弊端

雨课堂那些明显的优势在大学非英语专业研究生的英语课堂上并不能得以充分发挥。确切地说,在英语课堂上,这些优势恰恰变成了劣势。换言之,当雨课堂被应用于大学研究生英语教学中,其特点带来了相应的弊端,影响了教学效果,带来了更多问题,主要的弊端体现在以下几个方面。

3.1 不可控性

雨课堂之所以被广泛宣传和利用,一个主要原因在于雨课堂方便易用,节约成本。因为只需要PPT的插件和微信,所以教师和学生只要携带电脑和手机就可以创建雨课堂教学环境。但是,对于手机成为课堂活动的必备工具,很多教学工作者仍然持有不同的态度。作为一个工作在教学一线的教师,笔者就雨课堂应用于大学研究生英语课进行了近距离的观察和研究,发现利用手机进行研究生英语课程教学具有较大的不可控性。首先,手机的不可控性与操作手机的人有关。在大学研究生英语课堂上,学生大多是处于22~24岁年龄段的研究生,对于他们来说,手机本身就是一个不可或缺的生活必需品,无论是科研学习还是生活琐事,这群年轻人几乎利用手机上的各种软件打理自己的一切。而且,大多数处于这个年龄段的大学生休闲的重要方式就是玩手机,这既耗时又耗费精力。当教学活动也使用手机完成,学生们在进入雨课堂的同时,也可以同步利用手机做着自己的各种事情,而教师对此并不知情。作为课堂的建立者和主持者,教师使用雨课堂的点名功能只能看到学生是否在网上班级群里,而并不知晓学生的手机实际使用情况。要利用雨课堂的主功能,教师必须在课上推送教学幻灯片和教授课程,并无多余精力——核查每个学生是否在与教师同步学习。其次,相较于研究生的其他专业课,英语课上使用雨课堂的不可控性更明显,主要原因在于研究生的专业课程内容复杂、信息量大,老师的教授内容饱满,有时上课的时间非常紧张,学生根本没有一点空隙去开小差或者用手机做其他事情。相较之下,有的英语课的知识点不多,幻灯片相对简洁而有指示性,还给学生留有适当的思考缓冲时间。如果教师受雨课堂模式所限,不停发送教学课件,除了使得与学生交流时间缩减,也间接给学生创造了机会以利用手机去打开其他平台做和学习无关的私事。

3.2 干扰性

快捷的课上测验、弹幕、投稿、红包、点名、发题、拍照、语音、全景教学数据分析,这些都是在雨课堂上可以进行的教学活动,也是雨课堂最吸引人的亮点。对于其他科目教学,尤其是教学内容多、课时少的科目,充分利用雨课堂的这些优势可以延长学习时间,提高课堂效率,增加课堂趣味性,巩固学习效果。但是,外语语言教学与其他专业课教学不同。幻灯片在英语课上不是主角,主角是课堂的参与者——学生。老师考虑更多的是自己的课堂设计能否吸引学生去进行语言能力的实操。因此,一个合格的、良性的英语课堂需要学生积极地参与,需要学生与教师直面互动。如果在课堂上利用雨课堂发红包、投弹幕,课堂的确呈现出多样性和趣味性,但是也严重影响了学生的专注力,削减了课堂的有效学习时间,使得学生对于英语课堂本身的关注转移到对雨课堂功能的关注。除了对学生的专注力造成干扰,雨课堂还会分散教师的注意力。因为英语课堂的特殊性,英语教师必须在课堂上组织开展各种有趣的练习和活动,但是一旦使用雨课堂,教师必须分配一定量的课堂时间和个人精力去操作微信和电脑,也就是说,教师上课的状态很有可能是既要关注课件的推送,也要查看微信上与学生的互动,还要同时兼顾在真实课堂上的教学与交流。因此,与很多并不需要太多师生互动且教学知识点多的学科相比,在英语课上使用雨课堂对老师和学生都有不少干扰。

3.3 影响语言教学效果

雨课堂的灵活性使我们发现了课堂已不再是传统意义上的课堂,它突破了空间局限,变成了可以一直进行下去、永不下线的网上课堂。然而,即便是永不下线,这种模式也不适合于所有学科教学。众所周知,任何外语语言的学习都需要大量的操练,听说读写四个基本能力相辅相成,缺一不可。而对于国内很多非英语专业的研究生来说,他们最大的问题是在考研之前有两年的英语学习空档期,由于学校不作要求,大多数学生觉得不上英语课也无所谓,也没必要提升自己的英语能力,因此他们的英语口语和听力能力较差,有些学生甚至无法开口进行日常沟通,更不要说参加国外的学术会议或者用英文发言了。因此适合这些学生的英语课堂模式是:教师和学生是平等的主体,教师的角色在于引领学生、鼓励学生,让他们放下不安,敢于张口,面对面纠正学生的英语发音,积极创造机会让学生在课堂用英语对话,用英语进行口头报告、演讲、辩论等形式灵活的口语活动。只有在课堂上有效地操练并进行面对面互动,教师才会发现问题,学生才能意识到问题,只有在课堂上进行语言有声输出,学生才会增加说英语、用英语的信心,刺激他们利用课下时间、利用网络优质听说资源进行自我学习与训练。听说能力提高了,学生们才有自信和更扎实的基础能力去阅读专业文献,写出高水平的英文论文,进行高规格的英语学术交流,他们的科研能力和工作能力也提高了。另外,因为雨课堂的延时功能,英语口语作业在课后用语音发送并不能保证学生的学习效果,实际可能出现的情况是:学生可以从网络下载或是提前写好答案,边读边用语音录音,然后再发送。这样的结果是,口语练习的设置并没有达到预期效果,学生的口语能力不会得到提高。

4 结语

无线网络和智能手机是影响这个时代的伟大技术和产品,在未来,它们带给人类社会的变革将无法想象。但是对于大学教育来说,是否可以完全利用类似雨课堂的新方法去重新设计教学、重新改变课堂模式,仍然有待商讨。本文通过对雨课堂在大学研究生英语课堂中的应用研究,试图发现新技术应用于教学后产生的问题。将手机微信结合幻灯片来创造不下线的网上课堂,确实为大学教育注入了新的活力(周凤新,2018)。但是,在肯定优点的同时,希望教育者们也能正视其弊端,明确各个学科的特点,多多思考和探究在雨课堂使用过程中,教师应如何更好地发挥人的主观能动性,真正调动学生学习的积极性,优化教学效果,制订更人性化、更高效的教学方式,从而为高校英语和高校教育的可持续发展添砖加瓦。

参 考 文 献

多依丽、付晓岩、海军,2017,《"雨课堂"与传统教学模式的比较研究》,《大学教育》第 12 期。
胡杰辉、伍忠杰,2014,《基于 MOOC 的大学英语翻转课堂教学模式研究》,《外语电化教学》总第 160 期。
李鹏、易淑明、郑晓妮等,2018,《"雨课堂"在课前、课中、课后"三段式导学"中的应用效果评价》,《护理研究》第 4 期。
姚洁、王伟力,2017,《微信雨课堂混合学习模式应用于高校教学的实证研究》,《高教探索》第 9 期。
张彦青,2015,《基于网络资源平台的英语翻转课堂教学模式探讨》,《现代教育化》第 1 期。
周凤新、王兴辉,2018,《基于雨课堂智慧教学环境的课堂教学初探》,《中国教育技术装备》第 1 期。

口译教学中专题训练和技能训练对比及融合

王 茜[*]

摘 要:目前高等院校英语或翻译专业开设的口译课程多以专题训练或技能训练的教学模式授课,本文对以上两种口译教学模式进行对比,分析两种模式在口译人才培养上的优势和缺陷,以期对口译教学提供有益参考。

关键词:口译;专题训练;技能训练

持续扩大和发展的口译市场对口译人才的数量和质量提出了更高的要求,为实现市场和人才培养的双赢,高校纷纷在翻译专业、英语专业教学中开设口译课程。然而相对于传统的英语语言教学和已经发展相对成熟的笔译教学,口译教学仍然在实践中摸索前行。目前,国内高校的口译教学多采用专题训练或技能训练的教学模式,但这两种模式距离培养出市场满意的合格口译人才还有一定的距离(鲍川运,2004)。

口译教学的三个要素是教师、教材和学生,三者缺一不可(鲍川运,2004)。本文将从以上三个角度分析对比口译教学中的专题训练和技能训练。

专题训练是指口译的教学内容按专题划分,比如经济专题、法律专题、环保专题、旅游专题等。按专题划分的口译教学更偏向于专题知识、专题术语以及在交际能力培养的基础上进行口译训练。技能训练则是以口译活动中涉及的能力训练为主,比如听力理解能力训练、信息处理能力训练、短时记忆能力训练、笔记能力以及口译表达能力训练,以口译技能培训为主而非围绕口译训练的文本和话题。

专题训练模式对教师和学生的知识广度甚至深度都有很高的要求。比如在贸易专题口译中,涉及商业谈判、贸易术语甚至贸易规则的口译,这些内容需要教师和学生在教学和学习前进行相关资料的搜集、阅读、理解和记忆。这一部分的工作将助力课堂的口译训练,专业知识和信息将在口译活动的听力理解环节被激活,帮助译员理解原文。同时,搜索专题相关资料的能力虽不是口译活动最直接相关的能力,却也是培养口译员职业素养的重要内容之一。专题训练模式下,教师在课前扮演着引导者的角色,引导学生在正确的方向和合理的范围内进行资料的搜集和整理。比如课堂上要进行贸易专题的口译,但贸易是个相当宽泛的话题,教师应该根据原文指定学生搜集资料的方向和内容,如原文关键词有香港、GATT(General Agreement on Tariffs and Trade,关税暨贸易总协定)、贸易自由等,则应根据关键词搜集相关资料,了解专业词汇的表达以及专业词汇的内涵;比如风投专题的口译,可能译员会听到"天使投资""种子轮"等专业词汇,除了学习这些专业词汇的翻译,也要了解什么是"天使投资",什么是"种子轮"。在课堂上,教师的主要作用是组织口译训练、点评学生的口译表现。当然,专题训练并非

---

[*] 王茜:西安明德理工学院语言文化传播学院教师,主讲英语高级口译、英语精读、雅思口语等课程。

完全摒弃技能训练只专注口译话题，而是侧重话题，在话题中培养口译能力。

同理，技能训练模式也不可能脱离文本，而是在课堂上侧重于技能训练，不执着于某一专题下文本的口译，课堂上所训练的文本涵盖各种话题，所有的文本只为服务于口译某项技能的训练。事实上，口译所需要的能力在其他语言学习课程中都有涉及，比如听力理解能力在英语听力课上会得到锻炼，信息分类、发现逻辑关联的能力在英语阅读课上能得到提高。教授口译课程的教师则需要将语言学习技能融入口译技能训练。Gile(2011)提出的"认知负荷模型"认为，在口译活动中，口译员要将有限的注意力分配在听力、理解、记忆和产出等多个同时发生的任务中，若口译所需的精力超过了译员的精力总和，口译的质量就会下降。解决注意力分配的问题，就需要提高译员信息处理的能力。基于此，技能训练模式下的口译教学内容要放在口译所需各项技能的培养上。教师的教学目标即可拆分为多个子目标，如判断讲话人意图的能力、发现逻辑关联的能力、脑记能力、笔记能力和脱型达意能力等。课堂教学也是根据子目标设计的，而非直接的口译训练。

专题训练的口译教材按专题编写，比较权威的有全国翻译资格考试官方教材《英语口译实务》以及林超伦口译教材《实战口译》。此类教材通常用很少的篇幅对口译做一个基础介绍或对专题词汇和句子进行讲解，其余部分为不同专题下的口译训练原文和译文。以《英语口译实务》为例，教材按照专题进行单元划分，每个专题下分为对话口译、中译英和英译中篇章口译各一篇。以笔者之见，此教材本质上是口译原文和参考译文的堆砌，对口译涉及的技能训练并没有给出教学指导。林超伦的《实战口译》稍有不同，此教材总体上按照专题划分，但每个专题下除原文、译文外，分段落展示了林超伦的实战笔记，并对笔记进行了分析讲解。笔记是口译的重要技能之一，《实战口译》则是在专题训练中强调了这一技能的训练。然而口译除了笔记技能外，还涉及其他非常重要的技能，以专题训练为主的教材在技能训练上所给予的篇幅实在是太少了，但专题训练的教材亦有其优势。口译是一门实战性很强的课程，所涉及的话题确实也是方方面面的，学生在口译学习时练习的话题越全面，越能够了解自己在各个话题口译实战中面临的问题和解决方案，也越能够发现自己擅长或不擅长的口译话题，进而加强某一话题的训练。题海战术有其优势，尤其是那些要参加口译资格考试的学生是无法逃避专题训练的。

现实情况是，采用技能训练模式的口译教材非常缺乏，即使有些教材的初衷是按照口译能力分配进行编写，最后仍无法避免变成口译原文、译文的堆积，关于技能方面的阐述、训练方法和材料所占篇幅同样偏少，导致教材流于技能训练的形式，内核仍围绕口译文本。

基于口译课程的实战性质，该课程教材能否脱离传统纸质教材的形式而采用电子教材？市场上口译活动多为会议口译的形式，若能保留、收集、组织和编排真实的口译活动的视频文件，将其融于口译教材，并与时俱进，推陈出新，保证教材资源的稳步更新，将极大地帮助高校口译教学的发展和口译人才的培养。但电子教材恐涉及会议各方机密和利益，这一想法实现起来还需要多方努力。

英语或翻译专业学习口译的学生本身双语能力就参差不齐，专题口译训练对于平时多听、多看、多积累，语言水平比较高的学生而言是相对有优势的训练模式，这类学生一般只需对口译理论或技巧进行短时学习就能过渡到专题集训，通过对各类话题进行口译训练，这些学生的口译水平就能在练习中大幅提升。但对于语言水平比较差的学生而言，他们需要花更多的时间进行技能训练，在口译各项子能力达到一定水平才能顺利地进行口译训练。这并不意味着子能力训练与口译训练完全割裂，而应在口译训练中侧重于各项能力训练，二者是融合的。在教学实践中,一个班级的学生水平是有高有低的,将主题训练与技能训练融合起来,在口译教学中保持平衡,是实现教学效果最大化的途径。

高校口译教学面临种种困难,而能否培养出具备口译职业道德和素养的、受市场欢迎的口译人才这一问题显得格外严峻。口译教学无论是主题训练还是技能训练模式都应秉着因材施教的原则,找到适合学生的教学内容和方法,致力于培养出应用型口译人才。

参 考 文 献

鲍川运,2004,《大学本科口译教学的定位及教学》,《中国翻译》第 5 期。

Gile, D. 2011. *Basic Concepts and Models for Interpreter and Translator Training*. Shanghai: Shanghai Foreign Language Education Press.

过程教学法在德语写作课堂的运用

陈 婧[*]

摘 要：目前在我国高校德语教学中，有的教师在教学中只鼓励学生背诵常用句型和例文，导致学生缺乏自由创作的意识和热情。德语教师可以在教学的过程中运用过程教学法加强对学生写作思路的指导，关注作文形成的整体过程，从而真正提升学生的思维能力和写作水平。

关键词：过程教学法；德语写作；教学模式改革

目前的各类德语专业考试在写作考查方面越来越灵活，更加强调学生对知识的熟练运用。只靠死记硬背的篇章写作方法非常不受欢迎，学生得分极低，改革势在必行。在针对大学德语本科教学方法的探索过程中，笔者发现过程教学法更适合当下的写作教学。过程教学法强调交际的过程，将写作的过程表述为一种群体间的交际活动，主要对象就是学生和教师之间的交际，不能看作学生单方面的行动。教师应长期关注学生的写作过程，以提高学生的写作能力和思维能力为目标。教师的指导需要贯穿整个写作过程，直至最后成文（严若芳、欧光安，2018）。

1 德语写作课程存在的问题

受中学英语教学的影响，德语写作课堂教学主要使用结果教学法，过分重视结果，轻视过程。教师习惯于针对不同篇章的特点给出大量的例文、例句，或者限定特定的写作顺序，并不鼓励学生在写作中形成自己的思路，探索新的写作模式，形成了新一代的"八股文"。由于教师在教学过程中普遍强调写作技能的训练和速成，整个写作过程都是在教师的支配下完成的，学生为了得分则死记硬背、生搬硬套，缺乏创作的意识，写作就成了机械的输入和输出。

传统教学中，教师对学生作文的评改方式十分单一。教师对写作所持的陈旧观念和传统做法导致写作教学体系迟迟不能更新。鉴于德语语法结构之间具有互相制衡的特点，比如学生动词用错可能影响之后的动词配价，主被动态选错可能涉及主语、宾语的选择和相对应形容词的词尾，等等，这就导致教师在学生写作成文后进行批改的重点往往放在语法、拼写、配价等的错误上。虽然花费了大量的精力，却难免忽视了实际上最应重视的文章的实质内容（王凤，2010）。这也导致学生不注重内容框架的构建，拘泥于小的语法点而忽视全局。而且由于批改过程单向化，学生有时并不能完全理解教师的用意，教师也很难给出全部的建议方案，从而大大影响教学效果。久而久之，学生不愿意在写作前进行大量思考，反而愿意寻找相对固定的写作模式和顺序，影响了写作的积极性。最终导致学生在考试之前热衷于"押题"，背诵特定的作文模板或常用句型，缺乏深入的思考。

---

[*] 陈婧：西安明德理工学院语言文化传播学院副教授，主讲基础德语、德语阅读、德语报刊阅读等课程。

2 改革的方向

综上所述,改革德语写作课程的教学方法和考核模式十分必要。笔者认为应该从以下几个方面着手改革。

(1)为切实提高学生德语基础写作教学的效果,真正培养学生的写作能力,首先要推动学生主动学习写作的相关概念和做法,增加他们的兴趣,让学生真正参与到写作中去。从日常的教学活动可以看出,大部分大学生刚接触德语,他们对于德语的学习如同儿童学语,是一个吸收、模仿、再创造的过程。他们需要学习大量的语法结构,给自己打下坚实的语言功底,然后在不断模仿的过程中学会对于语言的运用,从而熟练运用各种写作技巧。而这一路布满艰辛,没有强大的内驱力很难坚持下去。

(2)教师应更新写作教学观念,优化写作教学过程,结合学生平时习作成绩、课堂表现等因素给出学生课程总评成绩,促进学生持续且有效地学习。教师需要从根本上认识到,最能提升学生写作水平的办法是允许学生自我创作,教师只是在他们创作的过程中给予引导,而不是填鸭式的灌输。教师的态度转变可以提升学生对于写作的积极性。

(3)教师要针对学生写作方面的错误进行分析和改正,在分析的过程中帮助学生进行一部分的自我改正。教师的指导要贯穿始终,在学生构思、写提纲、写初稿和修改等各个写作环节中帮助他们发现、分析和解决问题。在最终对成文进行批改的过程中要保证有效批改,即改正的内容要让学生充分理解,并且在可能的情况下给出更好的表达方式。

(4)提倡学生交电子版作业。有些学生在写作过程中没有预留足够的空间,有时教师的批注无法落笔或太多的批注会显得混乱,针对这一点,可以使用电子设备,让学生提交电子版的作文,从而可以更方便地增加批注,避免混乱。同时可以更好地保留写作数据,总结多数学生写作中可能的易错点,为下一届学生增加语料库资料。

(5)教师也应该与时俱进,熟练运用各类网络平台与学生进行联系,在课时不足或人数过多的情况下,可为学生提供在线咨询。教师通过网络也可在沟通的过程中提示学生句型或表达的其他方式,进而更好地指导学生进行写作。按照以往的教学模式,教师很难全面甚至正确地理解学生在写作中想要表达的意思,缺少面对面的交流,只是简单地批改作业。有时因为作业中语法方面的错误,忽视了学生整体或局部的想法,如果双方没有及时沟通,这些就有可能会被忽视。而这些学生表达得不太熟练的部分却恰恰是他们最需要得到教师指导、纠正的部分。

3 具体的设计和评价方式

笔者在写作教学活动中多次尝试运用过程教学法,尽力做到在讲授的过程中增加对学生的指导,增加互动环节,引导学生关注语篇的布局,期望可以增加学生写作的积极性和思维的灵活性,具体行动总结为以下几个方面。

(1)引入主题。教师组织学生针对某一写作主题进行讨论,可能包括但并不限于:为什么我们需要学习此类写作主题,此类文章在汉语中有什么特点,德语的写作特点和汉语的是否相同,德语此类文章写作主要会运用到哪些语法,等等。之后再给出一定量的固定搭配,例如议论文的开篇与结语、信件的格式、图表描述的固定句型等。从而改变以往的教学模式：教师针对写作主题直接给出若干篇例文和大量固定搭配，让学生选取其中一项用于自己的作文，不支持学生创新。

（2）写前准备。教师在课堂伊始就通过小组讨论、头脑风暴等方式引入所需讲述的题目，该过程中教师可以将以往教学中学生易犯的语法和语言错误展示出来，提示学生注意关注，然后可以让学生分组讨论提纲。为了激发学生的写作兴趣，教师可以设计多个问题场景，尽最大可能鼓励学生独立思考，激发其自我表达的欲望，从而使其所写的东西有意义，而不是简单的语言的堆砌。

（3）限时拟定草稿。在这个阶段，要求学生在限定时间内将所思所想草拟成稿。教师在这一阶段要鼓励学生尽量放开写，重视思维的过程和特点，不必过多思考语言、语法；此时教师可以关注部分学生，主动提出意见和建议，或鼓励学生提问，从而对班级所有学生起到启发作用，发现问题，随时解决。

（4）小组讨论。完成草稿后，教师将学生按照数量分成若干小组，由学生选取小组长，小组长负责组织组员进行商讨。在这一阶段，鼓励学生将讨论的重点放在内容结构上，例如文章的引言、论证、结语等，不要拘泥于对单词拼写或句子结构的讨论，从而让学生在源头上对文章整体有所把握。在这一过程中教师可以旁观或适当参与，但是要保证讨论的主体还是学生。

（5）初稿修改。在小组讨论之后，每位学生对于自己的文章一般会有新的认识，可以由此对第一稿内容加以修改。在这个环节，教师传授必要的修改策略，例如对以往学生在写作此类作文时易错的知识点加以提醒。成文之后要求学生自己检查语法、拼写等错误，要求其用红笔标示。

（6）互动分析及评价考核。教师在浏览之后，从数据库中提取部分典型的学生文本，在课堂上进行展示，组织讨论。一方面，教师在指导学生讨论的过程中，通过对学生反应的观察，针对部分学生不理解的内容要进行重点讲解；另一方面，鼓励学生发现并反思所看例文的优点和不足，让全体学生就典型语法或结构问题进行分析，最后教师给出指导性的建议。学生对优秀习作的思路和特色表达有了深刻印象，也为下一次的错误互动分析奠定基础。经过几次的练习，可以让学生在写作过程中形成自我质疑、自我改正的良好习惯。

（7）形成终稿数据库。教师收取学生终稿电子版，进行电子批改，形成有针对性的批注、评分和评语，并组建相应题材的学生终稿数据库，总结学生易犯的错误。学生语言错误不是学生不够努力的表现，反而是促进师生相互理解必不可少的环节（施益萍，2009）。教师与学生的思路常常相左，有时教师没见过特定的错误就根本不会想到学生还可以从某个角度思考问题，向学生展示以前学生易犯的错误也可以让学生自己从另一个角度更好地理解语法知识点。教师对学生的错误进行总结，可以在一定时间内更好地提升教师的教学水平，从而提高学生的写作水平。

（8）课后讨论。针对大部分院校德语写作课课时有限的现状，开辟课后"第二课堂"，让上课有问题但没有来得及提问的同学可以在课后接受教师的辅导，可以和教师就某一问题进行深入讨论。这样一方面可以解决学生当下的问题，另一方面让教师能够多接触新的想法，在以后的授课过程中可以多方位地针对主题进行讲解。教师在课后批改的过程中如果遇到问题也可以联系学生，有些看起来几乎不能理解的句子有时是因为学生自己的思路不清，有时是学生的德语水平不足以支撑其复杂的母语思维，这些也都是学生最需要被指导的地方。这类学生在多次与老师沟通、认清自己的不足之后,写作水平通常都会有质的提升。

通过这一教学模式的改革,教师能针对学生的实际情况因材施教,更加全面客观地对学生进行考核评价。而教师思路的这一转变也会引导学生真正关注写作的本质,而不是做一个辞藻的堆砌者。

不可否认,在过去的写作教学环节中,结果教学法起到了不可或缺的作用。但是采用结果教学法的弊端就是使整个教学过程完全受控于教师,作文的修改就是教师的单向行为,学生缺乏创作的自由和兴趣,导致写作过程枯燥乏味,学生不再愿意多思考,而思维深度是一篇好的作文必不可少的要点。结果性和过程性教学手法相结合,能有效地激发学生学习兴趣,使学生的信息检索能力、文本解读能力、自由表达能力、逻辑思维和批判思维均能得到更好的锻炼,最终提高其基础写作能力,在今后的考试、工作、生活中更好地运用所学。而教师也可以从多个角度更深入地了解学生的思路,精确地抓住学生的易错点,这将为后续的教学提供重要的参考。

参 考 文 献

王凤,2010,《谈基础德语写作课的教学改革——结果教学法和过程教学法分析》,《吉林华侨外国语学院学报》第1期。

严若芳、欧光安,2018,《过程教学法在大学英语写作教学中的应用研究》,《教育理论与实践》第6期。

施益萍,2009,《中国德语专业基础阶段学生作文错误分析》,硕士学位论文,浙江大学。

五、外语语言与教学研究

基于参数参照模式的口译质量及译员能力测评研究

孙 荧[*]

摘 要：随着全球化进程及我国"一带一路"倡议的不断深入，市场对口译人员的需求越来越大，而符合市场要求的高质量口译人员的缺口也越来越大。翻译质量评估研究一直是翻译研究的核心内容之一，但是针对口译质量评估的研究有限。本文基于威廉姆斯提出的参数参照模式，通过学术调研和问卷调查法对口译译文质量及议员能力中的指标进行量化研究，并在此基础上总结出对口译质量和译员能力影响较大的指标，从而制订出一套有实际意义的口译质量测评方法，提出口译人员能力提升侧重点。该研究旨在有效地指导今后的口译人员培训和技能评估的开展。

关键词：口译；质量；评估；测评

1 引言

随着全球化进程及我国"一带一路"倡议的不断深入，市场对口译人员的需求越来越大，而符合市场要求的高水平口译人员的缺口也越来越大。那么究竟何为高水平译员？何为高质量口译译文？翻译质量测评研究一直是翻译研究的核心内容之一，但是针对口译质量及译员能力的测评研究较为有限。

译界的领军人物霍斯把西方翻译质量评估模式分为四大流派：心灵主义、反应主义、语篇主义及功能－语用主义，而威廉姆斯在此基础上把翻译质量评估分为两大类：原则参照模式及参数参照模式。原则参照模式是在翻译质量评估的宏观层面上制订纲领性原则作为译文的评价标准；参数参照模式是评估人预先设计出一组最相关参数，赋予各个参数权重，然后以参数为参照，将原文与译文进行对比，最后对译文做出评价或定级。中西方翻译质量评估模式多以原则参照模式为主，但是由于各流派的理论切入点不同，让各流派评估原则难以整合，评估标准难以统一。而参数参照模式因更能客观地衡量翻译质量，使之成为国际上较为认可的评估模式，如加拿大翻译局研发的"加拿大语言质量测评体系"，2000年美国工程协会研发的"J2450翻译质量标准"等。

本文基于威廉姆斯参数参照模式，在对现有研究成果汇总的基础上，通过学术调研和问卷调查进行了口译工作中涉及的指标的量化研究，从口译译文及译员能力两个方面对口译进行测评研究，并在两个量化研究的基础上，总结出对口译质量和译员培训影响较大的指标，制定出一套有实际意义的口译质量测评评分标准，提出口译人员能力测评方法以及口译人员能力提升侧重点。该研究成果能够有效地指导今后的口译人员培训和技能评估的开展。

---

[*] 孙荧：西北工业大学外国语学院副教授，主讲本科大学英语相关课程，兼任MTI（翻译专业硕士）部分课程。

2 研究背景及现状

与其他形式的翻译工作不同,口译的现场交际功能和时限性决定了口译人员需要在极短的时间里完成听辨、理解、记忆和表达。任务的复杂性要求译员对信息进行有效、快速的加工和重新产出(宋缨,2012),因此对其的评判方法和标准也有其与众不同的特点。

笔者通过对大量的研究成果及文献的总结,发现大部分研究人员认为的评判标准是有一定之规的。首先,作为一个合格的口译翻译人员,其是否具备过硬的双语能力和扎实的语言基本功是不可或缺的最基本要求(波赫哈克,2010;勒代雷,2000;王建华,2012)。其次,广博的知识面是必不可少的,在此环节上对译员提出了两个要求:"专业学习宜专,知识掌握宜宽"(勒代雷,2000)。口译不同于其他类型的翻译,对临场能力要求较高,同时需要能够处理不同场合、背景下的翻译需求,能够处理突发或意外的翻译需求或情景,因此一个合格的口译译员还需要具备快速学习和运用知识的能力、敏捷的思维能力(李紫凌、刘淑倩、陈洁,2012)、灵活的应变能力(鲍刚,2005)、出众的记忆力(刘宓庆,2003;高春茹,2016)、丰富的实战经验(梅德明,2006),以及非智力因素(包括心理素质、身体素质等)(王斌华,2012)。在评判方法上,如何对口译译员进行合理又贴近现实需要的评判,国内外许多专家学者进行了大量研究。张维为(1999)指出,口译质量评估实际上就是对译员整体素质的评价;国际会议译员协会的章程中明确要求译员成为高素质的双语专家,熟练掌握各类口译技巧,深入了解会议专题知识并成为知识广博的"杂家",还要有稳定的心理素质和高尚的职业素养。卢敏(2007)认为,对译员的基本素质的测评,在命题时要设计与英汉互译尤其是与口译实务方法和技巧密切相关的基本素质考点,可大致按照重要的和实质性的内容(人名、职务、机构名称、时间、地点和数字等)翻译,主要的译词技巧(词类转译法、增词法、重复法、省略法、正反表达法等),主要的译句技巧(分句、合句、被动语态、名词从句、定语从句、状语从句、长句等)、习语、成语和俚语的翻译等几个较为突出的方面进行命题设计、安排与平衡。罗薇(2014)指出,在评估译员的口译能力时,除了考查他自身的语言素质和口译技巧外,更重要的是看他的交际能力;译员必须根据听众需求做自我调节;还应充分考虑主办方和听众因素,增加相应参数来对两者进行评估;三方人员取平均值,以得出最终口译效果的总分,这样一来口译质量评估显得更为合理和科学。苏伟(2011)的研究成果表明,口译评估的四个基本组成是:评估的客体(what to evaluate,即评估什么)、评估时间(when to evaluate)、评估形式(how to evaluate)、评估的主体(who evaluate,即谁来评估);其中,对评估的客体即口译职业能力的定义是评估体系构建的基础和起点。总之,在翻译研究领域,对于如何定义翻译(口译)能力及其子能力仍然没有达成一致意见,不过普遍认可的观点是,口译职业能力不仅包括进行双语转换的口译能力(interpreting competence),还应包括团队能力、应变能力、职业操守等内容丰富的职业技能,只有都具备这些子能力,才能成为一名职业译员,从这个角度而言,口译职业能力也被称为"译者能力"(interpreter's competence)(苏伟,2011)。

通过上述总结可以看出,对口译译员能力的要求主要有以下几个方面:过硬的双语能力、扎实的语言基本功、跨文化交际能力、百科知识能力、熟练的口译技巧、良好的记忆力、逻辑思维能力、灵活的应变力、过硬的身体素质和心理素质、职业素质、与时俱进的意识、较高的工作效率、合格的行为测评(衣着、表情、站位、走路与交流方式、讲话声音控制、采场经验)。

在此基础上,本文采用问卷调查和口译材料测试方式,分别对专业和非专业人员进行了口译质量调查。在测试材料制订和选择方面,一个是采用不同侧重点,另一个是需要考虑在内容上选择不同的侧重点材料,这是因为口译员必须具备丰富的语言外知识,也就是我们通常所说的百科知识(黄敏,2005)。

口译质量评判方面,国内外有大量专家学者开展了相关研究,并提出了不同的评判方法和指标。高亮、林郁如(1996)把口译评分标准划分为六个大项:"信息转换/完整性、准确程度、语言表达、流利程度/速度、清晰程度、应变能力"。刘和平(2002)把"现场口译质量评估"的评分标准划分为三个大项:讲话信息或内容转达准确、翻译表达的准确和流畅程度、满足听众的期待。陈菁(2002)根据交际法语言测试理论编制了一份《口译量化评估表》,把口译测试内容划分为知识能力(包括语言知识和言外知识)、技能能力(包括记忆、公众演说、口译笔记、意译、概述、应对策略和职业水平等)和心理能力。杨承淑(2005)把评分标准划分为四个大项:忠实(准确、完整)、表达(流畅、明确)、语言(语法、选词)、时间控制。Bühler(1986)对口译质量和译员评估进行了调查研究,该调查问卷共设定了十六项评估参数,包括语言和非语言(linguistic and extralinguistic)两个大类;其调查结果显示,语言评估类别中有六项评估参数被认定为"重要性显著",依次为——与源语的语义一致性、译语的逻辑性、信息的完整度、正确的语法性、术语的准确性、表达的流畅性;对译员进行评估的非语言评估类别中有三项参数被认定为"重要性显著",依次为——可靠性、会前准备的充分性、团队合作能力。Kurz(1993)对不同类别的几组口译用户进行用户期望(user expectations)调查;调查结果显示,排在"重要性显著"前六位的依次为——与源语的语义一致性、译语的逻辑性、术语的准确性、信息的完整度、表达的流畅性、正确的语法性。国际会议口译员协会(International Association of Conference Interpreters,AIIC)发布了其研究委员会进行的一项针对会议口译用户期望的大型调查报告。结果显示,口译用户认为,在口译与源语的"内容匹配"(content match)方面,有三项指标最为重要:翻译的完整度、术语的准确性、意义的忠实度;在"形式匹配"(formal match)方面,三项重要指标为:(同声传译的)同步性、口头表达技巧、声音的悦耳程度(Moser,1995)。Chiaro and Nocella(2004)通过互联网进行了一项大型的跨国调查,调查世界各地的译员对口译质量评估参数的看法。虽然在文献综述中,两位研究者对前人研究进行了方法论的反思,其研究结果却印证了Bühler和Kurz所统计的"重要性显著"的前六项口译质量评估参数,即与源语的语义一致性、信息的完整度、译语的逻辑性、表达的流畅性、正确的语法性、术语的准确性。国际会议口译员协会曾做过一项调查,研究用户如何评估口译服务,调查发现"理想"的口译员首先考虑对原语信息的忠实,这是最重要的标准。Bühler要求47名调查对象评定译员的各项素质的重要性(准备充分、耐力、镇定、令人愉悦的外表等)以及译员译文产出的九大特征(地道的发音、好听的声音、表达的流畅度、逻辑衔接、意思连贯、完整性、正确的语法、正确的术语、风格恰当)(曾思宇,2013)。

通过对中外学者对于口译质量评估标准的总结来看,口译质量评估标准主要包括以下几个方面。内容上:完整性、准确性(术语等)、忠实性、交际性;形式上:迅捷度、语音语调、流利度、语言使用(语法、选词)、简明度、清晰度、逻辑性、应急反应。

3 口译质量测评研究

本文以口译目标受众为指向,参考外语翻译专业或半专业人员的专业经验,对口译评判的指标参数的重要性进行了调研,调研形式包括问卷调研和口译译文质量测评两部分。问卷调研主要是调研测评标准重要性的主观和专业意见。口译译文质量测评采用设计了不同侧重点的翻译方式和译文的模型,由被采访人员选择所倾向的口译表达方式。根据广泛的调研情况,对调研结果进行数据分析,以期得到有针对性和指向性的口译测评指标。

3.1 口译质量问卷调研

口译指标重要性的主观调研问卷,共设计了 4 个问题;口译翻译质量评估方面共设置 10 道翻译例题,这些例题的内容尽可能地跨越多个领域,避免内容背景过于相似而导致调研的不准确。本次调研共收集了 238 份有效问卷/意见,其中包括 141 名在校学生和 97 名职业从业人员;男性 103 人,女性 135 人;因近半数受访者为在校学生,因此主要年龄分布在 24 岁以下;其学历主要为本科及硕士(包括在读)208 人,博士 7 人,专科 23 人;在专业分布方面,在校学生中语言类专业学生和非语言类专业学生各占一半。

3.2 口译质量主观问卷调研结果

本部分共设置了 4 个调研问题,分别对在校学生和从业人员进行了调研,各问题选项分布结果如下。

(1)在口译质量评价标准中,主要体现在两大方面:内容上和形式上。(结果如图 1 所示)

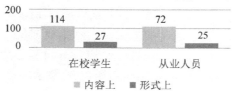

图 1 口译质量评价标准重要性(内容上与形式上)

(2)在口译质量评价标准中,内容上的完整性、准确性(术语等)、忠实性、交际性、客观性,您认为哪几项最重要?(结果如图 2 所示)

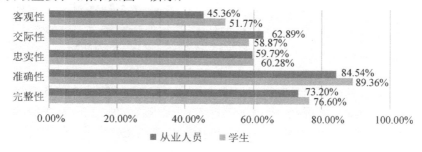

图 2 口译质量评价标准重要性(内容上)

(3)在口译质量评价标准中,形式上迅捷度、语音语调、流利度、语言使用(语法、选词)、简

明度、清晰度、逻辑性、应急反应、多样性,您认为哪几项最重要?(结果如图 3 所示)

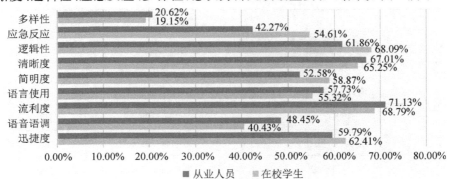

图 3 口译质量评价标准重要性(形式上)

(4)在口译质量评价标准中,以下选项中,按照各个标准的重要性进行排序,写出您认为的最佳排序。(结果如表 1 所示)

表 1 口译质量评价指标排序及打分

在校学生排序及打分		从业人员排序及打分	
排序	打分	排序	打分
准确性	11.38	准确性	10.85
完整性	9.38	完整性	9.49
忠实性	8.18	忠实性	7.96
客观性	7.33	客观性	6.38
交际性	6.34	交际性	6.16
逻辑性	5.68	流利度	5.89
迅捷度	5.52	逻辑性	5.61
清晰度	5.44	清晰度	5.49
流利度	5.31	迅捷度	5.46
语言使用	4.52	简明度	4.78
简明度	4.19	语言使用	4.71
语音语调	3.55	语音语调	4.57
应急反应	3.47	应急反应	2.57
多样性	1.21	多样性	1.48

3.3 口译案例调研结果

口译案例部分共包括 10 道翻译例题,包括 5 道汉译英和 5 道英译汉,每道例题都有 2~4 个翻译样稿,分别有不同的侧重点。10 道翻译例题所设置的选项的侧重点见表 2。

表 2　调研翻译案例选项侧重点设计

编号	选项			
	A	B	C	D
1	忠实性、专业性、完整性	迅捷度、流利度	—	—
2	清晰度、流利度	忠实性、语言使用	—	—
3	清晰度	迅捷度	忠实性	简明性
4	忠实性、完整性	简明性、迅捷度	—	—
5	忠实性	简明性、流利度	完整性	—
6	准确性、忠实性、完整性	迅捷性、流利度	—	—
7	准确性、清晰度	简明度	—	—
8	准确性	流利度、简明度	—	—
9	清晰度、逻辑性	忠实性	—	—
10	逻辑性、清晰度	流利度、迅捷度	—	—

通过对在校学生和从业人员进行调研后，根据被调研者的理解和偏好，选择其认为最容易理解并能更好地表达出原文含义的翻译形式。各选项所选人数见表 3。

表 3　翻译例题选择情况（S 为在校学生、P 为从业人员）

编号	选项							
	A		B		C		D	
	S	P	S	P	S	P	S	P
1	68	49	73	48	—	—	—	—
2	87	53	54	44	—	—	—	—
3	35	17	36	26	51	39	19	15
4	78	55	63	42	—	—	—	—
5	43	27	51	31	47	39	—	—
6	65	50	76	47	—	—	—	—
7	70	46	71	51	—	—	—	—
8	75	48	66	49	—	—	—	—
9	87	53	54	44	—	—	—	—
10	82	50	59	47	—	—	—	—

考虑到从业人员的专业水准与从业时间均高于在校学生，本文对在职人员的调研意见增加 50% 的权重。经过各选项归一、加权后，最终口译质量案例调研得分情况见表 4。

表 4 翻译例题指标得分

标准	平均分
忠实性	43.94
专业性	49.37
完整性	52.65
迅捷度	43.42
流利度	47.98
清晰度	46.51
简明性	38.52
准确性	49.56
逻辑性	56.51

4 口译人员能力测评研究

4.1 口译人员能力调研问卷

本次调研问卷共设置 4 个问题。本次调研共收集了 168 份有效问卷/意见,其中包括 80 名在校学生和 88 名职业从业人员;男性 28 人,女性 140 人;因近半数受访者为在校学生,因此主要年龄分布在 24 岁以下;其学历主要为本科及硕士(包括在读)154 人,博士 2 人,专科 12 人;在专业分布方面,在校学生主要包括语言类专业学生和非语言类专业学生。

4.2 问卷调研结果

(1)译员能力主要包括两个方面,口译能力和个人能力及素质,您认为口译能力和个人能力及素质哪个比较重要?(结果如表 5 所示)

表 5 译员能力重要性

排序	从业人员	学生
口译能力	25	25
个人能力及素质	63	55

(2)在口译能力(过硬的双语能力、扎实的词汇储备、熟练的口译技巧)中,如果给三者按重要程度排序,您会怎样排?(结果如表 6 所示)

表 6 口译能力重要性排序

排序	从业人员	学生
1	过硬的双语能力	过硬的双语能力
2	扎实的词汇储备	扎实的词汇储备
3	熟练的口译技巧	熟练的口译技巧

(3) 在译员个人能力及素质中,您认为最重要的是哪几项?(可多选)(结果如表 7 所示)

表 7 译员个人能力及素质重要性

排序	从业人员	学生	综合
灵活的应变力	71	64	135
跨文化交际能力	65	59	124
良好的记忆力	59	62	121
逻辑思维能力	56	55	111
过硬的身体素质和心理素质	56	51	107
百科知识能力	50	48	98
职业素质	36	38	74
与时俱进的意识	32	31	63
较高的工作效率	33	30	63
合格的行为测评	16	20	36

(4) 如果让您给译员个人能力及素质中的各项按重要程度排序,您会怎样排?(结果如表 8 所示)

表 8 译员个人能力及素质排序

排序	从业人员	学生	综合
良好的记忆力	6.48	7.41	13.89
逻辑思维能力	6.52	7.31	13.83
灵活的应变力	6.4	6.94	13.34
跨文化交际能力	6.55	6.08	12.63
百科知识能力	5.69	5.98	11.67
过硬的身体素质和心理素质	5.7	5.25	10.95
职业素质	4.83	4.56	9.39
与时俱进的意识	3.65	3.45	7.1
较高的工作效率	3.41	3.53	6.94
合格的行为测评	1.51	2.1	3.61

5 口译质量及译员能力测评标准

5.1 口译质量测评标准

综合以上调研数据和打分情况,进一步考虑翻译和口译的基本要求及特点,本文在口译质量评判标准选择方面,在内容性标准方面,选择准确性和完整性;在表现形式标准方面,选择逻辑性、专业性、流利性、清晰性、迅捷度、简明性和语音语调。其中完整性和准确性作为基础分占比最大,其余为加分项。最终测评设定标准如下。

(1) 准确性。对于口译质量而言,准确性是翻译的最基本条件也是要求,准确性评判指标占 40 分(百分制)。译文准确度在 95% 以上的认为是准确性较高,给 40 分。准确度在 70%~95% 的认为译文有一定缺失但能够反映原文意思,根据准确度的不同给 30~40 分。翻译准确度在70%以下的认为已经不足以表达原文含义,不予打分。

(2)完整性。完整性主要反映译文是否表达出原文全部内容,完整性评判指标占35分,分为"完整""较为完整"和"有较大缺失"三种情况,译文完整性在95%以上的认为是完整,给35分。完整性在70%～95%的认为有一定缺失但能够反映原文意思,根据完整性的不同给25～35分。完整性在70%以下的认为已经不足以表达原文含义,严重影响翻译交流,不予打分。

(3)逻辑性。满分5分。逻辑性的强弱主要体现在译文层次清晰明确,上下文衔接合理。此项根据强弱情况打分可分为三个层次,好、中、差,对应分值为5分、2.5分、0分。

(4)专业性。满分5分。专业性主要体现在词汇使用的准确性、专业术语翻译等方面,此项根据强弱情况打分可分为三个层次,好、中、差,对应分值为5分、2.5分、0分。

(5)流利度。满分4分。主要体现在口译过程中翻译的流畅性上,根据表现情况打分可分为三个层次,好、中、差,对应分值为4分、2分、0分。

(6)清晰度。满分4分。主要体现在语义表达的清晰程度上,根据表现情况打分可分为三个层次,好、中、差,对应分值为4分、2分、0分。

(7)迅捷度。满分3分。主要体现在口译表达的衔接速度上,根据表现情况打分可分为三个层次,好、中、差,对应分值为3分、1.5分、0分。

(8)简明性。满分2分。此标准只在"完整准确"的译文的基础上进行叠加,即当第一、二项打分为75分"完整准确"时,如有简明性特征,可加2分,否则不加分。主要是在不影响原意完整和清晰度的情况下,适用简明表达。但若过分强调该特点而影响到译文的完整准确程度,则不予给分。

(9)语音语调。满分2分。本标准根据现场口译实际效果酌情给分。

5.2 译员能力测评重点

口译译员能力评估有两方面作用。首先是能有相关的框架关从相关维度对译员的口译能力进行良好的评估。其次是在此基础上,指出了口译译员能力培养的侧重点和方向。本文在译员能力方面做初步探讨,根据大量的问卷调查调研结果,综合考虑译文质量评估指标,综合考虑译员能力评估,评估主要分为基本能力评估和个人素质评估。基本能力评估包括双语能力、词汇储备和口译技巧,三者的重要性依次降低。这是一名合格译员的基本能力,也是最具有锻炼成长空间的能力。译员个人能力和素质包含多个维度,其中良好的记忆力、逻辑思维能力、灵活的应变力是首要考虑的能力维度。另外,跨文化交际能力、过硬的身体素质和心理素质是对译员能力进行额外加分的能力维度。职业素质、工作效率等仅作为职业素养建议要点而不作为评估维度。

6 小结

本文在调研现有研究成果的基础上,总结了口译质量评估和口译人员能力评估的评测维度和参数,并在大量文件调查和听音调研的基础上,对各评判维度和指标的重要性进行了量化。在此基础上提出了一套具有较强操作性的口译质量评估打分体系,并提出了口译人员能力评估方法以及口译人员能力提升侧重点。但是,本文也有不足之处,如对口音的影响、心理素质及现场意外情况的应变能力的评估方法有待进一步开展。另外,本文收集的样本量有限,从业人员样本中翻译及口译专业从业人员较少,在校学生样本中翻译及口译专业学生较少,有待进一步扩大样本范围,进行进一步研究。

参 考 文 献

鲍刚,2005,《口译理论概述》,中国对外翻译出版公司。
陈菁,2002,《从 Bachman 交际法语言测试理论模式看口译测试中的重要因素》,《中国翻译》第 1 期。
弗朗兹·波赫哈克,2010,《口译研究理论》,仲伟合等译,外语教学与研究出版社。
高春茹,2016,《浅议口译译员基本素质》,《海外英语》第 2 期。
高亮、林郁如,1996,《英汉/汉英口译教程》,福建人民出版社。
黄敏,2005,《谈口译资格认证考试的规范性设计》,《中国翻译》第 6 期。
勒代雷,2000,《释意学派口笔译理论》,中国对外翻译出版公司。
李紫凌、刘淑倩、陈洁,2012,《论口译员必备的基本素质》,《科教文汇》第 2 期。
刘宓庆,2003,《口笔译理论研究》,中国对外翻译出版公司。
刘和平,2002,《科技口译与质量评估》,《上海科技翻译》第 1 期。
卢敏,2007,《全国翻译专业资格水平考试英语口译试题命制一致性研究报告》,《中国翻译》第 5 期。
罗薇,2014,《中国东盟合作背景下的英语口译质量评估所面临的问题和对策》,《佳木斯教育学院学报》第 1 期。
梅德明,2006,《高级口译教程》,上海外语教育出版社。
宋缨,2012,《语块在长时记忆中的状态与口译质量》,《天津外国语大学学报》第 3 期。
苏伟,2011,《以过程为导向的口译职业能力评估研究》,《上海翻译》第 3 期。
王斌华,2012,《从口译标准到口译规范:口译评估模式建构的探索》,《外语》第 3 期。
王斌华,2012,《从口译能力到译员能力:专业口译教学理念的拓展》,《外语与外语教学》第 6 期。
王建华,2012,《语块教学策略对提高学生会议口译准确性的实验研究》,《中国翻译》第 2 期。
杨承淑,2005,《口译教学研究——理论与实践》,中国对外翻译出版公司。
曾思宇,2013,《口译质量评估的"忠实"原则和"交际"原则》,《长沙铁道学院报(社会科学版)》第 3 期。
张维为,1999,《英汉同声传译》,中国对外翻译出版公司。
Bühler, H. 1986. "Linguistic (semantic) and Extra-linguistic (pragmatic) Criteria for the Evaluation of Conference Interpretation and Interpreters." *Multilingua*. Vol.5.
Chiaro, D., and Nocella, G. 2004. "Interpreters' Perception of Linguistic and Non-Linguistic Factors Affecting Quality: A Survey Through the World Wide Web." *Meta*. 49:278 – 293.
Kurz, I. 1993. "Conference Interpretation: Expectations of Different User Groups." *The Interpreters' Newsletter*.
Moser, P. 1995. "Expectations of Users of Conference Interpretation (Full report)." *Interpreting*. Vol 1(2):145 – 178.

德语语音入门阶段的理论基础和错误分析

刘无双[*]

摘　要：在经济文化全球化的大背景下，如何培养出会"听"、会"说"德语的专业型人才，是现今德语教学中值得思考的重要问题。本文以学生课堂中出现的发音错误为出发点，就德语入门教学进行了一些新的尝试，旨在阐明德语语音学理论在教学及实际交际中的重要意义。

关键词：德语入门教学；语音学理论；德语音素；发音错误

语言不仅是一种社会现象，也是一种认知现象，人们运用语言相互交流，不断加深对彼此、社会和世界的认知，可以说，语言是人与人、人与社会、人与世界之间沟通的桥梁。要想高效地传达和获取信息，最直观的方法便是"听"和"说"，而正确的语音是确保准确"听说"的基础。作为第二外语，德语在学习方法上和我们母语汉语的习得有着很大的不同，主要的区别在于语言环境的巨大差异：得益于成熟的语言环境，母语的习得是一个自然而连贯的过程，我们学习母语的过程一般总是先"听说"再"读写"；与之相反，在学习外语时，由于缺乏相应的语言环境，"听说"能力从一开始便无法与母语能力相匹配。因此，教习德语时，为了培养学生"听说读写"四项技能全面发展，必须在入门教学中带着学生打好扎实的语音基础，使学生不会因为害怕"听"岔或"说"错而逐渐失去对德语听说课的兴趣，从而导致"听说"和"读写"能力严重失衡。那么如何才能学好德语语音呢？最基础也最重要的便是准确理解和掌握德语音素。下文将对相关的德语语音学理论进行简单介绍，并在此基础上对学生的一些典型发音错误进行分析。

狭义语音学的主要研究对象是语言的发音原理和发音过程，具体来说，就是研究发音器官之间如何协同合作发出声音。图 1 所示是主要的发音器官。

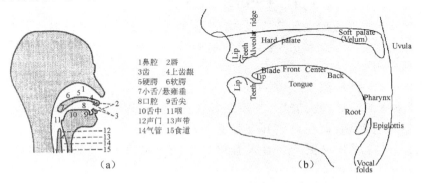

图 1　主要的发音器官（王京平，2002；Ladefoged，2001）

---

[*] 刘无双：西安明德理工学院语言文化传播学院教师，主讲德语听说、德语语法词汇等课程。

声音的产生过程:气流从肺部呼出,经过声带后穿过共鸣腔,在共鸣腔内,软腭、硬腭、牙齿和唇舌等发音器官通过不同的动作影响气流,从而发出声音。具体来说,发音过程分为以下两种情况:①气流在穿过咽腔和口腔时不受阻碍,同时振动声带,这种情况下发出的音为元音;②相反,如果气流在通过共鸣腔时受到某个发音器官的挤压或者短暂受阻,那么发出的就是辅音。需要注意的是,元音和辅音都被称为"音素",音素是语音的最小单位。音素不等同于我们通常意义上的字母,例如,德语的辅音[ʃ]只是一个音素,但其却是通过三个字母来表达的,写作<sch>;再比如,字母<z>和音素[z]虽然写法相似,但是字母<z>是书写单位,而音素[z]则是语音单位。

本文旨在对德语入门教学做一个新的尝试,即讲解元音和辅音的发音方法和与之相关的发音器官。在授课过程中,通过观察学生的发音情况,发现了一些对他们来说较难发音而且容易出错的德语字母,例如<ä><ö><ü><r><w><l><z>等。

在接下来的研究中将以这些字母为例,并以下列问题为切入点进行具体分析:频繁出错的字母或音素的发音位置通常在共鸣腔的哪些地方?学生在发音时是否了解相应的发音器官和正确的发音方法?导致错误发音的主要原因有哪些?老师在德语教学中应当如何纠正发音错误,并让学生掌握正确的发音方法?

1 德语元音

1.1 德语元音发音规律

按照嘴唇的形状、口腔的开度和舌位的高低这三个变量,德语单元音可分为 16 个(包含长短音)。德语单元音与国际音标相比有一些变化,如图 2 所示。

<ä><ö><ü>这三个变元音字母是德语特有的,其与我们所熟悉的其他字母的区别在于多出了"头上的两点"。这三个变元音字母分别从基础元音[a][o][u]变化而来,同时在发音上也有一些改变。从图 2 可以看出,左侧用小圆圈标记的是与<ä><ö><ü>相对应的变元音音素,右侧用大圆圈标记的是与<a><o><u>相对应的基础元音音素。具体分析如下:

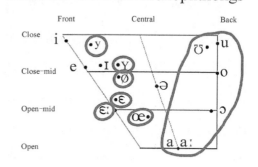

图 2 德语单元音(Kohler,1999)

(1)字母<ä>表示源自/a/的变元音[ɛː]与[ɛ],被称为"不圆唇半张前元音"。长短元音在发音位置上基本没有区别;而在口腔开合程度上,长音[ɛː]较短音[ɛ]嘴唇张得更开并且发音更靠近共鸣腔前部,例如长音 Ähre [ˋɛːrə],短音 Kälte [ˋkɛltə]。

(2)字母<ö>表示源自/o/的变元音[øː]和[œ]。与<ä>不同,这个字母长短元音的发音位置区别较大。长音[øː]是圆唇半闭前元音,例如 Höhle [ˋhøːlə];短音[œ]是圆唇半开前元音,例如 öffnen [ˋœfnən]。

(3)字母<ü>表示源自/u/的变元音,其长音[yː]和短音[y]的发音位置相对靠近。[yː]

更接近圆唇闭合前元音,例如 üben [ˈyːbn];[y]更接近圆唇半闭前元音,例如 Glück [glyk]。

从图 2 可以发现,以上六个变元音发音时的口腔开度主要是从全闭到半开,并且基本都是前元音,而从全闭到半开的后元音[uː][ʊ][oː][ɔ]和全开的元音[aː][a]则组成与变元音相对的六个基础元音。学习时需要注意这六个基础元音和六个变元音发音位置的区别,这样才能掌握正确的发音规律。

1.2 德语元音常见的发音错误

在学习了德语单元音音素的发音规律后,学生便跟着录音对图 2 中的每一个元音进行模仿式练习,效果十分显著。可以观察到,学生在理解、掌握和运用大部分单元音上基本没有问题。而在练习六个变元音的发音过程中,或多或少会出现一些发音错误,以下是对学生普遍容易出现的错误进行的归纳总结和分析。

(1)大多数学生会直接忽略变元音字母上的两点,而读成与之相对的基本元音,即将所有的变元音的发音位置移到了共鸣腔的后面(/ä/→/a/、/ö/→/o/、/ü/→/u/),导致在很多带有<ä><ö><ü>的单词中出现发音和听写错误,例如 wählen [ˈvɛːlən]→ wahlen [ˈvaːlən]、mögen [ˈmøːgn]→ mogen [ˈmoːgn]、üben [ˈyːbn]→ uben [ˈuːbn]等。如果忽视变元音上的两点,所发的语音与其对应的含义往往会产生改变,由此带来的最直观的影响就是在说话双方"听""说"德语时出现交流和理解上的偏差。

(2)学生在听读单独出现的变元音字母时,对其掌握情况也有不同:相比字母⟨ö⟩,学生更容易正确地读出字母<ä>和<ü>,因为在英语中有类似[ɛ]的发音,比如 bed 中的[e](英语中[e]是半闭前元音,比德语[ɛ]的口型小一些);同样汉语中也有跟[y]和[yː]相似的发音,比如汉字"鱼"[yú]的读音。以此作类比可以让学生更快更好地掌握德语字母<ä>和<ü>的读法。然而字母<ö>的发音对于德语初学者来说完全是新鲜的,由于很难从汉语和英语中找出发音类似的字或词,因此需要在大脑中为其构建一个新的概念,将其与已掌握的其他德语知识共同存储在大脑词库中。

(3)一部分学生在碰到变元音字母和其他辅音字母合成的词时会犯发音错误,错误率最高的组合是<f+ü+n>和<f+ü+r>。想要准确地读出这两个组合,首先需要拆开读准单个音素的发音。对照下文中图 3 的德语辅音音素表可以看出,字母<f>对应的辅音[f]是通过唇齿摩擦发出的清辅音,字母<n>对应的辅音[n]是带鼻音的齿龈音,字母<r>应读成通过大舌或小舌发出的颤音[r]/[R]。常见的发音错误有两种情况:①<f+ü+n> — *fünf*,正确的发音是[fynf],一些学生会直接忽视变元音 [y]而读成[fnf];②<f+ü+r> — *für*,正确的发音是[fyːɐ],在发音时,很多同学会自己添加或改变一些音素读成[fjuːɐ]。

2 德语辅音

2.1 德语辅音发音规律

按照发音位置(表格横向)和发音方法(表格纵向)的不同,德语辅音可以分为 25 个,也与国际音标有略微差异,如图 3 所示。

Consonants

	Bilabial	Labio-dental	Dental	Alveolar	Post-alveolar	Palatal	Velar	Uvular	Glottal
Plosive	p b			t d			k g		ʔ
Nasal	m			n			ŋ		
Fricative		f v		s z	ʃ ʒ	ç		χ ʁ	h
Approximant						j			
Lateral Approximant				l					

图 3　德语辅音(Kohler,1999)

2.2　德语辅音常见的发音错误

德语的辅音字母相较于英语来说虽然只多了一个 ß [ɛstsɛt],然而在发音上却相去甚远,例如有代表性的辅音字母<w><z><l><j><r>等,其在德语和英语中的发音截然不同。因此,德语辅音的发音学习对于初学者来说同样是一个构建新认知的过程。类比元音教学,同样的方法也适用于辅音的发音教学——用语音学理论指导教学,将德语辅音字母与图 3 中的辅音音素一一对应,让学生结合理论学习辅音字母的正确发音。接下来就学生在课中和课后练习中出现的辅音发音错误进行简要总结。

(1)字母<w>对应的音素是[v],是通过唇齿摩擦发出的浊辅音,声带振动,字母的读音是[veː]。这个音素特殊的地方在于其是一个唇齿音,上齿必须咬住并摩擦下唇才可以正确地发音。许多学生在读这个字母的时候由于受英语的影响,会不自觉地读成英语不咬唇的读法['dʌblju],从而使得以<w>开头的所有单词的发音都出现了偏差。

(2)字母<z>对应的音素是[ts],发音位置在齿龈间,即上下齿闭合阻断了气流所形成的**塞擦音**,声带不振动,为清辅音,字母的读音为[tsɛt]。这是在发音上出错率非常高的一个字母。例如学生在读 Zeit 这个单词时,几乎都会读成 [zait],而这个音标对应的单词是 seit,发音的错误会导致在"听说读写"四个环节中出现偏差。对此类发音错误的分析,得出以下两点结论:①英语发音对德语语音的影响较大,学生在看到字母<z>时第一反应便是对应英语中的音素[z];②学生对字母和音素的概念较模糊,因此对德语字母<z>和德语音素[z]的相似点和不同点无法清楚地认知。

(3)字母<l>对应的音素是[l],是德语中唯一的一个边音,发音时舌尖需抵住上齿根,舌前部尽量贴住硬腭的前部,气流由舌叶两侧送出,声带振动,字母的读音为[ɛl]。这个字母的发音与英语的<l>[el]虽然在音标的写法上差不多,但在发音上却有所不同,英语的发音较为含糊,德语的发音要更清晰、更重一些。很多学生在发德语<l>[ɛl]的时候很容易发成英语的<l>[el],导致发音错误。

(4)字母<j>对应的音素是[j],是气流通过硬腭与舌面之间时发出的擦音,声带振动。这个字母在德语中的发音主要分为以下两大类:①在德语本族语单词中,该字母的读音是

[jɔt]，例如 Jugend [juːgnt]；②在一些外来词中，字母＜j＞则是另一种读法，读作[dʒ]或[ʒ]，例如 Job [dʒɔp]，这种情况下字母＜j＞采用的是英语中＜j＞[dʒeɪ]的发音方法。有些学生对德语字母＜j＞的发音方法记忆不牢固，很容易将由其构成的德语单词全部读成英语的发音。

（5）字母＜r＞的发音很有特色，即平时所说的"小舌音"，它的音标一般情况下写作[er]，与之对应的音素有两个：一个是小舌颤动发出的[R]，一个是舌尖在上齿龈处颤动发出的[r]，声带振动。小舌音之所以被称为教学难点，是因为在汉语和英语中字母＜r＞并不会通过小舌发声，很多学生在大一接触到德语的时候才知道还有小舌这个发音器官的存在。基于字母＜r＞在德语中两种音素的不同发音方式，建议学生按照自己的实际情况选择性地练习小舌或者大舌。实践证明，在正确的理论指导下，加以正确的示范和经验的传授，学生对颤音[R]和[r]的理解和掌握的情况非常理想。有一点需要特别注意的是，德语字母＜r＞在＜e+r＞的组合中的发音切忌与英语中的卷舌音混淆，＜e+r＞组合里的＜r＞是平舌音而非卷舌音，这也是学生在学习＜r＞的发音时非常容易出错的地方。受汉语和美式英语的影响，很多学生在见到＜e+r＞的组合时，会毫不犹豫地读成卷舌音"er"，例如在读德语单词 Mutter 时，90%的学生都会发出和"儿子"或 better 同样的卷舌音，这样的发音是不符合德语发音规则的。

3 发音错误的原因分析及解决方法

从以上内容中学生对德语变元音字母＜ä＞＜ö＞＜ü＞和辅音字母＜w＞＜z＞＜l＞＜j＞＜r＞的发音情况出发，可以总结出发音错误的两点原因。

（1）母语和第一外语对第二外语的学习影响较大。作为母语的汉语和作为第一外语的英语已经在我们大脑中形成了十分稳定的语言认知系统，因此再为德语构建一个新的语言系统时会难上加难。在汉语和英语的负迁移作用的影响下，学生总是会不自觉地尝试用英汉的发音方法拼读德语单词。这是进行德语语音教学应当重点关注的地方。

（2）学生没有形成用语言学理论指导外语学习的思维习惯。在德语入门教学中，语音是重中之重，是"听说读写"的基础，也是人与人之间进行有效交流与沟通的保障，因此这个阶段的学习不能只以模仿式的发音为目的，而更需要从本质上理解德语语音学的发音理论，从而进一步掌握其发音规律。单纯的模仿式学习或缺乏系统的语音学理论，往往可能会导致学生课后出现一些记忆漏洞，忘记个别字母的发音规律，以至于在之后的练习中出现越来越大的偏差。

针对以上两点原因，本文对德语语音入门阶段的教学改革做了以下尝试。①用语音学理论指导实际德语教习。带领学生认识不同发音器官，将每一个字母或音素的发音位置与相应的发音器官对应，系统地学习德语元音和辅音的发音位置和发音方法，为"听说读写"打好基础。②在掌握理论知识的同时，模仿式的练习也十分重要。如何为德语构建一个新的语言系统？如何学习一门新的外语？最有效的途径便是跟读与模仿，听录音并对照"德语元音梯形图"调整口腔开合度练习元音，对照"德语辅音表"练习辅音的发音位置和方法。③在德语语音学习入门阶段，尽量避免对照英语发音方法来学习，应为德语构建独立的发音系统，这样才能最大限度地避免与英语发音混淆。④在练习德语音素的发音时，出错是不可避免的，因此需要学生养成小组学习的习惯，互相纠音，互相做对方的老师。其间可以让学生练习绕口令和诗歌，并将其录制成音频，在老师指导、纠错之后整理成学习文档作为平时成绩。

4 结论

中国有句古话:"授人以鱼不如授人以渔"。在教学中我们也需要时刻提醒自己,培养出新时代人才,不能只停留在教学生知识的层面,也应当教他们如何自主地学习知识。体现在德语语音入门教学中便是:把语言和语言科学结合在一起,教学生如何用理论指导实践,即用语音学理论指导具体语音的学习。德语语音学指出,德语学习者可以根据不同发音器官的协同合作找到各个元音和辅音的准确发音位置。在德语学习的入门阶段,理论与实践缺一不可,如果只单方面地注重理论或实践,便会出现一些典型的发音错误,例如变元音[yː][y][øː][œ][ɛː][ɛ]和辅音字母<w><z><l><j><r>等的发音错误。这些发音错误出现的原因是汉英的负迁移作用和德语学习者习惯性的模仿式学习方法。实践证明,单纯的模仿式学习并不能达到最好的效果,因此需要外语学习者用语言学理论作为指导,再配合大量的发音和听力练习进行模仿式学习和纠错,才能为之后的"听说读写"四大项及实际交际打下良好的语音基础。

参 考 文 献

皇甫宜均,2017,《实用德语语音教程》,西安交通大学出版社。
胡麟,2017,《德语二外语音教学的实践与思考》,《海外英语(上)》第 8 期。
黄利玲、胡颖群、廖倩,2015,《语音教学与跨文化交际——论语音教学在英语教学中的基础地位》,《景德镇高专学报》第 1 期。
穆兰、庄慧丽,1999,《德语语音》,外语教学与研究出版社。
王京平,2002,《德语语言学教程》,外语教学与研究出版社。
庄慧丽,1997,《略谈德语基础阶段教学法》,《外语与外语教学》第 6 期。
Kohler, K. J. 1995. *Einführung in die Phonetik des Deutschen*. Schmidt Erick Verlag.
Meibauer, Jörg. 2007. *Einführung in die germanistische Linguistik*. Verlag J.B. Metzler. Stuttgart · Weimar.
Kohler, K. 1999. *Handbook of the International Phonetic Association*. Cambridge: Cambridge University Press.
Ladefoged, P. 2001. *A course in Phonetics*, 4th Edition. Orlando: Harcourt.

英语口语教学与评估中的程式化词串

康 坛*

摘 要:程式化词串(或称"程式化语言")是语言中的一种常见现象,然而由于其形式的多样性和信息处理方式的不确定性,学术界虽多有研究,且与其他学科的交叉也较广泛,但仍存在诸多尚无合理解释的疑难问题。在结合 ESL/EFL 口语教学方面,因为语料库规模相对有限等现状,相关研究并不蓬勃。本文从程式化词串的权威操作定义发端,介绍了一些有代表性的研究成果,梳理了近年来被广泛讨论的重要理论,并尝试提出一些英语口语教学与研究方面的建议。

关键词:程式化词串;整体;存储;提取;口语水平

在第二语言研究和教学中,单词一直被认为是基本词汇单位,因为单词容易识别、学习和处理。然而人们逐渐认识到,语言使用者并不总是逐词处理语言,而是经常使用程式化语言。据估算,程式化语言在英语的口头和书面话语中所占比例超过 50%(Erman and Warren, 2000),而且这些语言与输出的流利度、交际性以及地道程度密切相关(Schmitt,2010)。因此,ESL 学习者需要掌握这些语言以提高英语水平,而 ESL 教学也应聚焦于此。

程式化语言种类繁多,Wray(1999)采用了一个概括性的术语:程式化词串(formulaic sequence),并给出如下定义——由单词或其他具有意义的元素构成的、连续或不连续的、预制的字符串,使用时在记忆中整体存储和提取,而非通过语法生成或解析。

识别并掌握程式化词串对于 EFL(而非 ESL)学习者来说尤为困难,因为他们的二语输入源以文本为主。在口头输入中,语速、间断、重音等语音特征可能标示程式化词串,而在书面输入中,某些词组无法显示为整体词块。

目前,针对程式化语言教学及其对学习者二语水平的影响的研究并不多见。其主要原因在于程式化词串是一种难以把握的语言现象,对其进行定义和操作不但困难,而且精确度达不到有效理论基础的标准(Dornyei,2009)。现有研究涉及利用课堂练习学习程式化词串及其对学习者意识的正面影响(Jones and Haywood,2004)、规定时间内学习者输出程式化词串的数量和范围(Taguchi,2007),以及学习者口语发展水平(Boers et al.,2006)。

其中 Boers et al.(2006)的一项实验研究为程式化词串在英语口语中的积极作用提供了实证支持。他们发现,英语学习者在面对面口语测试中对程式化词串的使用与他们得到的口语水平分数存在明显的相关性。受试者在表达时越多使用程式化词串,专业评分员就越认可其语言的地道程度、流利度和准确性。显而易见,二语教学中的程式化词串现象理应引起更多关注。

然而这类讨论仍然主要局限于英语教学。Stengers et al.(2011)研究了学习两种不同类

---

* 康坛:西北工业大学外国语学院教师,主要研究方向为应用语言学。

型外语(英语与西班牙语)的母语为荷兰语的学生的程式化语言使用情况与其该门外语口语水平之间的联系。研究结果验证了早先由其他学者(Boers et al,2006)提出的观点,即恰当运用程式化语言使英语学习者的口语流利且地道。该研究通过复述任务测试,发现受试者的口语水平与任务中程式化词串使用数量正相关,且相对于西班牙语,英语样本的相关性更强。数据显示,由于西班牙语样本中出现了较高的词法屈折变化错误,该组受试者使用的程式化词串对其口语水平的正面影响被削弱。同时,作为重要参考,作者也讨论了受试者第一语言与第二语言在类型上的差异。他们首先假设程式化词串的使用对西班牙语学习者的水平贡献度相对较低。这一假设基于两个原因。第一个原因是英语中包含大量习语。由于英语语法相对简单,对于英语学习者而言,真正的难点主要是掌握海量的标准化短语。第二个原因是两种语言的词法、句法类型差异。相对而言,英语偏重解析,而西班牙语强调合成。解析类语言的语法屈折变化较少,句法和语义主要取决于词序和介词运用,而非屈折变化。相反地,合成类语言词缀更多,词根变化也更多。词序相对较灵活,因为句法和语义通常由屈折变化体现。相对于英语,西班牙语语法的屈折变化更加丰富,比如形容词和名词在性别和数量上要保持一致;动词需根据人称、数量、语态等进行相应变化。而在上述研究中,受试者的第一语言(荷兰语)在语言类型上更加接近英语,与另一种目标语(西班牙语)差异较大。由于西班牙语中的屈折变化较多,学习者在实时环境中熟练掌握并运用该语种程式化词串的难度较大。

很多学者,如 Ellis(2002)和 Wray(2002),都认为程式化词串在语言习得和使用中扮演核心角色。这里的程式化词串(也称作词组或词块)涵盖很多相关语言现象,包括固定搭配(如 tell a lie、heavy traffic)、习语(如 turn the tide、back to square one)、双名词组(如 cuts and bruises、research and development)、标准化比喻(如 clear as crystal、dry as dust)、民谚俗语(如 When the cat's away …; That's the way the cookie crumbles)、话语组织词组(如 On the other hand、Having said that)以及社交套话(如 Nice to meet you; Have a nice day)(Stengers et al.,2011)。

虽然语言中的程式化词串并没有一个精确数量,但根据一些研究估计,对于成年英语本族语使用者,50%~70%的语言都包含程式化词串。

至于二语或外语学习中的程式化词串现象,学术界普遍认为掌握大量程式化语言是学习者精通一门语言的先决条件,因为这使他们能够产出大段自然纯正的话语,同时也能保证流利度(Wray,2002)。近年来,Willis(1990),Nattinger 和 DeCarrico(1992)等人相继提出了旨在促进二语程式化词串习得的教学方法。其中描述的"自然化"学习环境实际就是指学习者完全浸入二语氛围。虽然上述研究中的二语主要聚焦于英语,但程式化词串的使用与二语水平之间的关联显然不仅限于英语。

这里探讨的学习环境是指基于讲授的二语习得,即 Instructed Second Language Acquisition(ISLA)。学生主要在教室里通过听课接受较为规范的外语学习,辅以因人而异的课外二语学习,如多媒体、自主阅读、课后作业以及与二语国家人士交流等。Lewis(2000)提出了在这种学习环境下以程式化词串为导向的教学法。

频繁出现的程式化词串之所以在语言习得中扮演关键角色,是因为它们为学习者提供了基于范例的学习资料。这一观点来自 Ellis(2002),他认为对于一语习得而言,常规的发展路径是始于程式,继而小范围框架内代换,乃至创造性构建。根据 Skehan(1998)的看法,这种发展模式的结果就产生了一个双轨并行的语言处理系统。一边是基于语法规则,允许使用者创造全新话语的模式;另一边则是基于记忆,允许快速提取整体储存的范例的模式。至于哪一种模式优先运行,则要由语言使用的具体环境决定。在有充分准备时间的条件下,可以采用基于语法规则的模式。而在实时交际环境中,基于记忆的模式能够确保流利度,后者的特征就是大量使用程式化词串。大部分用于研究的语料都体现了上述两种处理模式的共存。

与 Skehan 类似,Wray(2002)也发现了第一语言处理中的两种互补模式。虽然本族语使用者可以根据需要采用语法解析模式,但他们却倾向于把词串作为整体进行处理,而这些词串单位在他们童年期就已储存于记忆当中。对于本族语使用者而言,海量的预制词串使他们在语言产出和接收两方面都能进行流畅的处理。实验证明,受试者能够在词串输入完全结束之前就完成对其识别和理解的过程(Conklin and Schmitt,2008)。这可以释放一定的处理空间,用于理解后面话语中较难预计的部分。

这里不免再次提出一个老生常谈但悬而未决的问题:程式化词串在人脑词库中是如何存在并拥有处理优势且在语言创造中起到跳板作用的?是否只有原型属于预制,而其众多变体需按步骤生成?或者说,这些变体是否也是作为整体单位储存,并等待作为成型整体被提取呢?目前尚不明确以上两种情况中的哪一种从自动性角度看更加可信(Dekeyser,2001)。这里的自动性是指快速并准确地进行字词流输出的能力(Segalowitz,2003)。关于自动化,目前存在两种理论,即记忆论和过程论。根据记忆论(Schmidt,1992),自动化就是不断增强记忆中特定要素之间的联系,直至这些要素作为一个单位被储存,并随时可以作为一个整体被提取。而过程论(Anderson,1993)则主张自动化是一种认知过程(比如运用语法规则)的反复训练,从而使其不断变快。根据 Ellis 和 Schmidt(1997)提出的"学习力法则",在达到某个极限值时,训练的加速作用停止,因为最优化的表现已经达到。按照第二种理论,流畅的程式化词串运用是高速聚合词语的结果,而不是从记忆库中整体提取。

Wray(2002)认为,本族语使用者和非本族语使用者对程式化词串的处理方式不同。她对本族语使用者整体处理程式化词串的阐述非常接近自动化记忆论。至于二语学习者,她认为只要具备强大的语言加工能力,就可能流畅使用程式化词串,而这一观点与过程论不谋而合。若真如此,二语学习者只要能高速聚合程式化词串,就能进行流利的语言输出并提高该外语水平。

当然还存在另一种可能性,即一部分二语程式化词串是作为整体被提取,而另一部分则是按步骤组合的。Schmitt 指出,词块可分为多种类型,每种类型的使用和处理方式不同。他对比研究了三种固化程度不同的程式化语言,分别为习语(如 packed like sardines)、可变短语(即包含开放性空位的短语,如 put ... to the test),以及"词束"(即语料库可识别的连续词串,如 the fact that)(Stengers et al.,2011)。

根据 Schmitt 的假设,整体存储在处理严丝合缝且不可变的程式化词串时发挥作用;而当出现变体时,则需借助于其他处理策略。拿习语来说,可能只有其原型作为模板被储存,凭借其中一个或多个词素即可提取,并且可衍生出若干变体。另外是可变短语,有的词块的所有变体都分别作为独立整体存储于词库中,例如 a week ago、a year ago、a minute ago 等;有的较高层次变体,如时态变体,则仅存储一个原型,但是包含语法空位以填充正确的屈折形式,如(stand 的屈折变体)shoulder to shoulder。最后是词束,它们很可能是以整体为单位存储的,因为它们相对固定,而且使用频率较高(Stengers et al.,2011)。

总而言之,相对于有多个变体的程式化词串,变化最少的程式化词串更容易被整体储存。

由于合成语言在屈折和词序方面的变化比解析语言更丰富,学习者要在前者中流畅且准确地使用程式化词串,就需要具备更丰富的语言处理知识,特别是当他们的母语和该语言在类型上差异较大时。简言之,在学习者进行口语交际时,程式化词串确实有助于提升流利度,但是对合成语言来说,很多词串相对更难掌握。

二语教学中的程式化语言教学策略要达到掌握词汇的目标,应遵循三个心理状态,即关注、提取、生成。正如 Nation(2001)所说,只有沿用学习孤立单词的思路,才能最有效地记忆词块。

在有限的课堂时间内,显然无法兼顾各类程式化词串。最现实的选择标准就是词串的出现频率,而且不仅限于通用英语,专门用途英语也应包括在内。其中一套实用的基于频率的词表是由 Martinez 和 Schmitt(2012)为教学目的而创建的 PHRASE 词表,其中汇总了英语中使用频率最高的 505 个程式化词串。当然,这类词表的规模和代表性非常重要,例如上述 PHRASE 词表是基于英国国家语料库(British National Corpus,BNC)。该语料库包含 1 亿单词量的英国英语样本,其中书面语和口头语分别占 90% 和 10%。

今后的研究应该在其他口语活动(如对话)中进一步寻求验证。另外,一些短语可能比另一些短语更能使评分者对学习者的口语水平产生判断,所以对程式化词串进行细分定性研究可能有助于更精确地建立程式化词串知识与口语水平之间的关联。

参 考 文 献

Anderson, J. R. 1993. *Rules of the mind*. Lawrence Erlbaum.

Boers, F., Eyckmans, J., Kappel, J., Stengers, H., and Demecheleer, M. 2006. "Formulaic sequences and perceived oral proficiency: Putting a lexical approach to the test". *Language Teaching Research*.

Conklin, K., and Schmitt, N. 2008. "The Processing Advantage of Formulaic Sequences". *Applied Linguistics*.

DeKeyser, R. 2001. "Cognition and second language instruction: Automaticity and automatization". *Computer Science*.

Dornyei, Z. 2009. *The Psychology of Second Language Acquisition*. Oxford: Oxford University Press.

Ellis, N. C. 2002. "Frequency effects in language acquisition: A review with implications for theories of implicit and explicit language acquisition". *Studies in Second Language Acquisition*.

Ellis, N. C., and Schmidt, R. 1997. "Morphology and longer distance dependencies: Laboratory research illuminating the A in SLA". *Studies in Second Language Acquisition*.

Erman, B., and Warren, B. 2000. "The idiom principle and the open choice principle". *Text*.

Jones, M., and Haywood, S. 2004. "Facilitating the acquisition of formulaic sequences: An exploratory study in an EAP context". *Formulaic sequences: Acquisition, processing and use*. pp. 269–300.

Lewis, M. 2000. *Teaching collocation: Further developments in the lexical approach*. England: Language Teaching Publications.

Martinez, R., and Schmitt, N. 2012. "A Phrasal Expressions List". *Applied Linguistics*.

Nation, I. S. P. 2001. *Learning vocabulary in another language*. Cambridge: Cambridge University Press.

Nattinger, J. R., and DeCarrico, J. S. 1992. *Lexical phrases and language teaching*. Oxford : Oxford University Press.

Schmidt, R. W. 1992. "Psychological mechanisms underlying second language fluency". *Studies in Second Language Acquisition*.

Schmitt, N. 2010. *Researching vocabulary: A vocabulary research manual*. Hampshire : Palgrave Macmillan.

Segalowitz, N. S. 2003. "Automaticity and second languages". *The handbook of second language acquisition*. Blackwell.

Skehan, P. 1998. *A cognitive approach to language teaching*. Oxford: Oxford University Press.

Stengers, H., Boers, F., Housen, A., and Eyckmans, J. 2011. "Formulaic sequences and L2 oral proficiency: Does the type of target language influence the association?" *International Review of Applied Linguistics in Language Teaching*.

Taguchi, N. 2007. "Chunk learning and the development of spoken discourse in a Japanese as a foreign language classroom". *Language Teaching Research*.

Willis, D. 1990. *The lexical syllabus: A new approach to language teaching*. Collins ELT.

Wray, A. 1999. "Formulaic Language in Learners and Native Speakers". *Language Teaching*.

Wray, A. 2002. *Formulaic language and the lexicon*. Cambridge: Cambridge University Press.

英语反身代词习得研究现状及前景展望

栾钧涵[*]　张　奕[**]

摘　要：国内学者对于二语习得者英语反身代词的习得研究主要包含多角度、多层次的理论探讨与实证研究。母语迁移在二语习得中起着重要的作用，因而大批研究者根据二语习得者不同的母语背景，对比研究其对于反身代词的习得情况，探究 Chomsky 提出的约束理论在反身代词习得过程中的作用，以此来验证人类大脑中所具有的普遍性语言机制。本文通过对该领域内主要文献中具有代表性的研究进行梳理及归纳，展示了该领域内主要的理论基础、研究视角、工具方法、存在问题及发展趋势，以期描绘国内有关反身代词习得研究的特点及所取得的成果，并为今后更进一步的实证研究提供理论支持与参考。

关键词：反身代词；二语习得；语言迁移；约束理论

1　引言

近年来，国内外学者针对二语习得者对英语反身代词的习得开展了多角度、多层次的理论探讨与实证研究（Manzini and Wexler，1987；Yuan，1994；李红，2002；王文斌，2000a）。根据 Chomsky（1981）的约束理论第一原则，反身代词的约束行为常被看作是人们与生俱来的语言知识。基于此，一批研究者根据二语习得者的不同母语背景，对比研究其对于反身代词的习得情况，探究 Chomsky 提出的约束理论在反身代词习得过程中的作用，以此来验证人类大脑中所具有的普遍性语言机制，即 Chomsky（1981，1986）所提出的普遍语法在二语习得过程中的作用。

众所周知，母语迁移在二语习得中起着重要的作用。英语反身代词与汉语反身代词"自己"的区别很大，因此，中国英语学习者极易将汉语中"自己"的用法迁移到英语中去，从而对其习得英语反身代词产生极大影响。本文通过对部分过往文献中具有代表性的研究进行梳理及归纳，展示了此领域内主要的理论知识、主要研究、研究视角、工具方法、存在问题及发展趋势，以期对中国英语学习者反身代词习得的有关研究做出综述，并为今后更进一步的实证研究提供理论支持与参考。

2　理论基础

中国英语学习者反身代词的习得研究大多以二语习得中的迁移理论，Chomsky 在提出普

---

[*] 栾钧涵：西北工业大学外国语学院硕士研究生。
[**] 张奕：西北工业大学外国语学院副院长，教授，研究方向为中外语言教育比较研究、教师教育与发展等，主讲英语专业研究生课程——应用语言学研究方法，英语专业本科生课程——论文写作、新闻视听、英语学习方法论等。

遍语法的基础上提出的又一理论——约束理论,以及 Progovac 提出的相对化大主语观点为主要理论基础。

2.1 迁移理论

迁移(transfer)是一个心理学概念,源于行为主义心理学,指学习过程中学习者已有的知识或技能会对新知识或新技能的获得产生影响。James(1980)借此描述语言迁移的概念:"第一语言的学习将影响第二语言的学习"。学界对于语言迁移的定义存在各种不同的表述,其中,Odlin(1989)给出的定义获得最广泛的认可:"迁移是指目标语和其他任何已经习得的或者没有完全习得的语言之间的共性和差异所造成的影响"。此定义表明,语言迁移不单指传统二语习得研究中来自学习者母语的影响,还指学习者已经习得的任何其他语言的知识对新语言知识习得的影响。

2.2 约束理论第一原则

根据 Chomsky(1981)的约束理论第一原则,反身代词必须在其管辖语域内受约束。虽然此原则为各种语言所遵守,但管辖语域却因语言而异,即不同的语言具有不同的管辖语域参数。

具体来说,英语反身代词(如 himself、herself)受局部约束,即先行语与反身代词处在同一个从句中,且该从句的主语和宾语都可以做它的先行语。例如:

例一:Julie k thought that [June j talked to Mary i about herself i/j/ * k]。

汉语反身代词(即自己)可以接受长距离约束,即先行语与反身代词可以放在不同的从句中,但反身代词的先行词一定是主语。例如:

例二:张扬 k 告诉王明 j[李伟 i 帮助了自己 i/ * j/k]。

而对于中国英语学习者来说,如果把汉语中的反身代词"自己"的一系列用法迁移到英语中,那么这将对他们习得英语反身代词的局部约束性产生负面影响。

2.3 相对化大主语观点

基于 Chomsky 的约束理论第一原则,Progovac(1992,1993)为解释各种语言中反身代词受约束现象提出了相对化大主语观点(relativized SUBJECT)。反身代词从形态角度看可分为简单反身代词(simplex reflexives)和复合反身代词(complex reflexives)。在形态上不存在数量、性及人称变化的反身代词属于简单反身代词,即 X^0 反身代词,如汉语中的反身代词"自己"和日语中的反身代词"zibun"等。相反,在形态上存在数量、性及人称变化的反身代词属于复合反身代词,即 X^{max} 反身代词,如英语中的反身代词。这样,反身代词在受约束方面就需要 X-bar 的彼此兼容。根据相对化大主语观点,大主语的概念依据反身代词的 X-bar 状态而产生相对化:简单反身代词只能接受 X^0 范畴作为其大主语,这一大主语就是表示一致关系的 AGR;而复合反身代词只能接受属于 X^{max} 范畴的句子成分作为其大主语,这一大主语就是具有人称和数特征的 X^{max} 标志语[NP IP]或[NP NP]。总之,简单反身代词和复合反身代词都受到大主语的约束,而这里的大主语是相对化了的大主语,在约束反身代词时需要在指代特征方面彼此匹配。

3 研究视角

对于二语习得者反身代词习得的研究主要从以下三大视角出发。

3.1 理论探索

早期研究有对理论知识的进一步研究和探索,如 Manzini 和 Wexler(1987)在其研究中指出跨语言反身代词的约束域不同,约束域参数也具有五个不同的值。基于此,开展了对跨语言反身代词约束域参数的验证。Progovac(1992,1993)为解释各种语言中反身代词受约束现象提出了相对化大主语观点(relativized SUBJECT),此观点被用于解释英汉反身代词受约束的差异,且受到越来越多的关注及认可。

进入新世纪以来,结合具体的语法知识对反身代词的习得过程进行解释依旧是研究的主流。如王文斌(2000a)以 Chomsky(1981,1986)的原则和参数为视野,从第二语言习得的不同方面考察普遍语法在第二语言习得过程中的通达情况。王文斌(2001)着重探讨了普遍语法中约束理论的各种修正观点,并以此分析英汉反身代词第二语言习得这一理论并展开了相关的研究工作。陈月红(2001)进一步验证了三种分析反身代词的语法理论。唐晋湘(2004a)则就二语习得是否受制于普遍语法这一论题,总结了学界最富争议的五种假说。通过对五种假说的逐一论证及运用早期学者 Progovac(1992,1993)提出的相对化大主语观点作为理论依据,进一步证实了普遍语法、第二语言输入和母语知识三者在二语习得过程中的互动作用,探讨了二语习得过程中普遍语法的有效性。与之类似,刘志平(2006)也探讨了普遍语法在反身代词习得中是否具有作用这一论题。李正权(2010)则进一步从语法理论的角度介绍并分析了反身代词的约束论、参数理论及实证研究。

二语习得领域内的正负迁移理论也被广泛应用,作为反身代词习得的理论支撑。如李金屏等(2010)以迁移理论为理论基础,将迁移视为在构建和验证假设过程中的一种学习策略,证明了学习者在构建新假设的过程中既依赖母语知识,也依赖现有的知识体系,与之前李红(2002)的研究结论一致。

3.2 理论探索与实证研究相结合

既有针对普遍语法在二语习得过程中有效性的讨论,如王文斌(2000a,2000b,2001)、刘志平(2006)及唐晋湘(2004a,2004b)。又有以迁移理论本身为理论基础,将其视为一种学习策略并加以讨论,如于娟(2014)基于中国英语学习者在反身代词使用过程中的常见错误,探究了错误出现的深层原因,从而正面证明了反身代词习得过程中母语负迁移现象的存在。李金屏等(2010)、李正权(2010)等也展开了相关研究。

同时,研究特定语法单位内反身代词使用的也逐渐增多。如李红(2002)采用英汉句子合乎语法性判断法研究了中国学习者习得反身代词过程中的迁移作用,并发现其在构建英语反身代词约束特征时既依赖于母语约束特征,又依赖于目的语约束特征,母语知识在习得过程中兼有正负迁移两种作用。唐晋湘(2004b)则通过对不同水平英语学习者对英语单子句中反身代词习得的测试,借助相对化大主语观点,探讨了第二语言习得过程中普遍语法的有效性。姜琳(2007)将中国学生对英语反身代词的习得与其对宾语代词的习得相结合,证实了学生对反身代词局部约束性的掌握远好于对宾语代词有形性的掌握,并通过语法分析理论解释了这一现象。吴明军(2017)则针对单双子句的语法单位内英语反身代词的约束特性习得开展了实证研究。

此外,研究者如姜琳(2007)并不仅仅局限于单一地研究英语反身代词的习得,而是将其与宾语代词的习得相结合,对二者进行对比,拓宽了该领域的研究思路。

3.3 不同母语背景下的对比研究

一些研究着眼于跨语言语境下的对比,如 Yuan(1994)对比了母语为汉语、日语及朝鲜语的二语习得者,发现他们在接触英语反身代词时能够将其与母语复合式反身代词的特征相联系。胡建华(1998)对比了中英英语学习者,研究了英汉两种语言中反身代词约束行为的异同。Yip 和 Tang(1998)研究了母语为广东话的英语学习者习得反身代词过程中的母语迁移现象,发现大部分英语学习者已经习得了英语反身代词的局部约束特征。此类研究在不同程度上表明,二语习得者的中介语法体系具有较强的母语特征,反身代词习得过程中存在着母语迁移的现象。

4 工具方法

4.1 图画指认法

早期 Finer 和 Broselow(1986)开创性地运用图画指认的方法开展二语照应成分习得的实证研究,主要研究了 6 名具有中、高级英语水平的韩国学习者对于反身代词和代词的习得。这在当时无疑是极为新颖的研究方法。

4.2 语法分析法

陈月红(2001)首先验证了三种不同分析反身代词的语法理论,在此基础上,李红(2002)采用英汉句子合乎语法性判断法这一全新方法,研究了中国学习者习得反身代词过程中的迁移作用,姜琳(2007)则通过语法分析理论解释了反身代词局部约束性的掌握优于宾语代词有形性的掌握这一现象。又如,唐晋湘(2004a,2004b)及姜琳(2007)均以 Progovac(1992,1993)提出的相对化大主语观点(relativized SUBJECT)为理论依据,验证普遍语法在二语习得中的有效性。

4.3 语料库研究法

近年来,语料库语言学的迅猛发展为研究者发展新的语料、更新研究对象创造了条件。比如,晏小琴和黄文静(2008)以三个不同语言背景的英语学习者书面语料库作为研究对象,对比研究了中国英语学习者反身代词习得的基本特征和使用功能异同,并探讨了母语知识在反身代词习得过程中的影响及英语水平与反身代词习得之间的关系。闫博文等(2016)以中国学习者英语语料库为基础,分析了不同层次学习者反身代词的使用频数和误用类型,进而对中国英语学习者在反身代词使用过程中经常出现的词类、范畴类、句法类等错误,以及中国英语学习者反身代词的整体习得情况展开了详尽分析。于娟(2014)也基于中国英语学习者语料库,探究了其在反身代词使用过程中常出现的典型错误及其背后的原因。

总之,近年来研究者们通过对研究视角、分析方法及研究对象或语料的创新,进一步加深和扩展了对于中国英语学习者反身代词习得研究的深度和广度。

5 存在问题

基于上述分析及举例可知,以往对于反身代词习得的研究主要存在四个方面的问题。

5.1 鲜有对学习者日常应用语境下的研究

以往的大多数研究都是将受试者置于一个规定的测试环境下考查其对于反身代词的掌握,鲜有研究真正关注学习者在学习、生活等应用场景中对于反身代词的实际运用。此种倾向使得许多研究结果偏于理性、书面性而缺乏普遍性、随机性。为此,笔者建议今后研究者可以从实际应用角度出发,例如,通过分析一组学生随机口语语料中反身代词的使用频数和语法特征,验证其在反身代词习得过程中表现出来的具体特点。

5.2 对语料库方法的应用不够充分

虽然现阶段国内出现了从语料库角度研究反身代词的尝试,但并不多见。众所周知,语料库中往往包含数量充足、来源真实的第一手语料,加之语料库检索工具(如 AntConc、Wordsmith 等)的日益普及使得语料处理方式变得方便快捷,基于语料库得出的研究结果将更具代表性和说服力。为此,笔者建议研究者们可在今后的研究中增加对语料库的使用,并借助相应的语料库检索分析工具对研究结果进行深入解读。

5.3 研究视角多局限于反身代词本身

根据约束理论,反身代词的使用与相应的人称代词之间有直接的联系,但现阶段大部分研究都只是单一地研究反身代词习得本身。因而笔者建议,研究者们在今后的研究中可结合相应的人称代词来研究反身代词习得,由此得出的研究结果将会更具有说服力。

5.4 研究对象多局限于英语本族语者

现阶段对于中外反身代词习得的对比研究多限于英语本族语者之中,鲜有涉及与其他母语背景下英语学习者的对比研究。诚然,英语本族语者对于反身代词的使用最具权威性,与之对比可以最大限度地体现出中国学习者在习得英语反身代词过程中的母语迁移作用。但若以英语本族语者对反身代词的使用为参照,对比中国英语学习者与其他更多不同母语背景下的英语学习者对反身代词的使用,更能挖掘出学习者在不同价值观、文化习俗、思维模式等背景下习得反身代词的特点和应用技巧。为此,笔者建议今后研究者们可多多关注如母语背景为阿尔泰语系(日语、韩语、朝鲜语等)、印欧语系(德语、瑞典语、丹麦语、挪威语等)等的受试者,在这种对比中得出的研究结果将更能凸显中国英语学习者的习得特点和使用特征。

6 发展趋势

总的来说,国内学者对于二语习得者反身代词的习得研究最早见于20世纪90年代,主要借鉴并参考了国外学者的研究。在此基础上,国内研究者开始有所探索。进入21世纪以来,国内学者对于英语反身代词的习得研究呈现出明显的上升趋势。

通过对以往研究的观察和总结可知,中国英语学习者反身代词习得的研究主要以二语习得中的迁移理论、Chomsky的约束理论以及Progovac的相对化大主语观点为理论基础,重点讨论反身代词习得过程中与普遍语法和母语迁移之间的相互作用。同时,在发展过程中将对反身代词的习得研究与探索其他句子成分的习得相结合,开展多角度对比。最后,伴随着近年来语料库资源的丰富和研究工具、方法的多样化,基于语料库探索反身代词习得的基本特征和使用功能也成为新的发展趋势。

参 考 文 献

陈月红,2001,《中国学生习得英语反身代词研究》,《外语与外语教学》第8期。
胡建华,1998,《汉语长距离反身代词的句法研究》,《当代语言学》第3期。
姜琳,2010,《中国学生对英语反身代词局部约束性及宾语代词有形性习得的实验研究》,《现代外语》第30期。
李红,2002,《中国英语学习者反身代词习得中的迁移作用》,《外语教学与研究》第2期。
李金屏、郅红、程怡,2010,《英语反身代词习得研究》,《教学与管理》第6期。
李正权,2010,《国内英语反身代词研究综述》,《西南农业大学学报(社会科学版)》第8期。
刘志平,2006,《英语反身代词习得实证研究》,《长沙铁道学院学报(社会科学版)》第7期。
唐晋湘,2004a,《从中国英语学习者习得英语反身代词看第二语言的句法习得》,《外语研究》第6期。
唐晋湘,2004b,《英语单子句中反身代词的照应习得》,《山东外语教学》第6期。
王文斌,2000a,《中国高级英语学习者对英语反身代词的习得》,《外语教学与研究》第4期。
王文斌,2000b,《约束论与反身代词第二语言习得理论研究纵观》,《四川外语学院学报》第16期。
王文斌,2001,《约束理论与英汉反身代词第二语言习得的理论研究》,《当代语言学》第2期。
吴明军,2017,《中国学习者英语反身代词约束特性的习得研究》,《语言科学》第6期。
闫博文、陈妮妮、杨廷君,2016,《以汉语为母语者英语反身代词习得研究——以中国英语学习者语料库(CLEC)为例》,《现代语文(语言研究版)》第4期。
晏小琴、黄文静,2008,《基于语料库的中国英语学习者的反身代词习得研究》,《疯狂英语(教师版)》第3期。
于娟,2014,《浅析中国英语学习者反身代词习得中的母语负迁移作用》,《考试周刊》第50期。
Chomsky, N. 1981. *Lectures on Government and Binding*. Dordrecht: Foris.
Chomsky, N. 1986. *Knowledge of Language: Its Nature, Origin, and Use*. California:

Praeger Publishers.

Finer, D., and Broselow, E. 1986. "Second language acquisition of reflexive binding." In *Proceedings of North Eastern Linguistic Society* 16. edited by S. Berman, J. W. Choe and J. McDonough. Amherst: Graduate Linguistics Students Association, University of Massachusetts.

James, C. 1980. *Contrastive Analysis*. London: Longman.

Manzini, M. R., and Wexler, K. 1987. "Parameters, Binding Theory, and Learnability". *Linguistic Inquiry*.

Odlin, T. 1989. *Language Transfer*. Cambridge: Cambridge University Press.

Progovac, L. 1992. "Relativized SUBJECT: Long-distance reflexives without movement". *Linguistic Inquiry*.

Progovac, L. 1993. "Long-distance reflexives: movement-to-infl versus relativized SUBJECT". *Linguistic Inquiry*.

Yip, V., and Tang G. 1998. "Acquisition of English reflexive binding by Cantonese learners". In *Morphology and Its Interfaces in Second Language Knowledge*. edited by M. L. Beck. Amsterdam/Philadelphia: John Benjamins.

Yuan, Boping. 1994. "Second language acquisition of reflexives revisited". *Language*. Vol. 70: 539–545.

语速对听力理解的影响

赵翙君[*]　党　弋[**]

摘　要：本研究旨在检视放慢语速对于中国大学生听力理解的影响。研究结果表明,慢于正常的语音速度(约 130 wpm)比平均语音速度(130～150 wpm)最大程度上提升了听力的理解。这一发现间接验证了放慢语速在提高语言学习者对真实材料听力理解方面的应用。在实际教学中,英语老师可以将语速放慢,以有效增进学生对真实新闻的听力理解。

关键词：听力理解；真实新闻；平均语音速度；适度缓慢语音速度；慢于正常语音速度

听力理解已成为第二语言和外语学习领域的一个核心要素；然而,与其他语言技能相比,它仍然是最不被理解的技能(Feyten,1991；Nunan,1999；Vandergrift,2004,2007)。越来越多的研究人员通过研究特定因素对听力理解的影响来探索听力的本质。在单向听力方面,因素包括听者因素和文本因素。在听者因素方面,语法知识(Mecartty,2000)、词汇知识(Kelly,1991；Mecartty,2000；Lin,2005)、背景知识(Chang and Read,2006；Chiang and Dunkel,1992；Dunkel,1986；Jensen and Hansen,1995；Long,1990；Markham and Latham,1987；Schmidt,1994；Yang,2002)和焦虑水平(Vogely,1998；Cheng,2005)一直是研究的内容。至于文本因素,句法复杂性(Blau,1988；Cervantes and Gainer,1992；Teng,2001b)、重复(Chang,1999；Chang and Read,2007；Chaudron,1983；Chiang and Dunkel,1992；Cervantes and Gainer,1992；Jensen and Vinther,2003；Parker and Chaudron,1987)、停顿(Blau,1990)得到了很大的关注。因为在不同的研究中都有一致的结果,这些因素的研究已经得出了相当令人满意的结论,但语音速度因子作为时间变量之一,产生了相互矛盾的结果。换句话说,语速对听力理解的影响还没有得出令人满意的结论,因此需要更进一步的观察与研究。

本研究旨在通过控制先前语音速度研究中未仔细处理的变量,探讨减慢的语音速度对听力理解的影响。本研究试图确定放慢语速与平均语速相比,放慢语速是否是一种能够提高听力理解表现的方法。"减速"语音进一步分为"适度缓慢"和"慢于正常"语速,以检验减速语音本身的细微差异并发现减慢语速能提升听力水平。

本研究的结果将揭示在 EFL 环境中语速对听力理解的影响,从而对语速的研究提供更深入的理解。

1　文献综述

听力理解是一个隐含的、隐蔽的、不可观察的过程,一般用自下而上、自上而下和交互处理

---

[*] 赵翙君：西北大学外国语学院教师,英国诺丁汉大学硕士毕业,主要研究方向为应用语言学、二语习得。
[**] 党弋：西北大学外国语学院讲师,西北大学外国语国际测试中心负责人,美国明尼苏达圣玛丽大学硕士毕业,主要研究方向为语言测试,深耕雅思、托福教学研究多年。

三种处理模型来说明。这三种处理模型是听力理解研究领域家喻户晓的术语,已被许多研究人员重新介绍和彻底解释(Brown,2001;Buck,2001;Field,2007;Flowerdew and Miller,2006;Hulstijn,2003;Lynch and Mendelsohn,2002;Rubin,1994;Rost,2002;Vandergrift,2007)。简单地说,这些广为人知的处理模型对听者处理传入语音信号的方式有不同的解释。

一些研究人员总结了影响语言学习者听力理解的主要因素(Boyle,1984;Parker and Chaudron,1987;Rubin,1994)。在他们总结的影响听力理解的主要因素分类中,语速是重要的因素之一。许多研究人员还从参与者的反馈和报告中得出结论,较快的语音速度是削弱听力理解的一个重要因素(Boyle,1984;Friedman and Johnson,1971;Flowerdew and Miller,1996;Graham,2006;Goh,1999;Hasan,2000;Teng,2002;Vogely,1995)。这表明,无论是研究者还是语言学习者都认识到,语速是影响听力理解的主要变量之一。因此,一些研究人员和教师为了提高语言学习者的听力理解,会扩大或放慢语速,这是合理的。由于语速所具有的教学意义,放慢语速一直是语速研究者的主要兴趣之一。

与此同时,压缩语音时间对听力理解的影响(Conrad,1989;King and Behnke,1989)的研究表明,较快的语速给听众处理传入信号带来了负担,从而降低了他们的听力理解水平。除了听力理解水平的下降外,研究者还观察到压缩语音时间对听力理解的额外影响。Conrad(1989)指出,时间压缩的言语会严重影响低熟练语言学习者的听力理解。此外,不同水平的学生会使用不同的策略来处理时间压缩的演讲。

速度控制训练的目标学员是那些处理输入语言信息较差的语言学习者,并且很难消化理解正常语音速度的口语文本。通过速度控制训练,期望在训练后能够开发大脑的听力信息处理功能,以达到较高的听力理解水平。这种速度控制的培训将持续一定的时间,在这段时间内,研究者将观察学员的听力理解进展,然而,能够证明速度控制训练有效性的研究却寥寥无几(Friedman and Johnson,1971;Huberman and Medish,1974;Pimsleur,1977)。

正如 Zhao(1997)和 Blau(1990)所指出的,以前的语速研究中显示的不一致和无法比较的结果是由不同研究人员采用的不同的语速分类所导致的。现在被认可的有两种语音速度分类:由学习者视角划分的语音速度以及以文本视角划分的语音速度。经验证据表明,学习者的感知语速与听力输入的实际情况之间存在差异(Drewing and Munro,1997,2001;Hasan,2000)。换句话说,语言学习者感知到的快或慢的语速可能与实际情况不对应。从文本的角度来看,不同文本类型的语音速度是不同的。Tauroza 和 Allison(1990)对讲英语的新闻播音员进行了语速分析,为英语提供了一个标准的语速分类(见表1)。

表1 The Range of Speech Rate in Tauroza and Allison(1990)

Categories	Speech rate/wpm
Faster than normal (above)	190
Moderately fast	170~190
Average	150~170
Moderately slow	130~150
Slower than normal (below)	130

本研究将广播新闻作为听力输入来衡量听力理解。第一个原因是新闻与文本的视角相一致。第二个原因是其具有教学意义。广播新闻被认为是一种难度更大的文本类型,这是由它的几个显著特征决定的。首先,广播新闻是一种具有某些类似书面语言特征的口头语言;其次,广播新闻主要以英语为母语的人为受众,具有丰富的文化参考。如前所述,广播新闻对语言学习者来说可能是一个真正的挑战。因此,在本研究中使用广播新闻作为材料可能会增加这些技术对其他听力材料的适用性。使用广播新闻的第三个原因是其具有真实性,这符合听力教学的最终目标,根据 Vandergrift(2006)的说法,即为语言学习者提供反映现实生活听力的技能。基于上述原因,本研究选择广播新闻作为主要的听力输入。本研究中使用的听力理解测试旨在激发参与者对广播新闻的听力理解水平。本研究采用了两种测试问题,包括真假(T/F)问题、简短回答问题。

2 研究问题和假设

本文提出了一个研究问题和三个假设,以此为目标,探讨了放慢语速和逐渐提高语速对听力理解的影响。

研究问题1:当文本以平均语音速度(150~170 wpm)、适度缓慢语音速度(130~150 wpm)和慢于正常语音速度(低于 130 wpm)播放时,听力理解是否有差异?

假设1:适度缓慢的语音速度(130~150 wpm)比慢于正常的语言速度(低于 130 wpm)能让听者有更好的听力理解。

假设2:与平均语音速度(150~170 wpm)相比,适度缓慢语音速度(130~150 wpm)的条件下有更好的听力理解。

假设3:当语音速度为慢于正常的语音速度(低于 130 wpm)和平均语音速度(150~170 wpm)之间时,听力理解没有差异。

3 方法论

西北大学共有60名大学生参与了这项旨在研究放慢语音速度对听力理解的影响的实验。在参与实验的60名参与者中,有50名是英语专业的学生。其他10名是非英语专业的学生。这60名参与者由26名大一新生、6名大二学生和28名大三学生组成。

本研究使用了6种数据收集方法:①背景问卷调查;②改编的 TOEIC(Test of English for International Communication,托业考试);③美国之音广播新闻;④酷编辑软件;⑤听力理解测试;⑥背景知识问卷调查。

4 结果

这一部分将介绍用 SPSS 12.0 计算的放慢语音速度对听力理解影响的数据分析的统计结果,包括前测和听力理解测试的结果。

采用单项方差分析(Analysis of Variance,ANOVA),分析前测分数,即 A 组、B 组和 C 组在适应 TOEIC 中获得的分数。如表2所示,无显著性差异($P=0.391$),结果表明,三组的英语听力水平均为同一水平。

表2 单向方差分析测量 A、B、C 组前测分数的结果

	SS	DF	MS	F	P
小组之间	207.608	2	103.804	0.958	0.391
小组内部	5 092.892	47	108.359	—	—
共计	5 300.500	49	—	—	—

关于听力理解测试的结果,描述性统计见表3。在低于正常语速的情况下,A 组获得的平均分数(M=160.33)高于 B 组(M=151.39)。C 组在平均语速下获得最低平均分(M=137.65)。

表3 A、B 和 C 组的平均值和标准差

小组	n	M	SD
A	15	160.33	25.246
B	17	151.39	24.959
C	17	137.65	32.745

注:A 组是比正常语音速度慢(低于 130 wpm);B 组是慢语音速度(130～150 wpm);C 组是平均语音速度(150～170 wpm)。

笔者对表4所示的单向方差分析对评分进行了分析,结果表明,三组中的两组之间没有显著性差异($p=0.82$)。这一结果印证了第三个假设,即慢于正常的语音速度(低于 130 wpm)和平均语音速度(150～170 wpm)之间的听力理解表现没有显著差异。另一方面,结果与第一个和第二个假设相冲突,即与慢于正常的语速(低于 130 wpm)相比,适度缓慢的语速(130～150 wpm)能让听者有更好的听力理解,而与平均语速相比,适度缓慢的语速能让听者有更好的听力理解。

表4 单向方差分析测量 A、B、C 组听力理解分数的结果

	SS	DF	MS	F	P
小组之间	4 214.182	2	2 107.091	2.643	0.082
小组内部	36 667.451	46	797.118	—	—
总计	40 881.633	48	—	—	—

因此,对于第一个探究慢语速对听力理解影响的研究问题的结果表明,与平均语速相比,适度缓慢语音速度和慢于正常语音速度都不能提高听力理解水平。换句话说,研究没有揭示放慢语速对听力理解的促进作用。然而,如表5所示,B 组和 A 组之间的 p 值与 C 组和 A 组之间的 p 值有很大的不同。虽然也有人指出,B 组和 C 组之间没有显著差异,但与 A 组相比,C 组的表现优于 B 组。因此,进一步审查这三组的原始分数被认为是适当的。

表5　A组、B组和C组听力理解分数的多重比较结果

比较	sig
A组 vs. B组	0.652
A组 vs. C组	0.071
B组 vs. C组	0.335

注：A组是比正常语音速度慢(低于130 wpm)；B组是慢语音速度(130～150 wpm)；C组是平均语音速度(150～170 wpm)

5　讨论

本节先说明混淆评分的处理方法，然后报告了放慢语音速度对听力理解影响的最终结果。

仔细检查听力理解测试的原始分数，研究者发现有一个分数对整体结果有很大的影响。这一分数明显高于其他分数，因此促使研究人员与收到分数的参与者进行访谈。访谈大约在正式考试后的第四周。访谈前，研究者邀请参与者再次参加听力理解测试，然后研究者检查了参与者给出的每一个答案，而参与者在回顾中解释了她是如何得到答案的，以及她在想什么。讨论表明，她在听力理解测试中没有猜测。研究人员询问了她的英语学习方法，发现她每天听BBC一个小时。据参与者说，这种做法已经坚持了近七年，这对她的特别高的分数有了合理的解释。

这个参与者的英语水平显然优于本研究中其他参与者的英语水平。因此，为了获得有效的结果，有必要排除她的分数。在省略了她的分数之后，毫无疑问，正如表6所显示的，A组听慢于正常的语音速度和C组听平均语音速度(P=0.016)之间存在显著差异。因此，不支持第三个假设：听力理解表现在慢于正常的语速和平均语速之间没有差异。

表6　多次比较测量听力理解测试分数的结果，没有混淆A组、B组和C组的数据

比较	sig
A组 vs. B组	0.611
A组 vs. C组	0.016*
B组 vs. C组	0.123

注：A组是比正常语音速度慢；B组是慢语音速度；C组是平均语音速度。

对于第一个假设，预测与慢于正常的语速相比，适度缓慢的语速将有更好的听力理解表现。然而，没有得到显著的结果来支持理解上的差异。第二种假设是，与平均语音速度相比，适度缓慢的语音速度将有更好的听力理解，但结果表明，这两种语音速度之间的理解水平没有显著差异。因此，与慢于正常或平均语音速度相比，适度缓慢的语速在加强听力理解方面并不有效。第三种假设也没有得到支持，如前一节所示。

虽然预测慢于正常的语速与平均语速之间在听力理解上没有差异，但这两种语速在听力理解上有显著差异。与平均语速相比，慢于正常的语速使听力理解水平显著增加，这表明提高听力理解能力的最适当的语速是慢于正常的语速。换句话说，结果表明，在两种减慢的语音速度之间，慢于正常的语音速度，而不是适度缓慢的语音速度，是提高听力理解的最有利的语速。

正如慢语速对听力理解影响的假设所建议的那样,本研究的主要预测是,如果语音速度太慢,听力理解水平就不会增加,以本研究中的适度缓慢语速为代表的适当的慢速语音可以有效地提高听力理解水平。当慢下来的语速被过度拉伸时,与平均语速的结果相比,听力理解能力不会得到改善。与平均语速相比,慢于正常的语速会使听力理解水平显著增加,这表明提高听力理解的最适当的语速是慢于正常的语速。换句话说,结果表明,在两种减慢的语速之间,慢于正常的语音速度,而不是适度缓慢的语音速度,是提高听力理解的最有利的语音速度。然而,听适度缓慢语速的听力材料的学生的得分没有超过听平均语速的听力材料的学生的得分,这表明,旨在提高听力理解水平的放慢语速必须到 130 wpm 左右,才能有效、显著地提高听力理解能力。总之,慢于正常的语音速度能有效地提高对真实新闻的听力理解。

6 结论

在两种减慢的语速中,慢于正常的语音速度(低于 130 wpm)比平均语音速度(150～170 wpm)能在最大程度上提升听力理解水平。这一发现间接验证了放慢语速在提高语言学习者对真实材料听力理解水平方面的应用。因此,Vandergrift(2007)关于放慢语速对听力理解产生不必要的促进作用的主张可能会受到怀疑。

对于教师而言,考虑到听力课的主要目标之一是使学生在理解受阻时更容易理解听力文本,将语速放慢到 130 wpm 以下对听力教师具有实践价值,旨在提高学生的听力理解水平,而不牺牲听力训练本身的时间。

本研究是以广播新闻为主要听力文本,未来的研究可能会考虑其他类型的听力文本,如故事或讲座,以探讨听力理解中文本类型与语速之间的相互作用。

参 考 文 献

Blau, E. 1990. "The effect of syntax, speed and pauses on listening comprehension". *TESOL Quarterly*.

Brown, D. 2001. *Teaching by Principle: An Interactive Approach to Language Pedagogy*. New Jersey: Prentice Hall Regents.

Buck, G. 2001. *Assessing listening*. New York: Cambridge University Press.

Chang C. S., and Read, J. 2006. "The effects of listening support on the listening performance of EFL learners". *TESOL Quarterly*.

Chang C. S., and Read, J. 2007. "Support for foreign language listeners: Its effectiveness and limitations". *RELC Journal*.

Chaudron, C. 1983. "Simplification if input: Topic and reinstatement and their effects on L2 learners' recognition and recall". *TESOL Quarterly*.

Cheng, Y. S. 2005. "EFL learners' listening comprehension anxiety". *English Teaching & Learning*.

Chiang, C. S., and Dunkel, P. 1992. "The effect of speech modification, prior knowledge and listening proficiency on EFL lecture learning". *TESOL Quarterly*.

Cervantes, R., and Gainer, G. 1992. "The effect of syntactic simplification and repetition on listening comprehension". *TESOL Quarterly*.

Conrad, L. 1989. "The effects of time-compressed speech on native and EFL listening comprehension". *SSLA*.

Derwing, T., and Munro, M. J. 2001. "What speaking rates do non-native listeners prefer?" *Applied Linguistics*.

Dunkel, P. 1986. "Developing listening fluency in L2: Theoretical principles and pedagogical considerations". *Modern Language Journal*.

Field, J. 2007. *Listening in the language classroom*. Cambridge: Cambridge University Press.

Feyten, M. C. 1991. "The power of listening ability: An overlooked dimension in language acquisition". *The Modern Language Journal*.

Flowerdew, J., and Miller, L. 2006. *Second language listening: Theory and practice*. New York: Cambridge University Press.

Friedman, L. H., and Johnson, L. R. 1971. "Some actually and potential uses of rate-controlled speech in second language learning". In *The Psychology of Second Language Learning*, edited by P. Pimsleur, pp. 157-163. Cambridge: Cambridge University Press.

Goh, M. C. C. 2000. "A cognitive perspective on language learners' listening comprehension problems". *System*.

Graham, S. 2006. "Listening comprehension: The learners' perspective". *System*.

Hasan, S. A. 2000. "Learners' perceptions of listening comprehension problems". *Language Culture and Curriculum*.

Huberman, G., and Medish, V. 1974. "A multi-channel approach to language teaching". *Foreign Language Annals*.

Jensen, C., and Hansen, C. 1995. "The effect of prior knowledge on EAP listening-test performance". *Language Testing*.

Jensen, E. D., and Vinther, T. 2003. "Exact repetition as input enhancement in second language acquisition". *Language Learning*.

Kelly, P. 1991. "Lexical ignorance: The main obstacle to listening comprehension with advance foreign language learners". *International Review of Applied Linguistic in Language Teaching*.

Lin, C. X. 2005. "Factors affecting listening comprehension and strategies for listening class". *Celea Journal*.

Markham, P., and Lathan, M. 1987. "The influence of religion-specific background knowledge on the listening comprehension of adult second-language students". *Language Learning*.

Mecartty. H. F. 2000. "Lexical and grammatical knowledge in reading and listening comprehension by foreign language learners of Spanish". *Applied Language Learning*.

Nunan, D. 1999. *Second Language Teaching and Learning*. Boston: Heinle & Heinle Publishers.

Parker, K., and Chaudron, C. 1987. "The effects of linguistic simplifications and elaborative modifications on L2 comprehension". *Psychology*.

Pimsleur, P., Hancock, C., and Furey, P. 1977. "Speech rate and listening comprehension". In *Viewpoints*, edited by M. K. Burt, H. C. Dulay, and M. Finocchisro.

Schmidt, R. 1994. "The effects of topic familiarity on second language listening comprehension". *Modern Language Journal*.

Tauroza, S., and Allison, D. 1990. "Speech rate in British English". *Applied Linguistics*.

Teng, H. C. 2002. "Effects of syntactic modification and speech rate on listening comprehension". Selected papers form the tenth international symposium on English teaching.

Vandergrift, L. 2004. "Listening to learn or learn to listen". Annual Review of *Applied Linguistics*.

Vandergrift, L. 2006. "Second language listening: Listening Ability or Language Proficiency?" *Modern Language Journal*.

Vandergrift, L. 2007. "Recent developments in second and foreign language listening comprehension research". *Language Teaching*.

Vogely, A. 1998. "Listening comprehension anxiety: Students' reported sources and solutions". *Foreign Language Annals*.

基于语料库的"BRING"语义韵比较研究

张晓红[*]　董俊虹[**]

摘　要：本研究基于中国学习者英语语料库（Chinese Learner English Corpus，CLEC）和美国当代英语语料库（Corpus of Contemporary American English，COCA），利用 AntConc 软件检索高频词 BRING 及其屈折变化的检索行及搭配，通过对比其使用频次、搭配名词和语义韵，揭示中国英语学习者和英语母语者对该词的使用特点和差异，指导中国英语学习者更好地掌握该词的使用，并为掌握其他英语高频词提供新思路。

关键词：语义韵；BRING；CLEC；COCA

1　引言

语义韵的概念最早是由 Sinclair 从英国语言学家 Firth 的语音学中借鉴而来。Sinclair（1991）根据多年编撰词典的经验得出，break out、happen、set in 有消极语义韵，set in 的搭配词语如 impoverishment、decay 等基本都是表达不愉快的事物，但他并没有公开使用"语义韵"。Louw(1993)第一次使用"语义韵"并将其定义为："一个词项倾向于和一定语义范畴的其他词项共现，习惯性地吸引某一类具有相同或相似语义特点的词项，这种现象就是语义韵。"Stubbs(1996)根据搭配词的总体语义特征将语义韵划分为积极语义韵（positive prosody）、消极语义韵（negative prosody）和中性语义韵（neutral prosody）三种。如果既有消极又有积极的词项，那么则认为该节点词具有错综的语义特点。

语料库语言学对语义韵的研究（Louw，1993；卫乃兴，2002）提供了词语搭配研究的一个崭新视角和途径，给定节点词的搭配行为都有规律可循，都隐含或明确表达语言使用者的态度与评价意义，实现某种语用目的或功能。

中国英语学习者与英语母语者使用某一词类的语义韵对比研究也是中国学者研究的热点。温玲霞(2007)对近义词的语义韵进行对比研究，发现 rather 和 fairly 两词除了在类连接及意义方面的区别外，还从语义韵的角度做了进一步的阐释。黄瑞红(2007)对中国英语学习者形容词增强语的语义韵进行了研究，发现随着学生水平的提高、搭配能力的增强，孕育词语搭配的语义韵的准确率也越高，同时指出在学习者使用 totally、very much 和 terribly 等词时，语义韵倾向与英语母语者不一致。王瑞和姜雪(2016)通过揭示 complete、finish、perform 三词在两类语料库中的使用特点，分析中国英语学习者与英语母语者在使用这三个词汇时的差异。

笔者发现，中国英语学习者在口语和书面语表达中，对 BRING 的运用非常普遍，也存在

---

[*] 张晓红：西北工业大学外国语学院硕士研究生。
[**] 董俊虹：西北工业大学外国语学院教授，主要研究方向为认知语言学、二语习得、高等教育管理等。

着搭配方面的问题。本研究借助 CLEC 和 COCA 语料库,旨在探索中国英语学习者和英语母语者在使用英语高频词 BRING 时的语义韵差异。

2　研究设计

本研究采用定量研究和定性分析相结合的方法,以 CLEC 和 COCA 语料库为基础,采用 COCA 的在线检索工具,以及 AntConc 3.4.3w 软件进行检索,提取出两个语料库中关于 BRING 及其屈折变化的所有索引行,对比发现 BIRNG 在使用频次上是否有差异。随后在 AntConc 和 COCA 在线索引上面限定节点词 BRING 左右 4 个词的范围内,提取共现频率为 5 次以上(包括 5 次),以及 MI 值 ≥ 3(表示和节点词为显著性搭配)的搭配词,并筛选出搭配词中的名词进行研究。再用 SPSS 软件对数据进行卡方检验,得出英语母语者和中国英语学习者在 BRING 使用上有哪些显著差异。本文试图回答以下问题:

(1)中国英语专业学习者在使用 BRING 时,其使用频次与英语母语者是否有差异?
(2)中国英语专业学习者对 BRING 搭配词的语义韵与英语母语者是否一致?

3　结果与分析

3.1　使用频数比较

本研究采用标准化频数来比较 BRING 在两个语料库中的使用频率,通过以上检索方式,得到使用频次的对比(见表 1)。

表 1　中国英语学习者与英语母语者使用 BRING 的频次比较

	库容量	观测频数	标准化频数
CLEC	1 070 602	1 366	1.276
COCA	560 000 000	247 575	0.442

注:COCA 库容量数据采用 2017 年官网数据。

其中:

$$标准化频数(每千词) = \frac{观测频数}{总体频数} \times 1\,000$$

注:观测频数即检索词项实际出现的次数;总体频数即语料库的库容量或总形符数。

如表 1 所示,在 COCA 中,BRING 一共出现 247 575 次,其标准化频次为 0.442;在 CLEC 中,BRING 一共出现 1 366 次,其标准频次为 1.276 次。BRING 在 CLEC 的标准化频数远大于 COCA,因此可以得出结论:BRING 在 CLEC 和 COCA 中出现的总体频数存在显著差异,即中国英语学习者对 BRING 的使用存在明显的超用情况。

3.2　语义韵比较

为了进一步研究中国英语学习者和英语母语者在使用 BRING 时的实际情况,我们需要比较 BRING 在两个语料库中的具体搭配和语义倾向度,通过检索和筛选降噪,得到样本容量分别为102(CLEC)和185(COCA)的搭配名词表,按照频数高低排列(见表2)。

表2 语料库中BRING高频搭配名词表(部分)

a. CELE数据

| \multicolumn{4}{c}{CELC(前20)} |||||
编号	频数	MI值	搭配
1	64	5.98	commodities
2	56	5.75	money
3	42	9.45	luck
4	42	3.85	water
5	38	4.07	life
6	36	8.21	trouble
7	34	3.72	job
8	30	8.03	happiness
9	26	7.57	effect(s)
10	24	6.54	harm
11	24	3.87	work
12	22	8.16	lunch
13	22	3.92	society
14	18	10.81	tombs
15	18	4.44	euthanasia
16	18	6.61	changes
17	18	6.38	clothes
18	18	5.46	food
19	16	9.69	convenience
20	16	5.33	human

b. COCA数据

COCA(前20)			
编号	频数	MI值	搭配
1	682	3.09	peace
2	508	4.34	pot
3	490	6.34	saucepan
4	430	3.48	mind
5	364	3.54	tears
6	350	5.32	broth
7	334	3.33	cups
8	309	4.3	lawsuit(s)
9	286	3.48	memories
10	245	3.12	joy
11	244	3.02	mixture
12	204	3.22	stability
13	146	4.35	closure
14	138	3.03	gifts
15	136	4.37	nightline
16	135	4.57	waiter/waitress
17	121	3.7	prosperity
18	121	3.02	happiness
19	106	3.04	charges
20	105	3.29	slaves

通过对样本中的搭配名词进行语义分类,并使用SPSS进行方差检验,结果见表3。

表3 BRING在CLEC和COCA中的搭配词语义倾向统计

	积极		消极		中性	
	频数	百分比/%	频数	百分比/%	频数	百分比/%
CLEC	45	44	21	21	36	35
COCA	49	26	51	28	85	46
P值	<0.01 (卡方值=9.28)		>0.05 (卡方值=1.70)		>0.05 (卡方值=3.06)	

表3统计数据显示,BRING在两个语料库样本中,都具有错综语义韵倾向,这和《朗文当代英语词典》对BRING的释义一致,词典中,BRING有"to take something or someone with you to the place"和"to cause someone or something to reach a particular state or condition"等释义,并不能看出有明显的语义倾向。在 CLEC 样本中,BRING 的高频搭配词有:commodities、money、luck、water、life、trouble、job 等,这些搭配名词有不同的语义含义,显示出 BRING 具有错综语义韵的倾向。结果表明,中国英语学习者对 BRING 的语义韵整体掌握良好。

其中,BRING 在 CLEC 的 185 个搭配词中,有积极含义的有 45 个,消极含义的有 21 个,中性的有 36 个。在消极含义和中性含义的搭配词的使用上,SPSS 卡方检验结果显示,P 值均大于 0.05,这说明 BRING 在两个语料库中,消极含义和中性含义的搭配词使用差异不明显。由此可知,中国英语学习者对 BRING 的消极和中性名词搭配掌握良好。

然而,在有积极含义的语义倾向上,卡方检验结果显示:卡方=9.28,p<0.01,远大于0.05,这表明在统计学意义上,BRING 在 CLEC 和 COCA 语料库中的积极语义韵方面的使用差异显著。这说明中国英语学习者在使用 BRING 时,搭配了过多具有积极含义的名词,存在过度使用情况。母语迁移对二语词汇选择的影响也很大。这也可能是由于学习者受到了母语迁移的影响。国内大部分的大学英语教材的作者通常将其直译为"带来",学习者在二语学习和运用中,只会生搬硬套。对 BRING 积极语义韵的过度使用,值得英语学习者注意和改正,英语教师在教学中也应适当引导。

通过进一步分析积极语义韵搭配名词发现,BRING 的词典释义:"to make a particular situation exist, or cause a particular feeling"的使用频率高,如在 CLEC 语料库中,高频搭配有 happiness、health、luck、relief 等;在 COCA 语料库中,有 peace、memories、stability、joy 等。其中,在 CLEC 中,最高频积极语义韵的搭配词为"bring luck";在 COCA 中,"bring peace"为最高频搭配,在搭配内容方面也有差异。笔者认为,这和语言使用者的生活环境有关:中国社会环境稳定,中国人关注自己在社会中的发展,所以 BRING 的具有积极意义的搭配名词都聚焦于人本身的感受或状态;美国参与越南战争、伊拉克战争等,并遭受"9·11"恐怖袭击等事件,促使美国人对 peace 有强烈的渴望。

4 结语

本研究使用语料库对比研究方法,聚焦于节点词 BRING 在 CLEC 和 COCA 语料库中的搭配词的语义含义倾向研究。结果表明,中国英语学习者对 BRING 有过度使用现象,但对 BRING 的语义韵掌握整体良好,呈现出和 COCA 语料库样本一样的错综语义韵倾向,而在消极语义韵和中性语义韵掌握上,和英语母语者使用差异不明显。不过在积极语义韵上,中国英语学习者使用过多,使该节点词在错综语义韵上更倾向于积极语义韵,这和英语母语者具有显著差异,值得中国英语学习者注意。

Louw(1993)指出:"语义韵存在于人们的感知之外,无法察觉"。众多学者的研究也表明,英语学习者很少注意到语义韵的存在。因此,对语义韵的学习和研究应该引起重视。对其进行研究可拓展词汇教学和学习的内容和深度,有助于英语学习者快速掌握词汇使用,也可以避免词语的误用。

参 考 文 献

黄瑞红,2007,《中国英语学习者形容词增强语的语义韵研究》,《外语教学》第 4 期。
王瑞、姜雪,2016,《基于语料库的 COMPLETE,FINISH,PERFORM 语义韵对比研究》,《外语电化教学》第 171 期。
卫乃兴,2002,《语义韵研究的一般方法》,《外语教学与研究》第 4 期。
温玲霞,2007,《基于语料库数据的近义词语义韵调查》,《沈阳大学学报》第 5 期。
Louw, Bill. 1993. "Irony in the text or insincerity in the writer? —The diagnostic potential of semantic prosodies". *Text and Technology: In Honour of John Sinclair*. Amsterdam: Benjamins.
Sinclair, J. 1991. *Corpus, Concordance, Collocation*. Oxford: Oxford University Press.
Stubbs, M. 1996. *Text and Corpus Analysis*. Oxford: Blackwell Publishers.

An Evaluation of Postgraduates' Global Competence and its Influencing Factors[*]

Lei Xiaolan[**]

Abstract: In the context of globalization and China's the Belt and Road Initiative, global competence is regarded as one of the core qualities for postgraduate students. In the framework of the global competence theory, employing a widely accepted assessment scale, a survey is carried out on the postgraduates in a key university in Xi'an City, Shaanxi Province. To be specific, a quantitatively analysis is done to find out whether there are significant differences among the three dimensions of global competence: knowledge and understanding, cross-cultural skills, attitudes and values. Then the main factors which might exert influences on global competence are explored qualitatively. The results show that there are significant differences among the three dimensions. Postgraduates perform worst in cross-cultural skills. The main factors affecting global competence might be as follows: participating in multinational activities, taking some intercultural communication or major-relevant frontier courses, reading original foreign works, etc. The purpose of this study is to broaden the global horizon and to improve the intercultural communicative competence of Chinese postgraduates.

Key Words: postgraduates; global competence; cross-cultural communication skills

1 Introduction

With the intensification of globalization and China's worldwide implementation of the the Belt and the Road Initiative, the cooperation between China and the countries along the Road has been strengthened day by day. In the future, exchanges in different fields such as economy, culture and education will become more and more frequent. In this context, an increasing number of high-level talents are required to engage themselves into the communication and cooperation of the international market.

Postgraduates are the main force of senior professional talents, and they are supposed to work and think on a global scale. In particular, engineering and the alike major's students

---

[*] This paper is supported by the Degree and Graduate Education Research Fund of Northwestern Polytechnical University(No. 18GZ050102).(西北工业大学学位与研究生教育研究基金)

[**] Lei Xiaolan:雷小兰,西北工业大学外国语学院副教授,主讲本科生课程——大学英语阅读、口语、网络视听说、英文电影赏析,英语专业研究生课程经济——分析语言学、篇章语言学等。

need to prepare themselves for the global society better (Lunn, 2008). Globalization and labor market internationalization also require postgraduate students to become international talents with core competencies such as intercultural communication and cooperation skills. This poses a challenge to the core literacy of postgraduate students. Only by possessing certain skills can the postgraduates meet the need for internationalized talents to participate in international cooperation. Therefore, international competence has become an important aspect of postgraduates' ability training. This study tries to answer the following questions: ①How could "global competence" be defined and interpreted? ②What are the criteria to evaluate the global competence of postgraduate students? What are the main influencing factors? By answering the above questions, this paper aims to broaden the international horizon of Chinese postgraduates and improve their intercultural communicative competence.

2 Research Design

2.1 Interpretation of Global Competence

Global competence is a term that refers to the knowledge, skills, and other capacities used to examine, appreciate, understand, and use local, national, and international elements to navigate the world successfully. A globally competent person should have an open mind while actively seeking to understand cultural norms and expectations of others, leveraging gained knowledge to interact, communicate and work effectively outside one's environment.

According to Hunter (2006), global competence is composed of three dimensions. The first is attitudes and values, which includes recognition of cultural differences, non-judgmental response and open-minded attitudes. The second is knowledge and understanding, which involves the cognition and understanding of the world's history and geography. The third is intercultural skills, which comprises the act of identifying cultural differences and evaluating cross-cultural behavior, cross-cultural cooperation and other skills and experiences. Deardorff (2006) and Li Yulong (2013) also insists the existence of three-dimensional structure: knowledge, skills and attitudes.

Following the above theory, we agree that a qualified postgraduate should, firstly, possess the knowledge of multinational languages, cultures, politics and economics, as well as an understanding of global issues; secondly, keep an open international consciousness and attitude and show respect for cultural diversity; and thirdly, apply relevant knowledge to effectively conduct cross-cultural learning, communication and work in a foreign cultural environment.

2.2 Research Design

2.2.1 Research subjects

Located in the historic city of Xi'an, a cradle of Chinese civilization and the starting point of the ancient Silk Road, Northwestern Polytechnical University (NWPU) is the only multidisciplinary and research-oriented in China that is simultaneously developing education and research programs in the fields of aeronautics, astronautics, and marine technology engineering. It was one of the first universities to enter into the 211 Project in 1995, the 985 Project in 2001 and Double Tops in 2015. Until September 2018, there are 23 doctoral authorization points and 32 authorized points for master's degree. Up to September 2020, there are, 17 541 postgraduates in NWPU, including 12 373 full-time postgraduates, 5 168 doctoral postgraduates.

The school attaches great importance to foreign exchange and cooperation. It has signed international academic exchanges and cooperation agreements with more than 100 universities and scientific research institutions in the United States, Britain, France, Germany, Belgium, Japan, Russia and Ukraine, etc. To enable postgraduate students to participate in scientific research practice, more than 120 well-known foreign scholars, professors and experts have been employed as honorary professors or consultant professors in the university. Every year, many famous international scholars come to give lectures and carry out international cooperation. There are many kinds of postgraduates training programs, such as joint training among state-sponsored overseas schools and exchange and cooperation among postgraduates tutors.

This study takes the postgraduates of NWPU as subjects, makes an analysis of their global competence and then explore its influencing factors.

2.2.2 Research questionnaire

Liu Yang and Wu Ruilin designed and validated the Global Competence Assessment Scale for College Students in 2015. On this basis, taking a consideration of the characteristics of postgraduate students, especially doctoral students, Liu Yang and others designed a specific assessment scale for postgraduate students, and tested its reliability and validity.

The questionnaire consists of two parts. The first part is the personal information of postgraduates, including gender, age, professional experience of visiting abroad and so on. The second part is the Global Competence Assessment Scale. The scale is designed according to the three categories mentioned above: ① attitudes and values; ② knowledge and understanding; ③cross-cultural skills. There is a total of 35 items. Among them, 10 items are contributed to explain "knowledge and understanding" dimension, which mainly assesses students' understanding of foreign culture, history, politics and economy, as well as globalization. 14 items are designed to evaluate students' intercultural communicative competence, scientific research communication and cooperation. The rest 11 items are used to judge students' attitudes and values which are related with students' open attitudes, willingness to engage with foreign cultures and values. The questionnaire adopts Likert-scale. Postgraduates can choose the degree of conformity between the description of international competence and their own situation. The five choices are "very inconsistent", "inconsistent", "average", "consistent", and "very consistent". Each is assigned a value of 1, 2, 3, 4, 5 respectively. This research adopts their assessment scale and passed the statistical test.

2.3 Research Methods

The survey employs stratified sampling. Sampling survey was conducted among postgraduates from every college of Northwestern Polytechnical University. A total of 2 000 questionnaires were distributed in this study and 1 900 questionnaires were collected, with a recovery of 95%. After excluded the invalid questionnaire, the valid ones amount to 1 519, which accounts for about 80%. The general description of the subjects is as shown in Table 1.

Table 1 A General Description of the Subjects

Items	Specified Items	Number	Percentage/%
Gender	Male	1 291	85.0
	Female	228	15.0
Level of students	Postgraduates (for master degree)	1 017	67.0
	Postgraduates (for PhD degree)	502	33.0
Disciplines	Engineering	890	58.6
	Science	486	32.0
	Liberal arts	143	9.4
Grades	Postgraduates Grade I (for master degree)	668	44
	Postraduates Grade II (for master degree)	349	23
	Postgraduates Grade I (for PhD degree)	303	19.9
	Postgraduates Grade II (for PhD degree)	199	13.1

The research employs both quantitative and qualitative methods to do the analysis. In quantitative analysis, the software of SPSS is used to do the statistical analysis of the collected data. The method used here is descriptive analysis. Qualitative method is employed to explore the factors which might affect the development of global competence.

3 Results and Discussion

3.1 Statistical Analysis of the Global Competence

As displayed in Table 2, postgraduates perform the best in the dimension of "attitudes and values", which indicates that postgraduates could be aware of cross-national distinctions. They are able to appreciate the cultural diversity and respect the cultural differences. The results prove that postgraduates do fairly well in knowledge and understanding dimension. They are ready to accept the concept "globalization". They know about the current world events and the world history. However, they behave the worst in "cross-cultural competence", which is only 3.01 in mean, which indicates that postgraduates needs improving their cross-cultural skills.

Table 2 Results of the Three Dimensions of Global Competence

Dimensions of global competence	Minimum value	Maximum value	Mean	St.dev
Knowledge and understanding	1	5	3.49	0.119
Cross-cultural competence	1	5	3.01	0.337
Attitudes and values	1	5	3.73	0.209

3.2 Discussion of the Influencing Factors

Global competence is the ability to employ some strategies to communicate and learn cross-cultures flexibly and effectively in a non-cultural environment. There are many factors that might affect the international ability of postgraduates, such as taking international courses, attending relevant lectures and training, presenting at international conferences, etc. Considering the factors mentioned in the related theory, empirical researches and the results of the questionnaire, this section focuses on the main factors which might affect the development of global competence.

3.2.1 Taking part in overseas study program

Taking Part in overseas study program is the most effective way to improve postgraduates' overall capabilities. In addition to broadening their academic horizon, studying abroad could, firstly, offer postgraduate students the opportunities to get to know more about the destination country's culture, geography, history, politics, economy, etc. What's more, it could help develop their skills of international academic exchanges with foreigners. Last but not the least, overseas visits could make them be more open and respectful to foreign cultures. To be specific, during the 1 to 6 months' stay, they are thrown into a pure foreign language environment, and they strive to adapt to foreign learning environment and scientific research environment, hence their cross-cultural ability and linguistic ability will be effectively enhanced.

3.2.2 Doing the reading of foreign literature and classics of original works

It has been evidenced that extensive reading of foreign original works has a positive effect on postgraduates' global competence. Being exposed to a sea of original works in foreign languages, postgraduates could not only increase their reading and writing ability in foreign languages, but also quickly improve their understanding of international issues in professional fields.

3.2.3 Participating in the cross-national research project

This research has shown that the participation of postgraduate students in international topics and projects will contribute to the promotion of their global capabilities. In fact, the participation of postgraduate students in the relevant research projects on international issues under the guidance of tutors will enhance their ability to comb and understand the international literature on professional issues. At the same time, postgraduates could substantively get involved in project cooperation in international cooperation, gaining more opportunities to exercise and enhance their international capabilities.

3.2.4 Taking the frontier major-relevant courses

Taking frontier academic courses can significantly expand the global horizon of postgraduate students. Moreover, it can bring postgraduates into the international frontier of specialty. These will help them build up a solid foundation to further participate in international conferences, seminars, international cooperation projects. In the meantime, it will facilitate postgraduates to have their academic paper published in international journals. Therefore, opening international frontier courses is serving as one of the important platforms to improve postgraduates' global competence. Of course, it will be better to increase the courses taught by foreign teachers because attending such courses will definitely improve postgraduates' communicative abilities both in foreign language and social skills.

3.2.5 Attending cross-cultural courses

Previous studies have shown that intercultural courses and teaching will have a positive impact on postgraduates' international competence. This could be implemented from two aspects: on the one hand, more cross-cultural courses could be opened to postgraduates to enhance their cross-cultural competence. On the other hand, knowledge about multinational history, culture and institutions can be added to the existing international courses to help postgraduates understand the value orientation, thinking mode and communication mode of different countries, hence increasing their knowledge and enhancing their ability to deal with international academic exchanges.

4 Major Findings and Suggestions

4.1 Major Findings

First, through factor analysis and regression analysis, this study confirms the basic hypotheses of the three dimensions of postgraduate students' international competence including knowledge and understanding, attitudes and values, and cross-cultural skills.

Second, there are significant differences in the three dimensions of international competence of postgraduates, and the results show that cross-cultural skills are the weakest dimension in the three dimensions.

Third, the experience of participation in the international programs and activities has a strong explanatory power to its global competence. The international activity factors have significant influence on the graduate students' ability include taking international courses and elective courses involving taking elective courses with foreign teachers, reading foreign language academic papers, reading the original foreign works, and participating in global scientific research projects. The same result can be seen in Liu Yang's study on *Internationalization of Higher Education: The Design and Examination on the Assessment Scale of College Students' International Competence*.

4.2 Suggestions for Improvement

Firstly, even though the effectiveness of short-term overseas study on global competence has been verified, a majority of respondents complained that the visit duration was too short, and they suggested extending the visiting stay in foreign countries. Also, participants of such overseas programs are too few due to the limited fund, thus, to increase the funding to ensure more postgraduates to benefit from the overseas programs is also a wish.

Secondly, since it is of great beneficial to do more reading of foreign, original literature and works, supervisors and instructors should recommend more original works to their students and hold seminars for discussion of the assigned reading tasks.

5 Conclusion

The cultivation and promotion of postgraduate students' global competence can initiate the objective requirements in the new situation. By analyzing the structure and influencing factors of postgraduate students' international competence, this paper provides some empirical basis and countermeasures for improving postgraduate students' international competence. However, based on time and sample questions, future research can further explore issues such as in-depth exploration of the course teaching process and the impact mechanism on postgraduate students' international competence.

References

Deardorff, D. K. 2006. "Identification and Assessment of Intercultural Competence as a student outcome of Internationalization." *Joural of studies in International Education*.
Feng, Weixing, et al. 2019. "Research on the Training Mode of Doctoral Innovative Ability Based on International Cooperation". *Education Teaching Forum*.
Hunter, B., White G. P., and Godbey, G. 2006. "What does it mean to be globally competent?" *Journal of Studies in International Education*.

Liu, Yang, and Ma, Ying. 2018. "Research on the evaluation and promotion strategies of postgraduate's international competence". *College education management*.

Liu, Yang, and Wu, Ruilin. 2015. "Internationalization of higher education—Design and test of international competence assessment scale for college student". *Fudan Education Forum*.

Liu, Yang, Wu, Peili, and Li, Mingyi. 2015. "Internationalization of higher education—An Empirical Study on the Influencing Factors of International Competence Assessment of College Students". *Fudan Education Forum*.

Lunn, J. 2008. "Global perspectives in higher education: Taking the Agenda Forward in the United Kingdom". *Journal of Studies in International Education*.

Li, Yulong. 2013. "Cultivating Student Global Competence: A Pilot Experimental Study". *Decision Sciences Journal of Innovative Education*.

Conceptualising Vocabulary Knowledge

Wang Xuan*

Abstract: This study aims to explore the relationship between receptive and productive vocabulary size and individual variance factors that might relate to this established relationship. Individual variance factors included reading ability, whether participants are studying in an arts or science stream, and the ratio of the score at the most frequent 2 000 words level to the overall vocabulary score. Two hundred and forty-six English as a Foreign Language (EFL) high school students in China were recruited to complete four tests to explore these research components. Participants completed the English-Chinese Vocabulary Translation (ECVT) and the Chinese-English Vocabulary Translation (CEVT) tests to measure their receptive vocabulary size and controlled productive vocabulary size. The Lex30 was used to investigate participants' free productive vocabulary size and participants' reading ability was identified according to their scores from one IELTS General Training Reading practice test. The current study found that participants' receptive and controlled productive vocabulary knowledge developed at an inconsistent speed and participants with a higher receptive score tended to have a larger gap between receptive and controlled productive knowledge. The findings of this study hope to provide additional insights that will assist language learning and teaching among intermediate EFL learners.

Key Words: receptive vocabulary size; productive vocabulary size; reading ability; English as a Foreign Language

1 Introduction

This paper considers the concept of vocabulary knowledge and discusses what processes are involved when learners encounter and learn to understand a new word. Vocabulary knowledge has been widely explored in recent empirical studies (Khezrlou, Ellis, and Sadeghi, 2017; Pellicer-Sánchez, 2016; Webb, 2015; Zhang and Lu, 2014) and review articles (Moghadam, Zainal and Ghaderpour, 2012; Schmitt, 2014; Walters, 2004). A consistent definition of vocabulary knowledge, however, has not yet been agreed upon because it is a complicated concept that can be defined via different approaches. Palmberg (1987) believed that knowing a lexical item was a process of building on a level of previous knowledge

---

* Wang Xuan: 王譞, 西北工业大学外国语学院教师, 主要研究方向为英语词汇学、对外英语教学、语言政策与规划、语言测试学等。

"starting with a superficial familiarity with the word and ending with the ability to use the word correctly in free production" (Laufer et al., 2004). Acquiring vocabulary knowledge as suggested by Nation (2001) and Coxhead (2007) involves knowledge of different components including phonology, morphology, syntax, and collocation. There are generally three kinds of approaches to categorising vocabulary knowledge in the literature: form, meaning, and use (Nation, 2001); breadth and depth (Anderson and Freebody, 1981); and receptive and productive vocabulary knowledge (Laufer, 1998).

2 Form, Meaning, and Use

The construct of vocabulary knowledge is complex with multiple dimensions (Zeeland and Schmitt, 2013). Meaning, form, and use are three commonly agreed dimensions that language learners should know (Nation, 2005). Specifically, the meaning of a word refers to how the language user understands it; form refers to its spoken and written forms and its parts including prefix and suffix; and the use of a word is defined by its associated grammatical functions, collocations and constraints on its use (Nation, 2001). Take the word "multicultural" as an example. The *Cambridge Dictionary* (2016) defines multicultural as including people who have many different customs and beliefs. In terms of form, the written form is m-u-l-t-i-c-u-l-t-u-r-a-l and the pronunciation of the word is /ˌmʌltiˈkʌltʃərəl/. This word form has "multi" as its prefix and "al" as its suffix. In addition, multicultural is an adjective and can be used with the word society as in a multicultural society, a term which is commonly related to the use of this word. It is demanding for learners to simultaneously acquire all the dimensions of a word, so the question of which dimension should be first introduced to assist in learning a word has garnered much attention and even debate in the literature.

It is commonly believed that word form and meaning are required first for language learners to use words correctly and appropriately (Schmitt, 2010). However, teachers and learners have adopted diverse approaches to the sequencing of form and meaning. Learners' vocabulary knowledge seems to develop differently, and some learners perform better with form than meaning whilst others are the opposite. Laufer (2005), for example, discussed two different approaches to vocabulary acquisition: Focus on Form (FonF) and Focus on Forms (FonFs). FonF encouraged language learners to learn English incidentally and to focus on meaning and communication, whilst FonFs focused on rules and grammatical knowledge of each lexical item. These two different approaches in vocabulary acquisition enabled language learners to develop their dimensions of vocabulary knowledge differently and the accuracy and correctness of L2 production are also influenced by whether L2 learners focused more on meaning or on form (Han, 2000; Salaberry and Lopez-Ortega, 1998).

Elgort et al. (2016) compared the effect of form-focused and meaning-focused elaboration in contexts where learners are exposed to new words. Form-focused elaboration involved writing the word, whereas meaning-focused elaboration involved inferring the meaning of a word from its context. Forty-seven intermediate proficiency Chinese ESL learners and fifty intermediate-to-high proficiency Dutch L2 learners were recruited and their performance was assessed after being exposed to form-focused or meaning-focused elaboration. Immediate measures, including dictation for the form of critical items and meaning generation for these critical items, were employed to compare the effect of the two approaches. Their research indicated that, although both groups of learners did gain better lexical quality of newly learnt target words, form-focused elaboration of word writing had more positive effects on their vocabulary acquisition than meaning-focused elaboration that involved inferring the meaning of a word from its context. Their findings also supported the importance of word copying in practical teaching and learning. Participants under the word-writing condition gained higher scores for both knowledge of form and meaning than participants under the condition of meaning-focused elaboration. Form-focused elaboration not only improved form acquisition but also enabled understanding of meaning more than meaning-focused elaboration. Such research illustrates that the interaction between form and meaning in acquiring vocabulary is more complicated than what has been understood.

3 Breadth and Depth

Anderson and Freebody (1981) introduced two dimensions to the concept of vocabulary knowledge: breadth and depth. Breadth refers to "the number of words for which the person knows at least some of the significant aspects of meaning"; in other words, the breadth of a learner's vocabulary reflects how many words that they know. In light of Nation's (2001) knowledge framework of vocabulary, this knowledge could include the oral and written forms of the words, as well as the surface meanings and basic uses of the words. However, while the breadth of knowledge relates to the overall vocabulary of a learner, the extent to which learners know individual words is not known. Vocabulary depth is "the quality or depth of understanding" (Anderson and Freebody, 1981) of a word and "reflects how well a learner knows individual words or how well words are organized in the learner's mental lexicon" (Stæhr, 2009). Learners within first and second language contexts do not tend to know each lexical item to the same extent as native language speakers, and they might understand some specific lexical items more deeply than others. Learners' understanding of particular lexical items may vary in precision, as can the extent of their knowledge of specific words (Read, 2000).

Researchers have noted the complexity and multidimensionality of vocabulary knowledge and measured its breadth using three major approaches: first, counting the words that are produced by the participants; second, counting the number of words in a dictionary and testing what proportion of them are known by the participants; and, third, taking samples at various frequency levels to estimate the amount of vocabulary known by the participants at each level. As vocabulary size plays an important role in language learning and use, there is an essential need to investigate how much vocabulary is actually held by language learners. Researchers have mainly approached the construct of depth in three different ways (Read, 2004). First, depth of vocabulary is measured based on degrees of word knowledge and with a principal focus on meaning, with the degrees represented by sensitivity grades (Haastrup and Henriksen, 1998) or self-assessment scales (Wesche and Paribakht, 1996). Second, depth is measured through a range of features such as orthography, phonology, morphology, syntax, collocation and pragmatics (Nation, 2001). Third, it is examined as a network in a learner's mental lexicon and their ability to build connections among relevant words. A learner's associative behaviour is perceived to reflect the depth of their knowledge, and researchers have looked at the degree of native-likeness in learner responses in word association tests as an indication of depth (Stæhr, 2009).

In terms of the feasibility and validity of measuring vocabulary, measuring the depth of knowledge requires testing diverse components of a specific word; thus, only a small number of target words can be assessed in order to be practical. Exploration of depth is also limited to small groups of participants compared to the investigation of breadth. Although it is challenging for vocabulary size tests to avoid being superficial (Read, 2000), tests that consist of larger samples of target words from many word frequency levels can provide a general picture of the overall state of the learner's vocabulary (Laufer et al., 2004).

Vocabulary breadth has a more significant role in lexical inferencing than the depth of vocabulary (Hatami and Tavakoli, 2012), and a more complicated interaction with vocabulary learning strategies (Zhang and Lu, 2015). Hatami and Tavakoli (2012) investigated the effect of breadth and the depth of knowledge on lexical inferencing and perceived ease of inferencing by analysing how well 50 EFL learners guessed 10 target words in a single passage. The Vocabulary Levels Test (VLT) was applied to measure vocabulary size; the Word Associates Test was employed to measure depth and the Likert-Scale Questionnaire was chosen to measure the degree of the perceived ease of inferencing. Their research showed that both breadth and depth of vocabulary knowledge positively affects lexical inferencing, but breadth could play a more significant role than depth. Results indicated that neither breadth nor depth significantly affected ease of inferencing. These findings suggest that increasing vocabulary size required more attention and building the form-meaning link is both valuable and necessary.

Zhang and Lu (2015) examined the effect of learning strategies on the breadth and depth of vocabulary through analysing 150 Chinese EFL learners. The VLT and the Meaning Recall Test (Schmitt, 1997) were adopted as measurements for meaning recognition and recall; the Depth of Vocabulary Knowledge Test was applied to examine the depth of receptive vocabulary knowledge and the Vocabulary Learning Strategies Survey was used for investigating strategies. Their research discovered that strategies on learning the forms and associative meanings of words were significant predictors of both breadth and depth of vocabulary. Although both meaning recognition and meaning recall could be used to measure the breadth of vocabulary knowledge, the effects of strategies of the same type on these two processes may be different.

4 Receptive and Productive Vocabulary Knowledge

Receptive and productive vocabulary relates to the different forms of word knowledge possessed by a language learner. Receptive knowledge relates to the receptive skills, such as listening to or reading words, through which a learner acquires vocabulary. In this process, learners develop an understanding of the form of a word and begin to learn its meaning, but they might not necessarily use this word. Productive knowledge, on the other hand, is gained through a learner implementing their productive skills, such as speaking and writing. In the literature, receptive vocabulary is also considered to be passive knowledge, whilst productive vocabulary refers to an active form of acquiring knowledge. Laufer et al. (2004) has categorised vocabulary knowledge into four dimensions based on the extent to which language learners can appropriately connect the form of a word with the concept that the form represents. These dimensions are active (productive) recall, passive (receptive) recall, active (productive) recognition, and passive (receptive) recognition. The difference between recall and recognition is that recall represents a learner's ability to recall the form or the meaning of a word without other support, whilst recognition relates to when they can recognise the form or the meaning in a set of options. This research focuses upon recall in regard to receptive forms of acquiring knowledge of words; only participants who could recall the form and meaning of a word were considered to know the words.

Studies (Webb, 2009; Zhong, 2016) have investigated the progression from receptive learning to productive use of vocabulary. Webb (2009) compared the effect of receptive and productive approaches to learning word pairs on the growth of a L2 learner's vocabulary. Sixty-two Japanese EFL university learners were recruited and randomly divided into two groups, and their knowledge of 15 target words was investigated and analysed. One group was required to learn 15 nonsense words receptively: they were asked to read these words first on the left column in English and then check their meanings in Japanese on the right column. Conversely, the other group learnt the same 15 nonsense words by reading their Japanese meaning first and then attempting to recall the forms of the nonsense target words in English. After six minutes of learning word pairs, the students participated in 10 tests that measured five aspects of their vocabulary-orthography, association, syntax, grammatical functions, and meaning and form—both receptively and productively. Results in Webb's (2009) study suggested that the type and amount of knowledge gained was significantly influenced by the direction of learning the word pairs. Receptive learning contributed more to receptive knowledge of meaning than productive learning, whilst productive learning resulted in higher achievements in both receptive and productive knowledge of orthography, and productive knowledge of meaning, syntax, and grammatical functions. These findings indicated that only employing productive learning of word pairs might be more effective than only employing receptive learning of word pairs.

Zhong (2016) further investigated the relationship between receptive and productive learning within a multi-aspect framework based on Nation (2001) and Coxhead's (2007) research. Six hundred and twenty EFL Chinese high school learners were recruited and their performance on 26 target words were examined in order to measure their meaning, form, word class, collocation and association, and controlled productive use of words when writing sentences. Results in Zhong's (2016) study suggested that productive word use in prompted sentence writing primarily related to receptive knowledge of form and meaning. Furthermore, these two dimensions contributed more to productive word use than the other aspects of class, association and collocation. Although class, association and collocation contributed to the statistical model of the internal structure of vocabulary knowledge along the receptive and productive continuum, it was suggested that restricting the study to meaning and form is still an effective and efficient test of vocabulary knowledge. Webb's (2009) and Zhong's (2016) studies both indicated the importance of productive learning in acquiring vocabulary, yet, the role of receptive learning in productive vocabulary knowledge still needs further exploration.

Studies (Webb, 2009; Zhong, 2016) have also investigated the relationship between receptive and productive vocabulary size. Morgan and Oberdeck (1930) were the first to measure the relationship between receptive and productive vocabulary size in a second language context. All the participants of their study were university students with German as a second language and a five-item multiple-choice test and a translation test were used to measure receptive and productive vocabulary size respectively. Vocabulary size was categorised into five frequency levels. Their analysis of the data indicated that the size of the participants' receptive vocabulary was larger than their productive vocabulary at all five frequency levels. However, their tests involved different cognitive formats. The five-item multiple-choice test that measured the size of receptive vocabulary allowed participants to guess, but they could not do so when completing the translation test used for measure productive vocabulary. The possibility that participants could have guessed when completing the test for receptive vocabulary may have influenced the accuracy of the results.

Laufer (1998) investigated the relationship between receptive and productive vocabulary by measuring the development of receptive, controlled productive, and free productive vocabulary knowledge of 48 participants over one year of school instruction. The results showed that their receptive vocabulary size (measured by the VLT) and controlled productive vocabulary size (measured by the productive version of the Levels Test) progressed very well. However, their free productive vocabulary (measured by the Lexical Frequency Profile) did not increase in size. Receptive vocabulary size in both advanced and less advanced groups was larger than controlled productive vocabulary size, but the gap between receptive and productive vocabulary size increased in the more advanced group. Scores for receptive vocabulary size positively correlated with those for controlled productive vocabulary size. Free productive vocabulary, on the other hand, did not correlate with either receptive or controlled productive vocabulary size.

Laufer and Paribakht (1998) further investigated the gap between receptive and productive vocabularies and found that it was smaller for EFL students than ESL students. Those learning English as a foreign language and those learning it as a second language have different learning processes, methods, and focuses. EFL learners are more likely to learn words through direct methods than ESL learners. EFL learners are usually provided with a comprehensive curriculum design encouraging them to make more of an effort to learn a new word, and as a result they gain more productive knowledge than ESL learners. Laufer and Paribakht suggested that vocabulary instruction and the proficiency level of the students are likely to have a substantial effect on vocabulary size.

Fan (2000) investigated the gap between receptive, termed "passive" vocabulary, and productive, termed "active" vocabulary, vocabulary knowledge by examining 138 Hong Kong Higher Diploma students. They used a modified VLT (Nation, 1990) and a modified controlled active vocabulary test (Laufer, 1990). The modified VLT included three levels of lexical frequencies: the 2 000, 3 000 and the University Word List (UWL) levels. Each level had 24 sets of words and each set had three target words and six options. Test participants chose the three most suitable options to match the three target words. Participants were classified into nine groups according to the majors that they were studying and their academic year, with different controlled productive vocabulary tests designed for each group. The target words for each group were the words that every participant in that group could recognise when they did their receptive vocabulary test. A sentence was designed for each target word and participants were required to complete gap-filling tests, that is, they were given the first few letters of the word, usually from one to three letters and were asked to fill in the missing letters in a given context. Results indicated that there was not a consistent ratio of the words recognised by participants to the words that they could recall. Thus, they surmised that the gap between receptive and productive vocabulary size could not be easily determined. Learners with a larger receptive vocabulary might actually have a smaller productive vocabulary than those with a smaller receptive vocabulary. The researcher reported that this result may have been influenced by the limitation that participants were generally low-proficiency learners.

Webb (2008) conducted a study regarding the relationship between receptive and productive vocabulary size of 83 EFL participants. Receptive and productive vocabulary size were tested using translation tests on 180 words from three frequency levels. Receptive and productive vocabularies were tested using translation tests on 180 words from three frequency levels. The target words were selected from the *Collins COBUILD* (*Collins Birmingham University International Language Database*) *English Language Dictionary*:

for word band 1, words were taken from among the 701st to the 1 900th most frequent words, word band 2 tokens fell within the 1 901st to 3 400th most frequent word range, and tokens in word band 3 were selected from the 3 401st to 6 600th most frequent words in English. Two versions of each translation test were used to ensure that there was no learning effect from a participant seeing the same target words in both the receptive and productive tests. Knowledge was measured by using approaches that included full and partial knowledge so that score responses could be scored at two levels of sensitivity. In the sensitive scoring system, words with spelling errors were marked as correct if the overall shape of the response was a close approximation of the target word. In the strict scoring system, responses were only marked as correct if the target words were spelt correctly. Responses in the wrong grammatical form were marked as correct for both scoring methods. Results showed that the total size of their receptive vocabulary size was larger than productive vocabulary. When responses were scored for fuller knowledge, the size of receptive vocabulary was also found to be greater than productive vocabulary in each of the three word bands. Further, as the frequency of the words decreased, the difference between receptive and productive knowledge increased. However, when responses were scored for partial knowledge, there was little difference between receptive and productive vocabulary size for each frequency band. The findings also indicated that receptive vocabulary size might give some indications of productive vocabulary size, that is, learners who have a larger receptive vocabulary are likely to know more of those words productively than learners who have a smaller receptive vocabulary.

Zhou (2010) tested receptive and productive academic vocabulary size of 72 Chinese non-English major college students. The VLT (Schmitt N., Schmitt D. and Clapham, 2001) and a modified version of the Productive Vocabulary Levels Test (Laufer and Nation, 1999) were used to investigate participants' receptive and controlled productive vocabulary size. The VLT was based on the Academic Word List (AWL) (Coxhead, 2000), whilst the Productive Vocabulary Levels Test (PVLT) was based on the UWL (Xue and Nation, 1984). Since these two tests are based on different word lists and the AWL has a wider coverage of academic text corpus and more consistent selection principles, Zhou (2010) modified the PVLT by using the same 30 words in the VLT but keeping the PVLT test format. For each lexical item a meaningful sentence was provided for each target word and the first few letters of the target words were given to the test participants. Participants were then divided into two groups according to their VLT scores. Participants with scores higher than the average score were placed in Group 1 and participants with scores lower than the average score were placed in Group 2. Results indicated that the students in Group 1 had more productive academic knowledge than those in Group 2. Moreover, the correlation between receptive and productive test scores was higher for Group 2 (0.595) than for Group 1 (0.446), indicating that receptive academic vocabulary size grows at a faster rate than productive academic vocabulary size.

Research has suggested that language learners' receptive vocabulary size is larger than their productive vocabulary size for two reasons: first, they have more opportunities to receive receptive knowledge; and, second, receptive knowledge is more easily acquired than productive knowledge (Fan, 2000; Laufer, 1998; Morgan and Oberdeck, 1930; Webb, 2008; Zhou, 2010). Despite this current understanding, it appears that three gaps remain that further research needs to comprehensively explore. Firstly, previous studies have suggested that the ratio between productive and receptive vocabulary size remains inconclusive. Secondly, the relationship between receptive and productive vocabulary size varies from study to study. For example, Laufer (1998) found that there was a positive and significant relationship ($r=0.78$) among these groups, whereas Fan (2000) found a mixture of positive and negative relationships between them. Little research in this area has focused on Chinese EFL students and all relevant studies conducted in China have recruited tertiary students; however, it is also important to conduct research with high school students in order to examine vocabulary acquisition at an early stage. Thirdly, the review of the literature indicates that different researchers have used different measures to estimate productive vocabulary size, for example, controlled (Fan, 2000; Laufer and Nation, 1999; Webb, 2008; Zhou, 2010) versus free productive (Laufer, 1998; Williams, Segalowitz and Leclair, 2014) measures.

5 Conclusion

Although the conceptualisation of vocabulary knowledge is complicated and not completely consistent in the literature, the approaches used to define dimensions of vocabulary knowledge are related to and based upon one another. Since the definition of receptive and productive knowledge is closely linked to the structure of form, meaning and use, the relationship between receptive and productive vocabulary knowledge also differs because of learners' different focuses in learning processes. Therefore, investigating the relationship between receptive and productive vocabulary knowledge can contribute to understanding it more widely. The specific differences between receptive and productive vocabulary can be explained with the help of the construct of form, meaning, and use. Therefore, understanding the relationship between receptive and productive vocabulary can also assist in understanding the construct of form, meaning and use.

References

Anderson, R. C., and Freebody, P. 1981. "Vocabulary knowledge". In *Comprehension and teaching: Research reviews*, edited by J. T. Guthrie, pp. 77–117. Newark: International Reading Association.

Coxhead, A. 2000. "A new academic word list". *TESOL Quarterly*.

Coxhead, A. 2007. "Factors and aspects of knowledge affecting L2 word use in writing". In *Teaching and Learning Vocabulary in another Language*, edited by P. Davidson, C. Coombe, D. Lloyd, and D. Palfreyman, pp. 331–342. Dubai: TESOL Arabia.

Elgort, I., Candry, S., Boutorwick, T. J. et al. 2016. "Contextual word learning with form-focused and meaning-focused elaboration". *Applied Linguistics*.

Fan, M. 2000. "How big is the gap and how to narrow it? An investigation into the active and passive vocabulary knowledge of L2 learners." *RELC Journal*.

Haastrup, K., and Henriksen, B. 1998. "Vocabulary acquisition: From partial to precise comprehension". In *Travaux de l'Institut de Linguistique de Lund*: Vol. 38. *Perspectives on lexical acquisition in a second language*, edited by K. Haastrup and A. Viberg, pp. 97–114. Lund: Lund University Press.

Han, Z. 2000. "Persistence of the implicit influence of NL: The case of the Pseudo-Passive". *Applied Linguistics*.

Hatami, S., and Tavakoli, M. 2012. "The role of depth versus breadth of vocabulary knowledge in success and ease in L2 lexical inferencing". *TESL Canada Journal*.

Khezrlou, S., Ellis, R., and Sadeghi, K. 2017. "Effects of computer-assisted glosses on EFL learners' vocabulary acquisition and reading comprehension in three learning conditions". *System*.

Laufer, B. 1998. "The development of passive and active vocabulary in a second language: Same or different?" *Applied Linguistics*.

Laufer, B. 2005. "Focus on form in second language vocabulary learning". *EUROSLA Yearbook*.

Laufer, B., Elder, C., Hill, K., and Congdon, P. 2004. "Size and strength: Do we need both to measure vocabulary knowledge?" *Language Testing*.

Laufer, B., and Nation, I. S. P. 1999. "A vocabulary size test of controlled productive ability". *Language Testing*.

Laufer, B., and Paribakht, T. S. 1998. "The relationship between passive and active vocabularies: Effects of language learning context". *Language Learning*.

Li, M., and Kirby, J. 2014. "The effects of vocabulary breadth and depth on English reading". *Applied Linguistics*.

Moghadam, S. H., Zainal, Z., and Ghaderpour, M. 2012. "A review on the important role of vocabulary knowledge in reading comprehension performance". *Procedia-Social and Behavioral Sciences*.

Morgan, B. Q., and Oberdeck, L. M. 1930. "Active and passive vocabulary". In *Studies in Modern Language Teaching*, edited by E. W. Bagster-Collins, pp. 213–221. Basingstoke: Macmillan.

Multicultural. 2011. In *Cambridge Dictionary*. Retrieved on September 27, 2016, from dictionary.cambridge.org/dictionary/english/multicultural.

Nation, I. S. P. 1990. *Teaching and learning vocabulary*. New York: Heinle and Heinle.

Nation, I. S. P. 2001. *Learning vocabulary in another language*. Cambridge: Cambridge University Press.

Nation, I. S. P. 2005. "Teaching vocabulary." *Asian EFL Journal*.

Palmberg, R. 1987. "Patterns of vocabulary development in foreign-language learners". *Studies in Second Language Acquisition*.

Pellicer-Sánchez, A. 2016. "Incidental L2 vocabulary acquisition from and while reading: An eye-tracking study." *Studies in Second Language Acquisition*.

Read, J. 2000. *Assessing vocabulary*. Cambridge: Cambridge University Press.

Read, J. 2004. "Research in teaching vocabulary." *Annual Review of Applied Linguistics*.

Salaberry, M. R., and Lopez-Ortega, N. 1998. "Accurate L2 production across language tasks: Focus on form, focus on meaning, and communicative control." *Modern Language Journal*.

Schmitt, N. 1997. "Vocabulary learning strategies." In *Vocabulary: Description, acquisition, and pedagogy*, edited by N. Schmitt and M. McCarthy, pp. 199 – 227. Cambridge: Cambridge University Press.

Schmitt, N. 2010. *Researching vocabulary: A vocabulary research manual*. New York: Palgrave Macmillan.

Schmitt, N. 2014. "Size and depth of vocabulary knowledge: What the research shows." *Language Learning*.

Schmitt, N., Schmitt, D., and Clapham, C. 2001. "Developing and exploring the behaviour of two new versions of the Vocabulary Levels Test." *Language Testing*.

Stæhr, L. S. 2009. "Vocabulary knowledge and advanced listening comprehension in English as a foreign language." *Studies in Second Language Acquisition*.

Van Zeeland, H., and Schmitt, N. 2013. "Incidental vocabulary acquisition through L2 listening: A dimensions approach." *System*.

Walters, J. 2004. "Teaching the use of context to infer meaning: A longitudinal survey of L1 and L2 vocabulary research." *Language Teaching*.

Webb, S. 2008. "Receptive and productive vocabulary size of L2 learners." *Studies in Second Language Acquisition*.

Webb, S. 2009. "The effects of receptive and productive learning of word pairs on vocabulary knowledge." *RELC Journal*.

Webb, S. 2015. "Researching vocabulary in the EFL context: A commentary on four studies for JALT Vocabulary SIG". *Vocabulary Learning and Instruction*.

Wesche, M., and Paribakht, T. S. 1996. "Assessing second language vocabulary knowledge: Depth versus breadth." *Canadian Modern Language Review-Revue Canadienne Des Langues Vivantes*.

Xue, G., and Nation, I. S. P. 1984. "A university word list." *Language Learning and Communication*.

Zhang, X., and Lu, X. 2014. "A longitudinal study of receptive vocabulary breadth knowledge growth and vocabulary fluency development". *Applied Linguistics*.

Zhang, X., and Lu, X. 2015. "The relationship between vocabulary learning strategies and breadth and depth of vocabulary knowledge". *The Modern Language Journal*.

Zhong, H. F. 2018. "The relationship between receptive and productive vocabulary knowledge: A perspective from vocabulary use in sentence writing". *The Language Learning Journal*.

Zhou, S. 2010. "Comparing receptive and productive academic vocabulary knowledge of Chinese EFL learners". *Asian Social Science*.

Analysis of Squealer's Discourse Strategies in *Animal Farm*

Chen Yindi*

Abstract: This paper intends to study the discourse strategies pig Squealer utilizes in the novella *Animal Farm* to reveal its effect on interpersonal relationship. By qualitative method, the research is carried out from three aspects, including self-selection strategy, incompletion-marker strategy and nomination strategy. The result indicates that to keep pigs' power, Squealer tends to use these three different strategies to muzzle other animals' thoughts on the farm. Finally, the paper is expected to provide a new perspective to study how the superior maintain and consolidate their despotism.

Key Words: discourse strategies; self-selection strategy; incompletion-marker strategy; nomination strategy; power

1 Introduction

Animal Farm, by George Orwell, was published in 1945 in England. It tells a story about a group of animals on the "Manor farm" driving their incompetent owner away and changing its name into "Animal Farm". Afterwards, pigs become leaders but they just scramble for power and wealth. Napoleon establishes a totalitarian and corrupted government, causing other animals to live miserable lives.

Animal Farm has attracted a large number of researchers and scholars' interests both at home and abroad. In reference to the previous studies, it can be mainly classified into two aspects, including researches on themes and rhetorical devices.

Some researchers keep a watchful eye on thematic discussion. Rodden (1999) points out that *Animal Farm* is a political allegory in the name of a beast fable. The characters of pig leaders on the farm is closely connected to the history of Soviet Union. Among domestic studies, Du Ning (2015) deems that the "Seven Commandments" which emphasizes all animals are equal is the official ideology. Since pig leaders revise it over and over again stealthily, they lay a clamp on the animals and keep their supremacy. Li Tian (2012) reveals pigs who keep the power, degenerate into the totalitarian governors; therefore, the goal to establish a liberal and equal society eventually fails. Jing Yuan (2013) concentrates on the

---

* Chen Yindi:陈引弟,西北工业大学外国语学院硕士研究生。

humanistic theme. He thinks that pig leaders bend themselves to violating the freedom and equality, suppressing individuality and degenerating humanity. Li Taotao (2017) attempts to explore the theme that female characters subordinate to the male characters and they are in a marginalized position.

Other researchers adopt the tool of rhetorical devices to discuss the novella. Wang Xueqin (2008) resorts to the figure of speech, including irony, simile, exaggeration and metaphor to make an analysis of *Animal Farm*. Guan Chao (2012) uses a symbol of absurdity when making a comparative analysis between *Animal Farm* and *1984*. Dong Lei (2013) analyzes *Animal Farm* from the perspective of the Rhetoric of Aristotle.

It can not be denied that the researches on themes and rhetorical devices from the different angles are conducive to the comprehensive interpretation and understandings to *Animal Farm*. However, very few scholars pay their attention to the research of characters' discourse strategies. In this novella, Squealer, a pig politician propagator, should not be neglected. Yang Min (2011) points out that Squealer utilizes the misleading function and shaping function of discourse to maintain their top class from the interactive relationships between language and power. Qiao Li (2013) reveals Squealer employs different discourse strategies, such as emotional language expression, presupposition, comparison and sophistry, to establish and consolidate pigs' priority position as powerful spokesman through critical discourse analysis. Huang Ye (2014) discusses Squealer's discourse based on the relationship between power and discourse. He emphasizes that Squealer, as the mouthpiece of powerful pigs' regime, is skilled in misleading the public.

But there is still plenty of room for interpretation and exploration of Squealer's discourse strategies. He unquestionably possesses an ability to deceive other animals using different discourse demagogue strategies. He sustains the pigs' ruling by hook or by crook through his claptrap. Therefore, the way he manipulates discourse strategies is worth studying from the aspects of self-selection strategy, incompletion-marker strategy and nomination strategy in detail.

2　Discourse Strategy Theory

Discourse has various definitions. Hasan (1996) defines that discourse is a spoken language which contains certain communicative goals. Put another way, it is a kind of practice. During the communicative exchange, the speakers need to use some tactics, either to push the conversation forward or to end it to reach communicative purposes. The tactics can be regarded as the discourse strategies.

Sacks, Schegloff and Jefferson are considered as the forerunner in the fields of discourse strategy theory. According to Sacks and Harris (1974), discourse strategy theory can fall into three categories, involving discourse-starting strategies, discourse-maintaining strategies and discourse-ending strategies. The first category is discourse-starting strategies, such as interruption strategy and self-selection strategy. It happens when the person fights for the chance to speak by some skills. The second one is discourse-maintaining strategies, usually including utterance-incompletor strategy, incompletion-marker strategy, mouth-hesitation filler strategy, repetition strategy and monologue strategy. It means the current speaker is unwilling to give up his chance of talking and would prefer to use some tactics to maintain his discourse. The third category is discourse-ending strategies, like nomination strategy. If the present speaker designates the listener by utilizing some means such as eye contacts, and the listener signals his willingness to convey his opinion and indeed grasps the chance, the speaker achieves the purpose of giving up his opportunity of talking.

In *Animal Farm*, Squealer utilizes some discourse strategies. The paper intends to analyze them as is shown in the following Table 1.

Table 1 The Relationship Between Discourse Strategy Theory and Squealer's Discourse Strategies

Discourse Strategy Theory	Squealer's Discourse Strategies
Discourse-starting strategies	Self-selection strategy
Discourse-maintaining strategies	Incompletion-marker strategy
Discourse-ending strategies	Nomination strategy

3 Analysis of Squealer's Discourse Strategies in *Animal Farm*

3.1 Squealer's Self-selection Strategy

Self-selection strategy is applied to such situation where the speaker chooses himself to continue the discourse. This strategy as well signifies the one who selects himself to endeavor to get the discourse is an active talker (Ian, 1998). Once the first speaker gives up his discourse, the next speaker catches the discourse-ending signal at the right transition relevance place. Example 1 is selected from the "Chapter V".

Somebody: He (Snowball) fought bravely at the Battle of the Cowshed.

Squealer: Bravery is not enough. Loyalty and obedience are important. And as to the Battle of the Cowshed, I believe the time will come when we shall find that Snowball's part in it was much exaggerated. Discipline ...

(Orwell, 2014)

Squealer captures a discourse-ending signal without delay. He starts his discourse by means of self-selecting the moment somebody gives up his discourse. There is no any pause. In their conversation, it can be found that Squealer is well-rounded in his logical order of the discourse. He hoaxes animals from two steps. For him, despite the fact that Snowball, the opponent of the incumbent leader Napoleon, performs bravely in the fight against humans, he does not give a corresponding evaluation or comment. Rather, he stresses the importance of loyalty and obedience to Napoleon. Then, he emphasizes the animals ought to comply with the discipline. Discipline is a specific technique of power which controls the operation of bodies by training and coercing(Huang, 2014). Beyond all question, Squealer has a clear mind in his response. In fact, the animals are gradually pressed on this limited farm and enslaved in an invisible tight rope.

Self-selection strategy demonstrates the speaker's intention and desire to give a discourse. It is to the benefit of showing the speaker's motivation. Hence, it is obvious that Squealer is rather sly in this example. He not only successfully avoids the animals' doubts, but persuades them to trust him.

Table 2 The Number of Self-selection Strategy in Discourse-starting Phase

Characters	Self-selection Strategy in All Chapters
Squealer	11 times
Other animals	6 times

As Table 2 displays, Squealer individually uses self-selection strategy 11 times in total to start the discourse while other animals adopt only 6 times. It indicates that Squealer is more talkative than other animals. Squealer often chooses himself as the talker after other animals expresses their doubts or raise questions. That also shows Squealer, as a member of powerful class, has more chance to start a discourse by adopting self-selection strategy.

3.2 Squealer's Incompletion-marker Strategy

The incompletion-marker strategy is relatively complex and formal. Accordingly, the length of the discourse is relatively longer. Subordinate conjunctions can be used to carry on the discourse in a certain context (Labov, 1972). Namely, when the present speaker adopts a subordinate clause, he will not be interrupted in a general way and succeeds in maintaining his discourse. That means, a speaker usually informs the hearers in advance with some words like "since", "when", "which", etc. Example 2 is selected from the "Chapter VII".

*Squealer: ... Snowball ... **who** is even now plotting to attack us and take our farm away from us! Snowball is to act as his guide **when** the attack begins ... We had thought **that** Snowball's rebellion was caused simply by his vanity and ambition. Do you know **what** the real reason was? ... It has all been proved by documents **which** he left behind him and **which** we have only just discovered. Did we not see for ourselves **how** he attempted?*

*Boxer: I do not believe **that** Snowball fought bravely at the Battle of the Cowshed. Did we not give?*

(Orwell, 2014)

Table 3 The Number of Incompletion-marker Strategy in Discourse-maintaining Phase

Characters	Incompletion-marker Strategy and Discourse-length in "Chapter VII"	Incompletion-marker Strategy and Discourse Length in Other Chapters
Squealer	7 (who:1; when:1; that:1; what:1; which:2; how:1), 129 words	26 (that:14; if:2; who:1; before:2; than:2; when:3; which:1; where:1); 402 words
Other animals	1(that:1), 29 words	5 (how:1; if:2; what:1; that:1); 43 words

As Table 3 shows, Squealer adopts incompletion-marker strategy 7 times totally to hold his discourse. And his discourse-length reaches to 129 words. He frames Snowball up in words and fools other animals into believing a fake story that Snowball is a secret agent of human race at the very beginning. Reversely, Boxer's adopts incompletion-marker strategy only once, and his discourse-length has merely 29 words. He shows his disagreement by using a subordinate conjunction "**that**". Next, he uses an interrogative sentence to prove Snowball is not a traitor. But the interrogative sentence also indicates his uncertainty about his own memory, implying the animals on the farm are brainwashed little by little. It is not difficult to draw such a conclusion that Squealer is a skillful propagandist. He succeeds to perplex and cheat other animals who only receive a low-level education.

The function of incompletion-marker strategy is to achieve some goals, such as demonstrate language proficiency, attract the public's attention and leave a profound impression on listeners. The dual purposes of Squealer's discourse can be explored in this example. First, the purpose Squealer attacks Snowball in words is to distort the history. It is true that Snowball once makes a contribution to drive human's aggression, but after contending for power and wealth, Snowball is ousted. Hence, once something bad happens on the farm, Squealer calls white into black with his silver tongue. He swears that everything unlucky is Snowball's fault. Second, he paves the way for the next purges because he knows some animals' thoughts are not in alignment with pig leaders. His discourse in this example is to warn animals and to consolidate the pigs' ruling.

In the column of the other chapters from table above, Squealer adopts incompletion-marker strategy 26 times, and the animals use just 5 times. That reveals the times Squealer makes use of this strategy is over 5 times than other animals. To sum up, Squealer is adept in lengthening his discourse and maintaining the discourse with the help of this strategy.

3.3 Squealer's Nomination Strategy

According to Harris (2007), nomination strategy means the current speaker can designate the next person to go on the topic after initiating the discourse, which is a helpful approach to begin a conversation naturally and smoothly. To fulfill this nomination strategy, two conditions should be co-occurred (Xu, 2017). The first condition is that the current speaker designates the listener by calling name or title. The second one is that the current speaker needs to ask a question, such as a yes-no question, wh-question, alternative question or tag question (Chen, 2014). To show politeness, the nominated person continues the topic as is required by answering the questions or offering some information. Only when both the speaker and the listener participate in the discourse will the conversation continue. Nomination strategy is conducive to creating a harmonious and cooperative atmosphere for further discussion. But there is an exception when social inequality occurs. Example 3 is chosen from the "Chapter V".

Squealer: ... One false step, and our enemies would be upon us. Surely, **comrades, you do not want Jones back**?
Boxer: If Comrade Napoleon says it, it must be right.

(Orwell, 2014)

Table 4 The Number of Nomination Strategy in Discourse-ending Phase

Characters	Nomination Strategy in "Chapter V"	Nomination Strategy in Other Chapters
Squealer	1	3
Other animals	0	0

Squealer firstly designates the next speaker with an intimate calling "comrades". Then, he ends his discourse by speaking intentionally "you do not want Jones back". Actually, "you do not want Jones back" is a declarative sentence which finishes with a full stop. But Squealer uses the raising tone. His words complete with a question mark as if he is eager to know what other animals think. Meanwhile, his discourse implies that the animals are not given room for disobedience. Under that circumstance, Boxer gives his comment as the response to Squealer's question. Simultaneously, he shows his loyalty and severe personality cult to Napoleon, which makes the conversation continue smoothly and acquire a natural effect.

The speaker uses nomination strategy for different purposes, such as to show his politeness or encourage the listener to speak up his opinion. In practice, however, the powerful speaker adopts this strategy by intention to show his social superiority or desires to suppress the listener's will of talking. Therefore, the purpose of Squealer is evident. He intends to require other animals to keep consistent with pigs in thought.

Throughout the novella, Squealer applies nomination strategy 4 times while the powerless animals have no chance to make use of this strategy. Of those 4 times of nomination, Squealer more than once declares the decisions made by pigs unilaterally. What is worse, Squealer ends his discourse for the purpose of political power. And some nominations even have intimidation intentions. Thus, the animals have no right to nominate Squealer to remove their doubt at all. In terms of a cooperative condition, out of the politeness, the speaker chooses to yield the discourse by nomination strategy. But in this example, Squealer exercises it out of power.

4　Conclusion

The reason why Squealer can always turn white to black is that he is one of the members of the powerful class. In the meantime, Squealer exercises power on other animals to build a kind of relationship between superior and subordinate. To put it simply, power is the decisive factor influencing and controlling the flow of discourse (Foucault, 1972). The ruling class has always adopted some discourse strategies to maintain and consolidate their despotism. The study reveals that Squealer starts his discourse with self-selection strategy, maintains his discourse using incompletion-marker strategy and ends his discourse with nomination strategy. By using all these strategies, he intends to claim the pigs' privilege and ruling role.

Besides, it can be noticed that as pig leaders degenerate into the totalitarian governors, Squealer mainly maintains his discourse and controls the topics over other animals. And the animals on the farm are deprived of the rights of speaking and have long time been silenced and sidelined. By discussing Squealer's discourse strategies, this paper is expected to provide a new perspective for the understanding of *Animal Farm*.

References

陈蕊莉，2014，《〈杨澜访谈录〉会话分析》，硕士学位论文，曲阜师范大学。
程雪娟，2018，《电视访谈节目〈杨澜访谈录〉的会话分析》，硕士学位论文，中南民族大学。
杜宁，2015，《从伊格尔顿的意识形态理论看〈动物庄园〉中的政治讽刺》，硕士学位论文，福州大学。
李桃桃，2017，《乔治·奥威尔〈动物庄园〉的女性主义解读》，硕士学位论文，河北师范大学。
李甜，2012，《〈动物庄园〉的权力关系研究》，硕士学位论文，鲁东大学。
管超，2012，《试论乔治·奥威尔小说的讽刺艺术——以〈动物庄园〉和〈一九八四〉为例》，硕士学位论文，中国传媒大学。
黄烨，2014，《堕落之途——〈动物庄园〉的权力话语关系解读》，硕士学位论文，华北电力大学。
景远，2013，《〈动物庄园〉人文主义主题研究》，硕士学位论文，河北师范大学。
谯莉，2013，《权力与语言之共生现象研究——以〈动物庄园〉中"声响器"的权力话语为例》，外国语文第4期。
奥威尔，2014，《动物庄园中文导读英文版》，方雨骁译，清华大学出版社。

徐策,2017,《〈吉米今夜秀〉的会话策略研究》,硕士学位论文,西安工业大学。

杨敏,2011,《穿越语言的透明性——〈动物农场〉中语言与权力之间关系的阐释》,《外国文学研究》第 6 期。

Foucault, Michel. 1972. *The Discourse on Language*. Smith, Sherdan trans. New York: Harper Colopphon.

Harris, Z., Labov, W., and Brown G. 2007. *Discourse Analysis*. Cambridge: Cambridge University Press.

Hasan. 1996. *English TV Conversation*. Oxford: Oxford University Press.

IanH. R. Wooffitt. 1998. *Conversation Analysis*. Cambridge: Polity Press.

Labov, W. 1972. "Some principles of linguistic methodology". *Language in Society*.

Rodden, J. 1999. *Understanding Animal Farm*. Conn: Greenwood Press.

Sacks and Harris. 1974. *Discourse strategies for Conversation Language*. Oxford: Oxford University Press.

Sacks, Schegloff, and Jefferson. 1974. "A Simplest Systematic for the Organization of discourse strategies in Conversation". *Language*.

Wang, Xueqin. 2008. "Analysis of the Figure of Speech in Animal Farm". *Sino-US English Teaching*.

An Empirical Analysis of Writing Errors of Non-English Majors Based on Error Analysis Theory

Li Fan[*]　Feng Zongxiang[**]

Abstract: The aim of this dissertation is to investigate the writing characteristics of non-English majors, and draws relevant enlightenments which are of practical significance to help them improve their learning ability and reduce the possibility of making mistakes. Based on the theory of error analysis, this paper conducts an empirical study by using quantitative analysis, with 95 non-English majors in NPU as the subjects. The authors asked them to submit their compositions on Juku Correction Network and then collect those data for analyzing. The main conclusion to be drawn from this work is that 16 common errors are mainly caused by interlingual errors.

Key Words: error analysis; empirical study; non-English majors; Juku Correction Network; interlingual errors

1 Introduction

Language is the most important communication tool. English writing is the actual reflection of students' English learning ability, and it's the most difficult one to master in the process of SLA (Second Language Acquisition) (Zhang Haiyan, 2012). Therefore, we must understand the factors that affect the improvement of students' English writing level and improve their English writing ability. One of the important and effective way is to analyze the errors in students' compositions. By analyzing learners' errors or mistakes made in the compositions, both teachers and students can notice those mistakes and find ways to reduce or avoid mistakes. For this reason, a lot of researchers and foreign language teachers try to conduct empirical experimental by using error analysis method in their researches and second language classrooms, which have aroused an upsurge in foreign language academic circles. In the field of SLA, the rise of error analysis theory provides a new perspective for teachers who are committed to language teaching. However, a lot of researchers put their emphasis on oral English (Wang Ying, 2006; Bian Kepan and Gao Linlin, 2015), word spelling (He

---

[*] Li Fan:李帆,西北工业大学外国语学院硕士研究生。
[**] Feng Zongxiang:冯宗祥,西北工业大学外国语学院副教授,研究方向为语料库语言学、英语测试学、计算机辅助外语教学。

Anping, 2001; Wang Xuewen and Sun Lan, 2004) and word collocation by the traditional way of face to face in the classroom (Huang Fuwei, 2008; Wang Haihua and Yang Xinhuan, 2007), few researchers use the network platform to systematically study the errors in learners' English writing, which is time-consuming and ineffective. Therefore, in this paper, the researchers would analyze the features or types of English compositions submitted on the Juku Correction Network, which were written by non-English majors; and try to investigate their common writing mistakes and the reasons. Specifically, by applying the error analysis theory, the objectives of this research are as follows:

(i) Identify the common mistakes which occurred in those compositions and features of those mistakes.

(ii) Explain the possibilities which causing that common mistakes.

(iii) Explore the rationale solutions and enlightening advices for both teachers and students in their second language teaching and learning.

This thesis consists of five parts. Here the researchers would like to supply the outline of this paper. This part will give the brief introduction of the background and significance of this research; and then the objectives and methodology will be mentioned in a much simpler way. Part two recaps the previous researches on Error Analysis (EA) both home and abroad, and conclude the features of those relevant literature, and the gap of those researches. The third part is the theoretical framework. It mainly introduces Error Analysis. The founder of this theory and the development process and some detail information would be presented here. Part four is an account of the research methodology. Research questions and instruments as well as the process of data collection and research design are presented in this part, while in Part five, results and discussion will be given. Errors made by students in their English compositions will be analyzed based on Juku Correction Network. Finally, Part six concludes the study. In this part, answers to the research questions are given, limitations of the resent study are discussed and suggestions for the future are put forward.

2 Literature Review

Research on Error Analysis has increasingly questioned the traditional teaching and Constructive Analysis (CA), which focuses on admitting and criticizing the errors in SLA and finding new perspectives to develop this theory. This paper will first state the origin of EA, and the connections of EA and CA will be clarified. Next, this paper will provide the overview of the research based on EA abroad and home, and research status in China will be well emphasized. In the final part, this paper will conclude the features of those existing researches and state the gaps between them.

2.1 The Origin of EA

As a branch of Applied Linguistics, EA came into being in the late 1960s and early

1970s. It has some relations with the comparative analysis which only pays attention to the external environment of language learning and ignores language learners due to the influence of structuralist linguistics and behaviorism psychology; while EA, instead of doing so (Tang Chengxian, 1997), shifts the focus of research to language learners, making up for the shortcomings of comparative analysis. Selinker (1972), Corder (1976) and Richard (1974) adopted a new research approach to analyze the language errors of middle school students in the learning process from the perspective of non-contrastive analysis, especially those that could not be explained by the "interference" of contrastive analysis. In the recognition and classification of errors, Corder (1967) divides the errors which people often say into two categories: mistake and error, and he points three significant way of errors. For teachers, they will make clear how far toward the goal the learner has progressed and, consequently, what reminds of him to learn; for researchers, errors could supply the evidence of how language is learned or acquired, what strategies or procedures that learner is employing in the discovery of the language; while for students, errors could be an indispensable part in the process of language learning, and making errors was served as a device by which the learner discovers the role of the target language, which all have important implications and positive effects on the teaching and research of English writing in China.

2.2 Research Status of EA

Tang Chenxian (1997) firstly discussed the interlanguage and procedure of EA as well as significance of that, and tried to used it in combination with teaching practice. In spite of the results was not so significant, it is a bold attempt. Dong Junhong (1999) focuses on analyzing the errors students made in connections and lexical devices in English composition and put forward critically some advices for improving discourse coherence in composition, which shed the light on the second language teaching and learning. Since then, research on analyzing error in the process of SLA has been growing at a rapid rate. Zhou Xin (2009) asserted learners could recognize and correct their errors in collocation aspects by pointed out errors. Men Haiyan (2010) and Guo Hong (2012) also analyze the errors in collocation from different ways. All those studies were all about the problem of collocation errors. Indeed, word collocation knowledge is an important part of vocabulary knowledge (Nation, 1990) and collocation ability is also an important part of language ability (Wei Naixing, 2002), however, it is difficult to fundamentally solve the problem of writing difficulties for Chinese students by simply studying collocation errors. Other studies are also only research one part of English writing, for example, spelling mistakes (He Anping, 2001; Wang Xuewen and Sun Lan, 2004; Huang Li, 2018; Deng Mengyao, 2018).

2.3 The Statement of Literature Review

From the overview of the literature, it can be seen that the precious researches focused on the specific one part or two parts alone in English writing, no much researchers systematically analyze the errors of students in the whole writing process, which has made it impossible to carry out satisfactory resolutions and methods for increasing the English writing proficiency. Thus, by analyzing the errors in the English compositions of non-English majors, this paper explores the writing characteristics of non-English majors, and provides some help and suggestions for foreign language teaching, so as to improve the English writing level of non-English majors.

3 Theoretical Framework

In the field of SLA, the emergence of EA provides a new perspective for scholars and teachers devoted to language teaching research. In the 1950s, American applied linguists Fries and Lado began to systematically study errors in second language learning and established EA theory. By the 1950s and 1960s, scholars such as Corder developed this theory, which brought research from the surface to the deep. According to Corder (1967), EA has two purposes: theoretical and applied. The purpose of theoretical research is to understand how learners learn second language. The purpose of application is to enable learners to use their professional knowledge more efficiently. At the same time, the empirical analysis of errors also satisfies two purposes: judgment and foreboding. EA theory regards language learners as the object of analysis. Through systematic analysis of the errors made by language learners in the process of using a second language, it finds out what stage the learners have reached in the process of learning the target language after mastering their mother tongue, and how much content they need to continue to learn.

Language errors can also be used as evidence of how learners learn or acquire language, so that teachers can understand the learning strategies and steps used by learners in the learning process. Therefore, the purpose of EA theory is to find out the strategies adopted by language learners in the process of language learning and the reasons for their mistakes, and to understand their common learning difficulties, so as to find out the corresponding strategies to help learners overcome the obstacles and improve their English proficiency. According to Corder, the earliest advocate of EA theory, language errors can be divided into three types, which are distributed in three stages. The pre-systematic stage, the systematic stage and the post-systematic stage of the formation system. In the first stage, that is, the pre-systematic stage, learners' errors refer to the errors caused by the use of incomplete second language knowledge to express and communicate in the process of SLA because learners have not mastered the second language completely. At this stage, learners do not know what mistakes they have made, so they cannot correct them by themselves. The second stage is the errors made in the formation stage, which means that learners have mastered some second language knowledge and have internalized into a certain system of language rules, but their understanding of second language knowledge is not accurate and complete enough, thus resulting in language errors in the process of learning. Such errors are mainly reflected in the use of special words.

The causes of errors are very complicated. Researchers' views on the sources or causes of learners' errors differ to a lesser or greater degree. However, there is a general agreement over the main diagnosis-based categories of error. There are four major categories—① Interlingual errors: the errors which are caused by mother tongue interference; ② Intralingual errors: the errors in learner language that reflect learner's transitional competence and which are the results of such learning processes as overgeneralization; ③ Communication strategy-based errors: the errors resulting from the use of communication strategy; ④ Induced errors: the errors arise in learner language when learners are led to make errors that otherwise they would not make by the nature of the formal instruction they receive. Application linguists have summarized the sources of language errors of language learners by studying the system characteristics of interlanguage. Applied linguists generally believe that the following eight factors can lead to learners' language errors (Xu Jun, 2002): mother tongue interference, overgeneralization, simplification by omission, communication strategy, pragmatic errors, pragmatic errors, hypercorrection, performance errors and cross-association.

4 Methodology

In this part, the procedure adopted to address the three questions presented in Part one, will be described in detail. In brief, 95 pieces of compositions submitted in Juku Correction Network will be analyzed.

4.1 Participants and Sample

With limited time and resources, 95 non-English majors' compositions of Northwestern Polytechnical University were selected as the subjects of this study. These 95 students are freshmen from different majors. Although they have just entered the University for one year and have not yet taken CET-4, they passed the College Entrance Examination smoothly and entered the double first-rate university, so we can see their English proficiency is not bad. Teachers assigned tasks to them and asked them to write an article with 100—500 words on the topic of "Information Security" after class, with a full score of 15. It should be noted that the composition must be submitted to Juku Correction Network, which provides feedback and scoring. According to the scores given by the Juku Correction Network, this paper finds the average score is 11.8 and there are more than 43 students' scores are higher than the average. Besides, 9 students scored above 13, which is high in the 15-point writing scoring system.

4.2 Instruments

(1) Juku Correction Network

Juku Correction Network is one of the online automatic marking tools widely used in the field of foreign language writing teaching in China. It is an intelligent online automatic marking system for English writing by using corpus data and corpus analysis technology. The system has been popularized in many colleges and universities in China, and has been upgraded according to the characteristics of Chinese learners. This paper will output all the data and save the data in word text.

(2) AntConc

AntConc is a kind of corpus retrieval tool. All the words in 95 essays will be transformed into ".txt" text and then they are input into AntConc.

By applying AntConc, this paper could collect all the information of those 95 essays with 16 166 tokens and 1 871 word types (a small corpus about the composition of non-English majors), such as the most frequent word used by students.

(3) TagConc

TagConc is a kind of corpus retrieval tool. All words in text will be tagged in TagConc. And this paper could explore the word collocations by analyzing the part of speeches.

4.3 Research Process

The corpus analysis tool used in this study are TagConc, AntConc and Juku Correction Network. The analysis methods are as follows: firstly, by applying AntConc, this paper could collect all the information of tokens and word, and through the systematic analysis of 95 essays by Juku Correction Network and TagConc, we can get the obvious common errors of 95 essays and frequent collocations of words; secondly, we would re-analyze all kinds of errors manually and find common errors appeared in this corpus; finally, we give explanations of errors and unmask the characteristics of English writing of non-English majors, which can reflect the strategies the learner possesses in his learning process and the teachers use in their classes; and through this we can conclude some regular rules responsible for L2 acquisition.

4.4 The Framework for Data Analysis

In order to answer the research questions, this paper has analyzed the number of all types of errors made by participants based on the Juku Correction Network. By applying AntConc, this paper finds the most frequent word in this small corpus, and analyzes the characteristics and explain the causes one by one.

(1) common errors in 95 compositions

By applying AntConc, this paper finds the most frequent word in this small corpus (the compositions of non-English majors), which is showed in Table 1.

Table 1   Frequent Word in the Corpus

Rank	Frequency	Word
1	805	information
2	752	the
3	577	to
4	381	of
5	364	and
6	345	is
7	323	security
…	…	…

From Table 1, we can see "information" and "the" are the two most commonly used notions. The reason for this is that the theme of the composition is "Information Security", when students conceive their compositions, they will write about this topic.

According to the English compositions submitted by the students on the Internet, which are entitled "Information Security", Juku Correction Network summarizes 16 types of errors. The results are showed in Table 2.

Table 2   Types of Errors from 95 Compositions

Category	Frequency	Rate/%
Spelling error	103	22.20
Article error	68	14.66
Mismatch	54	11.64
Subject-predicate agreement	50	10.78
Case error	37	7.97
Noun error	32	6.90
Sentence components	27	5.82
Part of speech misuse	21	4.53
Sentence structure	20	4.31
Conjunction error	18	3.88
Preposition error	9	1.94
Verb error	8	1.72
Pronoun error	8	1.72
Adjective error	4	0.86
Sentence voice	4	0.86
Sentence word order	1	0.22

According to Table 2, we can see that spelling mistake is the most common mistake, while the sentence word order is the least. This paper analyses the most frequency common mistakes. The most common mistakes are spelling mistake, article error, mismatch, subject-predicate agreement, case error, noun error, sentence components, part of speech misuse, sentence structure and conjunction error. Because of the limited time, this paper only analyses the first three common errors here.

(2) analysis of the main characteristics and causes of learners' errors

1) spelling errors

Spelling errors occur most frequently, accounting for 22.22% of the total vocabulary errors, and are negatively correlated with English writing. Spelling errors decrease with the improvement of learners' learning level and language proficiency. However, many students have made many spelling mistakes, which need to be noticed by learners. Wang Xuewen and Sun Lan (2004) classified spelling errors into three categories: phonological deviation, graphemic deviation and morphological deviation. If the error item causes a change in speech, it is regarded as a phonological deviation; if not, it will be classified as a graphemic deviation; while it would be viewed as morphological deviation if it only uses different shapes to mark the speech. These three kinds of errors can be further divided (see Table 3). For ease of analysis, the wrong cases are also categorized as spelling errors.

Table 3 Types and Examples of Spelling Errors

Types of Spelling Errors		Examples		Rate/%
		Error item	Target item	
Phonological deviation	summation tone	securarity	security	22.20
	reducing tone	envirnment	environment	
	sound replacement	imformation	information	
Graphemic deviation	silent letters	rong	wrong	
	double letters	reffer	refer	
	homophone substitution	benifit	benefit	
	alphabetical exchange	frist	first	
Morphological deviation	tortuous changes	choosed	chose	
	derivative change	regretly	regrettably	
	creative words	phenomenons	phenomena	
Case	wrong capital item	internet	Internet	7.97
Total	—	—	—	30.17

Chinese learners make many spelling mistakes, which can be attributed to three reasons. Firstly, there are too many differences between English and Chinese. Chinese belongs to the Sino-Tibetan language family and it is pictographic, while English belongs to the Indo-European language family. Secondly, Pinyin in Chinese is very complicated. The mapping of phonemes and morphemes in English is not one-to-one correspondence. There are far more letters and letter combinations used in phonetic notation than phonemes, that is to say, 40 phonemes correspond to 70 morphemes (He Huaqing, 2009). For example, the phoneme "k" can be showed as c, ch, ck, k and kh. Finally, English learners are careless in the process of writing and are lack of sensitivity to English. "Information" and "security" have been listed in writing requirements and is the theme of composition, but learners still make mistakes many times and someone write "imformation securarity" instead of "information security".

2) article errors

As can be seen from Table 2, article errors are the second most frequent errors in English theses, accounting for 14.66%. This shows that undergraduates of non-English majors generally have some obstacles in the acquisition and use of English articles, which should be paid attention to. Articles errors are generally classified into three categories: omission, redundancy and confusion. By studying the compositions, this paper lists some wrong sentences caused by article error in Table 4.

Table 4 Types of Article Errors

Type	Examples
Omission	First of all, do not take down your information carelessly *on Internet*.
	Only can we guard our information security safely, we can benefit from *Information Age* to a great extent.
	including name, age, address, telephone number, marital status, *account balance* and so on.
Redundancy	More and more people pay *a great importance* to information security.
	Besides, everyone *in the society* need are required to enhance their awareness of keeping the secret.
	Companies should promote *the awareness on* the information security.
Confusion	The information *in a newspaper* is easy to understand.
	In the eyes of *the a country*, nothing can be more important than *the information security*.

There are two main reasons of why article errors are the second most frequent error in non-English majors' compositions. First, there are no articles in Chinese, so Chinese students are more likely to make mistakes when using English in articles writing. Secondly, traditional English teaching emphasizes notional words rather than functional words, which makes the use of articles a weakness of students' English use. To some extent, article errors are influenced by the negative transfer of mother tongue and belong to interlingual errors.

3) mismatch

One of the most common features of language is the transverse combinational relationship between linguistic units—each linguistic unit co-occurs in a certain order to form a larger unit. These repeated combinations or (semi) preset phrases are often referred to as collocations (Wang Rui, 2014). Collocation is an important part of language learning. Collocation knowledge is an important part of vocabulary knowledge (Nation, 1990). Collocation ability is also an important part of language ability (Wei Naixing, 2002). With the help of TagConc and AntConc, this paper finds that the small corpus of non-English majors' English writing covers a variety of collocation forms, among which verb-noun collocation (V-N collocation), adjective-noun collocation (A-N collocation) and verb-preposition collocation (V-P collocation) are the most common. By correcting all the compositions, this paper finds that students' mismatch are mainly divided into two types, which are errors in grammatical collocation and semantic collocation.

Table 5 Errors in Grammatical Collocation and Semantic Collocation

Types of Errors	Number	Percentage/%
Grammatical collocation	17	30.35
Semantic collocation	39	69.64
Total	56	100

From Table 5, we can see that students make more errors in semantic collocation than in grammatical collocation. They have not mastered the collocation of nouns, verbs, adjectives and adverbs, which are widely used in students' compositions, resulting in more errors in collocation of word meanings.

(1) grammatical collocation

Grammatical collocation refers to the collocation of nouns, adjectives, verbs and prepositions, infinitives or clauses. Because students can't use prepositions and some fixed sentence structures in English correctly, grammatical mismatch occur. In order to investigate which kind of grammatical errors students made is more serious, we divide the eight types of grammatical collocation according to Benson et al., and calculate the number and proportion of grammatical mismatch in students' compositions (see Table 6).

Table 6 Errors of Grammatical Collocation

Types of Error	Number	Percentage/%
$n.+ prep$	6	35.19
$n.+ infinitive$	2	11.76
$n.+ that\ clause$	2	11.76
$prep.+ n.$	1	5.89
$adj.+ prep.$	5	29.41
$predic.\ adj.+ infinitive$	1	5.89
Total	17	100

From Table 6, we can see that the collocation of $n.+ prep$ and $adj.+ prep.$ are the most frequent in all types of collocation and the proportion is 64.60%. This shows that the use of prepositions is difficult for students to master collocation. Maybe it is because there are many kinds of prepositions in English and their usage is complex, which makes it difficult for students to master.

(2) semantic collocation

Semantic collocation is the collocation of nouns, verbs and adverbs. Benson et al. classified it into seven types. Table 7 shows the number and percentage of each collocation.

Table 7 Errors of Semantic Collocation

Types of Error	Number	Percentage/%
$v.+n.(pron./pp)$	13	33.33
$v.+n.$	6	15.38
$adj.+n.$	3	7.69
$n.+v.$	5	12.82
$n.+of+n.$	4	10.26
$adv.+adj.$	6	15.38
$v.+adv.$	2	5.13
Total	39	100

From Table 7, this paper gets the result that the mismatch between nouns and verbs [including $v.+n.(pron./pp)$, $v.+n.$, $n.+v.$] is as high as 61.53%. This is mainly due to the negative transfer of Chinese. Students create many Sinicism verb-noun phrases, such as:

(i) Always remember that never stop **learning the knowledge of** information security.

(ii) To sum up, we must **do preparation** of information theft prevention and emphasize the importance of information security too much.

(iii) By **passing the time**, our own private information is easy to be stolen, which makes us in danger.

Through the analysis of mismatch in students' compositions, this paper believes that mismatch are mainly affected by the following factors.

First, it is the negative transfer of native language. Influenced by the negative transfer of mother tongue mainly refers to the students' lack of knowledge in English mismatch and the misuse of Chinese collocation, which rigidly translates Chinese collocation into English collocation, ignoring the differences between Chinese and English in this respect. In the process of analysis, this paper finds that semantic errors reflect the interference of mother tongue more, such as "made a large mistake", "many differences on culture" and "because of many reasons". The correct expressions are "made serious mistakes", "many differences in/about culture" and "for many reasons" respectively. Second, learners' generalization of target language rules is too general of ignored. Students' generalization and neglect of some rules in English lead to some collocation errors (mismatch) (Gao Lili, 2009). The generalization of rules is mainly manifested in students' incorrect analogy of the combinations they have learned to match to other combinations. For example, some nouns in English can be collocated with verbs "have" and "take", which have no different meanings, such as "have/take a bath, have/take a rest". Therefore, students may think that other nouns can also be used in conjunction with two verbs, so that they may make mismatches like "take a fight" and "have a risk", but in fact they can only use such matches as "have a fight" and "take a risk".

5 Results and Discussions

This part reviews the data gathered on the AntConc and TagConc based on the Juku Correction Network. 95 essays with 16 166 tokens and 1 871-word types were analyzed. Based on the limited data available, we can see that a majority of errors were spelling error, article error and mismatch, and those common mistakes made by non-English majors were analyzed. The characteristics of those mistakes are seriously influenced by negative transfer of mother tongue (we think it is equal to the interlanguage errors).

As for the mistake of spelling error, it's because that Pinyin itself has the characteristics of complexity. In English, the mapping of phonemes and morphemes is not one-to-one. There are far more letters and letter combinations for phonetics than phonemes. 40 phonemes correspond to 70 morphemes. So some Chinese students cannot write words in the correct way. Besides, some of them write English compositions in a careless way. They may think that content is more important than accuracy in writing, thus they lack a careful attitude in writing. The potential influencing factors of the article error is that the Chinese English learners transfer the usage in Chinese that the nouns with zero marker can be regarded as the generic reference or specific reference to target language, and the overgeneralization on specific rules for English articles by Chinese learners may lead to their overuse or underuse of the article. For the reason of mismatch is that the non-English majors seemed more difficult to learn the verb-noun collocations in which the mother tongue is inconsistent with the semantics of the target language. Moreover, college students tend to confuse notional verbs by only reciting the literal meaning of those verbs and overly use these delexical verbs, and most non-English majors like creating new expressions according to their mother tongue, such as learn knowledge, study knowledge, know knowledge, etc.

Therefore, for teachers, they should pay special attention to language errors with high frequency, such as spelling errors, article errors, mismatch, incomplete sentence and so on, so as to help and guide students to correct these errors; for students, in order to reduce and avoid language errors, they should write more and practice more to cultivate language sense. Writing is a skill that needs a lot of practice, but at present, the amount of English writing exercises for undergraduates is far from enough. Only when teachers and students work together can students avoid mistakes and learn new knowledge from errors. Finally, this paper sincerely hopes that foreign language teachers could apply EA in English writing thoroughly for the reason that errors can tell them not only the degree of mastery but what needs to continue learning. Therefore, teachers should have a positive attitude towards errors and find out the defects in teaching plans, skills and textbooks by analyzing them.

6 Conclusions

This part concludes the present study. First, with the systematically analyze of the whole part of English writing, it provides the results that has been found in the study. Second, it points out the limitations of the present study. Third, it puts forward suggestions for the further studies of EA of English writing. Finally, autobiographical reflection would be supplied.

With the assistance of Juku Correction Network, this paper collects 95 kinds of English writings written by non-English majors in NPU. By analyzing the data, we know that the most common errors students make in English writing is spelling errors, which to some extend reflects that the students are careless when they write English compositions. In the process SLA, the teachers should play the role of instructor to help students avoid or reduce mistakes. Moreover, students should write more and practice more to cultivate language sense whenever they have time. However, the nature of this paper's data do not allow the authors to determine whether all the non-English majors in China have those common mistakes or not. The authors think possible areas for further research could collect much more data of English writings written by non-English majors from more new perspective aspects, which would be more reliable and comprehensible to prove the characteristics of English writings written by non-English majors. Fortunately, the research process has encouraged the authors to conduct an empirical study in a more scientific and objective way, and it also enlightens the authors to think in a critical way.

References

Corder, S. P. 1967. "The significance of learners' errors." International Review of *Applied Linguistics*.

Gao, Linlin. 2015. "Strategies of oral English Teaching under the guidance of EA theory". *Journal of Liaoning Education Administration College*.

Dong, Junhong. 1999. "EA of cohesion and coherence in college students' English Writing". *Foreign Language Teaching*.

Deng, Mengyao. 2018. "A corpus-based study of collocation errors of verbs and nouns in Senior High School Students". Master's thesis, accessed from CNKI (China national knowledge internet).

Guo, Hong. 2012. "Collocation errors in English Majors' compositions". *Journal of Heilongjiang Institute of Education*.

Huang, Fuwei. 2008. "An analysis of collocation errors in Chinese learners' English compositions". *Electric Power Education in China*.

Huang, Li. 2018. "A corpus-based study of collocation errors in senior one English Writing". Master's thesis, accessed from CNKI (China national knowledge internet).

Men, Haiyan. 2010. "Corpus based analysis of collocation errors of adverbs and adjectives in Chinese students' English Writing". *Network Wealth*.

Nation, I. S. P. 1990. *Teaching and Learning Vocabulary*. New York: Newbury House Publishers.

Selinker, L. 1972. "Interlanguage". *International Review of Applied Linguistics*.

Richards, J. C. 1974. "A non-constructive approach to EA". In *EA*, edited by Richards, J. C. London: Longman.

Tang, Chengxian. 1997. "EA and summary". *Foreign Language Teaching and Research*.

Wang, Xuewen, and Sun, Lan. 2004. "Chinese students' English spelling mistake revisited". *Foreign Language Teaching and Research*.

Wang, Ying. 2006. "Oral analysis of Chinese students". *Journal of Shaanxi Normal University (Philosophy and Social Sciences Edition)*.

Wang, Haihua, and Yang, Xinhuan. 2007. "An analysis of collocation errors of Chinese English learners". *Journal of Teaching and Management*.

Wei, Naixing. 2006. *The Definition and Research System of Collocation*. Shanghai: Shanghai Jiao Tong University Press.

Xu, Jun. 2002. "EA theory and foreign language remedy teaching". *Journal of Liaoning Educational Institute*.

Zhan, Haiyan. 2012. "A Revelation of the Error-Analysis Theory to English Writing Teaching for Postgraduates of Non-English Majors". *Theory and Practice of Education*.

Zhou, Xin. 2009. "A survey of collocation errors of English learners". *Consume Guide*.

The EMI Sphinx—Transforming the Challenge of English Medium Instruction into an Effective Approach to Learning to Meet the Needs of Our Time

Timothy Kingham[*]

Abstract: EMI can seem like a daunting challenge to both teachers and students whose mother tongue is not English. The difficulty of trying to use/follow the language compounds the problem of trying to explain/understand the subject. That loaded combination of subject plus English as the medium of instruction is what this paper terms the EMI Sphinx, and as more and more international programs are taught in English, the EMI Sphinx poses a riddle at the very heart of the educational debate: *how do language and knowledge connect*? Effective learning in any form depends critically on that connectivity. This paper suggests the notion of *"the inaudible tongue"* as a metaphor for the critical link, producing silent streams of thought that we "hear" as words and which we can communicate to others, and translating the words we hear or read back into some conscious experience of knowing. While making no claims to have any solution to the mysteries of consciousness, we explore the riddle of the Sphinx in a way that offers useful and practical insights for EMI purposes. Building on the "4 Cs" framework of CLIL (Content and Language Integrated Learning), our holistic approach brings the transformational thinking of *yin* and *yang* into a "Seven Seas" model that illustrates the dynamics of the learning process, and that teachers can easily adapt for their own use. And by setting EMI in the context of the emergence of English as a global *lingua franca*, the paper offers a deep historical perspective on how it can help to meet the needs of our time. Against the increasingly fraught and complex backdrop of globalization those needs include respect for linguistic and cultural diversity, with English serving as *"second among equals"* in a multilingual world. And they include the need for a healthy relationship with technology in view of the tremendous potential it now offers for both good and ill. Thru an informed and ethical discussion the EMI Sphinx is thus brought to life both as a practical tool for teaching and as an imaginative means for exploring the kind of education that a shared future for humanity requires.

Key Words: CLIL; the 4 Cs; the "Seven Seas"; *lingua franca*; holistic approach; *yin*

---

[*] Timothy Kingham：西北工业大学外国语学院英籍教师，主讲西方文明史、欧美文化、英语电影赏析等课程。

and *yang*; paradox metaphor; consciousness; the Chinese Room; *the inaudible tongue*

1 Introduction

The rapid growth of EMI in recent years has followed on from the spread of English as a global *lingua franca*, and the realization that education, like any other form of human activity, now takes place in a global context. To attract the most talented students and professors from around the world, and thus to build their international rankings and prestige, educational institutions feel they need to offer programs in English. The competitive element of that need is reinforced by the fact that in most countries' education systems, foreign students are seen to be more "lucrative" (Briggs et al., 2018)—the lucre coming from the widespread practice of charging foreign students higher fees than their domestic counterparts. So, as education has become increasingly international, EMI has become the "new normal" in international education. The question as to whether EMI can be justified on a pedagogical basis has until now been a secondary consideration. Perhaps that reflects something in the spirit of English itself: *"just do it—and learn by doing."* However, as we begin to share ideas as to what works and what doesn't—and why—from a wide variety of contexts and perspectives, there is clearly a need to address the fundamental question: *is EMI an effective way to learn and to prepare students for today's world*? While recognizing the many challenges that EMI presents, and respecting the fact that it is not right for everyone, this paper takes a highly positive view of its overall potential. EMI can offer an effective approach to learning that is very much in tune with the needs of our time. That view also echoes the generally positive mood of EMI teachers currently working in the field (Briggs et al., 2018).

This paper is a highly summarized version of a much longer first draft. The author has preferred to retain short accounts under a wide range of section headings so as to hopefully give a sense of his approach as a whole together with an intuitive feel for the dynamics of the learning process as illustrated in the diagram in Section 9.

2 Defining EMI

Born of the need to communicate knowledge and learning via a common language in today's global context, EMI has become a powerful presence that can take multiple forms on a wide variety of stages. Thus an MBA program at a business school will look very different from classes at an international primary school. Maths taught thru EMI will be very different from classes in music and drama. An online course in graphic design will be very different from a training session at a football club in England's Premier League. For the purposes of this paper they are all examples of EMI. But that's not how everyone sees it, and definitions will vary depending on the perspectives people take and the goals they want to achieve. Based on Dearden's paper of 2014, the Oxford EMI Centre defines EMI as:

The use of the English language to teach academic subjects (other than English itself) in countries or jurisdictions in which the majority of the population's first language is not English. (Macaro, 2015)

This definition reflects the aim of the Centre "to act as an observatory of the EMI phenomenon around the world" from a neutral standpoint—the UK is not deemed to be "an EMI country" (Macaro, 2015). Given the versatile nature of EMI in practice, and the fundamental issues raised by the riddle of the Sphinx, this paper prefers an open-ended "definition" coupled with a flexible pragmatic framework within which it can be adapted to take an appropriate form. The definition is thus simply: *the use of English as a medium of instruction in any learning context in which English is not the L1 of at least one of the parties involved.* That raises the key issue of learning and understanding in a foreign language, at least for that one party. The most typical case is naturally going to be a class of international students for many of whom English is L2, and, unless otherwise stated, that is the most useful picture to have in mind for the purposes of this paper. But note that the open-ended definition allows for the following possibilities:

(i) The teacher(s) may or may not have English as their L1.

(ii) The field may be academic, professional or technical—or any combination thereof.

(iii) The learning context includes the physical classroom, but may extend far beyond the classroom walls by including online elements, informal learning (e.g. *English Corners*), on-the-job training, class trips, visits, etc.

(iv) EMI may include the teaching of English as a Major, together with related fields (TESOL, EAP, ESP, etc.—not to mention EMI itself).

While thus encompassing most of the situations in which English is actually used as a medium of instruction, this broad definition allows us to focus on the central questions of how language and knowledge connect, and what kind of education we need to meet the needs of our time, on a deeper pedagogical and philosophical level. We can then consider how to apply the underlying principles involved to address the specific needs of any given context by asking:

Who is teaching what to whom? Why? Where? At what age/level? In accordance with what standards (institutional, national)? And online/offline or thru some combination of the two?

The answers will produce a complex matrix—sometimes even within a single institution. The need for content in teaching any language, for example, has recently led to a switch towards EMI expressly for the purpose of teaching English as L2—so the students do not major in English itself, but in a subject taught thru English (Briggs et al., 2018). Hence the distinction between English Majors studying thru content, let us say, in business, politics and science, and Business, Politics and Science Majors studying thru EMI, is becoming increasingly artificial. For some of the time, at least, the English Majors may find themselves attending the same classes as the Majors from the other Faculties. How effectively those classes are taught is the concern of this paper, not the Faculty to which the teachers and students belong.

3 Academic Review

Once the significance of EMI as a global phenomenon was realized in the early years of the millennium, it was natural "to map (its) size, shape and future trends worldwide" as a first step towards formulating an effective policy response (Dearden, 2014). Although many studies were available at national level, the Oxford EMI Centre of which Dearden is a Director saw the need for a systematic aggregation and review of data from around the world to build a more comprehensive global picture of EMI in Higher Education (Macaro et al., 2017). That picture is far from complete, but it is clear that to attract international students and teachers many EMI programs have been launched "without any real planning or thought for the potential implications" (Kirkpatrick, 2015). Among the problems thus arising the following are commonly cited:

(1) on a pedagogical level

English language competence of teachers and students; self-motivation and belief; sense of marginalization among students with poor command of English; lack of assessment of outcomes in terms of both English language proficiency, and content knowledge and competence

(2) on an organizational level

Top-down imposition of EMI programs on teachers and students often without consultation; lack of planning and coordination in the implementation of programs; lack of teacher preparation, support and development.

While the institution provides the primary context at organizational level, it is just one of many that can be framed within the overall global context that is of critical importance to the development of international education as a whole. In an increasingly complex multipolar world that has been aptly described as "multiplex" —interconnected and interdependent, but decentered with multiple overlapping nodes of power and authority (Archarya, 2014)—EMI can no longer take a free ride on the great tide of globalization.

Although EMI itself is a recent arrival in academia, it fits within the broader multilingual scope of Content and Language Integrated Learning on which there is a substantial body of work across many languages and disciplines, and which has been concisely summarized by Coyle, Hood and Marsh (2010).

This paper naturally draws on the author's own experience in EMI, TESOL and Steiner education. Steiner's central questions *"what is it that makes us human?"* and *"how do we grow and evolve into the fullness of that humanity?"* resonate throughout this work. Finally the author is much indebted to the university, NPU, Xi'an, for the opportunity to develop his thinking in a stimulating learning environment at a vital crossroads of cultures and civilizations.

4 Methodology

The methodology behind this paper mirrors the methodology of the author's approach as a whole. Both are based on the premise that the medium plus the content of instruction together form a distinctive whole greater than the sum of its parts. A holistic approach recognizes that wholeness, explores it from different perspectives and on different levels, pursuing and mapping out different paths of inquiry using a variety of appropriate means, and thus seeking to form an overall unifying view. It should be evident from the title and illustration at the top of this paper that metaphor and paradox have a key role to play in the holistic approach that the author adopts, and what brings them together—hopefully into an overall unifying view—is the wisdom of *yin* and *yang*.

5 The Riddle of the Sphinx

The sphinx is an ancient archetypal form found across Eurasia whose origins suggest there was a sensing on a subconscious or semi-conscious level of a creature with human intelligence emerging from an animal body i.e., the body of a lion. The presence of the Egyptian Sphinx alongside the Pyramids at Giza has ensured it has become a deeply embedded archetype within the human psyche, and it offers a captivating imagination of the phenomenon of emergence in an evolutionary process driven by the powers of mind. In the author's leading illustration the author has combined the two-fold lion-human hybrid of the Egyptian Sphinx with the Two Sisters riddle posed by the Greek Sphinx. The answer to the riddle comes from the fact that the words $\mu \rho \alpha$ (day) and $\nu \xi$ (night) are both feminine in Ancient Greek. So these are the two sisters that give birth to each other (Grimal, 1996). And they offer a beautiful image of the interaction—and mutual birth-giving—between language and content. But that is not the only reason why it makes a useful metaphor for the purposes of EMI. For all its weight in stone, the Sphinx hovers delicately between a perceived duality and an imagined unity. As an EMI teacher you need to be aware that you are teaching both language and content. You can focus on language issues or content issues as required at any given time. But in order for that work to be effective it is important to relate it to the context of the whole. And the key to grasping that wholeness is to see how it meets the needs of students building their lives and careers in a global context.

6 The EMI Challenge

6.1 Introduction

The challenges of EMI are well documented in the academic literature, as briefly outlined above in Section 3. Here the author delves more deeply into two challenges that are closely related on a philosophical level to the central question: "*how do language and knowledge connect?*".

6.2 The Chinese Room

The philosopher John Searle proposed the Chinese Room thought experiment to illustrate the impossibility of machines attaining any kind of conscious understanding in the field of AI (Searle, 1980). As an English teacher in China the author often finds himself in a position similar to John Searle executing the computer program in his thought-experiment—only the author is executing an actual program in his apartment. If the author needs to download a media player on his computer, for example, the screen presents him with a sequence of pages and options to check on each page—all in Chinese. By now the author knows which options to click on from their position on each page, and magically the computer downloads the required program. Does that mean the author can read Chinese? Perhaps fractionally more than John Searle, but basically the answer is no. So then the parallel to the question: "*what does an intelligent human have that an intelligent machine does not have?*" becomes "*what does a native Chinese speaker have that a non-Chinese speaker does not have (even if they can download something following screen displays in Chinese)?*". The answer in essence is the ability to reuse that same language in the screen displays freely and purposefully in other contexts. That echoes the notion of "intentionality" often cited as an answer to the first question in the AI debate. But here we need to consider the pedagogical implications. The Chinese Room illustrates an extreme case of being able to gain a desired outcome from the most superficial understanding of language that could be imagined, the "understanding" being based on a cursory—and purely visual—recognition of screen patterns. That presents a challenge both as to how we develop understanding in EMI and as to how we assess it.

6.3 Between Venus and Mars

Imagine the following scenario:

A TESOL teacher is observing a Maths teacher giving a lesson taught thru EMI to international students as part of an exchange program within a university. Both teachers have a shared L1 with English as their L2. The Maths teacher spends the entire lesson writing formulae on the board, and talking thru the logic and calculations behind them. On a technical level his English seems competent. Meanwhile the students dutifully listen and write them down. At the end of the lesson the two teachers go out for a chat, and after a polite exchange, the dialogue in their shared L1 goes as follows:

TESOL teacher: *How can that possibly be an effective way to learn if there is no interaction or discussion?*

Maths teacher: *How can interaction and discussion be an effective way to learn if neither the students nor myself are fully competent in English? How can I correct them if they make mistakes? What if I make mistakes, can they correct me? What if their English is better than mine? And besides, what is there to discuss in a series of mathematical equations?*

There is evidently a gaping chasm in attitudes between them, and, to borrow John Gray's well-known analogy, we might put it thus: "*TESOL teachers are from Venus. Subject teachers are from Mars.*" The challenge is to bridge that chasm not just thru a compromise that half-satisfies each side, but in a way that draws on the creative tension between Venus and Mars to fire students with the energy and enthusiasm to learn. That means seeking to understand what makes us human whatever planet we may be from—and the forces that bring our humanity to life here on Earth.

7 The Ethics of EMI

English as a global *lingua franca* belongs to everyone who speaks it, however well or however badly. That is not just a statement of moral principle. It is the basis on which the *lingua franca* evolves to serve as an effective means of communication outside their populations of native speakers, but with the language used by native speakers providing one of the many creative impulses—plus a critical standard for reference. In that light the author uses the term "second among equals" to give a sense of the actual role and use of English as a *lingua franca*—for most English speakers it is, after all, L2—together with the ethical status the author believes it should have in the world's family of languages.

The benefits of using English as a global *lingua franca*, and as a medium of instruction, depend critically on respecting the multilingual context from which they emerged. It is not the dominance of English that serves the global or any other community, but the vibrant linguistic, social, cultural and spiritual interaction that it fosters as a *lingua franca*, and the enhanced understanding of the world, and of our humanity as a whole, that such interaction brings. Thru its global perspectives and interdisciplinary connexions EMI thus serves to bring a unifying view to human diversity while respecting that diversity in its myriad different forms, not least in the unique individuality of each student. Language is both a medium for learning and a tool for living, and EMI should make effective use of both. By drawing on the social interaction that helps to bring lessons to life in TESOL it allows individuals to open up to each other—and discover themselves in the process while building a common understanding based on the shared focus of the lesson. Expand that focus to building a shared future together, and EMI becomes a vital tool for the key task that we now face as global citizens, and as human beings.

8 A Historical Perspective

As the world's first truly global *lingua franca* English is assured of a vital role at a time when humanity is awakening to the challenge of building a shared future together; and within that overall context EMI will have its own critical part to play in the field of education. Although those roles will in many ways be unique, there will also be parallels with other *linguas franca*, and lessons to be learnt from history. While Latin survived long after the Fall of the Roman Empire as the lingua academica and language of the Church—not to mention in the Romance languages that sprouted from its seeds—it is unlikely (touching wood) that the English-speaking world will suffer a catastrophe as devastating as the Sack of Rome in 410 AD. With Western political, economic and military power in relative, if not absolute, decline vis-à-vis China and the East, there is a closer historical parallel to Greek. When the empire of Alexander was divided between his generals, Koine Greek continued to flourish as the language of commerce, education and culture—above all in the city of Alexandria with its famed library and lighthouse. English, like Latin, has sown many seeds in the Englishes now spoken across the globe, but the global *lingua franca* is arguably now entering its Alexandrian phase with world cities from Sydney to San Francisco assuming the role of commercial, educational and cultural centres.

9 Building on the 4 Cs: A Holistic Model of EMI

9.1 Overview

In the schematic diagram (See Figure 1) content and language form a complementary duality, interweaving thru the primary cognition axis on the vertical and the primary communication axis on the horizontal, while the model itself is driven by the *yin/yang* transformations between the opposite poles of *word* and *world*, and *cosmos* and *self*. At the heart of the model stands the figure of the human being whose learning and understanding are born of that interweaving. Thus you cognize the world by speaking it into being in the form of words. You develop your own ideas by communication and discussion with others, and that learning process is in turn governed by the rhythms and cycles of the cosmos pulsing and turning thru the course of human evolution and human history, not to mention our daily lives.

We are working with an imagination of a vast interlocking cosmic whole in which what enables us to learn is what enables us to live, and what enables us to live is what enables the cosmos to evolve.

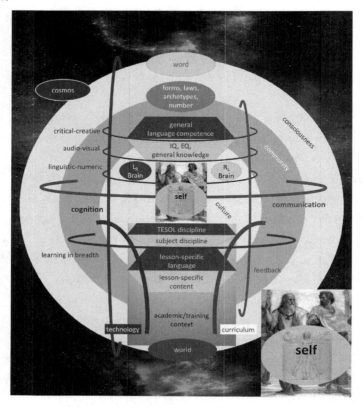

Figure 1　The Seven Seas Holistic Model of EMI with Centre Section Detail Inset

Humanity is represented by the classical-Renaissance trio of Plato and Aristotle (from Raphael's painting *The School of Athens*) framing Leonardo's *Vitruvian Man*. Seeming to explore how he fits within the perfect laws of proportion, Leonardo's figure serves to connect body, mind and soul thru the individual self to the cosmos—a connectivity made possible via the medium of consciousness that underlies the whole model. *Vitruvian Man* thus captures the genius of an individual whose passion for learning—for making the world his own in the highest ethical sense of understanding the cosmos in himself—has become not only an iconic evocation of the Renaissance mind, but also an archetypal symbol of universal wisdom.

We live in a globalized world. We live in the age of the selfie. It is important to see how they connect. How can you manage the forces of globalization if you can't see its partner in the dance? Technology today has enabled us to add a playful suffix to what lies at the very heart of our model. "*Know thyself*" was one of the maxims enshrined at the Temple of Apollo in Delphi, and it is echoed in the *Tao Te Ching*:

知人者智，自知者明。

Knowing others is wisdom. Knowing the self is enlightenment.

E-ducation from its Latin root lead out implies a twin path to that holy grail, i.e., drawing out (knowledge, competence, wisdom) from within as we are led out into the world, and thus nurturing a deep "under-standing" of the world by discovering the wonders it mirrors under our own skin. If it is consciousness that serves to connect those inner and outer worlds, it is language that enables us to navigate the ever-flowing streams of consciousness between them. Thus the dialogue between Plato and Aristotle opens into the axis of communication on a social level, while their gestures point to the two poles of the cognition axis (*world* and *word*) on the vertical. As streams of consciousness swirl thru our hearts and minds, and meet in our thinking, they drive the various contrasting mental faculties that have come to be symbolized by "Left Brain, Right Brain" in popular discourse. Among them are the critical/creative, audio/visual and linguistic/numeric faculties that are shown as circling the cognition axis by way of illustration. The author uses the terms "R_L Brain" and "L_R Brain" in recognition of the fact that, while they may be weighted more to one hemisphere than the other, they are considered to be neurologically far more complex. Bloom's taxonomy gives a much fuller account of that complexity based on three domains: cognitive (knowledge-based), affective (emotion-based), and psychomotor (action-based), and this has been widely adapted in various forms on education courses. Coyle, Hood and Marsh (2010) show how it can be applied to the field of CLIL in their practical "Tool Kit". Our diagram aims to illustrate the underlying dynamics: as streams of consciousness swirl between R_L Brain and L_R Brain in various forms (critical/creative, audio/visual, etc.), the key to making knowledge your own is to put it into your own words, and then discuss it with others. That involves many patterns of interaction suited to a variety of contexts on a number of levels.

9.2 Three Levels of EMI

Language is both a medium for learning, and a tool for living, and those functions are recognized here on three basic levels together with the corresponding forms of content (see Table 1).

Table 1 Three Levels of EMI

Level	Language-Content Pairing	Aim
General	general language competence (including grammar and vocabulary, communication and social skills ...)—general knowledge and intelligence	to nurture well-rounded culturally aware and socially adept human beings who can think freely, critically and creatively for themselves while working harmoniously and effectively with others

Continued Table

Level	Language-Content Pairing	Aim
Discipline	TESOL discipline—subject discipline	to enable students to explore and develop their chosen discipline using English as appropriate for the purposes of inquiry, discussion, research, presentations, etc.
Lesson	lesson-specific, language-lesson-specific content	to enable students to achieve the learning outcomes of any given lesson using English as appropriate

While reading across the table shows the aim of connecting and integrating language and content at each level, it is also important to see the connexions that can be made on a vertical level. Interlinking the lessons and discipline with general knowledge and intelligence fosters an interdisciplinary approach, and English is a particularly apt medium for doing this. Because it is a global language that is used to talk about virtually every conceivable area of human concern, and because TESOL courses naturally draw on that scope to stimulate interest and a sense of inclusivity, English can serve to interweave many disciplines with a wide variety of ways of thinking and cultural viewpoints. The secondary communication arc on the vertical marked "feedback" shows the importance of teachers and students discussing issues together at lesson, discipline and general levels—the last could include general issues (social, economic, environmental, etc.) together with the personal issues that inevitably impinge on our ability to learn effectively. Communication with the Admin department is also critical for both teachers and students particularly with a view to ensuring they have sufficient English language support.

The secondary cognition arc on the horizontal axis marked "learning in breadth" illustrates the importance of working together with, and learning from, the wider community. That includes the global community of which the class, the institution, the city ... may be a microcosm. Obviously such interaction requires careful handling and cultural sensitivity—the "soft" skills that go hand-in-hand with language learning—but it is one of the great gifts that EMI brings as education becomes increasingly international. Thru their contact with each other, and with the wider community, and thru a coherent interdisciplinary approach, students should have a vibrant sense of not only mastering their own discipline, but also developing as global citizens, and learning at the university of life.

9.3 The Seven Seas

In developing a holistic model of EMI based on the principle of *yin* and *yang* we have added certain key elements to the "4 Cs" foundation of *content*, *cognition*, *communication and culture*. Among these are *context*, *community*, *consciousness* and *cosmos*. They are not new ideas—the novelty is in how we put them together to construe the whole. And the seeming oddity that they all begin with the letter "c" gives a useful clue. *Content*, *communication*, *cognition*, *context*, *community* and *consciousness* are all built on the Latin prefix *"con"* which has the fundamental sense of *"together with"*. That sense of togetherness underlies our whole model because, like any holistic model, it is based on the principles of connectivity, completeness and harmony, or, let us say *"concordance"* to be phonetically consistent. To these we could add *symbiosis* and *synergy* (based on the Greek syn/sym = Latin con/com) which Coyle, Hood and Marsh stress as fundamental principles for their approach to CLIL. Together they enable the *comprehension* of the whole. Language, like life, has a playful quality, and that can often serve us well as teachers, but here it is not a question of trying to maximize the number of "Cs" however connected, complete and concordant we might want our model to sound. The author prefers to use a metaphor that gives a sense of both the holistic principles of EMI and its global nature, not to mention the maritime skills of the island people on whose language it is based.

10 Flipping Roles, Reconnecting the Parts, Synergizing the Whole: the *Yin* and *Yang* of Learning

Every teacher has been a student. Every parent has been a child. Every sunset has been a dawn. Flipping roles is as natural to the process of living and learning as speaking and listening, as producing a creative response to a critical insight, as breathing in and out, and it offers a key insight into the transformative power of *yin* and *yang* that underlies our holistic model. Learning—and our development as human beings—is part of a much deeper evolutionary process that is continually transforming and revitalizing itself within an overall cosmic frame. So we are not simply talking about a two-fold model. We are talking about a multi-dimensional model of transformation driven by the inter-action of *yin* and *yang* in a myriad forms on multiple levels.

While it is natural in the first instance to think of language as a medium for delivering knowledge/content, it is important to see how they are in practice continually flipping roles. Every word has a meaning, or meanings (content). Put the words into a sentence and that content serves as a medium for understanding the sentence as a whole (new content). Put the sentences together into a text, and they serve as a medium for grasping the gist (new content). That in turn serves as medium to build further understanding—and you can use it to refocus on any difficult words now that you know the meaning of the whole and the context.

If the *yin/yang* transformation in the above example works thru the mind going into question and answer—critical—creative—mode, there are many other *yin/yang* transformations that can empower the process of learning. In the classroom, for example, you need to ensure the students "*speak out to fix within*"—they need to get their tongues round the words, phrases, ideas that you are teaching so that they can be internalized and "recalled". They need to develop their own ideas thru discussing them with others, just as we develop ourselves thru engaging with and serving society. That is how we find our own voice—a voice that speaks from the heart, from our innermost self, and conveys a truth that resonates in the hearts of others. And let students be teachers, invite them up front, and have them explain things to their classmates, and yourself at the back.

The "flipped classroom"—in which instructional content is delivered outside of the classroom—can work well in conjunction with online courses watched in students' own time, especially for teachers concerned about their own competence in English. Students thus gain a healthy exposure to fluent or near-fluent English via the online courses, while the teacher ensures that what has been watched has been effectively understood by guiding discussion and feedback in class, and building on that understanding in whatever way they think appropriate, not least to tie back into the course online.

The key to it all is to ensure learners can express knowledge and ideas in English using their own words to make themselves understood. That is the surest sign they have mastered both content and language, and that they have found their own voice sufficient to develop their knowledge of the discipline in an international academic context, while developing themselves as global citizens in the process. Of course it takes time, but that seemingly banal phrase hides a kernel of great wisdom. Timing is of the essence in the drama of learning, as it is in the drama of life, and teachers, like actors, need to be masters of the art. We are working with the cycles of the cosmos thru the lives of human beings as they grow and evolve, we are following courses thru the seasons of the year, we are working with the rhythms of day and night, bringing rhythm into our lessons, and giving students the time they need to understand, and reflect on, the questions we ask. Mary Budd Rowe pioneered work on the importance of "wait-time" in her seminal paper on the subject in 1972. As has now been widely recognized in TESOL and EMI, allowing sufficient "wait-time" is even more important when students are learning in a foreign language. Whether we are dealing with historical ages, years, weeks, lesson "hours", or microseconds before a punchline, we need to get the timing right. That is how we engage forces of transformation far greater than ourselves.

11 The Inaudible Tongue

Silent sounds in black and white
ring true to a mind that can see
how meaning is woven from symbol
into the grammar of reality.

(The riddle of reading—TK)

名可名,非常名。

The name that can be named is not the eternal name.

Adam's Smith's famous metaphor of the invisible hand in economics has been applied by Keller (1994) to his work on language change, and the "twin idea" on which he draws echoes the paradoxical notion of "spontaneous order" in many fields of inquiry. From a universal perspective the cosmos imparts order to a myriad processes of spontaneous, and often seemingly random, change. From a pedagogical perspective the question is: *"how can we harness that cosmic order thru the medium of language to the freedom we have to think for ourselves?"* Although, as Laozi—and mystics thru the ages—have proclaimed, the ultimate knowing with which that could empower us would no doubt be beyond naming, what we learn in the process can still be immensely valuable in practical terms. In that process we can at least recognize that consciousness—in its human and cosmic forms—is bound to play a key role, and, without attempting to unravel the mysteries involved, we can gain an intuitive insight into its nature from the wisdom and the beauty of *yin* and *yang*.

Figure 2 The *taijitu* (*yin yang* symbol)

The classic symbol of the *taijitu* can be seen in many ways. In the realm of language (from *lingua* = *tongue* in Latin) we could see it as the interaction of two tongues. If the image of two tongues kissing evokes the emotive power of masculine and feminine—or self and other—in mutually balanced creative interaction, for our purposes here we can see it as the upper *audible tongue* engaging with its lower inaudible "other half". Linked into the field of consciousness, the latter produces silent streams of thought that we "hear" as words and which we can communicate to others—via the *audible tongue* in speech—while translating the words we hear (or read) externally back into some conscious experience of knowing. In that flickering mix of inner light and sound we "see" what words and ideas mean, they foster "under-standing"—let us say below the surface level of the tongue(s)—and "comprehension" as we "grasp" the sphere as a whole. The more such metaphors approach the actuality of our mental experience, the more we could argue they become an actual model of understanding rather than a mere aid to understanding.

The importance of the social dimension in the learning process is shown by the fact that, even if we are just thinking to ourselves, we still need a "listener" somewhere at the back of our mind—perhaps someone we actually know, perhaps an imagined composite of our students, or perhaps just a hovering shadow of our own self (our own "other"). As a guise thru whom we can speak to ourselves, "the listener" can serve as both our sharpest critic, and our most fruitful source of inspiration.

Imagine such an inner mental dialogue taking place between the contrasting faculties commonly associated with the right and left hemispheres of the brain. This helps to illustrate a useful analogy with Adam Smith's *invisible hand* in the field of economics. While from one side, let us say the critical side, our faculties pose questions (=demand), from the other—let us say creative side—they supply answers. Thus we learn thru language as a medium—and thru the interaction of questions and answers in response to the value of the knowledge we are seeking—just as goods are produced in response to the price mechanism of a market economy that equates supply and demand, and transacts thru the medium of money. Price may not be the same as value, but they both come together in the knowledge economy where AI is climbing ever upwards "thru the cloud" from data → information → knowledge → intelligence → wisdom. If it is now only wisdom that is the exclusive preserve of the human mind, that has major implications both for how we teach, and how we work with technology.

Expounding on his earlier ideas in *The Theory of Moral Sentiments*, in his major work *The Wealth of Nations* Adam Smith was particularly struck by the paradox that it is thru each individual pursuing their own interests in a market economy that society as a whole benefits from the wealth thus generated (Smith, 1759, 1776). The author would argue that in learning there is a similar paradox which we can see if we construe the mind as a kind of knowledge economy. It is thru the efforts of each individual to acquire their own knowledge, to understand the world for themselves, and to put that understanding into their own words, that human knowledge as a whole progresses. That progress, the author believes, is made possible thru the medium of consciousness in which *the inaudible tongue* plays the key role of translating words into an experience of knowing, and knowing into the phenomenon of words, and thus interweaving the processes of cognition and communication.

12 Technology

12.1 "*Human-led, technology-aided*": Integrating Technology within a Holistic Human-centered Approach

The power and speed of technology offer us convenient short-cuts in almost every field of human activity. As educationalists we need to make sure that technology does not cut out the learning process itself. By analogy with the problem outlined in Section 6.2, we might be getting amazing results using the computer in our "Chinese Room". But would we be learning Chinese? In this section we look at examples of how to work effectively with technology at classroom level, and at the level of a global arts and media initiative.

When you pose a question for discussion in an EMI class (whether offline or online), should you let students immediately resort to their mobiles (or laptops) for answers? The author recommends giving the students two phases of, say, 5 minutes each, to work on it. In the first phase they can't look anything up on the Internet via their mobile phone. So they have to draw on their own memory, knowledge, reason, imagination, etc. in discussion with classmates (or perhaps, at first, thinking it thru on their own). Then they can search on the Internet with a clear sense of what they are looking for. With online searches it is vital to be primed in advance with the question: *"what do I want from the Internet?"* in order to avoid unconsciously becoming the answer to: *"what does the Internet want from me?"*.

The Sunset Dawn is an arts and media initiative that the author founded based on the idea of linking the sunset and the dawn across the globe, and harnessing the potential this offers for Festivals, Creative Projects, and Education. In the paper *Connecting the hemispheres, minding the globe* the author makes clear how the Sunset Dawn makes an appropriate and sensitive use of technology to open fresh perspectives on the world in which we live in a way that fits well with a holistic and creative approach to education such as this paper advocates in EMI (Kingham, 2015). In organizational terms it is the kind of initiative that can help to integrate the fields of Media, Culture and Communication which are increasingly being brought together in academia in response to what is happening in society as a whole. And the multilingual festivals—with English serving as *lingua franca* and "second among equals"—offer a beautiful sense of global awakening that is very much in tune with the needs of our time, and the ethos of EMI.

12.2 To Humanize the Technology, or to Technologize the Human

If the original Egyptian sphinx can be interpreted as the human being emerging from the animal world—and as master of it—thru the power of intelligence, that form of intelligence today no longer reigns supreme. AI is increasingly joining forces with human intelligence, and the term *cyborg* has been coined to denote their coming together in a single integrated organism, i.e., a cybernetic organism (Clynes et al., 1960). From our perspective we might call it a *humanoid sphinx*, and we can sense its looming presence thru the integration of AI into the systems that govern our lives, not least as technology becomes increasingly wearable and implantable. So the principle of "humanity-led, technology-aided" needs to be applied with great care. The roles could very easily flip. And when we start asking *"how do we develop human beings to ensure the effectiveness of our technology-led systems?"*, we will be embarking on a very dangerous mission. That should never be a question for the EMI classroom.

13 Role Models

It is said that there are two kinds of teacher. There are teachers who teach a subject, and there are teachers who teach people. Students generally prefer the latter. But we need to do both. And the key lies in language: we need to find our own voice such that it resonates with our professional mastery of the subject, our empathy with our fellow human beings, and our passion for life. For examples of such role models the author would point to a profession that continually makes the news headlines although we don't often think of its members as EMI practitioners. The spectacular success of non-native English-speaking managers in English football has been consistently evident from the Premier League Tables. At the impassioned heart of English popular culture they have found their own English-speaking voice to convey their knowledge of, and passion for, the beautiful game, and their understanding of their fellow human beings.

14 Conclusion

The hybrid image of the Sphinx is intended to make EMI teachers aware that they are not merely teaching the content of their subject translated into another language. They have two halves to bring together into a vibrant and meaningful whole—a whole that resonates with a sense of the knowledge, the competences and the humanity that our age calls for. This paper has focused on building a holistic model for that purpose. Based on the transformative powers of *yin* and *yang* and a deep historical perspective of the evolution of English as a global *lingua franca*, the model takes an ethical human-centered view of the role of EMI as today's fraught and complex globalized world moves into a hi-tech future. On a practical level it shows how the dynamics of the learning process can be grasped by both teachers and students, and adapted to the wide variety of EMI contexts in which they pursue their lives and careers. Because it is an all-embracing model based on a holistic approach, it may seem somewhat overwhelming at first. But it has a master key—in the self at its heart. By attempting to understand the world in our own way, and sharing that understanding with others thru a language resonant with the consciousness of our time, we contribute to the development of human knowledge—and to the evolution of humanity and the cosmos—as a whole. And that in turn empowers us to learn. Hopefully in that light the model will inspire readers to transform the challenge of the EMI Sphinx into an abundance of opportunities from which we can all learn to meet the needs of the future we face together.

References

Acharya, A. 2019. "Causes of China-US tensions go beyond trade". *Global Times*, p.16.

Briggs, J. G., Dearden J., and Macaro, E. 2018. "English Medium Instruction: Comparing Teacher Beliefs in Secondary and Tertiary Education". *Studies in Second Language Learning and Teaching*. Accessed from https://pressto.amu.edu.pl/index.php/ssllt.

Clynes, M. E., and Kline, N. S. 1960. "Astronautics." Accessed from http://cyberneticzoo.com/wp-content/uploads/2012/01/cyborgs-Astronautics-sep.

Coyle, D., Hood, P., and Marsh, D. 2010. *Content and language integrated learning*. Cambridge: Cambridge University Press.

Dearden, J. 2014. "English as a medium of instruction—a growing global phenomenon". *British Council*.

Gray, J. 2002. *Men are from Mars, women are from Venus*. London: Harper Collins Publishers.

Grimal, P. 1996. *The dictionary of classical mythology*. Chichester: John Wiley & Sons, Ltd.

Keller, R. 1994. *On language change: the invisible hand in language*. Abingdon: Taylor & Francis Ltd.

Kingham, T. 2015. "Connecting the hemispheres, minding the globe". 2015 10th International Conference on Computer Science and Education (ICCSE). Accessed from http://ieeexplore.ieee.org/stamp/stamp.jsp? tp=&arnumber=7250243.

Kirkpatrick, A. 2015. Plenary Speeches. "The rise of EMI: challenges for Asia". Accessed from https://www.researchgate.net/search.Search.html? type = publication&query = plenary%20speeches%20english%20medium%20instruction%20global%20views%20and%20countries%20in%20focus.

Laozi. 2013. *Tao Te Ching*. Book 1.1. Suzuki DT, Carus P translation. Accessed from https://www.yellowbridge.com/onlinelit/daodejing01.php.

Laozi. 2010. *Tao Te Ching*. Book 1.33. In The world's greatest idea, John Farndon's English version. London: Icon Books.

Macaro, E. 2015. Plenary Speeches. "English medium instruction: Global views and countries in focus". Accessed from https://www.researchgate.net/search.Search.html? type = publication&query = plenary%20speeches%20english%20medium%20instruction%20global%20views%20and%20countries%20in%20focus.

Macaro, E., An, J., Curle S., Pun J., and Dearden J. 2017. "A systematic review of English medium instruction in higher education". *Language Teaching*. Cambridge: Cambridge University Press.

Rowe, M. B. 1972. "Wait-time and rewards as instructional variables". Accessed from http://eric.ed.gov/? id=ED061103.

Searle, John R. 1980. "Minds, brains, and programs". *Behavioral and Brain Sciences* 3 (3): 417 - 457. Accessed from http://cogprints.org/7150/1/10.1.1.83.5248.pdf.

Smith, A. 1759. *The Theory of Moral Sentiments*. Part IV, Chapter 1.

Smith, A. 1776. *The Wealth of Nations*. Book IV, Chapter 2, Paragraph 9.